M&E PROFESSIONAL STUDIES

Written by a team of practising lecturers and prepared under the General Editorship of a leading partnership of London accountancy tutors, the *M & E Professional Studies* series has been specially designed to meet the course needs of professional students in virtually all the examined subjects at appropriate professional, degree and diploma levels. The titles cover many of the subjects offered by the ACCA, ICA, ICMA, AIA, AAT, SCCA, ACEA, LCCI, RSA and numerous other bodies.

With carefully structured and thoroughly up-to-date contents, most titles include end-of-chapter progress tests based on the text, a large number of practice examination questions and suggested answers, a glossary of the more difficult key terms, and a very comprehensive index. An extensive programme of classroom testing, student surveys and independent assessment has been completed in relation to this series prior to publication.

With twenty substantial texts in the series, *M & E Professional Studies* constitutes a major contribution to business education, and will enable students throughout the English-speaking world gain the syllabus-related depth of knowledge and practice necessary to ensure a successful examination result.

GENERAL EDITORS

Emile Woolf

Emile Woolf first qualified in 1961 and joined the London Office of Deloitte Haskins & Sells. Since 1964 he has played a major part in pioneering accountancy education, first at Foulks Lynch and the London School of Accountancy, and then as founder and Chairman of the Emile Woolf Colleges in London and overseas. In 1984 he became a partner in Kingston Smith & Co with special responsibility for technical standards and training. He is an established author, and a regular contributor to numerous professional and student journals and magazines in the UK and overseas. In 1980 he received the Distinguished Services Award for Authorship at Hartford University, Connecticut, USA. Recently he was commissioned by the ACCA to produce a series of audio cassettes and workbooks for students throughout the world. Between 1973 and 1979 he was also an Examiner for the ACCA in Advanced Auditing and Investigations. Emile Woolf lectures regularly on accountancy, financial and economic matters in Ireland, the UK, USA, Trinidad, Jamaica, Singapore, Hong Kong, Malaysia, Nigeria, Ghana and elsewhere. He also conducts seminars on financial management topics for industrial and commercial clients as well as for professional accountancy firms.

Suresh Tanna

Suresh Tanna graduated in 1971 in chemical engineering from Edinburgh University. Following a career in business management he qualified as a chartered accountant in 1978. In 1981 he joined Karam Singh in setting up the City Accountancy Centre, which merged with the Emile Woolf Schools in March 1983, and is now Director of Studies on ACCA courses, and Financial Director of the enlarged FACT Group. He specialises in accounting, advanced accounting practice and advanced financial accounting.

Karam Singh

After a period of project planning with Burmah Oil as a graduate chemical engineer, Karam Singh obtained his MBA from the Liverpool Business School whilst also engaged in part-time consultancy work for clothing manufacturers and retailers and research at a P & O subsiduary. In 1971 he joined the London accountancy firm of Harmood Banner and Company which later merged with Deloittes. He qualified as a chartered accountant in 1974, and lectured for several years at the London School of Accountancy and the North East London Polytechnic. In 1981 he joined Suresh Tanna in the formation of the City Accountancy Centre, where he began to develop study material geared for in-school and home studies students. At present he is Principal Lecturer for the FACT schools for Level 2 ACCA courses, specialising in quantitative analysis. He has contributed numerous articles to the various professional and students' journals.

Contributing authors

The titles in this series have been prepared under the General Editorship of Emile Woolf, Suresh Tanna and Karam Singh in conjunction with the staff and tutors of the FACT Organisation, 23 Hand Court, High Holborn, London WC1V 6JF. All contributors and authors are practising lecturers with many years' experience of teaching accountancy at all levels.

M&E PROFESSIONAL STUDIES

COSTING

General Editors
Emile Woolf FCA FCCA FBIM
Suresh Tanna BSc(Hons) FCA
Karam Singh BTech MBC FCA

M&E MACDONALD & EVANS

M & E Professional Studies titles currently available

Advanced Accounting Practice
Advanced Auditing and Investigations
Advanced Financial Accounting
Advanced Taxation
Auditing
Company Law
Costing
Economics
Executorship and Trust Law and Accounts
Financial Management
Foundation Accounting
Law
Management Accounting
Managerial Economics
Numerical Analysis and Data Processing
Organisation and Management
Quantitative Analysis
The Regulatory Framework of Accounting
Systems Analysis and Design
Taxation

Macdonald & Evans Ltd
Estover, Plymouth PL6 7PZ

First published 1985

British Library Cataloguing in Publication Data
Costing.——(M & E Professional studies. Level 1,
ISSN 0266-8475)
1. Cost accounting
I. Woolf, Emile II. Tanna, Suresh III. Singh,
Karam IV. Series
657'.42 HF5686.C8

ISBN 0-7121-0456-9

Typeset by Latimer Trend & Company Ltd, Plymouth
Printed in Great Britain by
Redwood Burn Limited, Trowbridge, Wiltshire

Preface

Written to reflect the evolutionary nature of cost accounting this book indicates that the subject has moved from the classical role of product costing to the more complicated role of providing information for internal users.

This edition is presented in a revised format. Most chapters have been rewritten and new problems and illustrations included. Since the text is intended for students studying cost accounting for the first time it provides a wide range of illustrative problems which should reinforce the student's comprehension of basic concepts and their application.

The book has been prepared specifically for students of the Association of Certified Accountants costing courses; however, it would prove invaluable study material for any basic costing course. It is also a book that offers any interested reader a source of essential information, compressing as it does all the important aspects of costing into short, readable chapters.

The authors present the subject as a whole by dealing with the topics in a steady and logical sequence. Consequently, the text starts with a discussion of the accountant's role in an organisation and the accumulation of data for costing purposes. It then proceeds to a comprehensive coverage of elementary costing concepts for labour and for direct materials, and also includes an introduction to costing for decision making. In addition, the authors have recognised the need for a thorough analysis of the techniques applied to production overheads and the methods of product costing and variance analysis, all of which are areas of difficulty for students.

As with all accounting examinations the key to success is practice in answering questions against a time limit. In order to monitor progress each chapter has at least one example of an examination-type question with a suggested answer. These examples are based on past professional examination questions and should be carefully worked through, first without prior reference to the answers, before proceeding to the next chapter. By doing these examples students will not only test their knowledge and extend their understanding but also become familiar with the standard and type of questions they will encounter in their examinations.

Systematic use of this textbook should therefore not only lead to success in costing examinations, but also provide a solid framework on which to base further studies in management accounting.

Contents

List of Illustrations

CHAPTER ONE

The Purpose of Cost Accounting

1.0 FINANCIAL ACCOUNTING AND COST ACCOUNTING

1.1 Broad classification

The accounting system is the principal quantitative information system in any organisation. It can be broadly classified into:

(a) financial accounting,

(b) cost and management accounting.

1.2 Financial accounting

Financial accounting is mainly concerned with the provision of information for managers and for outside parties, including shareholders, suppliers, customers, employees, government departments and the general public. By and large the outside parties must accept the information that the business chooses to provide. The presentation of information, while accurate, shows only broad movements of income and expenditure over comparatively long periods of time. The information is expressed in three main types of financial statement:

(a) the profit and loss account (the income and expenditure attributable to activities undertaken by the firm during the period);

(b) the balance sheet (the financial position of the firm at a point in time);

(c) the statement of sources and application of funds (the flow of funds arising from activities during the period covered by the statement).

1.3 Cost and management accounting

Cost and management accounting may be defined as the provision of useful and relevant information to managers to enable them to perform their functions effectively and efficiently.

2.0 COST—DEFINITION AND THREE IMPORTANT IDEAS

2.1 Definition of cost

Cost is a measurement, in financial terms, of the amount of scarce resources used for some purpose.

2.2 The three important ideas

The above definition of cost embraces three important ideas:

(a) Cost measures the use of scarce resources. The resources are materials, labour and other *expenses*. Cost measures how much of these resources is consumed.

(b) Cost measurements are expressed in financial terms.

(c) Cost measurement is always related to the aims which it is to serve. The purpose must be known or stated when requests are made for cost information because the same cost information cannot serve all purposes. The information will take different forms for different purposes and a cost accounting system must provide for these multiple purposes.

3.0 COST ACCOUNTING—THE HISTORICAL ROLE—NARROW VIEW

3.1 The historical role of cost accounting

This is to determine the historical cost of manufacturing in terms of products or services, i.e. to relate cost units to cost centres or departments.

3.2 The expenditure incurred by a business

This may be broadly classified into:

(a) materials;

(b) labour;

(c) other expenses.

3.3 Cost centre and cost unit

(a) *Cost centre*. This is a location, person or item of equipment (or group of these) in or connected with an undertaking, in relation to which costs may be ascertained. Cost centres therefore embrace all of the persons employed by a business, all of the property owned by it and all of its areas of activity of a business.

(b) *Cost unit.* This is a unit of product, service or time in relation to which costs may be ascertained or expressed. We cannot have costs unless there are things to be costed. These units which the enterprise is set up to provide are termed cost units.

4.0 ORIGINS OF COST ACCOUNTING

The industrial revolution greatly assisted the development and use of cost accounting. The manufacturing industries and transport were transformed. "Thus the importance of buildings, plant, equipment, the supervision of overhead costs, had rapidly increased in relation to the prime cost of materials and labour. Larger bodies of labour had to be paid and controlled, complex processes had to be organised and administered. Moreover, the development of railways, with their enormous volume of fixed equipment, had brought the problem of overhead to the fore. These factors doubtless played a part in the development of cost accounting." (Prof. David Solomons.)

The major purposes of tracing costs to products were:

(a) *To provide information for setting prices for industrial products.* "Records of costing doubtless originated in the need for data required in estimating; especially in engineering and kindred trades where the work is specially contracted for and where there is no scale of market prices." (John Mann.)

(b) *For stock valuation and income determination.* "Originally the title Cost Accounting referred to ways of accumulating historical costs and tracing them to units of output and to departments, primarily for purposes of providing the inventory valuations used in balance sheet and income statements." (C. T. Horngren.)

5.0 TRACING COSTS TO PRODUCTS

5.1 Basic procedures

Tracing costs to products involves the following procedures:

(a) Broad classification of expenditure by function:

(i) Manufacturing costs (product costs);

(ii) administration, selling, distribution and other non-production costs (period costs).

(b) Further classification of manufacturing costs:

(i) According to their nature: into materials, labour, expenses.

(ii) As direct or indirect costs in relation to products:

(1) Direct costs: materials, labour and expenses which can be identified with products.

(2) Indirect costs: materials, labour, expenses which cannot be traced directly to products.

5.2 Product costing method

Product costing methods may be classified according to the nature of the cost unit into job and average (Fig. 1). All other product costing methods are variants of these two.

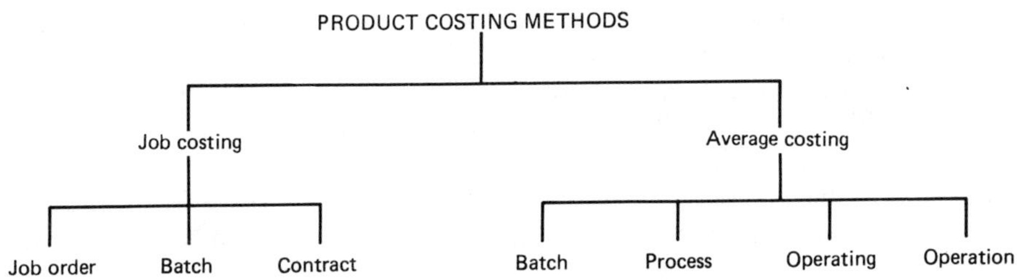

Fig. 1. *Product costing methods.*

(a) *Job costing* is a product costing method for the one-off type of product and is used when it is required to obtain the cost of a special order, batch or contract. The basic document is the job card. The job card is a form for recording and summarising the cost of materials, labour and overhead applicable to a specific job. The construction, furniture manufacturing, heavy machinery, printing and shipbuilding industries employ job costing.

(b) *Unit or average costing* is used in continuous or mass production of standardised or identical products. Costs are ascertained for a period of time by processes or departments. At the end of a period, because the units produced are homogeneous in nature, unit cost is determined as an average unit cost for the period. The average cost per unit is used to transfer output from one process to another for further processing.

The chemical, petroleum, textile, steel, rubber, cement, coal, flour and sugar industries, all assembly industries like those which manufacture household electrical appliances such as washing machines, refrigerators, electric irons, radios, TV sets, typewriters, automobiles and, finally, certain service industries such as gas, water, electric power and transport, cost their products by the process costing method.

5.3 Product costing systems

The list below and the text that follows indicate the main product costing systems:

UNIT COST UNDER DIFFERENT PRODUCT COSTING SYSTEMS

	Historical	*Normal*	*Standard*
Direct materials	Actual cost	Actual cost	Standard cost
Direct labour	Actual cost	Actual cost	Standard cost
Production overhead *OR* indirect cost of production	Actual rate to trace overheads	Predetermined rate to trace overheads	Predetermined rate

(a) *Historical product costing system.* Product costs are ascertained after they have been incurred.

(b) *Normal product costing system.* The normal product costing system differs from the historical in its treatment of indirect costs of production.

The normal costing system was introduced to overcome the main disadvantages of the historical costing system, namely:

(i) unit costs were determined only at the *end* of an accounting period;

(ii) the amount of overhead traced to identical products was often found to vary widely from period to period, owing mainly to seasonal fluctuations.

Illustration

Period	(month)	1	2	3
Factory	Rent and insurance	£10,000	£10,000	£10,000
	Units of output	10,000	8,000	5,000
	Cost per unit	£1.00	£1.25	£2.00

The normal costing system uses predetermined rates to apply a factory's indirect costs to products. The rate is determined at the beginning of the period and not at the end.

(c) *Standard product costing system.* Although standard costs are by definition scientifically predetermined costs, there are many different types of them, depending upon their use. Often two types of standard cost are used:

(i) Currently attainable standards—allowances are made for normal waste and are revised annually.

(ii) Ideal standard costs—do not allow for any inefficiencies, and demand perfection.

5.4 Product costing techniques

For stock valuation purposes there are two techniques of product costing. The major difference is the treatment of fixed production indirect costs.

(a) *Absorption costing.* Direct materials, direct labour, direct expenses, variable production indirect costs and fixed production indirect costs are traced to products and held as assets until the units are sold.

(b) *Marginal costing*. Direct materials, direct labour, direct expenses and variable production indirect costs are traced to products and held as an asset until the units are sold.

5.5 Summary table and chart

Table 1 lists in outline the systems, techniques and methods used in cost accounting while Fig. 2 charts the links between them.

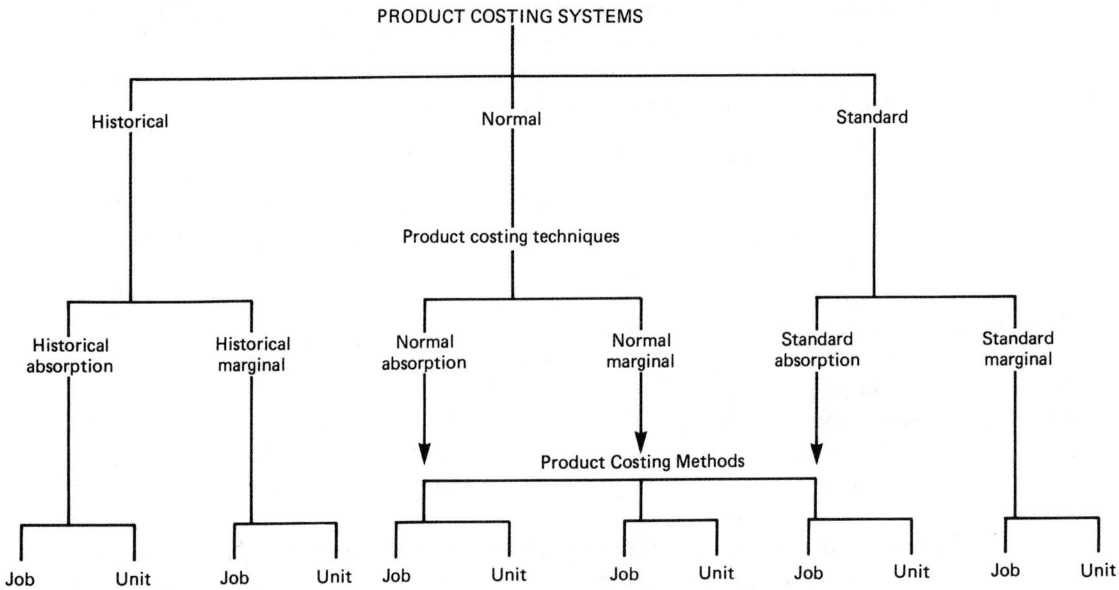

Fig. 2. *Product costing systems.*

6.0 MANAGEMENT ACCOUNTING—BROADER VIEW: THE EXTENSION OF THE BOUNDARIES OF COSTING

The purpose of cost accounting is not only to determine the cost of a product or service for pricing and stock valuation purposes but also:

(a) to show when, where and how costs are incurred, and

(b) to provide management with relevant information for *planning, control* and *decision making*.

Table 1. COST ACCOUNTING—METHODS, SYSTEMS AND TECHNIQUES

Cost Classification	*Product costs (assets)*	*Product costing methods*	*Product costing systems*	*Product costing techniques*
(a) *Direct production costs*				
Direct materials	Tracing of manufacturing costs to products	(a) Job Costing e.g. contract	(a) Historical	(a) Absorption
Direct labour			(b) Normal	(b) Marginal
Direct expenses			(c) Standard	For stock valuation purposes
(b) *Indirect production costs*				
Variable		(b) Unit Costing e.g. process		
Fixed				
Cost of production				
(c) Administration costs	Period costs			
Selling costs				
Distribution costs				

6.1 Planning

Planning is a basic function of management. It is the function by which the manager decides upon goals and the manner in which they are to be accomplished.

Planning gives the manager a warning of possible future crises and enables him to avoid having to take unplanned decisions.

6.2 Control

Control is the process of compelling events to conform to a plan. Planning is the basis for control, information is the guide for control and action is the essence of control.

6.3 The three essential requirements for control

(a) *Plan*—what goals are to be accomplished and how they can be reached.

(b) *Information*—to compare actual with plan.

(c) *Action*—to correct deviations from plan.

The accountant plays an important role in providing information at each of these three stages.

7.0 DECISION MAKING

The cost accountant *plays an important role* in the decision-making process. He acts in the capacity of an expert on cost analysis and is responsible for ensuring that all relevant data are passed to the manager responsible for making the decision. He may also be asked to offer his suggestions on what decisions to take.

7.1 Decision making as a goal-seeking process

Decision making is very much a goal-seeking process and entails choosing from among a set of alternative courses of action in order to achieve well-defined objectives. For this purpose the decision maker should:

(a) recognise why a decision is necessary;

(b) determine what alternative courses of action are available;

(c) evaluate the alternatives; and

(d) choose a particular course of action.

7.2 Relevance and decision making

To be relevant to decision making, a cost must normally meet two criteria:

(a) it must be an expected future cost;

(b) it must be an element of difference between the alternatives.

With reference to a particular cost the key question should be, "What difference does it make?" Once this question is answered, the relevance or irrelevance of a given cost in relation to a particular decision becomes much clearer. The objective of a decision may be to maximise net profit in the future, in which case all *past* costs will be irrelevant.

7.3 Decision making and the future

Decision making is always concerned with the *future*. If, for example, a decision is made to change the method of production in a factory, or to change selling prices, past and present costs are only of importance in so far as they assist in making predictions about the future costs.

8.0 COSTING TECHNIQUES FOR PLANNING AND CONTROL

8.1 Budget

This is a financial and/or quantitative statement, prepared prior to a given period of time, of the policy to be pursued during that period to attain a given objective.

8.2 Budgetary control

This means the establishment of budgets relating the responsibilities of executives to the requirements of a policy, and the continuous comparison of actual with budgeted results either to secure by individual action the objective of that policy or to provide a basis for its revision.

8.3 Kinds of budgets—planning budgets

(a) *Operating budget.* This is concerned with the use of economic resources and the products to be produced or the service to be rendered during the budget period (normally one year), e.g. sales, production, etc.

(b) *Cash budget.* This shows the estimated amount of cash which should be available during the budget period.

(c) *Fixed or static target budget.* A plan to achieve the objectives of a cost centre, or of the enterprise. A fixed budget is designed to remain unchanged, irrespective of the level of activity actually attained. It measures the effectiveness of the cost centres or of the enterprise.

8.4 Kinds of budgets—control budgets

Flexible budget. This budget, by recognising the difference between fixed, semi-fixed and variable costs, is designed to change in relation to the level of activity attained during the budgetary period.

9.0 REPORTING FOR CONTROL

9.1 Responsibility accounting

Responsibility accounting systems recognise various decision centres throughout the organisation and trace costs, incomes, assets and liabilities to the respective managers responsible for making decisions about factors involved. Responsibility accounting has three important characteristics:

(a) it fixes responsibility for cost control;

(b) the manager is made responsible only for those costs that can be directly affected by his decisions within a given time span;

(c) the information must be available at the correct time and at a reasonable cost.

9.2 Management by exception

A report to a manager should focus his attention on the most significant items in which actual performance is significantly different from plan. The exception principle is tricky in application, because the significant items must be clearly identified.

9.3 Timeliness and accuracy

To be useful, information must be presented before a decision is made. Information which is too late is useless, regardless of its precision.

10.0 COSTING TECHNIQUES FOR DECISION MAKING

10.1 Marginal costing

This is a technique which highlights contribution (sales minus variable costs) as the indicator of profitability. Knowledge of the techniques of cost–volume–profit relationships can provide valuable assistance in decision making.

10.2 Differential costing (incremental costing)

This is a technique which compares the profit before a particular decision is taken with the total profit, including the effect of the decision. For example, if a manager has to decide whether to accept a special order, he will compare the profit if the order is accepted with that if it is refused.

10.3 Opportunity costing

Opportunity costing is a technique for short-term decision making and is concerned with comparative rather than absolute costs. Opportunity cost is defined by the Institute of Cost and Management Accountants as "the net selling price, rental value or transfer value which could be obtained at a point in time if a particular asset or a group of assets were to be sold, hired or put to some alternative use available to the owner at that time". The opportunity cost of an asset is *not* the historical cost of the asset but *the alternative revenue forgone*.

In other words, the opportunity cost of using a particular resource in a particular way is the value of the best opportunity forgone by not using the resource in another way.

10.4 Relevant costing

The techniques above—marginal, differential and opportunity costing—are all applications of relevant costing.

11.0 CONTRAST BETWEEN COST ACCOUNTING AND FINANCIAL ACCOUNTING

(a) *Information.* Financial accounting is mainly the provision of information to external users. Cost accounting provides information to internal users.

(b) *Mandatory rather than optional.* Financial accounting—keeping a proper set of books—is mandatory. Cost accounting is optional. Information is collected, recorded and presented only if it serves a useful purpose.

(c) *Governed by accounting conventions.* Financial accounting statements follow accepted accounting practices and principles since they are used by outside parties. Cost accounting information follows one golden rule—*cost data must be useful to management.* Therefore different costings serve different purposes.

(d) *Historical information.* Financial accounting is based on historical costs and shows what has happened under an existing set of conditions. Entries are made only after transactions have occurred. Information is therefore historical. Cost accounting information represents future expected costs, as well as information about the past.

(e) *Focus on segments.* Financial accounting in the main focuses on the entire business. Cost accounting focuses on products, individual activities, departments, markets, etc.

(f) *Emphasis on precision.* Financial information should be true and fair. Cost accounting information serves as a guide in taking decisions.

(g) *Timing.* In financial accounting there is a lag between the time that the accounts are prepared and published and the period to which they apply. In cost accounting, the emphasis is placed upon the production of current, relevant information for control, planning and decision-making purposes.

(h) *Basic difference.* "One basic difference between cost and financial accounting is the extent to which the information reflects the degree of knowledge of the decision maker." Financial accounting must produce information that is used by many classes of people, none of whom have explicitly defined information needs. "The result is that reports are presented that do not precisely suit any particular decision maker's needs but rather reflect the average needs of all users of information." Cost accounting identifies the user, discusses his problems and needs, and provides tailored information.

CHAPTER TWO

The Elements of Cost

1.0 INTRODUCTION

1.1 Material, labour and other expenditure

In cost accounting it is convenient to consider expenditure under three headings:

(a) materials purchased;

(b) labour costs;

(c) other expenses.

However, it is necessary to realise that not all materials purchased become part of the product, not all labour incurred relates to actual manufacturing operations, and very few expenses can be regarded as being directly part of the product cost.

1.2 Direct and indirect expenditure

Expenditure may also be classified according to whether it is *direct* (identifiable with a particular cost unit) or *indirect* (not so identifiable).

2.0 DIRECT COSTS

2.1 Direct material costs

These are costs which can be identified with and allocated to cost units, i.e. the cost of materials which enter into and become part of the products, for example:

(a) materials specifically purchased for a particular job, order or process;

(b) materials bought and subsequently requisitioned from the stores for a particular production order;

(c) components purchased and/or produced and similarly requisitioned from the finished-goods stores.

In some cases it is not easy to determine whether a material is to be regarded as direct or indirect. The customs of the trade have to be taken into account, or a decision which appears fair and reasonable in the circumstances has to be made. For example, direct materials used in very small quantities or with a very low cost may be treated as a production indirect cost as a matter of convenience.

2.2 Direct labour costs

These are labour costs which can be identified with and allocated to cost units, i.e. direct labour is all labour expended in altering the construction, composition, conformation or condition of the product: in a *manufacturing* concern, the direct labour cost will be wages paid to operators who are immediately concerned with the manufacture of a product (who do something to the materials).

In a *service* industry, the term is related to those employees who directly carry out that service (bus drivers, postmen).

2.3 Direct expenses

These consist of any expenditure other than direct materials and direct labour directly incurred on a specific cost unit, e.g.

(a) hire of equipment for a particular job,

(b) cost of special layout, design or drawings

(i.e. expenses which can be identified with and allocated to cost centres or cost units).

2.4 Prime cost—cost in relation to a cost unit

The prime cost is the sum of direct materials, direct labour and direct expenses which can be identified with and allocated to cost units.

3.0 INDIRECT COSTS

Accountants use the words "overhead" or "burden" to cover materials, labour and expenses which it is either impossible or inconvenient to charge direct to a cost unit.

3.1 Classification of indirect costs

(a) *Production, factory or works overhead.* Factory overhead includes all production costs other than direct materials, direct labour and direct expenses.

(b) *Indirect materials.* These include:

(i) factory supplies;

(ii) lubricants for machines;

(iii) materials which form part of the product and which can be identified but are too insignificant in value, such as thread, glue and laces in producing shoes.

(c) *Indirect labour cost.* This is labour expended that *does not* alter the construction, conformation or condition of the product *but which contributes* generally to such work and to the completion of the product, its progressive movement and handling up to the point of dispatch. All factory wages which have not been charged direct to a product. Examples are:

(i) supervision;

(ii) inspection;

(iii) salaries of factory administration clerks;

(iv) holiday pay, employers' National Insurance contributions, pension contributions, sick pay, overtime premium of direct workers to the extent that they have not been charged as direct labour costs.

(d) *Indirect expenses.* These are expenses incurred by the undertaking which may be either allocated to the factory or partially apportioned to it.

Examples are rent, insurance of buildings and plant and machinery, depreciation of plant and machinery, maintenance and repairs, power, light and heat, small tools. Factory services such as welfare, first aid, canteen, printing and stationery, travel expenses.

3.2 Full factory cost

This comprises the sum of direct and indirect factory costs, i.e. prime cost plus production overhead.

3.3 Administrative expenses

These are indirect expenditure incurred in the direction, control and administration of an undertaking, for example:

(a) administrative and office salaries;

(b) rent and rates of administrative offices;

(c) printing and stationery;

(d) legal expenses;

(e) depreciation and repairs to office buildings and machinery.

3.4 Selling expenses

These are indirect costs incurred in soliciting and securing orders from customers and of efforts to find and retain customers, for example:

(a) salaries and commission to salesmen;

(b) advertising;

(c) bad debts and collection charges;

(d) samples and entertainment.

3.5 Distribution expenses

These comprise indirect expenses incurred from the time the product is completed in the factory until it reaches its point of sale, for example:

(a) freight and insurance charges;

(b) rent, rates and insurance of warehouses;

(c) salaries;

(d) wages of packers, dispatch clerks and cleaners;

(e) depreciation of delivery vans.

3.6 Analysis of total cost

	£	£
Direct materials	x	
Direct labour	x	
Direct expenses	x	
Prime cost		x
Production overhead		x
Cost of goods manufactured		x
Administration, selling and distribution		x
Total cost		£x

4.0 DISTINCTIONS BETWEEN PERIOD COST, PRODUCT COST AND PROFIT DETERMINATION

4.1 Period costs

These (sometimes called *expired* costs) are expenses (or losses) incurred during the accounting period and are not treated as assets of the company. They do not form part of the product cost because:

(a) their future benefits are unpredictable;

(b) the current period can bear the expenses;

(c) they do not represent future benefits.

4.2 Product costs

These depend on the technique of costing used:

(a) under *marginal* costing: variable manufacturing costs of the product;

(b) under *absorption* costing: total manufacturing cost of the product.

5.0 HISTORICAL ABSORPTION COSTING

Under absorption costing, manufacturing costs are charged to units of production and are held as assets of the company until the goods to which they are attached are sold. Non-manufacturing costs are treated not as product costs but as period costs.

Illustration 1

Manufacturing, trading, profit and loss account
for the year ended 31st December 19_7

Reference to notes	*Manufacturing Account*	£	£
	Direct materials		
	Opening stock 1.1._7	50,000	
	Purchases	150,000	
	Closing stock 31.12._7	(20,000)	
A	Cost of materials consumed during the period		180,000
	Direct labour		240,000
	Direct expenses		80,000
			500,000
	Production overhead		250,000
	Production costs incurred during year 19_7		750,000
	Add: Work in progress 1.1._7		250,000
			1,000,000
B	*Less:* Work in progress 31.12._7		(300,000)
	Costs of goods manufactured		£700,000

Trading Account

	Sales		2,400,000
	Finished goods—opening stock 1.1._7		400,000
	Cost of goods manufactured per manufacturing account		700,000
			1,100,000
C	Finished goods—closing stock 31.12._7		(300,000)
D	Manufacturing cost of goods sold		800,000
	Gross profit		1,600,000
	Less: Non-manufacturing costs		
E	Administration expenses	240,000	
F	Selling expenses	200,000	
G	Distribution expenses	60,000	500,000
	Net profit		£1,100,000

NOTE 1 PERIOD COSTS—EXPIRED COSTS

(D) Manufacturing cost of goods sold	£800,000
(E) Administration expenses	£240,000
(F) Selling expenses	£200,000
(G) Distribution expenses	£60,000

NOTE 2 PRODUCT COSTS—UNEXPIRED COSTS

(A) Raw materials carried forward	£20,000
(B) Work in progress carried forward	£300,000
(C) Finished goods	£300,000

6.0 DISTINCTIONS BETWEEN A MANUFACTURING CONCERN AND A MERCHANDISING CONCERN

6.1 Manufacturing concern (using absorption costing)

In a manufacturing concern raw materials are converted into products.

(a) The stock of raw materials at the end of the period is an asset of the company—*unexpired cost.*

(b) Work in progress at the end of the period contains cost of raw materials, direct labour and factory overhead—identified with units of products which are partly completed. It is treated as an asset of the company—*unexpired cost.*

(c) Finished goods. Cost of completed goods unsold—asset of the company—*unexpired cost.*

*Note: Manufacturing expenses such as depreciation on plant, insurance, wages and salaries of factory personnel, rent and rates, power, lighting and heating etc. form part of the product and are treated as assets of the company until sold (*unexpired until sold*).*

6.2 Merchandising concern

A merchandising concern performs no manufacturing function, i.e. goods are purchased ready for sale. Expenses such as depreciation of plant, insurance, wages and salaries, rent and rates, power, lighting and heating do not form part of the product and are treated as expenses of the period—*expired cost.*

Illustration 2: Merchandising company

Sales		£2,400,000
Opening stock	£500,000	
Purchases	900,000	
Closing stock	(400,000)	
Cost of goods sold		1,000,000
Gross profit		1,400,000
Administration, selling and distribution expenses		600,000
Net profit		£800,000

CHAPTER THREE

Accounting for Direct Materials

1.0 VALUATION OF PURCHASES

1.1 Guiding principle

All expenditure incurred in obtaining raw materials should form a part of the cost of materials. In other words, the cost of raw materials purchased should include not only the invoice price itself but also other expenses which are incurred in transporting materials to the purchaser.

(a) The costs incurred may be classified as follows:

(i) *Direct costs*, e.g. the invoice price and carriage.

(ii) *Indirect costs*, e.g. cost of ordering, storage, containers, insuring, unpacking, receiving and inspection. It is true that inclusion of these costs gives greater accuracy but the benefit received may be less than the clerical costs incurred.

These costs, therefore, are treated as production indirect costs.

(1) *Trade discount and quantity discount* are normally deducted from the quoted price and, therefore, are not recorded in the books of account.

(2) *Cash discount* is normally not deducted from the invoice price but treated as miscellaneous income (financial income).

(iii) *Carriage inwards* is a direct cost of materials but there are problems in allocating charges:

Illustration 1

1,000 kg of material A in 3 crates;
2,000 kg of material B in 5 crates;
300 kg of material C in 9 crates.

Invoice price (A + B + C)	£25,000
Carriage inwards	400

Freight is insignificant compared with the invoice price of materials and a practical method of accounting for carriage inwards on raw materials is to treat it as a manufacturing overhead.

(b) There are a number of reasons why some costs are excluded from the cost of materials purchased and treated as indirect expenses:

(i) Some of these costs are by and large fixed, e.g. inspection, storage, receiving and purchasing. If these costs are included then the cost per unit of material purchased during a period of relative inactivity would be higher, resulting in the same type of material bought at two different dates being at different prices in stock.

This would mean that two batches of the same type of material purchased at two different dates may have to be included in stock at different prices.

(ii) Allocation of the costs may be a problem. Size, value and weight of the material purchased may be used as a basis of apportionment, but none of these is applicable for all the various costs. For example, storage may be apportioned on the basis of area occupied and carriage on the basis of weight or distance.

(iii) Indirect costs are often insignificant in amount, as shown in Illustration 1 above relating to carriage.

2.0 PROCEDURE AND DOCUMENTATION

Procedure and documentation will cover:

(a) the ordering of material (*see* **2.1**);

(b) recording and checking (*see* **2.2**);

(c) payment.

2.1 Ordering of material

(a) The purchase requisition
A purchase requisition is the document which initiates the purchase of materials. It requests the purchasing department to purchase the wanted materials. In highly developed companies it is the responsibility of production control; in less highly developed companies it could be the responsibility of the production manager to determine the quantities of raw material to be ordered (*see* **5.0**).

ESSENTIAL INFORMATION ON A PURCHASE REQUISITION

(i) serial number;

(ii) name of department initiating requisition;

(iii) description of materials required;

(iv) date of delivery required;

(v) date of issue;

(vi) signature of responsible person.

(b) The purchase order

A purchase order is sent by the purchasing department to a supplier for specified materials. A copy of the order is sent to the department which initiated the purchase requisition.

ESSENTIAL INFORMATION ON A PURCHASE ORDER

(i) quantity and full description of goods;

(ii) date of delivery;

(iii) location where delivery is to be made;

(iv) terms of payment;

(v) price per unit and total cost of the order;

(vi) reference to purchase requisition;

(vii) signature of responsible person.

2.2 Recording and checking

(a) Receipt of goods

(i) *Delivery.* The materials are delivered with an advice note, and are accepted after checking by a responsible official.

(ii) *Inspection.* Some materials bought have to be inspected to establish that the quality of the goods is in accordance with the details on the purchase order.

(iii) *Stores—goods received note (GRN).* The materials are then sent to stores. It is the storekeeper's function to look after them. He accepts responsibility by entering the details on a goods received note (GRN).

Copies of the GRN are sent to the person responsible for initiating the purchase, the buying department and the accounts department and a copy is retained in the stores.

ESSENTIAL INFORMATION ON A GOODS RECEIVED NOTE

(i) serial number;

(ii) date of receipt of materials;

(iii) supplier and carrier;

(iv) description, quantity and code of materials;

(v) supplier's advice note number;

(vi) signature of a responsible person—usually the storekeeper.

(b) Materials returned to suppliers
Materials to be returned to suppliers are packed in the receiving department and a debit note raised immediately.

2.3 Payment

The supplier's invoice, when received, is checked by the accounts department against the purchase requisition, purchase order, advice note, inspection report and GRN. The invoice, if in order, is passed for payment.

2.4 Illustrative flowchart

The flowchart in Fig. 3 illustrates the whole procedure.

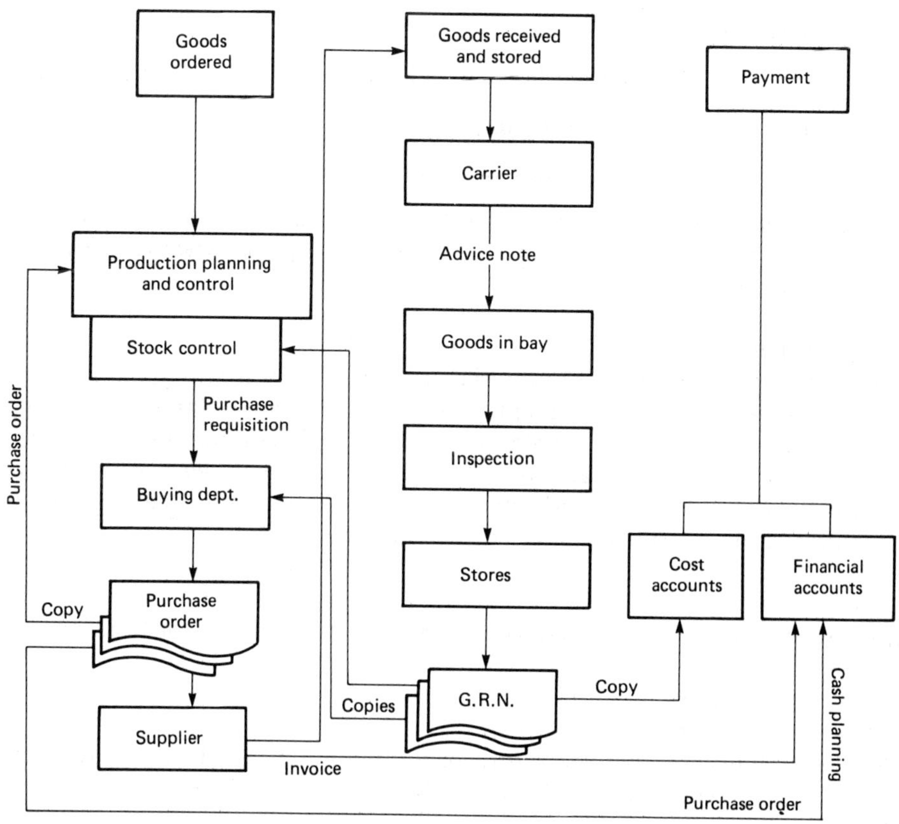

Fig. 3. *Flowchart—ordering, receiving and paying.*

3.0 MATERIALS ISSUES

3.1 Forms used

(a) Material requisition note

A document which authorises and records the issue of materials for use. It is both an authorisation and a record of usage.

ESSENTIAL FEATURES

Material requisitions should contain the following information:

(i) number of note;

(ii) date of requisitioning;

(iii) description of materials;

(iv) material code number;

(v) quantity required;

(vi) quantity issued;

(vii) job or departmental number;

(viii) stores from which issued;

(ix) signature of person authorised to issue a material requisition note;

(x) signature of person receiving materials.

There should also be space for unit price for pricing purposes.

Note: In most firms the material requisition note for direct materials is passed from the stores to the production control department for recording the issue in the perpetual inventory record cards and then to the cost office.

(b) Bill of materials

Some companies make a list of materials required for a specific job. This is normally done by a technical department, either production planning or engineering department. It serves as a single or blanket authorisation in lieu of a material requisition note. The advantages of bills of materials are: paper work is reduced, exact quantities can be requisitioned, storekeepers can be instructed to issue materials according to a plan, and risk of clerical error is reduced.

(c) Materials transfer note

A document used to transfer material from one job to another or from one cost centre to another.

(d) Materials return note

A document which records the return of unused materials. If materials requisitioned are in excess of requirements, it is the duty of the person in charge to return the materials to stores.

3.2 Pricing materials issues

The material requisition notes will be used to update the stores ledger and to charge the jobs with the cost of direct materials consumed.

There are a number of methods in common use for pricing material requisition notes:

(a) first in first out (FIFO)

(b) last in first out (LIFO)

(c) simple average

(d) weighted average

(e) periodic simple average

(f) periodic weighted average

(g) standard price

(h) replacement cost

(j) highest in first out (HIFO)

(k) next in first out (NIFO).

Each of these methods is explained in turn below, using Illustration 2.

Illustration 2

X Ltd had 100 units of item XY in stock at 1st January 19_1. They had cost £1 each.

During January the following transactions took place:

19_1	
3 Jan.	Bought 500 units at £2.00 each
5 Jan.	Bought 400 units at £2.50 each
6 Jan.	Issued 700 units
7 Jan.	Bought 300 units at £3.00 each
10 Jan.	Issued 400 units

You are required to calculate the price at which the issues on 6th and 10th January should be charged out, using the first six of the ten possible methods listed above in turn. The advantages and disadvantages of each method should also be stated.

The following stores ledger account shows the record of the above transactions:

RECORD KEPT IN THE COST OFFICE

Stores Ledger

Material: type
code
description

Date	RECEIPTS				ISSUES				BALANCE	
	GRN	Quantity	Price per unit	Amount	MRN	Quantity	Price per unit	Amount	Quantity	Amount
		Units	£	£		*Units*	£	£	*Units*	£
1 JAN	–	–	–	–	–	–	–	–	100	100
3 JAN	GRN	500	2.00	1,000						
5 JAN	GRN	400	2.50	1,000						
6 JAN	–	–	–	–	MRN	700	PROBLEM			
7 JAN	GRN	300	3.00	900						
10 JAN	–	–	–	–	MRN	400				

3.3 Factors to be considered in deciding on pricing method

(a) The method of costing:
   (i) unit process or average costing;
   (ii) job, batch or contract costing;

(b) policy of the company;

(c) cost of work involved;

(d) costing records to follow the physical movement of production;

(e) degree of price fluctuations;

(f) frequency of material issues;

(g) frequency of raw material purchases;

(h) report purchasing efficiency;

(j) quantities of materials to be purchased at any one time;

(k) need to comply with SSAP 9 in presenting financial accounts.

3.4 First in first out (FIFO)

(a) *Calculation*
The method assumes that materials bought earlier are the first to be issued and that the requisitions are priced at the earliest prices paid for the materials which are in stock. On this basis the 700 issue will be priced as follows:

100 units at £1.00 =	£100
500 units at £2.00 =	1,000
100 units at £2.50 =	250
	£1,350

Note: To use a price, materials bought at that price must be in stock.

The 10th January issue will be:

300 units at £2.50 =	£750
100 units at £3.00 =	300
	£1,050

(b) *Advantages and disadvantages*

(i) Advantages:
Closing stock represents the latest prices paid for the materials;
materials are priced at actual cost;
it is simple to understand.

(ii) Disadvantages:
Costly in operation: for example, it may be necessary to apportion a requisition to cost it; someone has to confirm that materials bought at that price are in stock;
it does not assist in fixing selling prices;
if prices fluctuate sharply then comparison of costs of one job with another may be difficult.

Note: In a period of rising prices, cost of materials charged to production will be low and closing stock will be valued at high prices.

In a period of falling prices, cost of materials charged to production will be high compared with current costs and closing stock of raw materials will be at low prices.

3.5 Last in first out (LIFO)

(a) *Calculation*
The last in first out method is virtually the opposite of FIFO. The method assumes that materials bought recently are the first to be issued and requisitions are priced at the most recent prices paid for the *materials which are in stock.*

Issue on 6th January (700) will be priced as:

400 units at £2.50 =	£1,000
300 units at £2.00 =	600
	£1,600

Note: To use a price materials bought at that price must be in stock.

Issue on 10th January will be priced as:

300 units at £3.00 =	£900
100 units at £2.00 =	200
	£1,100

(b) *Advantages and disadvantages*

(i) Advantages:
Materials are charged out at the latest prices paid for them;
the method may cause profit to be shown at a lower figure, thus saving tax if the tax authorities allow its use. (They do not in the UK.)

(ii) Disadvantages:
Closing stock is recorded at the earliest price paid for the materials and in periods of rising prices it may be well below current cost of replacement;
the method is costly in preparation. Each time a requisition is priced one has to identify that materials bought at that price are in stock;
in a period of falling prices stock may have to be written off to reduce stock values at cost to the current market values if such is lower than cost.

Note: In a period of rising prices, the cost of material charged to production would be high and closing stock would be valued at low prices.

In a period of falling prices, the cost of materials charged to production would be low compared with current costs and closing stock would be at high prices, resulting in high write-offs if the market price is lower.

3.6 Simple average

The total of the prices paid for the materials is divided by the number of prices used in the calculation. The prices paid for the materials fully issued from stock do not form a part of the calculations. It can be seen that this is similar to the FIFO method, with the difference that the simple average takes the average of all prices paid for materials which are in stock, whereas FIFO takes the earliest price of materials which are in stock.

Using simple averages,

the *issue on the 6th* will be priced as:

$$\pounds 1.00 + \pounds 2.00 + \pounds 2.50 = \frac{\pounds 5.50}{3} = \pounds 1.833 \text{ per unit,}$$

while the *issue on the 10th* will be:

$$\pounds 2.50 + \pounds 3.00 = \frac{\pounds 5.50}{2} = \pounds 2.75 \text{ per unit.}$$

3.7 Weighted average

This method of pricing, also known as the moving or running average method, is used by companies which seek to spread the cost of materials evenly. The moving average is calculated by dividing the cost of materials in stock by the quantities of materials in stock.

Procedure. Cost of materials purchased plus cost of material on hand is divided by the total quantity bought plus the quantity on hand. A new price is calculated when materials are bought and not when materials are issued.

Calculation of issue prices:

3rd January: $$\frac{£100+£1{,}000}{600}=£1.8333$$

5th January: $$\frac{£1{,}100+£1{,}000}{1{,}000}=£2.100$$

6th January: $$700\times £2.10=£1{,}470$$

7th January: $$\frac{£1{,}100+£1{,}000-£1{,}470+£900}{1{,}000-700+300}=£2.55$$

10th January: $$400\times £2.55=£1{,}020.$$

Closing stock balance:

Opening stock	100 units	£100
Add: Receipts	1,200 units	2,900
		3,000
Less: Issues	1,100 units	2,490
		£510

Note issues:

6th January	700	£1,470
10th January	400	1,020
	1,100	£2,490

3.8 Periodic simple average

The issue price is calculated at the end of the period. The total of the prices paid for the materials purchased during the *period* is divided by the number of prices used in the calculation. To use a price in the calculation it must be a price paid during the period.

The price of the materials in stock brought forward does not form a part of the calculation because it was not a price paid during the current accounting period.

$$\text{Periodic simple average: } £2.00+£2.50+£3.00=\frac{£7.50}{3}=£2.50 \text{ per unit.}$$

Issues during the period (i.e. on the 6th and 10th) would be priced at £2.50 per unit.

The method is simple to operate as material requisitions are costed at the end of the period; but this throws a great burden on the accounting staff at that time.

3.9 Periodic weighted average

The total cost of purchases made during the *period* is divided by the total quantity purchased during the period.

Notes

(a) The opening stock does not form a part of the calculation, as it was not purchased during the period.

(b) The term "weighted average" is used by some accountants to refer to two different systems, namely the weighted average and the periodic weighted average.

Receipts during the period:

	Units	*Amount*
3rd January	500	£1,000
5th January	400	1,000
7th January	300	900
	1,200	£2,900

Periodic weighted average price for pricing issues made during the period:

$$\frac{£2{,}900}{1{,}200} = £2.4167.$$

3.10 Standard price

This is a predetermined or an expected future price. Material requisitions are priced at this price regardless of the actual cost. The difference between the actual cost of materials bought and the standard cost is called a price variance.

The price variance is calculated at either:

(a) the time of purchase, in which case the stock accounts are at standard cost as also are issues; or

(b) the time of issue, in which case stock accounts are at actual cost. Price variance is calculated on quantity issued and issues to production are still at standard cost.

Illustration 3

Predetermined price £2.00 per unit.

1st January received	1,000 units at £2.50
10th January received	2,000 units at £3.00
19th January issued	500 units
24th January issued	1,000 units

PRICE VARIANCE CALCULATED AT THE TIME OF PURCHASE

		Dr	Cr
1st January	Stock account 1,000 × £2	£2,000	
	Material price variance	500	
	Trade creditors 1,000 × £2.50		£2,500
10th January	Stock account 2,000 × £2.00	4,000	
	Material price variance	2,000	
	Trade creditors 2,000 × £3.00		6,000
19th and 24th January	*Issues*		
	Work in progress 1,500 at £2	3,000	
	Stock control—raw materials		3,000

PRICE VARIANCE CALCULATED AT THE TIME OF ISSUE

		Dr	Cr
1st January			
Stock account	1,000 × £2.50	£2,500	
Trade creditors			£2,500
10th January			
Stock account	2,000 × £3.00	6,000	
Trade creditors			6,000
19th January			
Work in progress	500 × £2.00	1,000	
Material price variance		250	
Stock account	500 × £2.50		1,250
24th January			
Work in progress	500 × £2.00	1,000	
Work in progress	500 × £2.00	1,000	
Material price variance		250	
Material price variance		500	
Stock account	500 × £2.50		1,250
Stock account	500 × £3.00		1,500

Notes

(a) *Material price variance:* *£250 (£1,250 – 1,000)*
£500 (£1,500 – 1,000)

(b) *Material requisitions are priced at standard cost (charge to work-in-progress is always at standard cost)*

(c) *The issue price is fixed for use over a period of time regardless of the actual price paid during this period.*

3.11 Replacement price

This is the cost of replacing the materials issued. Under this method the replacement price at the time of each issue will have to be known.

3.12 Highest in first out

Issues are priced at the most expensive material in stock. To use a price materials bought at that price must be in stock.

Using HIFO, the issue on 6th January in Illustration 2 above will be priced as:

400 units at £2.50	£1,000
300 units at £2.00	600
	£1,600

3.13 Next in first out

This method attempts to value material issues at actual price, i.e. as near as possible to the market price. It prices material requisition at a committed price (the price of the materials which are on order but not yet received).

4.0 EXAMPLES

Example 1

The following information relates to material RAP 43 for the year 19_9:

Quantities				*Value in £*			
Date	*Received*	*Issued*	*Balance*	*Unit price*	*Receipts*	*Issues*	*Balance*
				£	£	£	£
Jan. 1			600	5.00			
15	900			6.00			
Feb. 12		150					
20		300					
Mar. 10		660					
Apr. 25	900			7.00			
May 20		600					
June 20		450					
Aug. 20	900			8.00			
Sept. 15		180					
Nov. 20		360					
Dec. 10		150					

Stock of RAP 43 has been charged on the FIFO basis until 1st January 19_9, but the system was changed on that date to the standard costing system to simplify data processing operations. The standard price was set at £5.00 per unit.

(a) What difference in cost charged to work in progress (WIP) for the year has been caused by the change?

(b) What is the closing stock value under the new system?

(c) Calculate the material price variance and state whether it is favourable or adverse.

(d) If a periodic weighted average basis had been used for charging out materials, what difference would this have made to the closing stock value?

(50 minutes)

Suggested answer

(a) *Standard cost of materials consumed*

Issues at £5.00 × 2,850 units			£14,250
FIFO issues			
Feb. 12	150 at £5.00	£750	
20	300 at £5.00	1,500	
Mar. 10	150 at £5.00	750	
10	510 at £6.00	3,060	
May 20	390 at £6.00	2,340	
20	210 at £7.00	1,470	
June 20	450 at £7.00	3,150	
Sept. 15	180 at £7.00	1,260	
Nov. 20	60 at £7.00	420	
20	300 at £8.00	2,400	
Dec. 10	150 at £8.00	1,200	18,300
Difference in cost charge to WIP			£4,050

(b) *Closing stock value under the new system*

It is assumed that the *price variance is calculated at the time of issue*

Opening stock units	600	
Purchases	2,700	
	3,300	
Issues	2,850	
Closing book stock	450	
Valuation 450 at £8 =		£3,600

(c) *Material price variance*

Total issues—units	2,850
Issued at STD prices	600
	2,250

	Price variance
900 units at £6 (£5–6)	£900
900 units at £7 (£5–7)	1,800
450 units at £8 (£5–8)	1,350
Price variance	£4,050

The material price variance is adverse. Actual price per unit incurred was more than the standard price specified.

(d) *Periodic weighted average*

Units		*Amount*	*Weighted average*
900 at £6	=	£5,400	
900 at £7	=	6,300	
900 at £8	=	7,200	
2,700		£18,900	£7

Opening stock	600 units at £5		£3,000
Receipts	2,700 units		18,900
	3,300		21,900
Issues	2,850 units at £7		19,950
Closing stock	450		£1,950
Closing stock under the new system:		450 × £8 =	£3,600
Closing stock as above		=	1,950
Difference in closing stock value			£1,650

Example 2

The newly appointed cost accountant of the Harrow Manufacturing Co. Ltd, Rodney Nelson, presented the managing director with five different schedules of gross profit for the half year ended 30th June 19–7.

	Sales	*Cost of sales*	*Gross profit*
Schedule 1	£720,000	£216,000	£504,000
Schedule 2	720,000	360,010	359,990
Schedule 3	720,000	320,000	400,000
Schedule 4	720,000	385,000	335,000
Schedule 5	720,000	360,000	360,000

The cost of goods sold in each schedule is based on the following data:

Opening stock b/f	1st January	10,000	£3	£30,000
Purchases	20th February	30,000	4	120,000
Purchases	20th April	10,000	5	50,000
Purchases	20th May	20,000	6	120,000
Purchases	10th June	10,000	7	70,000

Selling price per unit is £10.2857; standard cost per unit is £3.0857.

Jim Brown, the managing director, cannot understand how *five* different gross profit figures can be computed from the same information.

You are required to explain without using accounting jargon how different profit figures can be computed from the same accounting data. *(40 minutes)*

Suggested answer

SCHEDULE 1—STANDARD PRICE

Cost of goods sold is at standard price

70,000 × £3.0857 £216,000

SCHEDULE 2—PERIODIC WEIGHTED AVERAGE

Cost of sales: 70,000 × £5.143 = £360,010

Periodic weighted average price $\dfrac{£360{,}010}{70{,}000 \text{ units}} =$ £5.143

Note: Opening stock does not form a part of the calculation.

SCHEDULE 3—FIRST IN FIRST OUT

10,000 at £3	£30,000
30,000 at £4	120,000
10,000 at £5	50,000
20,000 at £6	120,000
70,000	Cost of sales £320,000

SCHEDULE 4—PERIODIC SIMPLE AVERAGE

$£4+£5+£6+£7=\frac{£22}{4}=$	£5.50
Cost of sales: 70,000 units at £5.50=	£385,000

SCHEDULE 5—LAST IN FIRST OUT

Stock at the end represents the earliest purchases:

10,000 at £7		£70,000
20,000 at £6		120,000
10,000 at £5		50,000
30,000 at £4		120,000
70,000	Cost of sales	£360,000

5.0 PURPOSE OF STOCK CONTROL

Stock control must meet two opposing needs:

(a) Sufficient materials are in stock to meet normal production and at times abnormal demands.

(b) In meeting the above requirements, the company does not tie up too much money in unnecessary large stocks.

5.1 Definition

The Institute of Cost and Management Accountants, in its publication *An Introduction to Budgetary Control, Standard Costing, Material Control and Production Control*, has defined stock control as the function of ensuring that sufficient goods are retained in stock to meet all requirements without carrying unnecessarily large stocks.

The objective is to be able to order materials at the right time from a dependable service to acquire the right quantity and quality at a fair price.

5.2 Functions of stock control

These are to ensure that:

(a) the minimum amount of capital is tied up;

(b) there are sufficient materials in stock to meet production demands;

(c) periods of short supply are anticipated (seasonal fluctuation);

(d) price changes are anticipated;

(e) slow-moving items are kept to a minimum;

(f) up-to-date records are kept;

(g) the necessary management reports are issued when action is called for.

5.3 Responsibility for stock control

(a) *Highly developed concerns.* Here stock control is the responsibility of the production planning and control department.

In addition to its other functions, it is the responsibility of production control to determine the quantities of raw materials to be ordered and to be maintained in stock.

(b) *Less highly developed concerns.* In these stock control may be the responsibility of:

(i) the production manager

(ii) the stores department.

5.4 Stock information requirements

Stock information requirements of management vary greatly. For example, the production controller, buyer and production manager all think by and large in terms of *quantities* in stock, on order or consumed, while financial controllers, top management and accountants are primarily concerned with the *money tied up in stock*.

Therefore, control information must be provided to both groups and it is most important that these two groups act in harmony with the overall objective of the company.

5.5 Basis of stock control

Figure 4 shows various methods by which control can be established.

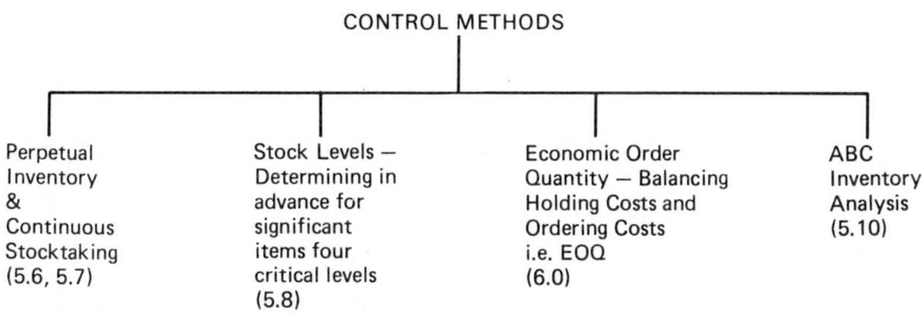

Fig. 4. *Methods of stock control.*

5.6 Perpetual inventory

The department responsible for stock control keeps records of each type of material in stock and records the day-to-day movements on the record card. Perpetual inventory is a stock recording system which provides an up-to-date record of the stock balances held at any given time.

The purpose of perpetual inventory is to control stock items from day to day. Therefore any movements must be recorded so that the stock card is up to date. The form and content of the perpetual inventory record card is to a very large extent dependent upon the particular circumstances of the company.

The card may show:

(a) description—code number;

(b) location in stock room;

(c) unit of measurement;

(d) maximum/minimum quantities;

(e) reorder level, reorder quantities;

(f) receipts, issues, allocated, balance in stock.

5.7 Continuous stocktaking

(a) Definition

Continuous stocktaking is the checking of stock items regularly, rather than at the end of the year or periodically. Sufficient items are checked each day so that in the course of a year all items are checked once, and fast-moving items several times.

(b) Purposes

(i) Stock control.

(ii) To check the accuracy of perpetual inventory records.

(c) System in operation

(i) *Checkers*. Independent personnel having no responsibility for stocks.

(ii) *Forms*. All differences are recorded and reported.

(iii) *Checking*. A few items are checked each day and all items are checked within a period of time (2, 4 or 6 months).

(d) Advantages of continuous stocktaking combined with perpetual inventory control

(i) If the system of perpetual inventory and continuous stocktaking works well, then an end-of-year physical count of stock can be dispensed with.

(ii) Fast-moving, valuable items can be checked more frequently.

(iii) Explanations for differences can be found with greater ease.

(iv) Satisfactory stock figures are available for periodic internal reporting.

(v) Losses are revealed much earlier.

(vi) Production dislocation due to stocktaking is avoided.

(e) The year-end stocktaking in a system of continuous stocktaking

In order to ensure accuracy of perpetual records, firms have introduced continuous stocktaking. The quantities shown on the perpetual inventory card are checked regularly with a physical stock count. As long as this is done throughout the year as company policy and any discrepancies have been investigated and adjusted, the balances on the perpetual inventory record card may be accepted as stock on hand and used for balance-sheet purposes.

5.8 Stock levels

It is one of the functions of stock control to ensure that sufficient goods are retained in stock.

Some of the considerations which will influence the level of stocks are:

(a) anticipated production demand;

(b) amount of capital available;

(c) reliability of suppliers;

(d) availability of storage space;

(e) cost of storing;

(f) minimum order quantities imposed by the supplier;

(g) procurement costs;

(h) risk of loss due to:

- (i) deterioration;
- (ii) evaporation;
- (iii) changes in fashion;
- (iv) fall in price.

The four critical levels in a stock control system

Stock control is based on determining in advance, for each significant item of stock, four critical levels:

(a) MINIMUM STOCK LEVEL

The level below which the stock should not be allowed to fall is essentially a base stock level and is set by:

(i) the reorder level;

(ii) delivery time;

(iii) rate of consumption.

To calculate the minimum stock level, deduct from the reorder level ((c) below) a figure representing the normal (or average) demand over normal (or average) delivery time.

(Reorder level less average usage for average reorder period.)

(b) MAXIMUM STOCK LEVEL

The upper limit above which the stock should not be allowed to rise. The following factors determine the maximum stock of an item:

(i) period of time between order and receipt;

(ii) rate of consumption;

(iii) cost of storage;

(iv) storage space available;

(v) availability of capital;

(vi) price fluctuation;

(vii) economic purchasing quantities.

From the reorder level (ROL) *deduct* the lowest likely demand for the shortest period and to the balance add the reorder quantity (ROQ).

(Maximum level = ROL + ROQ *less:* Minimum usage during minimum reorder period.)

(c) REORDER LEVEL

The first level to be fixed. This is a point that lies between maximum and minimum stock levels at which the purchase order must be placed to ensure that the goods ordered are received before the minimum level is reached. It is the level to which the uncommitted stock or free stock including goods on order is allowed to fall before an order for further stock is made.

There are two methods of calculating reorder level:

Method (i): Maximum usage × Maximum RO period

Method (ii): Maximum usage × Maximum RO period + minimum stock level.

(d) AVERAGE STOCK LEVEL

This is calculated as

$$\frac{\text{Maximum stock} + \text{Minimum stock}}{2}$$

5.9 Illustrations

The following illustrations show typical calculations involved, including the critical reorder quantity calculation (Illustration 4).

Illustration 4

Expected consumption:	Maximum	4,500 kg per week
	Minimum	2,400 kg per week
	Average	3,450 kg per week.
Expected delivery period:	Maximum	4 weeks
	Average	$2\frac{1}{2}$ weeks
	Minimum	2 weeks.
Maximum stock level:		22,000 kg.

REORDER LEVEL—METHOD 1

(Maximum usage × Maximum ROP)

4,500 kg × 4 weeks = 18,000 kg.

REORDER QUANTITY

Note: Maximum stock level equals ROL less minimum usage in minimum delivery period plus reorder quantity.

22,000 = 18,000 minus 2,400 × 2 + ROQ
22,000 = 18,000 minus 4,800 + ROQ
22,000 = 13,200 + ROQ
ROQ = 22,000 minus 13,200 = 8,800 kg.

ROL minus (NC × NRP) = (18,000 minus 3,450 × ($2\frac{1}{2}$) = 9,375 g.

Illustration 5

Two basic raw materials, L and S, are used as follows:

Normal usage	= 100 kg per week of each
Maximum usage	= 150 kg per week of each
Minimum usage	= 50 kg per week of each
Reorder quantity	= type L 600 kg
	type S 1,000 kg
Reorder period	type L = 4 to 6 weeks
Reorder period	type S = 2 to 4 weeks

Required: calculate for each type of material (a) reorder level; (b) minimum stock level; (c) maximum stock level; (d) average stock level.

Comment briefly on the difference in levels for the two types of material.

Suggested answer

REORDER LEVEL

Maximum usage × Maximum ROP

Type L = 150 × 6 = 900 kg

Type S = 150 × 4 = 600 kg

Reorder level of S is lower because reorder period is 4 weeks for S against 6 weeks for L.

MINIMUM STOCK LEVEL

ROL − NC × NRP Type L = 900 − 100 × 5 = 400 kg

Type S = 600 − 100 × 3 = 300 kg

Minimum level for S is lower mainly because of lower reordering level.

MAXIMUM STOCK LEVEL

ROL − (Minimum C × Minimum ROP) + ROQ

$$\text{Type L} = 900 - (50 \times 4) + 600 = \underline{\underline{1{,}300\text{ kg}}}$$

$$\text{Type S} = 600 - (50 \times 2) + 1{,}000 = \underline{\underline{1{,}500\text{ kg}}}$$

Maximum level for S is higher mainly because of its higher reorder quantity.

AVERAGE STOCK LEVEL

$$\frac{\text{Maximum} + \text{Minimum}}{2}$$

$$\text{Type L} = \tfrac{1}{2}(1{,}300 + 400) = \underline{\underline{850\text{ kg}}}$$

$$\text{Type S} = \tfrac{1}{2}(1{,}500 + 300) = \underline{\underline{900\text{ kg}}}$$

The average stock level of S is more because of the higher range between the maximum and minimum levels.

5.10 ABC inventory analysis

The ABC method attempts to control significant items in stock. This concept, known as Pareto analysis, or control by importance and exception (CIE), requires constant review of stocks. For example, it is not economical to control an item A which costs £0.20 per unit with an annual usage of 10,000 units as tightly as another item, B, which costs £20 per unit with an annual usage of 400 units:

Item	*Per unit*	*Annual usage*	*Total cost*	*% of total cost*
A	£0.20	10,000	£2,000	20%
B	£20.00	400	£8,000	80%
			£10,000	100%

This method concentrates *not* on the cost of each item but on the total annual usage cost of items of stock. The annual cost of each item in stock is determined and all the annual costs are then ranked on the basis of their descending order of importance. As a rule, about 20 per cent of items in stock account for about 80 per cent of the spending and hence 80 per cent of the items represents only 20 per cent of spending. Therefore, a greater degree of control can be effected by concentrating on only a few items.

Illustration 6

The following, although simplified, demonstrates the classification of items:

Item	*Annual requirements (units)*	*% of total*	*Cost per unit*	*Annual cost*	*% of total cost*
XY 1	7,500	5	£10	£75,000	35
XY 2	6,000	4	8	48,000	23
XY 8	8,250	5.5	4	33,000	16
XY 12	9,000	6	2	18,000	9
XY 32	10,000	6.67	1	10,000	5
XY 42	12,000	8	0.6	7,200	3
XY 52	15,000	10	0.4	6,000	3
XY 62	20,000	13.33	0.25	5,000	2
XY 72	25,000	16.67	0.18	4,500	2
XY 82	37,250	24.83	0.12	4,470	2
Total	150,000	100%		£211,170	100%

SUMMARY—THE CLASSIFICATION

Items	*% of total annual requirements*	*% of total annual cost*	*Relative value*
XY 1	5	35	
XY 2	4	23	
Total	9%	58%	High-value A items
XY 8	5.50	16	
XY 12	6.0	9	
XY 32	6.67	5	
Total	18.17%	30%	Medium-value B items
XY 42	8	3	
XY 52	10	3	
XY 62	13.33	2	
XY 72	16.67	2	
XY 82	24.83	2	
Total	72.83%	12%	Low-value C items

High-value or A items would come under very strict control. Low-value or C items would be under visual or physical control and medium-value or B items require average control measures. Clearly, it would be more beneficial to control A and B items which constitute about 27 per cent of stock rather than unnecessarily attempting to control all items of stock.

6.0 ECONOMIC ORDER QUANTITY—HOW MUCH TO ORDER

Economic order quantity (EOQ) is the size of the purchase order which minimises the combined annual cost of:

(a) placing orders;

(b) holding stock;

(c) purchase price (it is assumed that price per unit is constant over a wide range).

6.1 Cost of placing an order

It is assumed that it costs as much to place an order for a small quantity as it does for a large quantity. Certain costs would remain unchanged regardless of the quantity ordered. Examples of relevant ordering costs are: issue of order requests; stationery; postage; telephone; physical work involved in unloading; inspection and storage of goods; and typing the order.

6.2 Cost of holding or carrying stock

This cost includes such items as: storage costs; handling costs; damage; pilferage; obsolescence; administration costs in keeping records and interest on capital tied up in stock.

6.3 Balancing trick

As the size of an order increases, the number of orders needed is reduced and the total cost of placing an order is reduced. As the stock level increases cost of holding will increase. At some point, there is an ideal order size that will minimise the total cost over a given period of time; when the total cost of holding stock is equal to the ordering cost, total cost for a given period of time is minimised.

6.4 Concept of average stock

In order to demonstrate the concept one has to assume ideal conditions. It is assumed that usage takes place uniformly and that a new batch of materials will be received when stocks are fully used. For example, assume an initial stock of 8,000 units which is used at a constant rate of 500 units per week. It takes 16 weeks to exhaust the stock to nil. Average stock held during the period is half of 8,000, i.e. 4,000 units, on the assumption that a new batch of 8,000 units will be received when stocks are fully used.

Illustration 7

Week		*Level of stock*
0	Opening	8,000
1		7,500
2		7,000
3		6,500
4		6,000
5		5,500
6		5,000
7		4,500
8		4,000
9		3,500
10		3,000
11		2,500
12		2,000
13		1,500
14		1,000
15		500
16	Closing	nil
17		68,000

$$\text{Average stock} = \frac{68{,}000}{17} = 4{,}000 \text{ units.}$$

Where usage is not constant owing to seasonal variations in production, the average stock for a period will be greater or less than one-half the opening stock.

Average stock may be determined in two ways:

(a) Opening stock + Closing stock and divide by 2; or

(b) Opening stock + Stock at mid-period + Closing stock and divide by 3.

If the average stock is assumed to be half the order quantity, it is essential to determine what this order quantity should be.

SOLVING FOR EOQ

Assumptions:

(a) Conditions of certainty.

(b) Average stock held is half of order quantity.

(c) Price per unit remains unchanged over a wide range.

6.5 Methods used to determine EOQ

(a) Formula method:

(i) number of units per order

(ii) number of orders per year.

(b) Tabular solution.

(a) Formula method—Illustration 8

Frank plc buys component Arty from Potts Manufacturing Company at £2.00 per unit. Total annual requirements are 10,000 units at the rate of 40 units per working day. The following relevant information is available:

Ordering costs per order = £10.00

Interest on capital invested per annum = 10 per cent, i.e. £0.40 per unit in stock.

Other holding costs, taxes, insurance, storage etc. = £0.10 per unit.

FORMULA METHOD—OPTIMUM NUMBER OF UNITS PER ORDER

$$E = \sqrt{\frac{2AP}{S}}$$

where: E = EOQ
A = periodic usage in units
P = cost of ordering and handling one order
S = cost of holding one unit in stock for one period, including interest.

Now, substituting the values into the formula, we get:

$$E = \sqrt{\frac{2 \times 10{,}000 \times £10}{£0.50}}$$

$$E = \sqrt{\frac{200{,}000}{0.50}}$$

$$\text{EOQ} = \sqrt{400{,}000} \text{ units}$$

$$= 633 \text{ units (approx.).}$$

$\therefore$ Number of orders per year = 10,000 ÷ 633
= 16 (approx.).

(b) Tabular approach—Illustration 9

Annualised relevant costs of various orders.
Annual requirement 1,200 units of item Beauty.
Ordering costs per order: £50.00.
Carrying or holding costs per item: £0.50 per unit.

(a) *You are required* to prepare a schedule showing the associated costs if 1, 2, 3, 4, 5 or 6 orders were placed during the year.

(b) From your schedule, state the number of orders to be placed each year and the economic order quantity.

Note: Dividing the annual usage by the number of orders placed during the year gives different order sizes. The order sizes are therefore:

Number of orders per annum	*1*	*2*	*3*	*4*	*5*	*6*
Annual requirements—items	*1,200*	*1,200*	*1,200*	*1,200*	*1,200*	*1,200*
Order size—units	*1,200*	*600*	*400*	*300*	*240*	*200*

Suggested answer

SCHEDULE OF ORDER COSTS PER ANNUM

Number of orders per annum	(A)	1	2	3	4	5	6
Number of items per order (i.e. order size)	(B)	1,200	600	400	300	240	200
Average stock: $\frac{1}{2}$ of order quantity	(C)	600	300	200	150	120	100
Annual carrying cost per unit	(D)	£0.50	£0.50	£0.50	£0.50	£0.50	£0.50
Total annual carrying costs ((D) × (C))	(E)	£300	£150	£100	£75	£60	£50
Ordering costs at £10.00 per order ((A) × £50)	(F)	£50	£100	£150	£200	£250	£300
Total annual costs ((E) + (F))	(G)	350	250 ↓ minimum	250 ↓ minimum	275	310	350

The tabulation shows minimum costs at two levels. The next step would be to see if total cost is lower, somewhere between 600 units and 400 units, say 500 units:

(i) Holding costs − Average stock $\frac{500}{2}$ = 250 units × £0.50 = £125.

(ii) Ordering costs = Number of orders to be placed $\frac{1,200}{500}$ = 2.4 orders × £50 = £120.

Total cost, therefore, is £125 + £120 = £245.

Although the cost differences are insignificant the approach is useful to determine the EOQ.

CHAPTER FOUR

Accounting for Wages

1.0 LABOUR COST CLASSIFICATION

Essentially labour cost consists of:

(a) basic pay—the daily, weekly or monthly salary, plus

(b) labour-related costs—holiday pay, overtime premium, employer's contribution to National Insurance, shift bonuses, production incentives, training costs, company pensions and insurances such as accident, health and life.

For costing purposes, labour costs are classified broadly into two groups, *direct* labour and *indirect* labour.

1.1 Direct labour

This is labour which can be directly identified with products. In practice, not all labour costs which can be directly identified with products are treated as direct labour; to be treated as a direct labour cost, it must be practicable and economically feasible to collect the data.

In a manufacturing concern direct wages will be wages paid to the operators immediately concerned with the manufacture of a product. In a service industry, the term is related to those employees who directly carry out that service, e.g. bus drivers, postmen, plumbers.

1.2 Indirect labour

This is labour expended that does not *alter* the construction, conformation or condition of the product, but *contributes generally* to such work and to the completion of the product and its progressive movement and handling up to the point of despatch.

Examples are: wages and salaries of personnel at the service department; salaries and wages of supervisors and other personnel who are not directly involved in the manufacturing operations of the production departments; employer's contribution to National Insurance of all direct and indirect workers; holiday pay; sick pay, overtime premium (if spasmodic) of direct workers to the extent that they have not been charged as direct labour costs.

2.0 TIMEKEEPING

Timekeeping has two main purposes:

(a) For *payroll* purposes—the provision of necessary information for the payroll departments for the preparation of the payroll:

  (i) to show the normal pay, overtime pay, overtime premium pay, bonus pay and other related costs, e.g. shift premium;

  (ii) to provide evidence of compliance with legal requirements.

(b) *Costing* purposes—the provision of information to assist in the distribution of labour costs to jobs, departments and cost centres:

  (i) to show the hours spent on production;

  (ii) to show idle time hours;

  (iii) to show the cost of work done;

  (iv) to show the cost of idle time.

2.1 Basic documents to record time

(a) Timekeeping for direct labour

(i) Clock card: evidence of the time an employee spends in the factory.

(ii) Time sheets: evidence of the time an employee spends on production. The clock card records the hours he spends in the factory and the time sheet records the specific use made of the time spent in the factory.

(iii) Idle-time cards—to record time not spent in production.

EXAMPLES OF TIME SHEETS

Single time sheet per employee for each payroll period and when workers perform repetitive work regularly.

Daily time sheets for each employee for each day when a worker moves from one department/job to another many times during the day.

Job cards: the employee fills in as many job cards as there are jobs he works on. Job cards normally carry instructions to the worker as to how the job he is required to do should be carried out.

Route job cards: the card follows the job through the factory and includes details of all operations to be carried out.

(b) Timekeeping for indirect labour

Since indirect labour costs are charged to products via factory overhead absorption rates, timekeeping for indirect labour is not as elaborate as for direct labour. The emphasis is mainly on the correctness of the amounts paid and on seeing that the expenditure on indirect labour is well under control.

The basic documents are:

(i) clock card;

(ii) idle-time card.

2.2 Financial accounting

(a) Timekeeping department

The main function of this department is to record the time an employee spends in the factory. To do so it uses the clock card and supervises the clock punching.

(b) Payroll department

The payroll department has as its main functions the preparation of the company payroll and the distribution of the payroll to departments and processes (*see* Illustration 1).

To do so it uses the following information:

(i) an employee's record card, giving details of the clock number, date hired, wage rate, department in which the employee will work, holiday entitlement, PAYE code (P45), hours of employment, voluntary wage deductions agreed by the employee, etc.

(ii) A clock card, recording the information on the basis of which the payroll department prepares the weekly or monthly payroll.

(c) Prevention of fraud

When preparing the payroll for the payment of wages, certain safeguards should be introduced to prevent fraud:

(i) Where possible, a mechanised form of time recording should be introduced.

(ii) Recording time should be properly supervised.

(iii) Clock cards should be checked and signed by the supervisor before they are sent to the payroll section.

(iv) Preparation of the payroll and the payment of wages should be separated.

(v) Bonus calculations or deductions from gross wages should be prepared by personnel who are not responsible for the preparation or payment of wages.

(vi) Bonus payments should be checked against production records.

(vii) The supervisor should be present at the time of payment to ensure that wages are paid to the right person.

(viii) A record of unclaimed wages should be maintained.

(ix) The dates of employees joining and leaving the company should be checked against personnel records.

(x) At regular intervals a responsible person from the personnel department should be present when wages are being paid.

2.3 Cost department

The clock cards record the time spent by employees in the factory. The cost department records how the departments utilised the employees' time by the introduction of:

(a) time sheets/job cards;

(b) idle-time cards.

At the end of a period the total of the hours recorded on the clock card must, therefore, equal the total of the times recorded on the time sheets and idle-time cards.

On the basis of this information the cost department prepares the wages analysis, a document which is a classified record of time and/or wages compiled from labour time records (*see* Illustration 1).

On the basis of the wages analysis sheet the cost department charges the wages which can be directly identified with job to work in progress. The wages paid to direct workers which *cannot* be identified with jobs (WIP) plus wages of other employees are treated as factory overheads.

Illustration 1

Wadduwa Merchants Limited operates a job/order costing system. RC, RG, and RK are operators employed in a production department, RJ is the foreman and RD is employed on material-handling duties.

Clock cards for week ended 30th June, year 8, showed the following hours of attendance:

Name	*Monday*	*Tuesday*	*Wednesday*	*Thursday*	*Friday*	*Total*
RC	10	12	12	12	10	56
RG	10	10	10	10	10	50
RK	8	8	8	8	8	40
RJ	12	12	12	12	12	60
RD	10	10	10	10	10	50

It is the company's practice to pay hours in excess of eight on any day at "time and a half", such overtime being necessary to enable the company to meet the general pressure for delivery of customers' orders. A shift premium of £20 is payable to RC and RJ.

The hourly rates of pay are: RC £5; RG £4; RK £4; RJ £5; RD £2.

In preparing the payroll it may be assumed that the following deductions were made from the gross wages of employees:

SUMMARY OF THE DEDUCTION

Employee	*PAYE*	*National Insurance*	*Union*	*Sports club*	*Total*
RC	£40	£34	£2	£1	£77
RG	20	22	2	1	45
RK	20	16	2	1	39
RJ	60	48	2	1	111
RD	12	11	2	1	26

The employer's National Insurance contributions on behalf of the employees were as follows:

RC £50; RG £30; RK £20; RJ £80; RD £20.

The company operates an integrated accounting system.

Required (a): Prepare the payroll for the week and journal entries to show how each item is recorded in the books.

TIME SHEETS—HOURS WORKED

The time sheets of operatives show time spent on production as indicated below; any time not allocated is to be regarded as idle time:

	Work in progress				*Other*	*Total*
Name/ Job No.	*Job 123*	*Job 333*	*Job 444*	*Special purpose machine job XY747*	*Machine repairs*	
	hours	hours	hours	hours	hours	hours
RC	10	20	16	10	nil	56
RG	10	10	10	15	nil	45
RK	nil	nil	nil	20	15	35

Required (b): Prepare the wages analysis and show journal entries to indicate clearly how each item is dealt with in the cost accounts.

Suggested answer

(a) *Payroll*

Department: Production — *Week ended 30th June, year 8*

Name	*Clock No.*	*Rate*	*Normal hours*	*OT hours*	*OT Premium hours*	*Bonus hours*	*Normal pay*	*OT pay*	*OTP pay*	*Bonus pay*	*Shift premium*	*Gross wage*
		£					£	£	£	£	£	£
RC	–	5	40	16	8	–	200	80	40	–	20	340
RG	–	4	40	10	5	–	160	40	20	–	–	220
RK	–	4	40	–	–	–	160	–	–	–	–	160
Sub-Total		–					520	120	60	–	20	720
RJ	–	5	40	20	10	–	200	100	50	–	20	370
RD	–	2	40	10	5	–	80	20	10	–	–	110
Sub-Total		–					280	120	60		20	480
Total	–	–					£800	£240	£120	–	£40	£1,200

Name	*Statutory deductions*		*Other deductions*		*Net pay*	*Employer's contribn. NI*	*Total wage*
	PAYE	*NI*	*Union*	*Sports club*			
	£	£	£	£	£	£	£
RC	40	34	2	1	263	50	390
RG	20	22	2	1	175	30	250
RK	20	16	2	1	121	20	180
Sub-Total	80	72	6	3	559	100	820
RJ	60	48	2	1	259	80	450
RD	12	11	2	1	84	20	130
Sub-Total	72	59	4	2	343	100	580
Total	£152	£131	£10	£5	£902	£200	£1,400

(b) *Wages analysis*

Name	*Rate per hour*	*Work in progress*					*Production overhead—indirect wages*					*Total wages*
		Job 123	*Job 333*	*Job 444*	*Job XY747*	*Employer's contribn. of NI*	*Idle time*	*OT premium*	*Shift premium*	*Machine repair*	*Other*	
	£	£	£	£	£	£	£	£	£	£	£	£
RC	5	10 × £5	20 × £5	16 × £5	10 × £5		*					
		50	100	80	50	50		40	20			390
RG	4	10 × £4	10 × £4	10 × £4	15 × £4		5 × £4					
		40	40	40	60	30	20	20	–			250
RK	4	–	–	–	20 × £4		5 × £4			15 × £4		
					80	20	20	–	–	60		180
		90	140	120	190	100	40	60	20	60		820
RJ											450	450
RD											130	130
Total				£540					£860			£1,400

* Idle time: clock hours less time spent on production, e.g. RG clock hours 50, time booked on job 45.

Suggested answer (continued)

JOURNAL ENTRIES

(a) *Payroll*	*Dr*	*Cr*
Total wages (gross pay *plus* employer's contribution of NI)		
Wages control a/c	£1,400	
Wages payable a/c		£1,400
Wages payable a/c	1,400	
Net pay cash		902
PAYE (tax)		152
National Insurance (£131 + £200)		331
Union		10
Sports club		5
(b) *Wages analysis*		
Work in progress control a/c	540	
Production overhead control a/c	860	
Wages control a/c		1,400

Note: Employer's contribution of National Insurance, cost of idle time, overtime premium and shift premium are treated as indirect labour costs because they cannot be allocated to any job, unless *wage rate per hour is grossed up in preparing the analysis to include these items.*

Illustration 2

The following totals were extracted from a weekly payroll for 400 employees at an ACMA Factory:

Gross pay		£40,000
Deductions:		
Employees' National Insurance contributions	£1,460	
Superannuation contributions	1,760	
Income tax	4,800	
Trade union dues	60	
Social club	40	
Total		8,120
Net pay		£31,880
Total of employees' and employer's National Insurance contributions		£4,600

The wages analysis gave the following summary breakdown of the gross pay:

	Direct workers	*Indirect workers*
Ordinary time	£20,000	£7,000
Overtime	3,700	2,500
Overtime premium	800	900
Shift allowance	1,600	800
Sick pay	800	200
Idle time	100	–
Capital items	1,600*	–
	£28,600	£11,400

* This represented work on building a special purpose machine for the toolroom and the machine is not yet complete.

You are required to show journal entries (narrations are *not* required) to indicate clearly how each item is dealt with in the accounts.

Suggested answer

NOTE 1

Total wages: £40,000 gross pay, plus employer's contribution of National Insurance £3,140 = £43,140.

NOTE 2

Wages analysis

	Direct wages (WIP)	*Production overhead*
Ordinary time	£20,000	£7,000
Overtime	3,700	2,500
Overtime premium	–	800 + 900
Shift allowance	–	1,600 + 800
Sick pay	–	800 + 200
Idle time	–	100
Capital item	1,600	–
Employer's NI contribution	–	4,600
Total	£25,300	£17,840

JOURNAL ENTRIES (ASSUMING THE COMPANY OPERATES A FULLY INTEGRATED HISTORICAL COSTING SYSTEM)

		Dr	Cr
Total wages:	£44,600		
	Wages control	£43,600	
	Wages payable		£43,600
Wages payable:		43,140	
	Net pay (cash)		31,880
	NI (Employees £1,460 Employer £3,140)		4,600
	Superannuation contributions		1,760
	PAYE (tax)		4,800
	Union dues		60
	Social club		40
Wages analysis:	Work in progress control a/c	25,300	
	Production overhead control a/c	17,840	
	Wages control a/c		43,600

3.0 ACCOUNTING FOR DIRECT LABOUR RELATED COSTS

3.1 Direct labour—the rate per hour for costing purposes

The times recorded by direct labour on time sheets must be valued before they can be charged to jobs. The problem arises as to how overtime premium, shift premium, idle time, incentive payments, holiday pay, employer's National Insurance contribution etc. should be treated in the cost accounts.

Methods used

(a) BASIC RATE

For costing purposes use the basic rate of pay as used in the payroll department and treat wages which cannot be identified with jobs as factory overhead.

(b) EFFECTIVE HOURLY RATE

For costing purposes calculate an effective hourly rate which absorbs these costs.

Illustration 3: Effective hourly rate (normal idle time)

The factory procedure of RB Limited provides for employees to clock on and off jobs at time of commencement and completion. In the machine department the employees are paid an hourly rate of £2.00 and work 08.30 to 12.30 and 13.30 to 17.30 each day for five days per week.

CALCULATION OF THE EFFECTIVE HOURLY RATE FOR COSTING PURPOSES (i.e. ABSORBING NORMAL IDLE TIME)

(a) Gross wages for week ending 30.6.19_7:
40 hours × £2.00 = £80

(b)		*hours*
	Productive time	
	Clock hours	40.00
	Idle time	
	15 min per day × 5 days	(1.25)
	Productive hours per week	38.75

Effective hourly rate for costing purposes is £80 ÷ 38.75 or £2.06.

3.2 Direct labour—bonuses and holiday pay

Bonuses and holiday pay may both be treated as a production overhead or as a direct labour cost.

(a) Treatment as production overheads

(i) BONUSES

If a direct worker is paid a monthly or weekly salary and a bonus at the end of the year of, say, 10 per cent of his monthly salary, his earnings might be:

	Per month	*Per annum*
Salary	£400	£4,800
Bonus	–	480
Total wages	£400	£5,280

Average earnings per month $\frac{£5{,}280}{12} = £440$.

£400 will be treated as a direct labour cost per month,
£480 will be treated as a production overhead in calculating predetermined overhead absorption rates.

(ii) HOLIDAY PAY

Holiday pay is non-productive. The holiday pay of the direct labour force may be treated as a production overhead.

For example, if a productive worker has a basic monthly pay of £400 and is entitled to a paid vacation of 4 weeks, £4,400 (11 × £400) may be treated as direct labour and the remaining £400 as production overhead in determining the predetermined factory overhead absorption rates.

(b) Treatment as direct labour cost

If the bonus and holiday pay of direct labour is to be treated as a direct labour cost, then an effective hourly rate for direct labour will have to be calculated for costing purposes, for example:

Salary including bonus £5,280

Expected direct labour hours per annum per employee:

Hours payable	40 × 52 =	2,080	
Less: Normal loss	40 × 4 =	160	(4 weeks paid holidays)
		1,920	

Effective hourly rate: $\frac{£5,280}{1,920} = £2.75$

The rate of £2.75 per hour includes not only the bonus pay but also holiday pay.

3.3 Direct labour—employer's National Insurance contribution

Employer's National Insurance contribution may be treated either:

(a) as a production overhead and included in determining the factory overhead absorption rates; or

(b) as a direct labour cost by calculating an effective hourly rate for costing purposes which include the employer's contribution of National Insurance.

Illustration 4

Gross annual wages per employee	£4,800
NIC employer's	240
Total wages payable	£5,040

(a) £240 may be treated as a production overhead. The direct labour hourly rate remains constant.

(b) £240 may be treated as a direct labour cost. An effective hourly rate will have to be calculated which includes the employer's contribution.

$$\frac{\text{Total wages payable} \quad £5,040}{\text{Expected hours} \quad 1,920} = £2.625 = \text{Effective hourly rate.}$$

3.4 Overtime premium

Overtime pay consists of two elements:

(a) pay for the hours worked in excess of normal hours;

(b) incentive pay and premium pay for working in excess of normal time.

For example, if an employee is paid £3.00 per hour for a 40-hour week and he works 50 hours during the week, time worked in excess of the 40 hours in any week might be paid for as follows:

The first 6 hours	time and a third
Additional hours	time and a half

Normal pay	$=40$ hours $\times$ £3.00 $=$	£120.00
Overtime pay	$=10$ hours $\times$ £3.00 $=$	30.00
Overtime premium		
First 6 hours	$=6\times$ £3.00 $\div 3=$	6.00
Next 4 hours	$=4\times$ £3.00 $\div 2=$	6.00
		£162.00

3.5 Overtime premium payable to indirect labour

The question here is whether to charge the cost of overtime premium to the product or treat it as a period cost. It is a fundamental principle of costing that non-recurring and/or extraordinary costs should not form a part of the cost of the product. Therefore, if overtime was not planned, the premium should be kept separate and treated as a period cost and charged as such to the profit and loss statement. But if overtime is planned then the premium should be treated as a production overhead and indirectly forms a part of product cost.

3.6 Overtime premium payable to direct labour

The proper treatment of overtime premium depends on the reason for the overtime. The question here is whether to charge the overtime premium:

to a specific job or customer;

to a department as a production indirect cost;

as a direct labour cost;

as a period cost.

The effect of each of these alternatives is explained, with illustrations, in **3.7** to **3.10** below.

3.7 Charging overtime premium to a specific job or customer

If the factory is operating at practical capacity, and overtime is worked at the customer's request, the premium should be charged as a direct labour cost to the customer.

Illustration 5

A company whose average wage rate for direct labour is £4.00 per hour, worked during the year 200,000 normal hours and 5,000 overtime hours. Overtime was worked at the customer's request to expedite delivery of job number JOE 747, on which 15,000 normal hours were booked. The overtime premium is equal to one-half the normal rate. Required: to determine the direct labour cost of job number JOE 747.

DIRECT LABOUR COST

Normal hours	15,000 at £4.00 =	£60,000
Overtime hours	5,000 at £4.00 =	20,000
Overtime premium	2,500 at £4.00 =	10,000
	Direct labour cost	£90,000

Note: For costing purposes, basic rate of pay is used and not an effective hourly rate.

3.8 Overtime treated as production indirect cost

If overtime is planned and undertaken irregularly to meet the company's commitments from time to time, the premium may be treated as an element of factory overhead. This is the most common treatment.

Illustration 6

A company whose expected direct labour hourly rate is £4.00 expects to work irregularly during the year 50,000 overtime hours in addition to 250,000 normal hours. You are required to determine the direct labour cost of job number RD 747 on which 10,000 normal hours and 5,000 overtime hours were booked by the direct labour force.

DIRECT LABOUR COST

Normal hours	10,000 at £4.00 =	£40,000
Overtime hours	5,000 at £4.00 =	20,000
		£60,000

Notes:

(a) The total overtime premium = $\frac{1}{2}$ × 50,000 hours at £4.00 = £100,000 is treated as a production overhead.

(b) If the premium is treated as production overhead, the basic rate of pay is used for costing direct labour hours, and not an effective hourly rate.

3.9 Overtime treated as a direct labour cost

If, as a policy to avoid increasing the labour force employed during normal hours, overtime was undertaken evenly throughout the year the premium may be treated as a direct labour cost.

Illustration 7

A company whose average expected and actual rate for direct labour is £4.00 worked overtime during the year for which the company paid time and a half.

PLANNED HOURS FOR YEAR

Normal hours	240,000
Overtime hours	40,000

ACTUAL HOURS DURING PERIOD 1

Normal hours	20,000
Overtime hours	3,000

On job number RJ 742 2,000 direct labour hours were worked in normal hours and 300 in overtime. You are required to determine the direct labour cost that should be charged to job number RJ 742.

If overtime is planned and undertaken regularly throughout the year, for costing purposes the overtime premium is treated as a direct labour cost, i.e. an effective hourly rate is used.

EFFECTIVE HOURLY RATE FOR COSTING PURPOSES

Planned normal hours	240,000 at £4 =	£960,000
Planned overtime hours	40,000 at £4 =	160,000
Overtime premium 50%	20,000 at £4 =	80,000
		1,200,000
Planned direct labour cost		£1,200,000
Planned effective direct labour hours		280,000
Effective hourly rate	$\frac{£1,200,000}{280,000}$ =	£4.2857

For job number RJ 742 the direct labour cost is therefore:

DIRECT LABOUR COST

Normal hours	2,000 at £4.2857 =	£8,571.40
Overtime hours	3,000 at £4.2857 =	1,285.71
	Direct labour cost	£9,857.11

3.10 Overtime treated as a period cost

If overtime is the result of inefficiency or wasted normal time, and non-recurring, then the premium should be treated as a period cost, i.e. excluded from cost of production and charged against gross profit.

4.0 LABOUR TURNOVER

Every firm experiences the process of recruiting staff and employees leaving. Labour turnover is the change in the labour force during a specified period of time measured against a suitable yardstick, e.g. labour turnover in the industry or locality; past periods, etc.

4.1 Methods of expressing labour turnover

The labour turnover rate is often expressed as a percentage, but some companies express it as a fraction, e.g.:

$$\frac{\text{Number of employees leaving}}{\text{Average number on payroll}}.$$

Other methods of calculation are listed below:

(a) $\dfrac{\text{Number of employees replaced}}{\text{Average number on payroll}} \times 100$

(b) $\dfrac{\text{Number joining plus number leaving}}{\text{Average number on payroll}} \times 100$

(c) $\dfrac{\text{Number of employees leaving}}{\text{Average number on payroll}} \times 100.$

In some cases it may be helpful to analyse the labour turnover:

(a) departmentally;

(b) by age groups and sex;

(c) by length of service;

(d) by trades, grades;

(e) by methods of payment: monthly, weekly, piece workers etc.

4.2 Causes of labour turnover

(a) Uncontrollable causes

(i) redundancies;

(ii) retirement due to age and illness and death;

(iii) family troubles and personal problems;

(iv) disciplinary grounds, e.g. long absences from work;

(v) change for betterment.

(b) Controllable causes

(i) pay—methods and/or rates;

(ii) dislike for the job due to the nature of work;

(iii) lack of promotion prospects;

(iv) unsatisfactory working conditions, e.g. hours of work;

(v) relationships with other employees;

(vi) lack of suitable facilities, accommodation, transport, etc.;

(vii) lack of social amenities.

4.3 Cost of labour turnover

Broadly, the cost of labour turnover may be analysed under two headings:

(a) *Preventive costs.* These are costs incurred to keep the employees happy and discourage them from leaving.

(b) *Replacement costs.* These consist of recruitment and training costs, scrap and defective work during training, loss of production etc.

(a) Preventive costs

(i) *Medical services*—availability of fulltime doctors and nurses not only reduces labour turnover but also increases efficiency and productivity.

(ii) *Sports, recreation and other welfare activities*—subsidised canteens and better meals, housing scheme, educational facilities, social club.

(iii) *Environment*—general improvement in working conditions such as lighting, heating, air conditioning, flexible working hours and increase in holiday entitlement.

(iv) *Pension scheme*—replacement of the present scheme by one giving improved benefits on retirement.

(v) *Transport*—company providing transport facilities (to and from premises) to the rail/road transport terminals.

(vi) *Personnel department*—role of the department in helping to develop and maintain a contented workforce. The employees remaining contented if they are looked after and are respected and their grievances sympathetically considered and supported. Part of the expenditure of the department may be treated as preventive costs.

(b) Replacement costs

(i) *Administration*—advertising, recruitment, selection, engagement, medical examination.

(ii) *Training*—even if skilled workers are engaged, employees have to be given some training.

(iii) *Scrap and defective work*—new employees may take time to attain the degree of efficiency of the employees they have replaced.

(iv) *Cost of tools and machine breakages*—while on training and during the early periods after completion of training.

(v) *Accidents due to inexperience*—the costs include under-recovery of overhead, idle time, compensation, etc.

4.4 Measuring the cost of labour turnover

It must be noted that it is difficult to separate the labour turnover costs from those of normal operations. The aim should, therefore, be to obtain as true an indication as is possible.

Specimen Labour Turnover Report

Labour turnover report

Location:	Harrow Factory	To:
Period:	March, year 19_7	c.c.:
Date prepared:		From:

	Mar. 19_7	Feb. 19_7	Mar. 19_6
Number of employees on 1st of month	966	960	965
Number of employees on last day of month	950	965	980
Average labour force	958	963	973
Number recruited during month	64	66	48
Number left during month	80	60	34
Labour turnover rate*	8.35%	6.23%	3.49%
Analysis of number left			
Uncontrollable			
Redundancies	10	–	–
Retirement	5	–	10
Disciplinary grounds	–	–	–
Family and personal	20	10	–
Other reasons	10	8	8
Controllable			
Pay	20	22	2
Working conditions	–	–	–
Lack of prospects	15	20	10
Lack of amenities	–	–	–
Other reasons	–	–	4
	80	60	34

* Calculation of labour turnover rates:

March 19_7: $\frac{80}{958} \times 100 = 8.35\%$.

February 19_7: $\frac{60}{963} \times 100 = 6.23\%$.

March 19_6: $\frac{34}{973} \times 100 = 3.49\%$.

5.0 INCENTIVE WAGE PAYMENT SYSTEMS

All wage systems including those for wages paid on a time basis have an element of incentive payments. These systems are based upon payments of wages, not only on time spent but also (mainly) on output. Any system in which payment is made by results, or according to work done, can be classified as an incentive wage payment system. Wages paid to employees may be calculated broadly in one of three ways; these are compared in Table 2.

Table 2. METHODS OF REMUNERATION

Time basis	*Incentive plans*	
	Results basis (time + work basis)	*Work basis*
Employee is remunerated on the basis of time spent in the factory not on production. (a) Rate per hour *or*, (b) Rate per day *or*, (c) Rate per week. *An extra premium is paid for overtime.* Employer benefits from labour efficiency and accepts all the loss arising from labour inefficiency.	A bonus calculated in relation to the time saved is paid in addition to time wages. Individual bonus system—bonus calculation (a) Halsey = 50% of time saved. (b) Halsey–Weir = $33\frac{1}{3}$% of time saved. (c) Rowan = (i) $\frac{\text{Time taken} \times \text{Time saved.}}{\text{Time allowed}}$ (ii) Percentage of time saved × Time wages. *Group bonus systems*	(a) Straight piecework (number of pieces × rate per piece). (b) Piecework with guaranteed day rates/weekly wage. (c) Differential piecework (rates change at different levels of output). Systems using differential principle are: (a) Taylor (b) Merrick (c) Gantt. Produce more earn more. Produce less earn less.

5.1 Purpose of incentive wage payment systems

The fundamental objective is to reduce the cost of production per unit by providing an incentive for the workers to earn more by producing more. The higher wages paid are compensated by greater output. The fixed overhead of the company will be spread over a greater number of units.

Illustration 8

Manufacturing fixed overhead per week (rent, rates, etc.): £40,000.

Present system: 100 employees on an 8-hour day are paid £4.00 per hour and each employee is expected to produce 64 units per day or 8 units per hour.
Proposed system: the company wishes to increase the hourly rate to £4.75 if a worker produces 10 units per hour or 80 units per day.

PRESENT SYSTEM

Expense	*Amount per week*	*Production per week*	*Cost per unit*
Direct labour	40 hours per week × 100 employees = 4,000 × £4.00 = £16,000	64 units × 5 days = 320 units per week per employee = 32,000 units	£0.50
Fixed overhead	£40,000	32,000 units	1.25
			£1.75

PROPOSED SYSTEM

Expense	*Amount per week*	*Production per week*	*Cost per unit*
Direct labour	40 hours per week × 100 employees = 4,000 × £4.75:	80 units × 5 days = 400 units per employee = 40,000	
	£19,000		£0.475
Factory overhead	£40,000	40,000 units	1.000
			£1.475

Although the weekly wages have increased by £3,000 (£19,000 − £16,000), the cost of a complete unit of product is reduced by £0.275 (£1.75 − £1.475).

The reduction of the cost per unit is the result of three factors:

(a) Output has increased by 25 per cent: increase in output 2 units

$$\frac{2}{8} \times 100 = 25 \text{ per cent.}$$

(b) Percentage increase in wages

$$= £0.75 \text{ per hour} = \frac{75}{400} \times 100 = 18.75 \text{ per cent.}$$

Note: The increase in output more than compensated the increase in wages.

(c) The fixed cost of £40,000 is now spread over 40,000 units instead of 32,000 units.

SUMMARY

	Cost per unit of output		
	Present	*Proposed*	*Difference*
Direct labour	£0.50	£0.475	£0.025
Fixed overhead	1.25	1.000	0.250
Total	£1.75	£1.475	£0.275

In evaluating the merits and demerits of incentive plans, one has to consider the additional clerical costs and increased spoilage costs. In addition, increased supervision may be necessary to maintain quality with increased output.

5.2 Requirements of a good incentive plan

(a) The scheme must be accepted by the employees—it should be simple and understandable by the employees and it must be seen to be a fair system by them.

(b) It must cover not only direct workers but also indirect workers.

(c) The standard of performance must be fair and work units must be arrived at which fully reflect the varying levels of effort required to finish each work unit. Work units can be made up in a number of ways, e.g. standard hours or units of products produced.

(d) High reward should be paid for performance above standard and must be flexible. Rewards should be paid without delay after being earned.

(e) Not only quantity standards but also quality standards must be set and only standard quality production should be considered in determining the bonus.

(f) Standards should remain in force unless there are changes in methods.

(g) The plan must be fairly and intelligently administered.

(h) It must not be too costly.

Several incentive wage plans are described in **6.0** and **7.0** below. It should be accepted that there are many variations of these plans currently in use.

6.0 INDIVIDUAL BONUS SYSTEMS

Under the individual bonus systems a given time called the standard time is allowed for the completion of a job by an individual employee. If the work is completed in less than the time allowed for the job (standard time), a percentage of time saved is paid as a bonus, in addition to the normal pay.

The individual bonus systems differ in the method of the calculation of the bonus entitlement. The main characteristic of this method of incentive payment is that the saving in time is shared between the employer and the employee and the payment is made to the employee on the basis of work completed by himself.

The three main systems are Halsey, Halsey–Weir and Rowan.

6.1 Halsey

Bonus: 50 per cent of time saved.

(a) A standard time is set for the completion of a job.

(b) If the time taken is greater than the time allowed the worker receives time wages.

(c) If the time taken is less than the time allowed the worker receives a bonus of 50 per cent of the time saved.

6.2 Halsey–Weir

Bonus: $33\frac{1}{3}$ per cent of time saved.

(a) A standard time is set for the completion of a job.

(b) If the time taken is greater than the time allowed the employee receives time wages.

(c) If the time taken is less than the time allowed the worker receives a bonus of $33\frac{1}{3}$ per cent of time saved.

6.3 Rowan

This is basically similar to the Halsey system:

(a) A standard time is set for the completion of a job.

(b) If the time taken is greater than the time allowed an employee receives time wages.

(c) If the time taken is less than the time allowed the employee receives a bonus. The Rowan system differs from the Halsey and Halsey–Weir systems in the calculation of the bonus:

Halsey: Bonus = 50 per cent × Hours saved × Time wages.

Halsey–Weir: Bonus = $33\frac{1}{3}$ per cent × Hours saved × Time wages.

Rowan: $\text{Bonus} = \dfrac{\text{Time taken}}{\text{Time allowed}} \times \text{Time saved} \times \text{Time wages.}$

Illustration 9

Time allowed for Job No. 345 49 hours.

Hourly rate £2.00 per hour.

Bob Hugett takes 40 hours to complete the job. His bonus is calculated as follows:

Halsey		*Halsey–Weir*		*Rowan*	
Time wages 40 × £2.00 = £80.00		Time wages 40 × £2.00 = £80.00		Time wages 40 × £2.00 = £80.00	
Bonus: 50 per cent of time saved × Rate per hour		Bonus: $33\frac{1}{3}$ per cent of time saved × Rate per hour		Bonus: Time taken × Time saved ÷ Time allowed, all × Rate per hour	
$= 9 \times \frac{50}{100} \times £2.00$		$= \frac{33\frac{1}{3}}{100} \times 9 \times £2.00$			
$= 4\frac{1}{2} \times £2.00 =$	£9.00	$= 3 \times £2.00 =$	£6.00	$= \frac{40 \times 9}{49} \times £2.00 = £14.70$	
Total	£89.00		£86.00		£94.70

Note:	*Hours taken*	*Hours allowed*	*Hours saved*
Bob Hugett	*40*	*49*	*9*

7.0 GROUP BONUS SYSTEMS

It is impossible for a worker on an assembly line or conveyor belt system to increase his output without the assistance and co-operation of the entire group of workers—*the team*. In such situations companies have successfully introduced group incentive schemes.

7.1 Common characteristics of group bonus schemes

(a) A standard time is set for the completion of a job.

(b) If the time taken is greater than the time allowed, the workers in the group receive time wages.

(c) If the time taken is less than the time allowed, the group receives a bonus on time saved.

7.2 Advantages of group bonus systems

(a) Encouraging team spirit. Mutual dependence engenders mutual trust.

(b) Good group incentive plans assist in the reduction of labour turnover, accidents, spoilage, waste and absenteeism.

(c) Good output will qualify for bonus and this can be earned only if each member has performed his/her task satisfactorily. There is therefore a built-in system of inspection and such a scheme reduces the amount of supervision necessary.

(d) High output should result as the slower workers in the group follow the example of faster workers. The cost per unit should decrease as the fixed overhead will be spread over a greater number of units.

7.3 Disadvantages of group bonus schemes

(a) A faster worker in the group may feel dissatisfied with his earnings; this may cause dissension within the group. In such cases he may be paid a higher rate; alternatively, he may be transferred.

(b) Sickness of members may cause the output of the group to suffer. For the incentive scheme to be successful, it is necessary to have able substitutes to cover sickness, holidays and other absences.

(c) Additional administrative costs may result.

(d) In attempting to produce greater output, quality of the work may deteriorate and there could be excessive material wastage.

Illustration 10

Albert & Co. plc operates in department three a group bonus system. A minimum hourly rate is guaranteed to each employee in the group if actual output is less than standard output of 12,000 units for a 40-hour week. If actual output is greater than standard output the hourly rate of each employee is increased by 8 per cent for each additional 600 units of output produced:

Employee	*Actual output units, week 4*	*Minimum hourly rate*
RB	2,500	£2.00
RD	2,700	£2.50
RR	2,400	£3.00
RJ	2,500	£2.00
RS	2,460	£2.50
RN	2,440	£3.00
	15,000	

Actual output of the group	15,000 units
Standard output	12,000 units
Additional output	3,000

HOURLY RATES

Increased by 8 per cent for each additional 600 units.

$\therefore$ Percentage increase $= \frac{3,000}{600} \times 8 = 40$ per cent.

$\therefore$ Bonus is 40 per cent of the hourly rate.

$\therefore$ Earnings of employees are as follows:

		Normal wages	*Bonus*	*Total earnings*
RB	40 × £2.00	£80.00	40 × £0.80 = £32	£112
RD	40 × £2.50	100.00	40 × £1.00 = £40	140
RR	40 × £3.00	120.00	40 × £1.20 = £48	168
RJ	40 × £2.00	80.00	40 × £0.80 = £32	112
RS	40 × £2.50	100.00	40 × £1.00 = £40	140
RN	40 × £3.00	120.00	40 × £1.20 = £48	168
		£600.00	£240	£840

How effective is the group incentive scheme to the company?

12,000 units per week cost £600

15,000 units cost $£600 \times \frac{15,000}{12,000} = £750$

Actual wages paid $= £840$

Loss £90

There is a loss of £90 (12 per cent of £750) but this could be more than compensated by increased output as production fixed costs would be spread over a greater number of units.

Example 1

Matara Merchants Ltd make electrical components. The company has been producing 300 components per week; fixed production overhead was estimated to be £1,200 per week. The following is a schedule of the hourly rates of pay of three direct employees:

Employee	*Hourly rate*
Hendry	£4.00
David	£5.00
William	£6.00

A major customer has been requesting the company for faster deliveries but management does not want to introduce overtime to meet demand. The company works a 40-hour week. In order to increase production it is decided to institute an incentive pay plan. The following schedule describes the pay plan formulated and started on a trial basis.

Employee	*Hourly rate*	*Bonus (per unit)*
Hendry	£2.75	£0.25
David	£3.75	£0.25
William	£4.75	£0.25

The first week the plan was put into operation production increased to 330 units. The works manager studied the results and believed the plan too costly; production had increased 10 per cent but labour costs had increased by approximately 16.25 per cent. He wanted the accountant to redesign the pay plan to make labour cost increases proportionate to productivity increases.

Required: to show by figures whether the works manager was correct in assuming the incentive plan too costly. *(40 minutes)*

Answer guide

(a) *Without the incentive plan*

On the basis of a 40-hour week, direct labour costs per week are:

Hendry	40 hours × £4.00 = £160
David	40 hours × £5.00 = £200
William	40 hours × £6.00 = £240
	Total direct labour £600

(b) *Under the incentive plan—330 units*

	Basic	*Bonus*		*Total*
Hendry	40 × £2.75 = £110	330 units × £0.25 =	£82.50	£192.50
David	40 × £3.75 = £150	330 units × £0.25 =	£82.50	£232.50
William	40 × £4.75 = £190	330 units × £0.25 =	£82.50	£272.50
	£450	Total bonus	£247.50	£697.50

LABOUR COST INCREASE

Increase in labour cost = £697.50 − £600.00 = £97.50.

Percentage increase in labour costs $= \frac{£97.50}{£600.00} \times 100 = 16.25$ per cent.

Judging by the increase in labour costs alone, the incentive plan is costly. Labour cost has increased by 16.25 per cent, but in order to evaluate the effectiveness of the incentive plan it is essential to analyse its effect on the cost per unit produced. It may be possible that a rise in labour costs is more than compensated by distributing the fixed cost of production over a greater volume.

COMPARISON OF THE TWO PLANS AND THEIR EFFECT ON THE UNIT COST OF PRODUCTION

	Production units	*Direct labour cost*	*Fixed production cost*	*Total*	*Conversion cost per unit*
Present	300	£600	£1,200	£1,800	£6.00
Proposed	330	£697.50	£1,200	£1,897.50	£5.75

Under the proposed system the conversion cost per unit has decreased by £0.25. The increase in labour cost was more than compensated by the increase in output. Therefore the works manager was not correct in assuming the incentive plan too costly.

Example 2

A factory operates a group bonus scheme in which 20 skilled, 25 semi-skilled, 20 unskilled operatives and 10 junior operatives participate. Time saved on good units produced on group bonus jobs is shared in proportion to the time spent on them. In a certain week when 50 hours were worked by each employee, the following information is recorded:

	Male skilled	*Male semi-skilled*	*Male unskilled*	*Juniors*
Number in the group	20	25	20	10
Hours spent on bonus jobs	24	24	30	40
Base rate per hour	£4.00	£3.00	£2.00	£1.00
Percentage of base rate at which hours saved are paid (bonus)	50%	40%	30%	20%

PRODUCTION DETAILS FOR THE WEEK

Product (unit)	Standard	Super	Deluxe
Bonus time allowed per unit (in minutes)	15	20	30
Gross units produced (bonus)	1,200	3,500	3,100
Units rejected on which bonus time allowance withdrawn	200	500	100

ADDITIONAL INFORMATION

The company operates a 40-hour week.
Overtime is paid for at:

(a) Time plus one-half for the first 8 hours in excess of 40 hours.

(b) Double time for hours in excess of 48 hours.

Calculate:
(a) Bonus hours entitlement of each grade of labour.
(b) Bonus payable to: (i) each grade of labour,
(ii) each operative.
(c) Gross wages payable to each operative. *(45 minutes)*

Answer guide

(a) *Bonus hours entitlement*

(i) *Time allowed:*

	Standard	*Super*	*Deluxe*	*Total*
Gross units produced	1,200	3,500	3,100	
Rejects	200	500	100	
Good units produced	1,000	3,000	3,000	
Bonus time allowance per unit (min)	15	20	30	
Bonus time allowance (hours)	250	1,000	1,500	2,750

(ii) *Time taken (bonus jobs):*

Male skilled	20 × 24 =	480
Male semi-skilled	25 × 24 =	600
Male unskilled	20 × 30 =	600
Juniors	10 × 40 =	400
		2,080

(iii) *Time saved:* (2,750 − 2,080) = 670 hours.

The bonus hours entitlement of each labour grade is therefore as follows (time saved is shared in proportion to the time spent on bonus jobs):

	Total	*Male skilled*	*Male semi-skilled*	*Male unskilled*	*Juniors*
Time taken	2,080	480	600	600	400
Time saved	670	155	193	193	129

(b) *Bonus payable (to the nearest £):*

Grade	*Skilled*	*Semi-skilled*	*Unskilled*	*Juniors*
Bonus hours entitlement	155	193	193	129
Base rate	£4.00	£3.00	£2.00	£1.00
Percentage of base rate at which hours saved are paid (bonus)	50%	40%	30%	20%
Rate per hour (bonus)	£2.00	£1.20	£0.60	£0.20

Grade	*Skilled*	*Semi-skilled*	*Unskilled*	*Juniors*
Bonus payable to each grade of labour	£310	£232	£116	£26
No. of operatives	20	25	20	10
Bonus payable to each operative (nearest £)	£15	£9	£6	£3

(c) Gross wages payable (to nearest £) (*see* page 77)

Example 3

ACCA plc is a small company manufacturing a single product in a single operation. The company employs 20 operatives on a basic 40-hour week at £4 per hour, with a guaranteed minimum weekly gross wage of £160 per operative. The maximum amount of overtime which may be worked, paid at time rate plus one-half, is in total of 400 hours per week. Additional workers cannot be recruited.

The average time for one operative to produce one unit of product is 40 minutes. Demand for the product varies; the minimum weekly output is 1,000 units, but for a significant part of the year the company cannot satisfy total demand despite working the maximum overtime hours available. The nature of the product is such that stocks of WIP or finished goods cannot be stored.

Required:

(a) Under the present wage scheme the weekly profits at the following activity levels:

(i) minimum weekly output,

(ii) maximum weekly output.

(b) Under the proposed wage scheme with labour achieving standard efficiency weekly, profits at the following activity levels:

(i) minimum weekly output,

(ii) current maximum output,

(iii) proposed maximum output.

After appropriate studies have been made, an incentive scheme has been proposed based upon a standard operator-time of 30 minutes per unit, in which operatives will be paid £2.75 for each component produced. The guaranteed minimum wage will still apply, and, if required, overtime will continue to be worked, up to the maximum shown above, and be paid at the previous time rate premiums.

The selling price of the product is £20 per unit. Material costs are £5 per unit; variable overheads varying with hours worked are £2 per direct labour hour and fixed overheads £8,000 per week.

(c) *Gross wages payable (to nearest £):*

DEPARTMENT — PAYROLL — PERIOD: WEEK ENDED

		Hours payable					*Wages payable*			
	Rate per hour	*Normal*	*Over-time*	*Overtime premium*	*Bonus hours (see Note)*	*Normal pay*	*Over-time pay*	*Over-time premium*	*Bonus (see Note)*	*Total wages payable per employee*
		hours	hours	hours	hours	£	£	£	£	£
Skilled, per employee	£4.00	40	10	6		160	40	24	15	239
Semi-skilled, per employee	£3.00	40	10	6		120	30	18	9	177
Unskilled, per employee	£2.00	40	10	6		80	20	12	6	118
Junior, per employee	£1.00	40	10	6		40	10	6	3	59

Suggested answer

WORKINGS—PRESENT SYSTEM:

Note 1	Normal hours 20×40	=	800
	Overtime	=	400
	Total hours available	=	1,200.
Note 2	Gross wages—minimum guaranteed = 800 × £4	=	£3,200.
Note 3	Maximum output: 1,200 hours ÷ 40 minutes per unit	=	1,800.

PROPOSED SYSTEM:

Note 4	Maximum output: 1,200 hours ÷ 30 minutes per unit	=	2,400.
Note 5	Hours required to produce the current maximum output of 1,800 units $= 1{,}800 \times \frac{30}{60}$	=	900 hours.
Note 6	Overtime hours required to produce 1,800 units (900 − 800)	=	100 hours.

COMPARISON OF WEEKLY PROFIT UNDER THE PRESENT AND PROPOSED SYSTEMS OF WAGE PAYMENT: PROFIT/LOSS STATEMENT

	Present		*Proposed*		
	Minimum	*Maximum*	*Minimum*	*Current maximum*	*Proposed maximum*
Units produced/sold	1,000	1,800	1,000	1,800	2,400
Hours required	667	1,200	500	900	1,200
	£	£	£	£	£
Sales at £20	20,000	36,000	20,000	36,000	48,000
Direct materials £5	5,000	9,000	5,000	9,000	12,000
Direct labour (Note 3)					
Normal (minimum)	3,200	3,200	3,200		
Overtime 400 × £4	–	1,600	–		
1,800 × £2.75				4,950	
2,400 × £2.75					6,600
OT premium					
100 × ½ × £4	–	–	–	200	
400 × ½ × £4	–	–	–	–	800
400 × ½ × £4		800			
Variable overhead:					
Hours required × £2	1,334	2,400	1,000	1,800	2,400
Fixed costs	8,000	8,000	8,000	8,000	8,000
Profit (loss)	£2,466	£11,000	£2,800	£12,050	£18,200

8.0 PIECEWORK SYSTEMS

8.1 Piecework with guaranteed day rate or guaranteed weekly wage

Guaranteed day rate

In a scheme based on piecework with guaranteed day rate, the employee is guaranteed his *day* wages regardless of output. Each day stands on its own and he is paid either the day wage or piecework wages per day whichever is higher.

Guaranteed weekly wage

Here the employee is guaranteed his *weekly* wage regardless of output. Each week stands on its own and he is paid either the weekly guaranteed wage or piecework wages per week whichever is higher.

Illustration 11

Guaranteed rate per day £20 or a corresponding guaranteed weekly wage of £100. Rate per piece £0.50.

	Guaranteed	*Based on output*		*Paid*
Monday	£20	50 × £0.50	£25	£25
Tuesday	20	30 × £0.50	15	20
Wednesday	20	60 × £0.50	30	30
Thursday	20	10 × £0.50	5	20
Friday	20	20 × £0.50	10	20
	£100		£85	£115

EMPLOYEE'S WAGE ON A GUARANTEED DAY RATE

Each day stands on its own, so the weekly wage is the total of the days, i.e. £115.

EMPLOYEE'S WAGE ON A GUARANTEED WEEKLY WAGE

Each week stands on its own and an employee will be paid the guaranteed weekly wage of £100, which is higher than the wages based on production (£85).

8.2 Differential piecework systems

The objective is to provide a strong incentive to reach high levels of output. This is an extension of the straight piecework system to give an added incentive for greater effort. For example:

£0.50 per unit if production is below 50 units per hour,
£0.75 per unit if production is between 50 and 75 units per hour,
and £1.00 per unit if production is above 75 units per hour.

Illustration 12

RS Limited operates a day-rate system of employee remuneration at the factory at Galle Face. The employees are paid at £12.00 for an 8-hour day and on average each employee produces 15 units of good output per day. Production overhead is absorbed at a rate of £3.00 per direct labour hour. The works manager proposes to introduce a differential piece rate system. Under the proposed system, an increase in good output will lead to increased remuneration according to the following scale:

Production in units of good output	*Remuneration per unit*
16	£0.84
17	£0.88
18	£0.92
19	£0.96
20	£1.00

COMPARISON OF PRESENT AND PROPOSED SYSTEMS

Systems	*Daily level of output units*	*Direct labour rate per unit (£)*	*Labour cost (£)*	*Factory overhead absorbed (£3 × 8 hours) (£)*	*Total cost (£)*	*Average cost per unit (£)*
Present day rate	15	0.80	12.00	24.00	36.00	2.40
Proposed differential piece rates	16	0.84	13.44	24.00	37.44	
	17	0.88	14.96	24.00	38.96	
	18	0.92	16.56	24.00	40.56	2.2533
	19	0.96	18.24	24.00	42.24	
	20	1.00	20.00	24.00	44.00	2.2000

Note: Increased remuneration is more than offset by the spread of factory overhead over increased output.

8.3 Main differential systems

The main differential systems are:

the Taylor system (later modified by Merrick and Gantt);

the Merrick system;

the Gantt system.

(a) The Taylor system
The system is based on two piece rates:

(i) a lower piece rate for output below standard (−20 per cent);

(ii) a high piece rate for output above standard (+20 per cent);

(iii) day wage is not guaranteed.

(b) The Merrick system
The system is a modification of the Taylor system and uses three rates instead of two.

(i) Piece rates are paid on output up to target output.

(ii) On output above target up to 120 per cent of target output a *bonus* of 8 per cent is paid.

(iii) On output above 120 per cent of target output a *bonus* of 20 per cent is paid.

(iv) There is no lower rate.

(c) Gantt task and bonus plan
This is a combination of time, piece rate and bonus plan using the differential piece-rate principle.

(i) If output is below target output, time rate is guaranteed.

(ii) If output reaches target output a bonus of 20 per cent on time rate is paid.

(iii) If output is above target output a high piece rate operates.

Illustration 13—Comparison of the three differential systems
The following data apply:

Employee	*No. of hours*	*Target or standard output units*	*Actual output units*	*Rate per hour*
DW	40	400	350	£2.50
DJ	40	400	450	£2.50

Note: Units per hour = 10 units. Hourly rate per unit = £0.25.

COMPARISON OF SYSTEMS

Employee	*Taylor*	*Merrick*	*Gantt*
DW	350 × £0.20 = £70	350 × £0.25 = £87.50	40 × £2.50 = £100
DJ	450 × £0.30 = £135	450 × £0.25 = £112.50 *plus* Bonus = 9.00 £121.50 (8% × £112.50 = £9.00)	450 units × a high piece rate

Employee	*Taylor*	*Merrick*	*Gantt*
DW	Output is below target output; thus the rate is 20% below the standard rate, i.e. £0.25 less 20% = £0.20.	Output is less than target output, so he gets the piecework wages.	Output is below target output, so time wages.
DJ	Actual putput is greater than target output; then the rate per unit is plus 20%, i.e. £0.25 + 20% = £0.30.	Output is greater than target output but less than 120% of target output which is 480. He therefore gets a bonus of 8% and *not* 20%.	Output is greater than target output. Therefore a *high* piece rate operates.

CHAPTER FIVE

Production Overhead I – Characteristics and Methods of Absorption

1.0 INTRODUCTION

In a manufacturing concern raw materials flow through the factory where direct labour and other factory costs are incurred to convert them into a finished product.

1.1 Absorption costing

This is a technique of product costing that attempts to trace manufacturing costs to products. These expenses are traced to products and are held as assets of the company until the units to which they are attached are sold.

1.2 Manufacturing overhead: characteristics of indirect costs of production

(a) *Various items:* indirect materials, indirect labour, direct labour related costs (holiday pay, sick pay, idle time, overtime premiums, shift premiums, bonus, employer's NI contribution), rent, rates, insurance, maintenance, depreciation, light and heat, power, and other.

(b) *Their behaviour:* most of the items are more related to time than to levels of activity, i.e. fixed costs.

(c) *Common costs:* they benefit more than one product or department. They cannot be allocated directly to departments.

(d) *Various classes of departments:* in the manufacturing function there are two broad classes of departments. Figure 5 shows the broad classification and the various cost centres under each department.

(e) *Indirect costs of products:* although they are as much a part of a product as direct materials or direct labour, they cannot be directly allocated to products. In order to find the total cost, these costs have to be allocated to products.

Figure 5 shows a typical production unit.

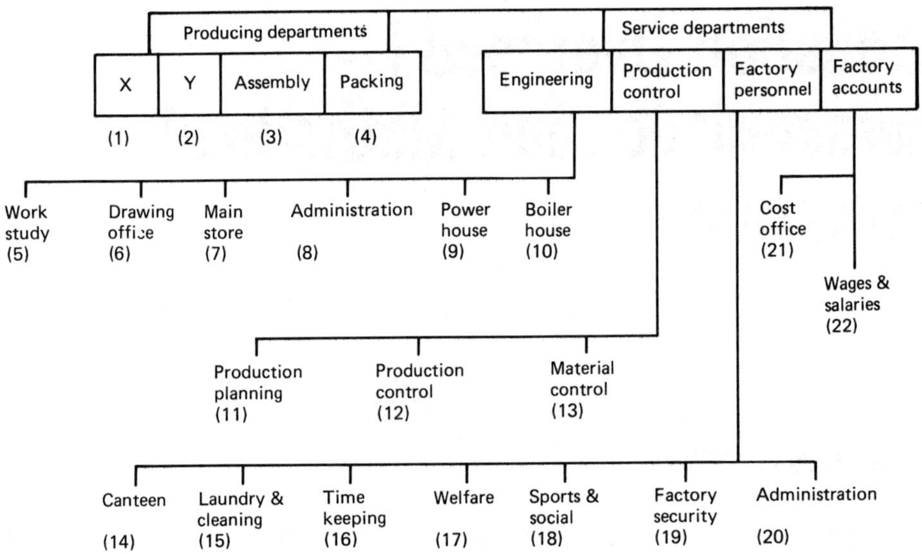

Fig. 5. *Typical production unit.*

1.3 The problem

Materials, labour and expenses incurred in the four producing departments (Fig. 5) which cannot be identified with products, and the materials, labour and expenses incurred in the eighteen service departments, are termed "manufacturing overheads" or "indirect production expenses". The problem is how to trace these costs to products, i.e. how to apportion these costs to cost units. For example, costs incurred in a timekeeping department, the canteen etc. have to be absorbed by cost units.

1.4 Tracing production overheads to products

This process can be studied in stages. Overhead is traced to products by means of an overhead rate. The function of the overhead rate is to allocate an equitable share of overhead to each product; it is calculated as follows:

$$\text{Overhead rate} = \frac{\text{Total overhead cost } (\pounds)}{\text{Level of activity}}.$$

For its calculation, the basic information required is:

(a) Total overhead cost and level of activity (production).

(b) Product costing system.

Stages consist as follows:

Stage one Methods of absorbing overhead.
Stage two Actual rate or predetermined rate. (A single rate or plant-wide rate (which is either actual or predetermined) and the operation of the system.)
Stage three Departmental overhead absorption rates and the operation of the system.
Stage four Single rate versus departmental rates.

2.0 METHODS OF APPLYING OVERHEADS TO PRODUCTS

The function of the overhead rate is to allocate an equitable share of overhead cost to each product. The base selected should be closely related to the functions of the overhead cost being applied. If the overhead cost tends to vary with the amount of labour hours worked, the proper basis is probably direct labour cost or direct labour hours. If the overhead costs tend to vary with machine time, then the proper basis is probably machine hours.

Having selected the most suitable basis, the overhead absorption rate is calculated by dividing total overhead cost by the total amount of activity.

2.1 Characteristics of good methods of overhead absorption

(a) The method of overhead absorption selected should result in the most accurate application of overhead to products.

(b) It should be easily computed and minimise clerical effort and costs.

(c) If the factory is departmentalised, departmental overhead absorption should be used rather than a single rate for the whole factory.

(d) Many indirect costs are period costs. They are related more to time than to a level of activity. The overhead rate of absorption should have some relation to the time factor.

2.2 Expression of the level of activity

Methods of overhead absorption depend on how the denominator (level of activity) in the overhead rate calculation is expressed. Figure 6 illustrates the variety of ways possible.

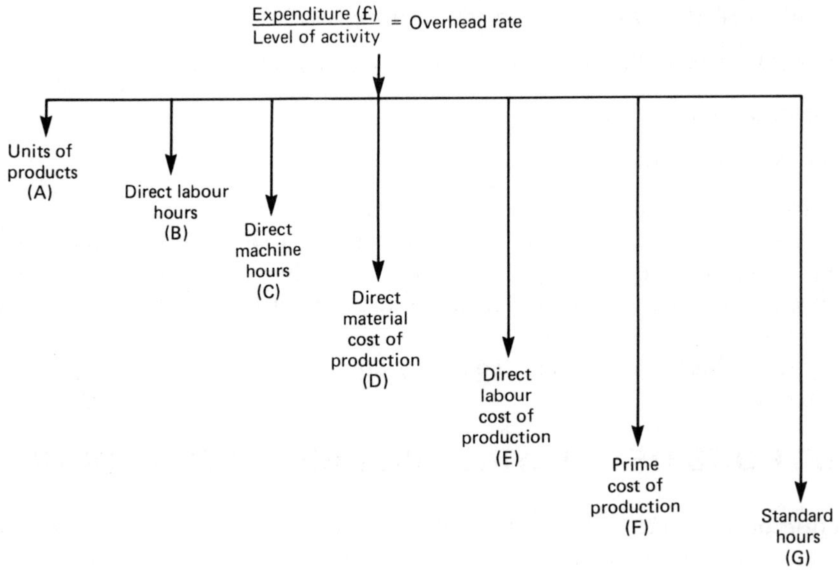

Fig. 6. *Expressions of the level of activity.*

(A) Overhead rate per unit
(B) Overhead rate per direct labour hour
(C) Overhead rate per machine hour
(D) Overhead rate—percentage of direct material
(E) Overhead rate—percentage of direct labour cost
(F) Overhead rate—percentage of prime cost

} Product costing system may be either historical or normal.

(G) Overhead rate per standard hour

Product costing system—is a standard costing system.

Illustration 1—Predetermined single overhead absorption rate

Ramsu Ltd manufactures two products, Standard and Super, to which the following details relate:

Product	*Standard*	*Super*
Direct materials cost	£30	£60
Direct labour cost:		
machining £1.50 per hour	10 hours	20 hours
assembly £1.25 per hour	5 hours	5 hours

The company plans to produce 200,000 of Standard and 100,000 of Super during the forthcoming year and estimates its overheads for that year at £600,000.

(a) You are required to calculate the overhead absorption rates on the following alternative bases:

(i) rate per unit;

(ii) rate per direct labour hour;

(iii) rate per machine hour;

(iv) percentage of direct material;

(v) percentage of direct wages;

(vi) percentage of prime cost.

(b) Compile a comparative statement showing, for each of the methods, the total production cost attributable to a unit of Standard.

Suggested answer

(a) (i) Rate per unit $= \frac{£600{,}000}{300{,}000} = £2$ per unit of product.

(ii) Rate per direct labour hour $= \frac{£600{,}000}{5{,}500{,}000} = £0.1091.$

	Machine hours	*Assembly hours*
200,000 × 10	2,000,000	
× 5		1,000,000
100,000 × 20	2,000,000	
× 5		500,000
	4,000,000	1,500,000

(iii) Rate per machine hour $= \frac{£600{,}000}{4{,}000{,}000} = £0.15.$

(iv) Percentage of direct materials $= \frac{£600{,}000}{£12{,}000{,}000} \times 100 = 5$ per cent.

Note

Standard	*£30 × 200,000 =*	*£6,000,000*
Super	*£60 × 100,000 =*	*£6,000,000*
		£12,000,000

(v) Percentage of direct wages $= \frac{£600,000}{£7,875,000} \times 100 = 7.619$ per cent.

Note

Machine dept	*4,000,000 × £1.50 =*	*£6,000,000*
Assembly dept	*1,500,000 × £1.25 =*	*£1,875,000*
		£7,875,000

(vi) Percentage of prime cost $= \frac{£600,000}{£12,000,000 + £7,875,000} \times 100 = 3$ per cent.

3.0 ADVANTAGES AND DISADVANTAGES OF DIFFERENT METHODS

3.1 Per unit of output

This is the simplest and the most direct method of absorbing overhead. Its usefulness however is limited to companies manufacturing one product.

3.2 Per direct labour hour

This may be used if labour is the predominating factor and work is done manually. The method takes time into consideration and allocates overhead to production according to the time spent by direct labour (DL). Work is measured in units of time (DL hours) and therefore can be used where production is not uniform. The method requires detailed records of labour time and may be expensive in terms of clerical costs.

3.3 Per machine hour

The method may be used if machinery is the most significant factor in production. Again, this method absorbs overhead on the basis of time spent. If a company uses a single rate of absorption (e.g. machine hour rate) it is possible in such circumstances that any non-machine production would be charged no overhead at all.

3.4 Percentage on direct wages

This is a simple and easy method of overhead absorption. It could be used with great advantage if the company employs similar grades of direct labour and/or their rates of pay are not subject to great variations.

If there exist grade differences and rate differences then the jobs upon which highly paid workers are employed will be charged with a greater burden than those on which lower paid employees are employed. This in itself is inequitable because employment of lower grades of labour may cost the company less in terms of wages, but may lead to greater expense in the form of factory overhead—e.g. greater scrap, wastage of materials, training, defective units, etc.

Suggested answer—Illustration 1 (contd)

(b) *Comparative production cost—product standard*

Overhead rate	*Per unit*	*Per direct labour hour*	*Per machine hour*	*Percentage of direct wages*	*Percentage of direct materials*	*Percentage of prime cost*
	£	£	£	£	£	£
Direct materials	30.00	30.00	30.00	30.00	30.00	30.00
Direct labour						
Machine dept						
10 × £1.50	15.00	15.00	15.00	15.00	15.00	15.00
Assembly dept						
5 × £1.25	6.25	6.25	6.25	6.25	6.25	6.25
Production overhead	2.00	(15 × £0.1091) = 1.6365	(10 × £0.15) = 1.50	(7.619% × £21.25) = 1.619	(5% × £30) = 1.50	(3% × £51.25) = 1.5375
	£53.25	£52.8865	£52.75	£52.869	£52.75	£52.7875

3.5 Percentage of materials basis

The method may be used if the cost of materials consumed by each unit of product is the same. In other cases, it is a crude method of overhead absorption. The cost of materials is often subject to fluctuations, which may not be followed by overhead costs. This method ignores *time*—the most important factor to be considered in allocating overhead.

3.6 Percentage of prime cost

This is a simple and easy method of overhead absorption. The method gives weight to costs (material and labour) and does not make use of the time factor.

CHAPTER SIX

Production Overhead II – Historical versus Normal Costing Systems

1.0 HISTORICAL VERSUS PREDETERMINED SINGLE ABSORPTION RATES

1.1 Product costing systems

These may be classified as follows:

(a) Historical
These are based on the ascertainment of unit costs after they have been incurred.

(b) Normal
These take as their basis the ascertainment of unit costs with predetermined overhead absorption rate.

(c) Standard
These are based on the setting up of predetermined unit costs for each cost element.

1.2 Unit cost under different production costing systems

See Table 3.

Table 3. COMPARISON OF DIFFERENT PRODUCTION COSTING SYSTEMS: UNIT COST

	Historical	*Normal*	*Standard*
Direct materials	Actual quantity × Actual rate	Actual quantity × Actual rate	Standard quantity specified × Standard rate
Direct labour	Actual hours worked × Actual rate	Actual hours worked × Actual rate	Standard hours specified × Standard rate
Variable overhead	Actual input × Actual rate	Actual input × Predetermined rate	Standard hours specified × Standard rate
Fixed overhead	Actual input × Actual rate	Actual input × Predetermined rate	Standard hours specified × Standard rate

2.0 HISTORICAL PRODUCT COSTING SYSTEM

2.1 Historical overhead rate (i.e. actual overhead rate)

This is an actual overhead rate computed after the end of the period and this rate is used to apply the actual costs of the period.

Illustration 1

EW Rod Limited worked on three jobs during the past accounting period. Cost records indicate that total overhead of £24,000 was incurred and that 12,000 direct labour hours were worked. These 12,000 direct labour hours are used as follows:

Job 123	4,000 hours
Job 345	5,000 hours
Job 567	3,000 hours

The historical overhead rate per direct labour hour is:

$$\frac{£24{,}000}{12{,}000} = £2.00.$$

The factory overhead would be charged to the individual jobs:

Job 123	4,000 at £2.00 = £8,000
Job 345	5,000 at £2.00 = £10,000
Job 567	3,000 at £2.00 = £6,000
	£24,000

2.2 Disadvantages of the use of historical overhead rates

(a) There is a delay in product cost evaluations at least until the end of the accounting period because overhead cannot be charged to work in progress until records of all production for the period have been compiled.

(b) The overhead rate may fluctuate from one period to another. Some of the overheads are fixed and do not change with changes in the level of activity. Thus, when there are fluctuations in volume the factory overhead rate will fluctuate.

Illustration 2

	Period 1	*Period 2*	*Period 3*
Direct labour hours	36,000	48,000	24,000
Factory overhead:	£	£	£
Fixed	72,000	72,000	72,000
Variable	36,000	48,000	24,000
Total	108,000	120,000	96,000
Factory o.h. rate per direct labour hour:			
Fixed	2.00	1.50	3.00
Variable	1.00	1.00	1.00
Total	3.00	2.50	4.00

The illustration shows that the factory overhead rate fluctuates because of the interaction of the level of activity with fixed costs. This will result in fluctuations in product costs.

3.0 NORMAL PRODUCT COSTING SYSTEM

To overcome the disadvantages of the historical (i.e. actual) overhead rate, a predetermined factory overhead rate is often used. The rate is computed in advance of the period to which it will apply:

$$\text{Predetermined factory o.h. rate} = \frac{\text{Predetermined factory overhead for the coming accounting period}}{\text{Predetermined level of activity for the coming accounting period}}.$$

3.1 Advantages and disadvantages arising in the use of predetermined overhead rates

Advantages

(a) Calculation of an overhead rate once a year requires less effort than going through the same calculation every period.

(b) Permits product costs to be calculated more promptly with the use of a predetermined rate; overhead costs can be charged to products at the same time as the direct costs are assigned to them.

Disadvantages

When a predetermined overhead absorption rate is used to determine the product cost, it would be highly unusual for factory overhead actually incurred to agree exactly with factory overhead absorbed or applied.

3.2 Under-/over-absorbed overhead

This is the difference between the amount of overhead absorbed and the amount of overhead incurred.

Definitions

(a) *Overhead absorbed:* overhead charged to work in progress.

(b) *Overhead under-applied or under-absorbed:* the amount by which the actual factory overhead incurred during the period exceeds the total factory overhead charged to work in progress.

(c) *Overhead over-applied or over-absorbed:* the amount by which the actual factory overhead incurred during the period falls short of the total factory overhead charged to work in progress.

Illustration 3

Let us assume that RH Limited used a predetermined overhead absorption rate of £2.50 per direct labour hour.

$$\frac{\text{Predetermined expenses} \quad £120{,}000}{\text{Predetermined level of activity} \quad 48{,}000} = £2.50 \text{ per direct labour hour}$$

Let us examine the consequences of using this predetermined rate in a number of alternative actual situations:

PREDETERMINED OVERHEAD ABSORPTION RATE

			Under- or over-absorption	
(a)	Actual expenditure Actual level of activity	£120,000 48,000 DL hours	nil	
(b)	Actual expenditure Actual level of activity	£140,000 48,000 DL hours	Under-absorption	£20,000
(c)	Actual expenditure Actual level of activity	£120,000 40,000 DL hours	Under-absorption	£20,000
(d)	Actual expenditure Actual level of activity	£100,000 48,000 DL hours	Over-absorption	£20,000
(e)	Actual expenditure Actual level of activity	£120,000 50,000 DL hours	Over-absorption	£5,000
(f)	Actual expenditure Actual level of activity	£130,000 52,000 DL hours	nil	
(g)	Actual expenditure Actual level of activity	£100,000 40,000 DL hours	nil	

3.3 Analysis of under-/over-absorbed overheads

It is most unlikely that actual overheads incurred will be exactly the same as the predetermined figures. It is necessary to analyse the reasons for the difference which will almost certainly arise.

Two separate variances are computed in making the analysis: expenditure or spending variance; volume variance.

3.4 Expenditure or spending variance

This is a variance due to a budget or expense factor:

(a) when the actual expenditure is *greater* than budgeted then the variance is *unfavourable*;

(b) when the actual expenditure is *less* than budgeted then the variance is *favourable*.

3.5 Volume variance

This is a variance due to a volume or activity factor:

(a) when the actual level of activity is *greater* than the budgeted level then the variance is *favourable*;

(b) when the actual level of activity is *less* than the budgeted level then the variance is *unfavourable*.

3.6 Example of analysis over- or under-absorption

This uses the figures calculated in illustration 3.

Situation	*Actual*	*Budget*	*Absorbed*	*Over (Under)*	*Analysis*	
					Expenditure	*Volume*
	1	2	*3*	*4* (*3*− *1*)	*5* (*2*− *1*)	*6* (*3*− *2*)
A	£120,000	£120,000 / £48,000	48,000 × £2.50 = £120,000	nil	nil	nil
B	140,000		48,000 × £2.50 = £120,000	£(20,000)	£(20,000)	nil
C	120,000		40,000 × £2.50 = £100,000	(20,000)	nil	£(20,000) = 8,000 hours × £2.50
D	100,000		48,000 × £2.50 = £120,000	20,000	20,000	nil
E	120,000		50,000 × £2.50 = £125,000	5,000	nil	£5,000 = 2,000 hours × £2.50
F	130,000		52,000 × £2.50 = £130,000	nil	(10,000)	£10,000 = 4,000 hours × £2.50
G	100,000		40,000 × £2.50 = £100,000	nil	10,000	£(10,000) = 4,000 hours × £2.50

Study the above table in relation to the explanations in **3.4** and **3.5** until you have clearly understood the derivation of the figures in the analysis columns.

Illustration 4

The demand for the products of South West Company have increased substantially in the recent past, and the firm is now working at full capacity within the normal 40-hour week for 50 weeks a year. Sixteen operatives are employed in the factory and are paid £2.00 per hour of *attendance time*. In view of the high quality of workmanship required, overtime working is not permitted.

The company is having additional premises built and when these are completed there will be space for up to 50 operatives. In the meantime, however, the company wishes to expand its output and is considering employing 20 part-time operatives to attend for 4 hours in each of the 5 evenings of the week, for which they would be paid the normal hourly rate plus one-half. It is expected that this arrangement would apply for the whole of the forthcoming year, i.e. 50 weeks.

The time spent by each operative on production is booked to the appropriate production order and it is estimated that this accounts for 80 per cent of the time for which operatives are paid.

Production overhead for the forthcoming year has been estimated as follows:

	Without the extra shift	*Addition for extra shift*
Factory supplies	£20,000	20 per cent
Power	12,000	10 per cent
Materials handling	8,000	20 per cent
Lighting and heating	20,000	Proportionate to direct labour hours
Production control	30,000	£4,000
Miscellaneous expenses	10,000	Proportionate to direct labour hours
Plant maintenance	10,000	25 per cent
Indirect labour	40,000	Proportionate to direct labour hours
Rent and rates	54,800	No change

You are required to:

(a) Calculate the overhead absorption rate per direct labour hour for the forthcoming year, assuming the evening shift is *not* worked.

(b) (i) Prepare the production overhead estimated for the forthcoming year, assuming the evening shift *is* worked, and
(ii) Calculate the production overhead absorption rate using the direct labour hour basis.

(c) Discuss the main advantages and disadvantages of using a predetermined absorption rate.

(d) Define the following:

(i) overhead absorbed
(ii) overhead under-absorbed
(iii) overhead over-absorbed

(e) State the factors which give rise to over- or under-absorption of factory overhead.

Suggested answers (numerical)

BUDGETED PRODUCTION OVERHEAD

Overhead items	*Without shift work*		*Shift (increase)*	*With shift work*
Factory supplies	£20,000		£4,000	£24,000
Power	12,000		1,200	13,200
Material handling	8,000		1,600	9,600
Light and heat	20,000	(Note 1)	12,500	32,500
Production control	30,000		4,000	34,000
Miscellaneous expenses	10,000		5,250	16,250
Plant maintenance	10,000	(Note 5)	2,500	12,500
Rent and rates	54,800		54,800	54,800
Indirect labour	40,000	(Note 5)	25,000	65,000
Idle time (Note 1)	12,800	(Note 4)	8,000	20,800
Shift premium	–	(Note 4)	20,000	20,000
	£217,600			£302,650
Direct labour hours	25,600			41,600
Overhead absorption rate per direct labour hour	£8.50			£7.2752 per DL hour

Note 1 *Available capacity* (without shift work)

16 × 40 × 50	= 32,000 hours
Less: 20 per cent idle time	= (6,400)
Direct labour hours	25,600
Cost of idle time 6,400 × £2	= £12,800

Note 2 *Available capacity* (with shift)

Shift work

20 × 4 × 5 × 50	= 20,000 hours
Less: 20 per cent idle time	= (4,000)
	16,000

Note 3 Available capacity with shift = 25,600 + 16,000 = 41,600 hours.

Note 4 Wages payable with shift (gross pay)

Basis	20,000 × £2 =	£40,000
Premium	10,000 × £2 =	20,000
Total		£60,000

Analysis of gross pay:

Idle time 4,000 × £2	= £8,000	production overhead
Premium	20,000	production overhead
Direct labour	32,000	direct labour cost
	£60,000	

Note 5

	Without shift	*Shift*
Direct labour hours	25,600	16,000
Light and heat	£20,000	$\frac{£20,000}{25,600} \times 16,000 = £12,500$
Miscellaneous expenses	£10,000	$\frac{£10,000}{25,600} \times 16,000 = £2,500$
Indirect labour	£40,000	$\frac{£40,000}{25,600} \times 16,000 = £25,000$

4.0 EXAMPLE

The budgeted activity and cost data for each half-year of X Ltd were as follows:

Direct labour hours	68,000
Direct wages	£42,500
Overhead: fixed	£37,400
variable	£64,600

During the 6 months January to June the following actual results were achieved:

Direct labour hours incurred	65,000
Direct wages	£45,500
Overhead: fixed	£38,700
variable	£65,800

(Number of units produced—not applicable.)

The existing method of absorbing overhead is by a direct wages percentage rate. A proposal has been made to change the overhead absorption to a direct labour hour rate analysed into fixed and variable overhead.

You are required, for the period January to June:

(a) to calculate, under the present system:

(i) the budgeted direct wages percentage rate of overhead absorption;

(ii) the absorbed overhead;

(iii) the over- or under-absorbed overhead;

(b) to calculate under the new proposal (i.e. using direct labour hour rates of absorption):

(i) the budgeted direct labour hour rate of overhead absorption for:

fixed overhead

variable overhead;

(ii) the absorbed overhead;

(iii) the over- or under-absorbed overhead;

(c) to state which of the answers to (a) (iii) or to (b) (iii) you consider gives the better indication of the company's achievement and explain *very briefly* why you think this is so.

Answer guide

Predetermined overhead absorption rate.

(a) (i) $\frac{£102{,}000}{£42{,}500} \times 100 = 240$ per cent of direct wages.

(ii) *Absorbed overheads January–June*

Actual overhead	£104,500
Overhead absorbed 240 per cent × £45,500	£109,200
(iii) Over-absorbed	£4,700+

(b) (i) *Proposed method—budgeted direct labour hour rate of overhead absorption*

Fixed overhead $\frac{£37{,}400}{68{,}000} = £0.55$ per DL hour

Variable overhead $\frac{£64{,}600}{68{,}000} = £0.95$ per DL hour

Note: Total rate per hour £1.50.

(ii) Actual overhead	£104,500
Overhead absorbed 65,000 at £1.50	97,500
(iii) Under-absorbed	£(7,000)

(c) The under-absorption of £7,000 in (b) (iii) rather than the over-absorption of £4,700 in (a) (iii) gives a better indication of the company's achievement.

ANALYSIS OF OVERHEAD VARIANCE BY CAUSES

	Actual	*Budget*	*Absorbed*	*Over (Under)*	*Expenditure*	*Volume*
(a) (iii)	£104,500	£102,000	£109,200	£4,700 +	£(2,500)	£7,200
(b) (iii)	104,500	102,000	97,500	(7,000)	(2,500)	(4,500)

Overheads are in excess of the budget to the extent of £2,500 in both cases; the higher degree of absorption in (a) (iii) is due to a higher rate of pay in the January–June period.

	Budget	*Actual*
Direct labour hours	68,000	65,000
Direct wages	£42,500	£45,500
Rate per hour	£0.625	£0.70

If the original rate had continued in operation the amount of overhead absorbed as a percentage of direct wages in (a) (ii) would have been:

Direct labour hours worked—65,000 × £0.625	=	£40,625
Overhead absorbed £40,625 × 240 per cent	=	£97,500
Overhead incurred	=	£104,500
Under-absorbed		£(7,000)

CHAPTER SEVEN

Production Overhead III – Departmental Rates

1.0 DEPARTMENTAL OVERHEAD ABSORPTION RATES

1.1 Concept of departmentalisation

In the production function there are two broad classes of departments. Departmentalisation of production overhead means the division of the production function into departments to which costs are charged:

(a) *Producing departments* actually convert raw materials by adding labour and overheads to create a finished product.

(b) *Service departments* do not directly work on the finished product but assist the producing departments by providing the necessary services.

The main reasons for departmentalisation of overhead are:

(a) cost control and responsibility accounting;

(b) more accurate costing of products.

Illustration 1

Assume, for instance, that machinery in the press shop is divided into two categories, A and B. Estimated costs at practical plant capacity are as follows:

PRESS SHOP OVERHEAD BUDGET

	Cost centres *A*	*B*	*Total*
Building services	£400	£400	£800
Indirect wages	800	600	1,400
Depreciation	4,000	1,000	5,000
Repairs	800	200	1,000
	6,000	2,200	8,200
Normal capacity			
Machine hours	2,050	2,050	4,100
Overhead rates	£2.9268	£1.0732	£2.00

If overhead is absorbed at a single rate of £2.00 per machine hour, orders processed in centre B would be overcharged and orders processed in centre A would be undercharged. A better method would be to use departmental rates. Thus an order going through centre A and centre B would be charged at £2.9268 and £1.0732 per machine hour respectively.

2.0 STEP-BY-STEP PROCEDURE FOR CALCULATING AND OPERATING DEPARTMENTAL RATES

(a) Prepare the *budgeted overhead* at the volume selected.

(b) Prepare the *primary distribution*—allocation/apportionment of each item to various departments of the factory.

(c) *Secondary distribution*—transfer of costs charged to service departments, to producing departments.

(d) *Levels of activity*—production budget and method of absorption.

(e) Departmental rates—*final step*.

(f) Operation of the system during a period of time.

(g) Over-/under-absorption, analysis and treatment at the end of the accounting period.

3.0 PRIMARY DISTRIBUTION—LINKING PROCESS

3.1 Allocation and apportionment

The primary distribution involves the allocation and/or apportionment of overhead costs on various bases deemed reasonable to all departments of the factory to which they apply. In making the primary distribution, the distinction between producing departments and service departments is ignored.

The two terms *allocation* and *apportionment* are now defined before we proceed any further:

(a) *Allocation.* Charging a cost centre with those overheads that result solely from the existence of that cost centre: e.g. salary of a supervisor who supervises one centre entirely.

(b) *Apportionment.* Most of the overheads are not caused solely by one cost centre (they are *joint costs*) and it is therefore not possible to allocate costs directly to individual cost centres, but rather only to *apportion* these joint costs on a reasonable basis.

3.2 Basis of apportionment

Some overheads can be apportioned on more than one basis. Any basis that is chosen should meet these tests:

(a) it should be equitable;

(b) it should be practicable;

(c) it should not be costly;

(d) it should result in charges to each department, that will be reasonable in view of the benefit the department receives;

(e) in some cases a much more costly method of apportionment, perhaps involving the continued collection of data, may result in a slightly more accurate apportionment. But the small increase in accuracy may not justify the much greater cost of this method.

3.3 Bases most commonly used

These are:

(a) floor area;

(b) weight of materials—material handling and storekeeping;

(c) number of employees;

(d) book value;

(e) number of radiators—heat;

(f) technical estimates—power.

3.4 Sources of information for the primary distribution

Basic information for primary distribution is as follows:

(a) *Statistical* information pertaining to the factory:

buildings and departmental occupancy;
floor area of buildings.

(b) *Statistical* information relating to machinery and equipment:

location of equipment in departments.

(c) *Statistical* information relating to personnel.

(d) *Accounting* information relating to property:

plant ledger;
property ledger;
patents ledger.

(e) *Direct allocation* (from original records):

purchase voucher: coal for power house;
stores requisition: small tools, supplies and repair materials for use in specific producing or service departments;
payroll or indirect labour analysis.

3.5 Comprehensive illustration of primary distribution

Illustration 2

Emile Woolf Ltd, a manufacturing company, has four production departments and four service departments, one of which, the engineering department, serves producing departments X and Y only.

BUDGETED TRADING ACCOUNT FOR THE YEAR ENDING 31ST DECEMBER 19_8

Sales				£1,500,000
Direct materials		£100,000		
Direct labour		500,000		
Direct expenses		50,000		
Prime cost			£650,000	
Other identifiable costs of production	(Note 1)		240,000	
Other joint costs of production	(Note 2)		121,000	
Total cost of production				1,010,000
Budgeted factory profit				£489,000

NOTE 1 OTHER IDENTIFIABLE COSTS OF PRODUCTION

	Total	*Wages and salaries*	*Consumable supplies*	*Overtime premium*	*Depreciation of machinery*	*Holiday pay and National Insurance*
Department X	£53,000	£20,000	£5,000	£4,000	£20,000	£4,000
Department Y	49,000	20,000	5,000	4,000	16,000	4,000
Assembly	34,000	20,000	2,000	4,000	4,000	4,000
Packing	26,000	10,000	8,000	2,000	4,000	2,000
Engineering	19,000	10,000	1,000	2,000	4,000	2,000
Production control	15,000	10,000	1,000	2,000	–	2,000
Factory personnel	21,000	15,000	1,000	2,000	–	3,000
Factory accounts	23,000	15,000	1,000	2,000	2,000	3,000
	£240,000	£120,000	£24,000	£22,000	£50,000	£24,000

NOTE 2 OTHER JOINT COSTS OF PRODUCTION:

Rent and rates	£60,000
Power	10,000
Lighting and heating	30,000
Insurance of building	6,000
Insurance of machinery	15,000
	£121,000

NOTE 3 FURTHER DATA AVAILABLE

Departments	*Original book value of machinery*	*Area (sq. ft)*	*Effective holiday pay hours*
Department X	500,000	30,000	40
Department Y	400,000	30,000	40
Assembly	100,000	10,000	10
Packing	100,000	10,000	10
Engineering	100,000	10,000	–
Production Control	–	10,000	–
Factory Personnel	–	10,000	–
Factory Accounts	50,000	10,000	–
	1,250,000	120,000	100

NOTE 4 PRODUCTIVE CAPACITY (PRACTICAL, NORMAL OR EXPECTED CAPACITY)

Departments	*Machine hours*	*Direct labour hours*
Department X	200,000	50,000
Department Y	300,000	50,000
Assembly	–	200,000
Packing	–	400,000

NOTE 5

After study it is decided that the costs of the service cost centres should be apportioned as follows:

	Production departments				Service departments			
Service rendered	*X*	*Y*	*Assembly*	*Packing*	*Engineering*	*Production control*	*Factory personnel*	*Accounts*
Engineering	40%	60%	–	–	–	–	–	–
Production control	30%	30%	20%	20%	–	–	–	–
Factory personnel	10%	10%	20%	30%	10%	10%	–	10%
Factory accounts	10%	10%	20%	30%	10%	10%	10%	–

You are required, using relevant information, to prepare the primary distribution.

RELEVANT INFORMATION REQUIRED TO PREPARE THE PRIMARY DISTRIBUTION

(a) other identifiable costs of production (Note 1).

(b) other joint costs of production (Note 2).

(c) the basis of apportionment of joint costs (Note 3).

Note: Productive capacity (Note 4) and the distribution of the costs of service departments (Note 5) are not relevant at this stage.

Suggested answer

PRIMARY DISTRIBUTION: PRODUCTION OVERHEAD DISTRIBUTION SUMMARY

			Productive departments				*Service departments*			
Expense	*Basis of allocation/ apportionment*	*Total*	*X*	*Y*	*Assembly*	*Packing*	*Engineering*	*Production control*	*Factory personnel*	*Accounts*
Wages and salaries	Direct allocation	£120,000	£20,000	£20,000	£20,000	£10,000	£10,000	£10,000	£15,000	£15,000
Holiday pay and National Insurance	Direct allocation	24,000	4,000	4,000	4,000	2,000	2,000	2,000	3,000	3,000
Overtime premium	Direct allocation	22,000	4,000	4,000	4,000	2,000	2,000	2,000	2,000	2,000
Consumable supplies	Direct allocation	24,000	5,000	5,000	2,000	8,000	1,000	1,000	1,000	1,000
Depreciation	Direct allocation	50,000	20,000	16,000	4,000	4,000	4,000	–	–	2,000
Rent and rates	Floor area	60,000	15,000	15,000	5,000	5,000	5,000	5,000	5,000	5,000
Lighting and heating	Floor area	30,000	7,500	7,500	2,500	2,500	2,500	2,500	2,500	2,500
Insurance—building	Floor area	6,000	1,500	1,500	500	500	500	500	500	500
Insurance—machinery	Capital cost	15,000	6,000	4,800	1,200	1,200	1,200	–	–	600
Power	HP	10,000	4,000	4,000	1,000	1,000	–	–	–	–
		£361,000	£87,000	£81,800	£44,200	£36,200	£28,200	£23,000	£29,000	£31,600

4.0 MANUFACTURING OVERHEAD—SECONDARY DISTRIBUTION

We have now set the stage for product costing.

In the factory (Illustration 2) there are two broad classes of departments:

(a) *Producing departments:* actually work on products.

(b) *Service departments:* e.g. factory personnel, accounts, engineering and production control. They support the producing departments but do not work directly on the final product. Their purpose is to make the producing departments more effective.

4.1 Secondary distribution defined

It is necessary to analyse all the overheads according to producing departments.

Therefore the costs charged to service departments have to be apportioned to the producing departments on a suitable basis termed *secondary distribution.*

4.2 Bases for secondary distribution

(a) Service rendered

If the engineering department services machine shop A 70 per cent, and machine shop B 30 per cent, it seems reasonable that the relative share of the engineering department costs should be borne 7:3 by the two departments.

(b) Readiness to serve

The capacity of a service department is determined by the demands that would be made by the other departments. The cost of maintaining this capacity to serve may be apportioned on the basis of the expected use by other departments.

4.3 Examples of service departments and bases of apportioning their costs

Service department	*Basis of apportionment*
(a) Stores	Number of requisitions; number of units handled; cost of materials.
(b) Factory office and personnel canteen	Number of employees; labour hours; labour cost.
(c) Building services	Floor area.
(d) Machine maintenance	Machine hours.

Illustration 3—Comprehensive illustration of different methods of secondary distribution

Using the figures from the comprehensive illustration, you are required to calculate the total overhead chargeable to each production cost centre by each of the following methods:

(a) Ignoring the service that each of the service cost centres gives to the other (*see* Note 1 below).

(b) Using a "step" method of apportionment whereby costs of the service cost centre that serves most cost centres is apportioned first, and the other service cost centres are then apportioned to the cost centres.

(c) Using the "repeated distribution" or "continuous allotment" method of apportioning the costs of service cost centres (*see* Note 2 below).

Relevant information required to prepare the secondary distribution is as follows:

(a) Primary distribution.

(b) The distribution of service department costs.

(c) Note that there are different methods of distributing the service department costs.

NOTE 1

Ignoring the service that each of the service cost centres gives to the other:

(a) Accuracy of costing products is not increased by elaborate methods of secondary distribution.

(b) For purposes of cost control, primary distribution is sufficient.

(c) This method apportions the cost directly to the producing departments. It is easy and straightforward.

NOTE 2

Repeated distribution—the steps involved are as follows:

(a) Apply the percentages to allocate the primary distribution total of the service department that serves the most number of departments (regardless of whether a department is a service or producing department).

(b) Apply the percentages to the second service department that serves the most number of departments to allocate the primary distribution total plus charges from service department (Note 1).

Suggested answer

SECONDARY DISTRIBUTION—IGNORING INTERSERVICE TRANSFERS

		Productive departments				*Service departments*			
Basis	*Total*	*X*	*Y*	*Assembly*	*Packing*	*Engineering*	*Production control*	*Factory personnel*	*Accounts*
Primary distribution	£361,000	£87,000	£81,800	£44,200	£36,200	£28,200	£23,000	£29,000	£31,600
Engineering (ratio) 40:60	–	11,280	16,920	–	–	(28,200)	–	–	–
Production control (ratio) 30:30:20:20	–	6,900	6,900	4,600	4,600	–	(23,000)	–	–
Factory personnel (ratio) 10:10:20:30	–	4,143	4,143	8,286	12,428	–	–	(29,000)	–
Accounts (ratio) 10:10:20:30	–	4,514	4,514	9,028	13,544	–	–	–	(31,600)
	£361,000	£113,837	£114,277	£66,114	£66,772	–	–	–	–

SECONDARY DISTRIBUTION—STEP METHOD

		Productive departments				Service departments			
Basis	*Total*	*X*	*Y*	*Assembly*	*Packing*	*Engineering*	*Production control*	*Factory personnel*	*Accounts*
Primary distribution	£361,000	£87,000	£81,800	£44,200	£36,200	£28,200	£23,000	£29,000	£31,600
(a) Factory accounts (the one which serves most departments) 10:10:20:30:10:10:10	–	3,160	3,160	6,320	9,480	3,160	3,160	3,160	(31,600)[a]
(b) Factory personnel (ratio) 10:10:20:30:10:10	–	3,573	3,573	7,147	10,721	3,573	3,573	(32,160)[b]	
(c) Production control (ratio) 30:30:20:20	–	8,920	8,920	5,946	5,947	–	(29,733)[c]		
(d) Engineering (ratio) 40:60	–	13,973	20,960	–	–	(34,933)[d]			
	£361,000	£116,626	£118,413	£63,613	£62,348	–	–	–	–

SECONDARY DISTRIBUTION—REPEATED DISTRIBUTION

		Productive departments				*Service departments*			
Basis	*Total*	*X*	*Y*	*Assembly*	*Packing*	*Engineering*	*Production control*	*Factory personnel*	*Accounts*
Primary distribution	£361,000	£87,000	£81,800	£44,200	£36,200	£28,200	£23,000	£29,000	£31,600
Cycle one									
Accounts 10:10:20:30:10:10:10	–	3,160	3,160	6,320	9,480	3,160	3,160	3,160	(31,600)
Factory personnel 10:10:20:30:10:10:10	–	3,216	3,216	6,432	9,648	3,216	3,216	(32,160)	3,216
Production control 30:30:20:20	–	8,813	8,813	5,875	5,875	–	(29,376)	–	–
Engineering 40:60	–	13,830	20,746	–	–	(34,576)			
Cycle two									
Accounts	–	322	322	643	963	322	322	322	(3,216)
Personnel	–	32	32	64	98	32	32	(322)	32
Production control	–	106	106	71	71	–	(354)	–	–
Engineering	–	147	207	–	–	(354)			
Cycle three									
Insignificant	–	8	8	8	8	–	–	–	(32)
Arbitrary Apportionment	£361,000	£116,634	£118,410	£63,613	£62,343	–	–	–	–

5.0 THE FINAL STEP—OVERHEAD RATES

These are now calculated as follows:

Productive department	*X*	*Y*	*Assembly*	*Packing*
Budgeted overhead (repeated distribution summary)	£116,634	£118,410	£63,613	£62,343
Budgeted level of activity (given)	200,000 machine hours	300,000 machine hours	200,000 direct labour hours	400,000 direct labour hours
Predetermined overhead rates	£0.5832 per machine hour	£0.3947 per machine hour	£0.3181 per direct labour hour	£0.1559 per direct labour hour

Illustration 4

Shown below is next year's budget for a small engineering factory manufacturing two different products in two production departments, namely a machine shop and an assembly department. A canteen is also operated as a separate department.

Product	A	B
Sales volume	4,500 units	3,000 units
Increase (decrease) in finished stocks	500 units	(500) units
Material cost per unit	£8	£5
Direct labour:	hours/unit	hours/unit
Machine shop (£3 per hour)	5	6
Assembly dept (£2 per hour)	4	4
Machining:		
Machine shop	3	8
Assembly dept	1	–

You are required to express the budgeted level of activity in terms of units, machine hours, direct labour hours, direct wages, direct materials and prime cost in order to determine appropriate overhead rates.

Suggested answer

STEP 1 PRODUCTION BUDGET (IN UNITS)

Product	*Sales budget*	*Stock increase (decrease)*	*Production budget*
A	4,500	500	5,000
B	3,000	(500)	2,500

STEP 2 DEPARTMENTS

		Machine		Assembly
(a) Units		7,500		7,500
(b) Machine hours:				
Product A: 5,000 × 3	=	15,000	5,000 × 1 =	5,000
B: 2,500 × 8	=	20,000	2,500 × 0 =	nil
		35,000		5,000
(c) Direct labour hours:				
A: 5,000 × 5	=	25,000	5,000 × 4 =	20,000
B: 2,500 × 6	=	15,000	2,500 × 4 =	10,000
		40,000		30,000
(d) Direct wages:				
40,000 × £3	=	£120,000	30,000 × £2 =	£60,000
(e) Direct materials:				
A: 5,000 × £8	=	£40,000	5,000 × £8 =	£40,000
B: 2,500 × £5	=	£12,500	2,500 × £5 =	£12,500
		£52,500		£52,500
(f) Prime cost:				
Labour		£120,000		£60,000
Materials		£52,500		£52,500
		£172,500		£112,500

Illustration 5—Predetermined departmental overhead absorption rates of companies (without service departments)

One of your clients, ACCA Engineers Ltd, has hitherto based quotations on cost of materials and labour plus a percentage to cover overheads and profit. The company has now accepted your advice to relate costs to departments (A, B and C) through which the work passes and, in pursuance of this policy, to charge overheads to jobs on the basis of departmental direct-labour hours.

The following data have been produced for the forthcoming year:

Expense	£	*Proposal basis of departmental apportionment*
Rent, rates and insurance	6,200	Floor area
Indirect labour	3,900	Direct labour hours
Depreciation	2,200	Plant valuation
Repairs and maintenance	1,200	Technical estimate, viz. A £540; B £378; C £282
Consumable stores	900	Direct labour hours
Canteen	2,000	Number of employees
Works manager's salary	2,600	Allocation, viz. A £700; B £1,100; C £800
National Insurance	400	Number of employees
General administration	6,000	Ratio of quotations, based on past experience, viz. A 5/12; B 4/12; C 3/12

Your client estimates that department A will work 6,000 direct labour hours in the year, department B 4,000 and department C 2,000. Wage rates are: department A £0.50; department B £0.45; department C £0.40. The number of employees in each department is: department A 40; department B 25; department C 15.

Departmental floor areas are: department A 15,000 square feet, department B 18,000, and department C 17,000. The value of the plant and machinery used in each department is: department A £20,000; department B £18,000; department C £6,000.

You are required to:

(a) Calculate the hourly overhead rates to be charged for work in each department; and

(b) to prepare a quotation for a job to which the following data relate:

Direct material	£274.84
Direct labour	
Department A	20 hours
B	12 hours
C	4 hours

Profit—20 per cent on selling price.

Suggested answer

(a) *Overhead distribution summary*

Expense	*Basis of apportionment*	*Total*	*Department* A	B	C
Rent, rates and insurance	Floor area	£6,200	£1,860	£2,232	£2,108
Depreciation	Plant values	2,200	1,000	900	300
Indirect labour	Direct labour hours	3,900	1,950	1,300	650
Consumable stores	Direct labour hours	900	450	300	150
Canteen	Number of employees	2,000	1,000	625	375
National Insurance	Number of employees	400	200	125	75
Repairs and maintenance	Technical estimates	1,200	540	378	282
Works manager's salary	Technical estimates	2,600	700	1,100	800
General administration	No. of quotations	6,000	2,500	2,000	1,500
		£25,400	£10,200	£8,960	£6,240
Direct labour hours			6,000	4,000	2,000
Overhead absorption rate per hour			£1.70	£2.24	£3.12

(b) *Quotation for job*

Direct materials			£274.84
Direct labour:	Dept A (20 × £0.50)	£10.00	
	Dept B (12 × £0.45)	5.40	
	Dept C (4 × £0.40)	1.60	17.00
Overhead:	Dept A (20 × £1.70)	34.00	
	Dept B (12 × £2.24)	26.88	
	Dept C (4 × £3.12)	12.48	73.36
Total cost			£365.20
Profit:	25 per cent of total cost		91.30
Selling price			£456.50

Example 1

A draft budget for ICMA Ltd, a company with four production centres, included the following data for the year:

Cost centre	*Directly allocated overhead*	*Apportioned overhead (%)*	*Direct labour hours*
A	£32,800	20	60,000
B	45,200	40	75,000
C	28,400	10	30,000
D	14,400	30	100,000

The total overhead to be apportioned amounted to £352,000.

As a result of technical developments it was decided to reorganise the production centres. A revised budget was therefore developed incorporating the following changes from the draft budget:

(a) A new cost centre, E, was established.

(b) £13,200 of overhead previously allocated directly to cost centre A is to be transferred to cost centre E.

(c) An additional £30,000 of overhead is to be allocated directly to cost centre E.

(d) An additional £60,000 of overhead will be incurred and should be apportioned:

Cost centre	A	B	C	D	E
Percentage	–	10	10	20	60

(e) Overhead will be absorbed on a machine hour rate for all cost centres except A. Revised budgeted hours are:

Cost centre	A	B	C	D	E
Machine hours	–	40,000	17,400	60,000	22,500
Direct labour hours	50,000	–	–	–	–

You are required to calculate:

(a) cost centre direct labour hour rates of overhead absorption based on the draft budget;

(b) cost centre direct labour hour rates and/or machine hour rates of overhead absorption (as relevant) based on the revised budget;

(c) the overhead chargeable to unit of product Z, (i) under the draft budget, (ii) under the revised budget.

The time taken in each cost centre for production of one unit of product was budgeted as follows:

Cost centre	*Draft budget direct labour hours*	*Revised budget direct labour hours*	*Machine hours*
A	5	5	–
B	10	–	3
C	5	–	2
D	7	–	3
E	–	–	5

Answer guide

DRAFT BUDGET

Expenses		*Cost centre*				
Basis	*Total*	*A*	*B*	*C*	*D*	*E*
Direct allocation	£120,800	£32,800	£45,200	£28,400	£14,400	–
Apportioned (basis given)	352,000	70,400	140,800	35,200	105,600	–
	£472,800	£103,200	£186,000	£63,600	£120,000	–

REVISED BUDGET

	Total	A	B	C	D	E
Original budget	£472,800	£103,200	£186,000	£63,600	£120,000	–
Change (b)	–	(13,200)	–	–	–	£13,200
Change (c) Direct allocation	30,000	–	–	–	–	30,000
Change (d)	60,000	–	6,000	6,000	12,000	36,000
	£562,800	£90,000	£192,000	£69,600	£132,000	£79,200

(a) *Cost centre direct labour rate of overhead absorption on the draft budget*

Cost centre

A $\frac{£103,200}{60,000} = £1.72$

B $\frac{£186,000}{75,000} = £2.48$

C $\frac{£63,600}{30,000} = £2.12$

D $\frac{£120,000}{100,000} = £1.20$

(b) *Cost centre direct labour hour rates and/or machine hour rates of overhead absorption (as relevant) based on the revised budget*

Cost centre

A $\frac{£90,000}{50,000} = £1.80$

B $\frac{£192,000}{40,000} = £4.80$

C $\frac{£69,600}{17,400} = £4.00$

D $\frac{£132,000}{60,000} = £2.20$

E $\frac{£79,200}{22,500} = £3.52$

(c) *Overhead chargeable to unit of product Z*

(i) *Under the draft budget*

Cost centre	*Direct labour hours*	*Overhead rate per hour*	*Amount*
A	5	£1.72	£8.60
B	10	2.48	24.80
C	5	2.12	10.60
D	7	1.20	8.40
			£52.40

(ii) *Under the revised budget*

Cost centre		*Direct labour/ machine hours*	*Overhead rate*	*Amount*
A	(Direct labour)	– 5	£1.80	£9.00
B	(Machine hours)	– 3	4.80	14.40
C	(Machine hours)	– 2	4.00	8.00
D	(Machine hours)	– 3	2.20	6.60
E	(Machine hours)	– 5	3.52	17.60
				£55.60

Example 2

Y Ltd uses an absorption costing system with a predetermined rate for the application of factory overhead to production. Factory overhead is on a machine-hour basis in department A and a direct labour-hour basis in department B. The following information is available:

ESTIMATES AT BEGINNING OF YEAR

	Department A	*Department B*
Direct labour cost	£64,000	£96,000
Factory overhead	72,000	75,000
Direct labour hours	2,000	10,000
Machine hours	500	2,500

ACTUAL OVERHEAD DATA

	Department A	*Department B*
Direct labour cost	£72,000	£84,000
Factory overhead	84,000	72,000
Direct labour hours	2,400	9,600
Machine hours	600	2,200

THE COST SHEET FOR JOB RD 674 SHOWS ACTUAL COSTS AND ACTIVITY AS FOLLOWS

	Department A	*Department B*
Direct material–	£36	£64
Direct labour	48	32
Direct labour hours	6	4
Machine hours	2	24

You are required:

(a) to calculate the predetermined factory overhead rate for each department;

(b) to calculate how much overhead should be allocated to job RD 674;

(c) to calculate the total cost of job RD 674;

(d) to determine the amount of under- or over-applied factory overhead by department, and indicate if it was over-applied or under-applied.

(e) to determine the historical factory overhead rate based upon single factory overhead rate using direct labour cost as basis of application. If this historical rate is used, how much factory overhead would be applied to job RD 674?

Answer guide

(a) *Overhead absorption rate*

	Department A	*Department B*
Estimated overhead	£72,000	£75,000
Estimated DL hours		10,000
Estimated machine hours	500	
Overhead rate of absorption	£144	£7.50

(b) *Overhead charged to job RD 674*

Department A	2 × £144	=	£288
Department B	4 × £7.50	=	30
			£318

(c) *Total cost of job RD 674*

	Department A	*Department B*	*Total*
Direct materials	£36	£64	£100
Direct labour	48	32	80
Prime cost	84	96	180
Manufacturing overhead	288	30	318
	£372	£126	£498

(d) *(Under-)/over-absorption*

		Department A		*Department B*
Incurred		£84,000		£72,000
Absorbed				
600 × £144	=	86,400		
9,600 × £7.50			=	72,000
Over-absorbed		£2,400		nil

(e) *Single rate—historical rate*

Factory overhead	£
Department A	84,000
Department B	72,000
Incurred	156,000

Direct labour cost	£
Department A	72,000
Department B	84,000
	156,000

Historical (actual) overhead absorption rate:

$$\frac{£156{,}000}{156{,}000} \times 100 = 100 \text{ per cent of direct wage.}$$

Job RD 674:

$$100 \text{ per cent of direct wages} = 100 \text{ per cent} \times £80 = \underline{\underline{£80}}.$$

6.0 OPERATION OF DEPARTMENTAL OVERHEAD RATES

At the end of a control period or year-end:

(a) Overhead incurred is recorded in the ledger.

(b) An overhead distribution summary of the actual overhead, i.e. primary and secondary distribution summaries, is prepared.

(c) As the period progresses, the work in progress control account is charged with overhead traced to products at predetermined departmental rates, and producing departments are credited—overhead absorbed.

(d) A comparison is made of actual overhead against overhead absorbed departmentally.

(e) Analysis.

Example 3

Z Ltd has two production departments, machining and finishing, and two service departments, maintenance and materials-handling.

The overhead budgets per 4-week period are £9,000 for the machining department and £7,500 for the finishing department. The machining department overhead is absorbed on a machine hour basis (300 per period) and finishing department overhead is absorbed on the basis of direct labour hours (3,000 per period).

In establishing the overhead budgets of the production departments, service department costs have been dealt with as follows:

Maintenance	60 per cent to machining department 30 per cent to finishing department and 10 per cent to materials handling.
Materials handling	30 per cent to machining department 50 per cent to finishing department 20 per cent to maintenance department.

During period VI, the machining department was in operation for 292 hours and the number of direct labour hours worked by finishing department personnel was 3,100. Overhead incurred during period VI was as follows:

	Machine	*Finishing*	*Maintenance*	*Materials handling*
Materials	£2,000	£3,000	£1,000	£200
Labour	3,000	900	2,000	3,000
Other allocated costs	600	400	800	300

You are required to:

(a) Prepare an overhead distribution summary.

(b) Determine the amount of over- or under-absorbed factory overhead by department and indicate if it was over-applied or under-applied.

(c) State the factors which gave rise to the under-/over-absorption, and

(d) Analyse the under-/over-absorption under the headings you have stated in your answer to (c).

Answer guide

(a) *Factory overhead distribution summary*

			Productive		*Service*	
Expenses	*Basis of ALL/APP*	*Total*	*Machining*	*Finishing*	*Maintenance*	*Handling*
Materials	DA	£6,200	£2,000	£3,000	£1,000	£200
Labour	DA	8,900	3,000	900	2,000	3,000
Other	DA	2,100	600	400	800	300
		17,200	5,600	4,300	3,800	3,500
		–	1,312	2,188	–	(3,500)
		–	2,533	1,267	(3,800)	
		£17,200	£9,445	£7,755		

Note: Secondary distribution (distributing service department costs). The service department costs are distributed directly to producing departments. There is a saving of time and effort in contrast to alternative methods. For example,

> *Handling £3,500 is distributed to the two producing departments in the ratio of 3:5 and maintenance £3,800 in the ratio of 6:3.*

(b) *Under-/over-absorption*

Department	*Actual*	*Absorbed*	*Difference*	
Machining	£9,445	£8,760	£685	Under-absorbed
Finishing	7,755	7,750	5	Under-absorbed

Note: Absorbed overhead

Machining $\quad 292 \text{ hours} \times \frac{£9{,}000}{300} = £8{,}760$

Finishing $\quad 3{,}100 \text{ hours} \times \frac{7{,}500}{3{,}000} = £7{,}750$

(c) *Factors*

(i) Due to expenditure.

(ii) Due to level of activity, or

(iii) due to both (i) and (ii).

(d) *Variance analysis by causes*

Department	*Actual*	*Budget*	*Recovered or absorbed*	*Variance*	*Variance analysis* Expenditure	*Volume*
	1	*2*	*3*	*4* (3–1)	*5* (2–1)	*6* (3–2)
Machining	9,445	$\frac{£9,000}{300}$ = £30	8,760	(685)	(445)	(240) 8 hours × £30
Finishing	7,755	$\frac{7,500}{3,000}$ = £2.50	7,750	(5)	(255)	£250 + 10 hours × £2.50

Example 4

A manufacturing company absorbs overhead into the cost of its three productive departments by means of estimated departmental rates. In view of a large difference between overhead incurred and overhead absorbed for the year, you are asked to investigate. You discover the following information for the year:

Dept	*Overhead incurred*	*Actual direct labour hours worked*	*Predetermined rate per DLH*	*Overhead absorbed*	*Direct labour hours contained in stock* WIP	*Finished goods*
1	£46,530	84,600	£0.35	£29,610	14,500	8,300
2	18,700	37,400	0.60	22,440	6,500	3,000
3	30,160	35,400	0.50	17,700	4,000	1,000

You are required to calculate:

(a) the extent to which the values of the

(i) year-end WIP and
(ii) year-end finished goods

should be increased or decreased for each department for the year;

(b) the amount of factory overhead transferred to the profit and loss account.

Answer guide

Dept	Overhead incurred	Overhead absorbed	Overhead absorbed: WIP	Overhead absorbed: Finished goods	Overhead absorbed: Profit and loss A/c: cost of goods sold	Over-/under-absorbed	Adjustment—Over-(under-): WIP	Adjustment—Over-(under-): Finished goods	Adjustment—Over-(under-): Profit/loss A/c
1	£46,530	£84,600 × £0.35 = £29,610	14,500 × £0.35 = £5,075	8,300 × £0.35 = £2,905	84,600 (14,500) (8,300) 61,800 × £0.35 = £21,630	£(16,920)	£2,900	£1,660	£12,360
				Under-stated					
2	18,700	37,400 × £0.60 = £22,440	6,500 × £0.60 = £3,900	3,000 × £0.60 = £1,800	27,900 × £0.60 = £16,740	3,740	(650)	(300)	(2,790)
				Over-stated					
3	30,160	35,400 × £0.50 = £17,700	4,000 × £0.50 = £2,000	1,000 × £0.50 = £500	30,400 × £0.50 = £15,200	(12,460)	1,408	352	10,700
				Under-stated				Refer to Note	

NOTE ADJUSTMENT—ON THE BASIS OF DIRECT LABOUR HOURS

Dept	Overhead (under-)/over-absorbed	WIP	Finished goods	Cost of sales
1	(16,920)	$\frac{£16,920}{84,600} \times 14,500$	$\frac{£16,920}{84,600} \times 8,300$	$\frac{£16,920}{84,600} \times 61,800$
	Increase	£2,900	£1,660	£12,360
2	£3,740	$\frac{£3,740}{37,400} \times 6,500$	$3,000 \times \frac{£3,740}{37,400}$	$27,900 \times \frac{£3,740}{37,400}$
	Reduce	(£650)	(£300)	(£2,790)
3	(£12,460)	$\frac{£12,460}{35,400} \times 4,000$	$\frac{£12,460}{35,400} \times 1,000$	$\frac{£12,460}{35,400} \times 30,400$
	Increase	£1,408	£352	£10,700

BALANCE SHEET

Dept		WIP	Finished goods
1	Balance b/f	£5,075	£2,905
	Adjustment	2,900	1,660
		7,975	4,565
2	Balance b/f	3,900	1,800
	Adjustment	(650)	(300)
		3,250	1,500
3	Balance b/f	2,000	500
	Adjustment	1,408	353
		£3,408	£852

PROFIT AND LOSS ACCOUNT—TO AVOID DISTORTION IN NET PROFIT

Department	1	2	3
Cost of goods sold b/f	£21,630	£16,740	£15,200
Under-absorbed—Dept 1 (add)	£12,360	–	
Over-absorbed—Dept 2 (deduct)	–	£(2,790)	
Under-absorbed—Dept 3 (add)			£10,700
Total	£33,990	£13,950	£25,900

CHAPTER EIGHT

Production Overhead IV – Single versus Departmental Rates

1.0 INTRODUCTION

A cost centre is defined as a location, a person or an item of equipment, or a group of these, in relation to which costs may be ascertained for purposes of cost control. In some firms each expensive machine is a cost centre; in some a group of these expensive machines may be a cost centre; or in some factories it may extend to departments (location, persons and items of equipment). At the other extreme, all production and service departments of the production functions may be treated as a cost centre. Between these extremes there are many choices.

Illustration 1

Assume a factory with two producing departments (assembly department and machine department) and four service departments. In the assembly department hand labour predominates.

The manufacturing indirect cost budgeted for the forthcoming year is as follows:

Producing and service departments: £180,000.
Predetermined level of activity: direct labour hours, 36,000.

The plant-wide or single rate of absorption rate

$$=\frac{£180,000}{36,000}=£5.$$

If a unit of product requires 400 hours of labour in the assembly department and

80 hours in the machine department then the overhead charged to the job would be

480 hours at £5 = £2,400.

2.0 SINGLE (PLANT-WIDE) OVERHEAD RATE OF ABSORPTION

2.1 Predetermined overhead rate

If a plant-wide rate is used then the *estimated* overhead for the entire plant is divided by a predetermined level of activity to determine the overhead rate of absorption.

2.2 Historical overhead rate

If a historical overhead absorption rate is used then the overhead *incurred* during the period is divided by the *actual* level of activity attained.

Note: The apportionment of service department costs to producing departments would not be necessary.

2.3 Conditions for use of plant-wide basis

(a) where only one product is made;

(b) where all producing departments contribute in *uniform* proportion to the fabrication of every product.

3.0 DEPARTMENTAL OVERHEAD ABSORPTION RATES

The use of departmental overhead absorption rates has advantages and disadvantages:

3.1 Advantages

(a) *Better control:* closer control is made possible because the departmental manager has clear responsibility for the costs incurred.

(b) *Better costing of products:* it makes possible the charging of overheads on a departmental basis rather than a plant-wide basis.

3.2 Disadvantages

(a) the managers of the producing departments often have very little influence over the apportionment process. They have no control over joint costs.

(b) The process of apportionment may be neither fair nor true; we search for cause and effect relationships, but they are not always apparent and clear.

(c) May not identify controllable and non-controllable costs.

Illustration 2

(Refer to Illustration 1.)

Predetermined overhead rate at the end of the secondary distribution, on the assumption that the company has two producing departments and four service departments, is:

			Producing depts		*Service depts*			
Expenses	*Basis*	*Total*	*Assembly*	*Machine*	*1*	*2*	*3*	*4*
					20	40	10	5
					(20)	(40)	(10)	(5)
		£180,000	£60,000	£120,000	nil	nil	nil	nil

Estimated direct labour hours: 24,000—assembly department
Estimated direct labour/machine hours: 12,000—machine department
Predetermined level of activity plant-wide: 36,000 hours.

DEPARTMENTAL OVERHEAD RATES

Assembly dept: $\frac{£60,000}{24,000} =$ £2.50 per direct labour hour.

Machine dept: $\frac{£120,000}{12,000} =$ £10.00 per machine hour.

If the product requires, as in Illustration 1, 400 hours in the assembly department and 80 hours in the machine department, then the overhead charged to the job would be:

Assembly	400 × £2.50 =	£1,000
Machine	80 × £10.00 =	800
		£1,800

4.0 COMPARISON OF PLANT-WIDE AND DEPARTMENTAL RATES

Refer to Illustrations 1 and 2.

The £1,800 charged to the job using a departmental rate is *more equitable* than the £2,400 charged using a plant-wide or single absorption rate. Eighty per cent of the direct labour required on this job was done in the assembly department, where the overhead rate was only £2.50 per hour, compared with a plant-wide rate of £5.00 per hour.

Illustration 3

R. B. Marcus Manufacturing Company has four producing departments: R, M, T and U. The manufacturing costs budgeted for year 19_7 are as follows:

	Total	*R*	*M*	*T*	*U*
Direct materials	£230,000	£40,000	£50,000	£60,000	£80,000
Direct labour	480,000	100,000	100,000	120,000	160,000
Overhead	160,000	30,000	50,000	40,000	40,000

Overhead is absorbed on the basis of direct labour cost and the company uses predetermined rates of absorption.

The actual material and labour cost of producing job number CEY 132 during period one was as follows:

Direct materials		£4,000
Direct labour:	dept R	£400
	dept M	£600
	dept T	£800
	dept U	£300

You are required to:

(a) Determine the total manufacturing overhead chargeable to job number CEY 132 on each of the following alternative assumptions:

(i) the company uses a single overhead rate of absorption;

(ii) the company uses departmental overhead rates of absorption.

(b) Determine the over- or under-absorption of overhead for the year for each alternative assumption, using the following actual costs for year 19_7:

	Total	*R*	*M*	*T*	*U*
Direct materials	£330,000	£50,000	£80,000	£80,000	£120,000
Direct labour	500,000	80,000	120,000	120,000	180,000
Production overhead	180,000	40,000	45,000	60,000	35,000

Suggested answer

(a) (i) *Single overhead absorption rate:*

$$\frac{£160,000}{£480,000} \times 100 \text{ per cent} = 33.33 \text{ per cent of direct wages.}$$

Job No. CEY 132

Total wages: £2,100 (£400 + £600 + £800 + £300)
Overhead chargeable to job CEY 132:
33.33 per cent × £2,100 = £700.

(ii) *Departmental overhead absorption rates as a percentage of direct wages:*

Department R: $\frac{£30,000}{£100,000} \times 100$ per cent = 30 per cent.

Department M: $\frac{£50,000}{£100,000} \times 100$ per cent = 50 per cent.

Department T: $\frac{£40,000}{£120,000} \times 100$ per cent = 33 per cent (approximately).

Department U: $\frac{£40,000}{£160,000} \times 100$ per cent = 25 per cent.

Overhead absorbed by job CEY 132:

Department R:	£400 × 30 per cent =	£120
Department M:	£600 × 50 per cent =	300
Department T:	£800 × 33 per cent =	264
Department U:	£300 × 25 per cent =	75
Total overhead chargeable		£759

(b) (i) *Single rate:*

Overhead incurred	£180,000
Overhead absorbed:	
33.33 per cent × £400,000	133,320
Under-absorbed	£46,680

(ii)

	Total	*R*	*M*	*T*	*U*
Actual overhead	£180,000	£40,000	£45,000	£60,000	£35,000
Overhead absorbed					
30% £80,000	24,000	24,000	–	–	–
50% £120,000	60,000	–	60,000	–	–
33% £120,000	39,600	–	–	39,600	–
25% £180,000	45,000	–	–	–	45,000
(Under-)/over-absorption	£(11,400)	£(16,000)	£15,000	£(20,400)	£10,000

5.0 EXAMPLE

Q Ltd, a company with three departments, uses a single production overhead absorption rate expressed as a percentage of direct wages cost. It has been suggested that departmental overhead absorption rates would result in more accurate job costs. Set out below are the budgeted and actual data for the previous period, together with information relating to job No. 657:

			Hours (000)		
		Direct wages	*Direct labour*	*Machine*	*Production overhead*
Budget:		(£000)			(£000)
Department:	A	25	10	40	120
	B	100	50	10	30
	C	25	25	–	75
Total		150	85	50	225
Actual:					
Department:	A	30	12	45	130
	B	80	45	14	28
	C	30	30	–	80
Total		140	87	59	238

Estimated costs and times of job No. 657 in the departments are as shown below:

		Direct material	*Direct wages*	*Direct labour hours*	*Machine hours*
Department:	A	£120	£100	20	40
	B	60	60	40	10
	C	10	10	10	–

After adding production overhead to prime cost, one-third is added to production cost for gross profit. This assumes that a reasonable profit is earned after deducting administration, selling and distribution costs.

You are required to:

(a) Calculate the predetermined overhead absorption rate.

(b) Using the rate obtained in (a), (i) calculate the production overhead charged to job No. 657 and (ii) state the production cost and expected gross profit on this job.

(c) Compute predetermined departmental absorption rates.

(d) Using the rates calculated in (c), show the overhead, by department and in total, that would apply to job No. 657.

(e) Show the over-/under-absorption, by department and in total, for the period using:

(i) the current rate in your answer to (a) above, and

(ii) your suggested rates in your answer to (c) above.

Answer guide

(a) Current overhead absorption rate

Single overhead absorption rate.

Percentage of direct wages cost $= \frac{£225,000}{£150,000} \times 100 = \underline{\underline{150 \text{ per cent.}}}$

(b) (i) Overhead charged to job No. 657

Direct wages incurred:

Department A	100
B	60
C	10
	170

150 per cent of £170 = £255.

(b) (ii) *Cost of production—job No. 657*

	Direct material	*Direct labour*	*Factory overhead*	*Total*
Dept A	£120	£100	–	£220
B	60	60	–	120
C	10	10	–	20
Prime cost	190	170		360
Overhead	–	–	255	255
Cost of production				615
Gross profit (⅓ production cost)				205
				£820

(c) *Predetermined departmental overhead absorption rates*

	A	*B*	*C*
Planned overhead	£120,000	£30,000	£75,000
Planned level of activity:			
Direct labour (hours)	10	50	25
Machine (hours)	40	10	nil
Ratio of direct labour hours to machine hours	1:4	5:1	1:0
Overhead rates:			
Dept A (machine hours)	£3.0	–	–
Dept B (direct labour hours)	–	£0.60	–
Dept C (direct labour hours)	–	–	£3.0

(d) *Job No. 657*

	A	*B*	*C*	*Total*
Cost:	(£000)	(£000)	(£000)	(£000)
Direct materials	120	60	10	190
Direct wages	100	60	10	170
Prime cost	220	120	20	360
Overhead:				
40 × £3.00	120	–	–	120
40 × £0.60	–	24	–	24
10 × £3.00	–	–	30	30
Cost of production	340	144	50	534

(e) (i) *Single overhead absorption rate:*

	(£000)	(£000)
Actual overhead:		
Dept A	130	
B	28	
C	80	238
Overhead absorbed:		
150 per cent of direct wages: 150 per cent × £140		210
Under-absorption		28

(e) (ii) *Using predetermined departmental rates:*

Dept	*Actual*	*Budget*	*Absorbed*	*(Under-) over-absorbed overhead*	*Expenditure*	*Volume*
	1	*2*	*3*	*4* (*3–1*)	*5* (*2–1*)	*6* (*3–2*)
A	£130,000	£120,000	£135,000	£5,000 +	£(10,000)	£15,000 +
B	28,000	30,000	27,000	(1,000)	2,000 +	(3,000)
C	80,000	75,000	90,000	10,000 +	(5,000)	15,000 +

CHAPTER NINE

Methods of Product Costing I – Job and Batch Costing

1.0 INTRODUCTION

A major purpose of cost accounting is product costing. This is the process of linking expenditure with cost units. A cost unit is defined as a unit of *product, service* or *time* (or combination of all three) in relation to which costs may be ascertained or expressed.

1.1 Methods of cost accumulation

There are two methods of cost accumulation:

(a) *Job costing:* the essential feature is that expenditure is linked to the job, contract or batch.

(b) *Unit costing:* the essential feature is that expenditure is charged to departments or processes and not directly to cost units. The cost of a unit of product is determined by dividing the total costs by the number of units produced.

2.0 JOB COSTING DEFINED

Job costing is the process of determining the cost of materials, labour and other expenses incurred to produce a specific order or contract.

3.0 TYPES OF JOB COSTING

These are as follows:

(a) *Job order costing*. Used for job work in factories. The job consists of a single unit of product.

(b) *Contract costing*. This is a form of job costing; the term is used in the construction industry. The job may extend over more than one Accounting Period.

(c) *Batch costing*. A special type of job costing. The job consists of a number of units of similar products covered by a single job number, for example a batch of a thousand books produced by a printer. A batch is a cost unit which consists of a group of identical items which maintains its identity throughout one or more stages of production.

4.0 ESSENTIAL FEATURES OF JOB COSTING

These may be described as follows:

(a) The method assumes the possibility of physically identifying each job.

(b) There is an accumulation of expenditure incurred to the job.

(c) Each job may represent different manufacturing specifications.

(d) Each job has its own characteristics that cause it to differ from any other.

(e) In order to identify the expenditure incurred on a job, a separate job card or cost sheet is established for it.

(f) Each job card or cost sheet is given a job number.

5.0 ACCUMULATION OF COSTS

5.1 The job cost sheet

The basic document is the job cost sheet. This is a form for recording and summarising the cost of materials, labour and factory overhead applicable to a specific job, batch or contract.

Each job cost sheet is numbered so that costs can be linked correctly.

(a) Material requisition note—records the job number.

(b) Labour time sheet—records the job number.

(c) Direct expenses—invoices, records the job number.

(d) Factory overhead—through an overhead rate.

The cost sheet becomes a summary of all costs incurred in completing a job, batch or contract.

5.2 Illustrations of use of job cost sheets

Illustration 1

The job cost sheet in Fig. 7 forms part of the question and candidates are required to explain the entries appearing therein.

Demonstrate your knowledge of cost accounting by commenting in detail on the information provided by the job card reproduced here (Fig. 7). Your comments should cover what the job card tells you about the system of costing in operation and what control action you would initiate on job No. 342.

JOB CARD

Customer: Green & Co. Ltd.	Job No. 342
Description: Transfer Machine	Promised delivery date: 3.11.19-2
Date commenced: 15.9.19-2	Actual delivery date: 13.11.19-2
Price quoted: £2,400	Despatch Note No. 7147

Date 19x2	Ref.	Material		Labour			Overhead		Other charges	
		Estimate £1.250		Estimate £100			Estimate £176		Estimate £25	
							DLH rate £1.1			
		Cost £	Cum. £	Dir. lab. hrs.	Cost £	Cum. £	Cost £	Cum. £	Cost £	Cum. £
	B/F		1,200	170		110		187		13
Nov. 6	MR1714	182	1,382							
7	Consultant's Test Fee								10	23
8	MR1937	19	1,401							
9	MRN213	(26)	1,375							
10	Labour Analysis			50	28	138	55	242		

SUMMARY | COMMENTS

	£
Material	1,375
Labour	138
Overhead	242
Other charges	23
	1,778
Invoice Price (Inv. No. 7147 dated 12.12.x2	2,400
Profit	622

Fig. 7. *Job cost sheet (job card) for a non-departmentalised company.*

Suggested answer

(a) The system in operation is a job order costing system.

(b) Jobs are performed on the basis of customer specifications.

(c) Each job can be identified and charged with its own costs.

Thus it has been possible to link the direct materials via direct material requisition notes, labour via wages analysis sheet, direct expense via invoices (e.g. Consultancy fees).

CONTROL ACTION

Note: The card provides cost estimates in terms of direct materials, direct labour, overhead and other charges, price quoted to the customer, and in addition promised delivery date and the actual delivery date.

From the data recorded on the job cost sheet, the following can be seen:

(a) *Cost of direct materials* is £125 more than the estimated figure of £1,250.

(b) *Direct labour hours:*

Estimate	160 hours	(£176 ÷ £1.10)
Actual	220 hours	
Variance	60 hours	

In other words, it has taken 60 direct labour hours more than expected, with the rate per hour remaining constant at £0.625 (£100 ÷ 160 hrs).

(c) *Overhead:* As a result of the increase in direct labour hours, the overhead charged to job number 342 was £66 more than the estimate (60 hours × £1.10).

(d) *Other charges:* the difference is not significant.

(e) Job No. 342:

Cost of production (actual)	£1,778
Estimated cost of production	1,551
Difference	£227

The difference is due to:

Direct material	£125
Direct labour	38
Overhead	66
	229
Other charges	(2)
	£227

Consequently, instead of the planned profit of £849 (£2,400 − £1,551) the actual profit was:

£849 − £227 = £622.

(f) *Delivery date:* promised on 3rd November 19_2, actual delivery 10 days after.

(g) *Invoice:* date of delivery 13th November 19_2, was not invoiced until 12th December 19_2—nearly a month after the date of despatch of goods.

CONCLUSION

In terms of material, labour and overheads, costs are in excess of estimate on job No. 342 prior to 6th November, indicating that management should have taken action.

A review of the invoicing procedure is also necessary. Each day's delay in calculation affects both the overall needs for liquid funds and profitability. A firm with a turnover of £5 million per year adds almost £13,700 from sources other than internal cash flow for every calendar day's delay in collection and thus incurs additional interest charges.

Illustration 2

Rod Sylon Ltd uses a job order costing system. At the beginning of January 19_5 the company has the following balances in the ledger:

Raw materials	Control account	£9,500
Other materials	Control account	£1,500
Work in progress	Control account	£19,032

The job cost sheets (e.g. Fig. 8) show the following detail:

	Job RA	*Job RB*	*Total*
Direct materials	£6,816	£3,240	£10,056
Direct labour	3,435	645	4,080
Factory overhead	4,122	774	4,896
	£14,373	£4,659	£19,032

TRANSACTIONS FOR THE MONTH OF JANUARY

(a) *Purchase of raw materials*	£22,000		
Raw materials control account		£22,000	
Trade creditors			£22,000

Note: Individual stock ledger cards record the details, i.e. quantity received, price per unit and amount.

(b) *Materials returned to suppliers*	£2,000		
Trade creditors		£2,000	
Raw materials control account			£2,000

Note: An entry for the returned materials is also made on the appropriate stock ledger cards.

(c) *Issues of materials to jobs* £22,000

The production schedule for January called for the completion of jobs RA and RB and for the start of jobs RC and RD (for job cost sheets refer to Fig. 8(a)–(d)).

The materials required for the order are issued by the storekeeper on receipt of requisitions bearing the job number, type, and quantity of materials required. The cost office then prices the requisitions and prepares a material issue analysis in job number order summarising issues during a period. For January the analysis showed the following direct materials issued to the jobs:

Job RA	£7,000
Job RB	£2,000
Job RC	£5,000
Job RD	£8,000
	£22,000

The following journal entry records the issue:

Work in progress control account	£22,000	
Raw materials control account		£22,000

Note: The issue column of the stores ledger record cards will record the issue of £22,000 worth of materials.

(d) *Issue of indirect materials to factory* £500

Factory overhead control account	£500	
Other materials control account		£500

Note: The above entry is made when indirect materials are issued from stock.

(e) *Returns to stores* (raw materials) £500 (job RD)

Document used: material returned note.

Raw material control account	£500	
Work in progress control account		£500

This also calls for entries on the stores ledger cards as well as on the job card for job RD.

(f) *Payment for time spent* £55,000

Wages control account	£55,000	
Wages payable		£55,000

JOB SHEET No: RA

Customer: Sunil & Sons (Sri Lanka) Price quoted: £56,000

Description: Date and invoice: 30.1. –5

Date commenced: 15.12. –4 Invoice number: H 1234

Promised date of delivery: 15.1. -5

Actual date of delivery: 25.1. –5

Date	Ref.	Materials		Labour			Overhead		Other charges		Total
		Estimate £15,000		Estimate £10,000			Estimate £14,000		Estimate Nil		Estimate £39,000
							DLH	Rate £1.50			
		Cost £	Cum. £	Dir. lab. hrs.	Cost £	Cum. £	Cost £	Cum. £	Cost £	Cum. £	Cost £
1.1.–5	B/F		6,816			3,435		4,122			14,373
	M R	7,000	13,816								
	T S			6,000	6,000	9,435					
							9,000	13,122			
	TOTAL	-	13,816	-	-	9,435	-	13,122	-	-	36,373

SUMMARY **COMMENTS**

	Estimate £	Actual £	Difference £
Materials	15,000	13,186	1,184+
Labour	10,000	9,435	565+
Overhead	14,000	13,122	878+
	39,000	36,373	2,627+
Selling price	56,000	56,000	-
Gross profit	17,000	19,627	2,627+

Fig. 8. *Example of job cost sheet: (a) Job No. RA.*

JOB COST SHEET — No. RB

Customer: Manel & Co. (Germany)
Description:
Date commenced: 2.12.-4
Promised date of delivery: 10.1.-5
Actual date of delivery: 15.1.-5

Price quoted: £30,000
Date and invoice: 20.1.-5
Invoice number: E3456

Date	Ref.	Materials		Labour			Overhead		Other charges		Total
		Estimate £6,000		Estimate £5,000			Estimate £7,000		Estimate		Estimate £18,000
							£1.50 per DLH				
		Cost £	Cum. £	Hrs. £	Cost £	Cum. £	Cost £	Cum. £	Cost £	Cum. £	Cost £
1.1.-5	B/F	-	3,240	-	-	645	-	774	-	-	4,659
	MR	2,000	5,240								
	TS			4,000	4,000	4,645					
							6,000	6,744	-	-	
		-	5,240	-	-	4,645	-	6,744	-	-	16,659

SUMMARY	Estimate £	Actual £	Difference £
Materials	6,000	5,240	760+
Labour	5,000	4,645	355+
Overhead	7,000	6,774	226+
	£18,000	£16,659	£1,341+
Selling Price	£30,000	£30,000	-
Gross Profit	£12,000	£13,341	£1,341+

COMMENTS

Fig. 8. *Example of job cost sheet: (b) Job No. RB.*

JOB COST SHEET No. RC

Customer: Theja & Co. (West Berlin)
Description:
Date commenced: 1.1.-5
Promised date of delivery: 5.3.-5
Actual date of delivery:

Price quoted: £175,000
Date and invoice:
Invoice number:

Date	Ref.	Materials		Labour			Overhead		Other charges		Total
		Estimate £20,000		Estimate £40,000			Estimate £60,000		Estimate £1,000		Estimate £121,000
							£1.50 per DLH				
		Cost £	Cum. £	Hrs. £	Cost £	Cum. £	Cost £	Cum. £	Cost £	Cum. £	Cost £
1.1.-5	B/F		Nil			Nil		Nil		Nil	Nil
	M R	5,000	5,000								
	T S			12,000	12,000	12,000					
							18,000	18,000			35,000

SUMMARY **COMMENTS**

	Estimate £	Actual £	Difference £
Materials			
Labour			
Overhead			
Selling Price			
Gross Profit			

Fig. 8. *Example of job cost sheet: (c) Job No. RC.*

JOB COST SHEET No. RD

Customer: Nimal Rodrigo (South America)
Description:
Date commenced: 5.1.-5
Promised date of delivery: 10.3.-5
Actual date of delivery:

Price quoted: £125,000
Date and invoice:
Invoice number:

Date	Ref.	Materials		Labour			Overhead		Other charges		Total
		Estimate £10,000		Estimate £25,000			Estimate £37,000		Estimate £2,500		Estimate £75,000
							£1.50 per DLH				
		Cost £	Cum. £	Hrs. £	Cost £	Cum. £	Cost £	Cum. £	Cost £	Cum. £	Cost £
5.1.-5	B/F	-	-	-	-	-	-	-	-	-	-
	M R	8,000	8,000								
	SRN	(500)	(500)								
	T S			14,000	14,000	14,000	21,000	21,000	-	-	42,500

SUMMARY

	Estimate £	Actual £	Difference £
Materials			
Labour			
Overhead			
Selling Price			
Gross Profit			

COMMENTS

Fig. 8. *Example of job cost sheet: (d) Job No. RD.*

(g), (h) *Wages analysis*

	£	*hours*
Direct employees:		
Job RA	6,000	6,000
RB	4,000	4,000
RC	12,000	12,000
RD	14,000	14,000
	36,000	
Treated as indirect	4,000	
	40,000	
Indirect employees	15,000	
	£55,000	

Work in progress control account	£36,000	
Factory overhead control account	£19,000	
Wages control account		£55,000

(j) *Factory overhead (indirect expenses)* £35,000

In addition to the £500 of indirect materials issued to the factory and the indirect labour of £19,000, the following additional indirect costs were also incurred:

Heat and light	£4,000
Company pension	2,000
Insurance—factory	2,000
Rent and rates	15,000
Depreciation—building	5,000
Depreciation—plant and machinery	5,000
Cleaning	2,000
	£35,000

Factory overhead control account	£35,000	
Sundry creditors		£25,000
Provision for depreciation: buildings		£5,000
plant and machinery		£5,000

(k) *Transfer of factory overhead to work in progress*
The predetermined overhead recovery rate for the company is £1.50 per direct labour hour.

Direct labour hours (per (f) above):

		Hours	Overhead absorbed at £1.50 per hour
Job	RA	5,000	£9,000
	RB	4,000	6,000
	RC	12,000	18,000
	RD	14,000	21,000
		36,000	£54,000

Work in progress control account	£54,000	
Factory overhead control account		£54,000

(l) *Under- or over-recovery of factory overhead*

Actual factory overhead was:

Indirect material	£500
Indirect labour	19,000
Factory overhead	35,000
	£54,500

There is accordingly an under-recovery of £500.

Under-absorbed factory overhead	£500	
Factory overhead control account		£500

(m) *Procedure for completed jobs*

The factory production report shows that job RA and job RB were completed during the period and job RC and job RD were still in progress.

As the jobs are completed, job cost sheets are transferred from the work in progress file to the finished goods file.

	RA	RB	Total	RC	RD	Total
Cost of completed jobs	£36,373	£16,659	£53,032			
Cost of uncompleted jobs	–	–		35,000	42,500	77,500

Finished goods control account	£53,032	
Work in progress control account		£53,032

Note: The cost of work not yet completed (jobs RC and RD) will be carried forward in the work in progress control account (£77,500).

(n), (p) *Sale of finished products*

Cost of sales	£53,032.
Sale value	£86,000.

Rod Sylon Company sold the product of job RA for £56,000 and that of job RB for £30,000 during January.

On delivery, the following entry is made (n):

Cost of goods sold account	£53,032	
Finished goods control account		£53,032

On despatch of the invoice to the customer, the following entry is made (p):

Debtors	£86,000	
Sales account		£86,000

(r) *Additional costs*

In order to prepare the monthly income statement it is assumed that the company incurred the following additional costs during the period:

General administration	£10,000		
Selling and distribution	£5,000		
Administration cost account		£10,000	
Selling and distribution cost account		£5,000	
Cash			£15,000

The monthly income statement
Rod Sylon Company
The income statement
for the month of January 19_2

	Job RA	*Job RB*	*Total*
Sales	£56,000	£30,000	£86,000
Less: Cost of sales	36,373	16,659	(53,032)
Trading profit	19,627	13,341	32,968
Less: Under-absorption	–	–	(500)
Gross profit			32,468
Less: Selling and distribution expenses	–	–	(5,000)
Administration expenses	–	–	(10,000)
Net profit for the month	–	–	£17,468

SCHEDULE 1—LEDGER ACCOUNTS

Raw Material Control a/c

Balance	£950		
(a)	22,000	(b)	£2,000
(e)	500	(c)	22,000

Other Materials Control a/c

Balance	£1,500	(d)	£500

Wages Control a/c

(f)	£55,000	(g)	£36,000
		(h)	19,000

Wages Payable a/c

		(f)	£55,000

Work in Progress Control a/c

Balance	£19,032	(e)	£500
(c)	22,000		
(g)	36,000	(m)	53,032
(k)	54,000		

Factory Overhead Control a/c

(d)	£500	(k)	£54,000
(h)	19,000	(l)	500
(j)	35,000		

Over-/Under-Absorbed Overhead a/c

(l)	£500		

Provision for Depreciation

		(j)	£10,000

Trade Creditors

(b)	£2,000	(a)	£22,000

Trade Debtors

(p)	£86,000		

Cost of Goods Sold

(n)	£53,032		

Finished Goods Control a/c

(m)	£53,032	(n)	£53,032

Sales a/c

		(p)	£86,000

Admin. Selling and Distribution Control a/c

(r)	£15,000		

Sundry Creditors

		(j)	£25,000

Cash

		(r)	£15,000

6.0 WORK IN PROGRESS CONTROL ACCOUNTS

Work in progress accounts represent the cost of raw materials, labour and factory overhead applied to jobs which are in the process of manufacture at the end of the accounting period.

Many variations of work in progress accounts are to be found in practice. For example, it is possible to maintain a single work in progress account, covering costs of direct materials, direct labour and factory overhead, or to maintain three separate work in progress accounts to show clearly each cost element:

Work in progress—materials;
Work in progress—labour;
Work in progress—factory overhead.

6.1 Illustration of separate work in progress accounts

Illustration 3

The PR Manufacturing Company had the following balances in the ledger on 1st May 19_5:

Raw materials control a/c	£500
Finished goods control a/c	£2,000
Work in progress—materials	£150
labour	£200
overhead	£100

Work in progress account details from cost sheets are:

	Job R200	*Job R300*	*Job R400*	*Total*
Direct materials	£50	£60	£40	£150
Direct labour	50	100	50	200
Factory overhead	25	50	25	100

Finished goods control account details from job cost sheets are:

	Job R110 £	*Job R220* £	*Job R330* £	*Total* £
Direct materials	100	400	150	650
Direct labour	200	600	100	900
Factory overhead	100	300	50	450
	£400	£1,300	£300	£2,000

The following relate to the month of May 19_5:

Materials purchased, £1,000; direct wages paid, £1,000; factory overhead including depreciation of plant, machinery and buildings, £615.

Raw material issue analysis indicates:

Job R200	£20
Job R300	£30
Job R400	£40
Job R500	£150
Job R600	£150
	£390

The wages analysis shows:

Job R200	£50
Job R300	£100
Job R400	£150
Job R500	£400
Job R600	£300
	£1,000

The company absorbs factory overhead at the rate of 50 per cent of direct wages.

Jobs R200, R300 and R400 were completed and transferred to finished goods store.

Required:

(a) Provide the work in progress account for:

(i) direct materials;
(ii) direct labour;
(iii) factory overhead.

(b) Provide the job cost sheets.

Suggested answer

Work in Progress—Materials

Balance b/f	£150	Finished goods	£240
Stores control	390	WIP c/f	300
	£540		£540
WIP b/f	£300	*Note: Finished goods:*	
		Job 200	£70
		Job 300	90
		Job 400	80
			£240
		WIP c/f	
		Job 500	£150
		Job 600	150
			£300

Work in Progress—Labour

Balance b/f	£200	Finished goods	£500
Wages control	1,000	WIP c/f	700
	£1,200		£1,200
WIP b/f	£700		

Work in Progress—Overhead

Balance b/f	£100	Finished goods	£250
Other creditors and provision for department	615	Under-absorption	115
		WIP c/f	350
	£715		£715
WIP b/f	£350		

JOB COST SHEETS

Job No.	*Ref.*	*Materials*	*Labour*	*Overhead*	*TOTAL*
R200	b/f	£50	£50	£25	£75
	This period	20	50	25	95
		£70	£100	£50	£170
R300	b/f	£60	£100	£50	£210
	This period	30	100	50	180
		£90	£200	£100	£390
R400	b/f	£40	£50	£25	£115
	This period	40	150	75	265
		£80	£200	£100	£380
R500	b/f	–	–	–	–
	This period	£150	£400	£200	£750
R600	b/f	–	–	–	–
	This period	£150	£300	£150	£600

7.0 SERVICE ORGANISATIONS

Some service organisations use job order costing systems. Examples are garages for servicing and repairing motor vehicles, or hospitals, which often maintain a job cost record for each patient.

Methods of allocating costs are exactly as for manufacturing concerns.

8.0 COSTING FOR RESEARCH AND DEVELOPMENT

8.1 Research cost

The cost of searching for new or improved products, new applications of raw materials, or new improved methods.

8.2 Development cost

The cost of the process which begins with the implementation of the decision to produce a new or improved product or to employ a new or improved method and ends with the commencement of formal production of that product or by that method.

Research and development costs therefore are costs associated with efforts to find new or improved products or processes.

8.3 Accumulation of costs—project cost card (Fig. 9)

The unit of costing is generally the individual research and development project. The project cost card includes estimates taken from a project request form and provides for the accumulation of the actual costs of the project.

Each project is a *job*, to which is assigned its direct costs and an apportionment of the indirect costs of the research and development functions.

Since each project is a job the direct cost of the project is allocated directly to the job and the other costs of the research and development department (indirect in relation to the projects) are charged to the individual projects by calculating a research and development overhead rate, using a procedure similar to the absorption of manufacturing overhead.

9.0 BATCH COSTING

A batch is a cost unit which consists of a group of identical items which maintains its identity throughout one or more stages of production.

9.1 Essential features

(a) In job costing each job keeps its identity and is treated separately. Expenditure incurred is entered on individual job cost sheets.

In batch costing (a variation of job costing) each batch of products is

Project Number:			
Description:			
ESTIMATED COST:	*Hours*	*Rate*	*Amount*
Laboratory technicians;			
Work study engineers			
Other personnel			
Equipment – depreciation			
Materials			
Outside services			
Other			
ACTUAL COSTS:	*Hours*	*Rate*	*Amount*
Laboratory technicians			
Work study engineers			
Other personnel			
Equipment depreciation			
Materials			
Outside services			
Other			

Fig. 9.· *Research project cost card.*

treated as a job and the expenditure incurred is identified with the batch and not with individual units of products.

(b) Batch costing is concerned mainly with making a quantity of products of identical specifications which, after being placed in stores, are sold later.

(c) In order to identify the expenditure incurred on a batch, a separate batch cost card is established for each batch.

(d) Each batch cost card is given a batch number.

9.2 Accumulation of costs

The basic document is the batch cost card.

This is a form of recording and summarising the costs of materials and labour, and indirect factory expenses applicable to a specific batch.

Each batch cost card is numbered so that costs can be identified with the batch:

(a) Material requisition notes — record the batch number
(b) Labour time sheets — record the batch number

(c)	Direct expenses	record the batch number
(d)	Factory overhead	through an overhead rate

The cost sheet becomes a summary of all costs incurred in finishing a batch.

Notes

(a) One major cost in producing a batch of articles is the cost of initially setting up the necessary jigs and tools. This will be spread over the number of units of products made in that batch.
(b) Cost per unit: The total cost of the completed batch is divided by the total number of units in the batch. The cost per unit is an average cost. This method therefore combines job costing and unit costing or average costing.

9.3 The relationship between (a) batch size, (b) setting up cost, and (c) unit cost

This is displayed in the comparative batch cost sheet, as follows:

COMPARATIVE BATCH COST SHEET

(a) Batch size (units)		500	5,000	10,000
(b) Setting up cost:	100 hours at £5	£500	£500	£500
Overhead:	100 hours at £12	£1,200	£1,200	£1,200
Subsequent cost of production				
Materials:	500 × £3.00	£1,500		
	5,000 × £2.50		£12,500	
	10,000 × £2.00			£20,000
Labour:	500 hours at £4	£2,000		
	5,000 hours at £4		£20,000	
	10,000 hours at £4			£40,000
Overhead:	500 hours at £12	£6,000		
	5,000 hours at £12		£60,000	
	10,000 hours at £12			£120,000
Total cost of production		£11,200	£94,200	£181,700
(c) Cost per unit		£22.40	£18.40	£18.17

Note: Cost per unit has dropped significantly from £22.40 to £18.17 per unit. But consideration must be given also to the speed with which the products can be sold or used, because undue delay in disposal results in valuable storage space being occupied and ties up capital.

10. EXAMPLE

K Limited designs and manufactures Deluxe containers for various industries. The company has been requested to submit quotations for supplying a specially designed container to which the following data relate:

ESTIMATED DESIGN AND DEVELOPMENT COSTS

Engineer's time, 50 hours at £6 per hour.
Draughtsman's time, 30 hours at £3 per hour.
Materials, £30.
Engineering machine shop time, 20 hours at £5 per hour.
Project supervision, £200.
General overhead allocation, £350.

MANUFACTURING COSTS INCLUDING SETTING UP COSTS

The production machine to be used requires 20 hours of an engineer's time at £3 for setting up and has an output of 50 containers per hour; it will be used exclusively on the production of this type of container for eight hours per day, five days per week, until the order is completed.

Operatives are paid an hourly rate of £1.50 and production overhead is absorbed at £2.50 per direct labour hour worked. The direct material cost per container is £1.25.

It is the company's practice to provide for a profit of 10 per cent on design and development costs, and 30 per cent on production costs.

REQUIRED:

Calculate the price to be quoted per 100 containers for the supply of:

(a) 5,000 containers,

(b) 20,000 containers,

(c) 50,000 containers.

Suggested solution

QUOTATION CALCULATIONS

		5,000	20,000	50,000
Batch size (units)		5,000	20,000	50,000
Production (hours)		100	400	1,000
Design and development costs				
Engineers 50 × £6		£300	£300	£300
Draughtsman 30 × £3		90	90	90
Materials		30	30	30
Engineering machine shop (20 × £5)		100	100	100
Project supervision		200	200	200
General overhead allocation		350	350	350
		£1,070	£1,070	£1,070
Setting-up costs				
Engineer's time: 20 × £3		60	60	60
Manufacturing costs				
Direct materials at £1.25 per container		6,250	25,000	62,500
Direct labour	100 × £1.50	150		
	400 × £1.50		600	
	1,000 × £1.50			1,500
Manufacturing overhead	100 × £2.50	250		
	400 × £2.50		1,000	
	1,000 × £2.50			2,500
Total cost		£7,780	£27,730	£67,630
Average cost per unit		£1.5560	£1.3865	£1.3526

CHAPTER TEN

Methods of Product Costing II – Contract

1.0 INTRODUCTION

Contract costing may be regarded as costing in relation to jobs which are large in value and extend over more than one accounting period. A significant part of the work will normally be carried out on the customer's site. The contract becomes the cost unit as well as the cost centre and it is relatively easy to trace costs and ascertain the total cost incurred. The basic document detailing the accumulation of cost is the Contract Cost Sheet.

2.0 MAIN FEATURES

2.1 Direct expenses

A high proportion of *direct expenses*, in addition to direct materials and direct labour, will normally be incurred, e.g.:

(a) hire of machinery;

(b) specialist subcontractors' charges, e.g. heating engineers, interior decorators;

(c) site office expenses;

(d) local purchases.

The main cost will consist of:

(a) Direct materials

(i) Most of the materials will be delivered direct to the site—the contract will be charged from the suppliers' invoices.

(ii) *Materials from the main store:* a material requisition will be made; these may be charged-out in the normal way.

(iii) *Materials on site* (materials delivered but not used): these must be valued at cost and carried forward for the next period.

(iv) *Material returned to the stores:* cost of materials returned should be credited to the contract.

(b) Direct labour

Nearly all labour will be direct labour. Often wages are paid in arrears to give staff time to prepare the payroll and to make up the pay packets. At the end of the period it is therefore necessary to accrue for all wages due but not paid.

(c) Plant and machinery used

Building contractors usually only have one store, a plant store, which may be a separate legal entity. From here such items as shovels, wheelbarrows, picks, scaffolding, saws, protective clothing, lights, buckets, transport hire and plant and machinery are charged out to the contracts on the basis of plant requisitions.

Each contract will be charged for these by one or more of the following methods:

(i) a hire charge for each article according to the time on site, e.g. transport;

(ii) at cost and considered as unreturnable as most small plant is stolen or easily worn out, e.g. consumable tools;

(iii) at cost or the written-down value and credited at the written-down value at the time the article is returned to store. Thus the contract bears the depreciation during the period it uses it (usually larger plant).

(d) Works overhead

This consists of expenses such as the site telephones, electricity, repairs, water, etc. *Note: These are normally allocated to the contract—no need for overhead absorption methods.*

(e) Other overhead

Costs relating to the business as a whole will have to be apportioned on a suitable basis among contracts.

(f) Contract price

This is usually agreed in advance of the works. Tenders will have been invited and the lowest (if reliable) quotation accepted.

Rarely, except in local government and central government work, will the price be on a cost-plus basis.

2.2 Architect's certificate

Periodically (usually monthly or quarterly) the builder's surveyor in charge of the contract prepares a formal copy of the costs incurred to date and submits it to the architect.

The architect or engineer acting for the client *inspects* the work done and certifies that this amount of work has been satisfactorily completed (this is the value of the work completed).

The contractor submits the invoice, claiming these amounts as progress payments, and encloses the certificate or certificates as evidence of work done.

2.3 Retention

The amount to be paid will normally be the amount certified by the architect (value of work), less a percentage withheld by the client (*retention*) which will be paid on final completion of the contract and acceptance by the client.

The purpose of the retention is to safeguard against the risk of loss or faulty workmanship. It is not immediately due and should not be treated as a current asset until the release date for the retention money is imminent.

If the main contractor sub-contracts work, he may himself withhold money when paying sub-contractors.

3.0 PROFIT ON INCOMPLETE CONTRACTS

(Refer to SSAP 9.) When a contract extends over a number of years, it may be necessary to take profit each year in order to avoid wide fluctuations in reported profits and to comply with the matching principle.

3.1 Rules

The following rules apply:

(a) Take no profit in the very early stages.

(b) In the contract's maturity the amount of profit to be taken (refer to Illustration 1 below) is:

$$\tfrac{2}{3} \times \text{Notional profit} \times \frac{\text{Cash received}}{\text{Value of work certified}}$$

Note: With work certified, it is possible that additional work may arise in the future. This is usually achieved by withholding one-third of notional profit.

(c) When the contract has reached an advanced state, use is made of one of the following formulas for the amount of profit to be taken:

(i) $\text{Estimated total profit} \times \dfrac{\text{Value of work certified}}{\text{Contract price}}$;

(ii) $\text{Estimated total profit} \times \dfrac{\text{Cost of work to date}}{\text{Estimated total cost}}$.

See Illustration 2 below. (Estimated total cost = actual expenditure to date plus estimated future costs plus contingencies.)

(d) Individual firms may have their own particular basis of calculations.

3.2 Illustrations of profit-taking on incomplete contracts

Illustration 1: calculation of profit—mature stage

Contract price	£600,000
Cost of work to date	200,000
Cost of work not yet certified	50,000
Cost of work certified	150,000
Value of work certified by the architect	250,000
Notional profit	£100,000
Cash received	
Value of work certified	£250,000
Less: 10 per cent retention	25,000
Cash received	£225,000

Profit to be taken:

$$\tfrac{2}{3} \times \text{Notional profit} \times \frac{\text{Cash received}}{\text{Value of work certified}}$$

$$= \tfrac{2}{3} \times £100{,}000 \times \frac{£225{,}000}{£250{,}000} = £60{,}000.$$

Illustration 2: calculation of profit—advanced stage

Contract price:	£600,000
Cost of work to date	350,000
Cost of work not yet certified	25,000
Cost of work certified	325,000
Value of work certified by the architect	525,000
Notional profit	
Value of work certified	£525,000
Cost of work certified	325,000
Notional profit	£200,000

Profit to be taken:

$$\text{Notional profit} \times \frac{\text{Value of work certified}}{\text{Contract price}}$$

$$= £200{,}000 \times \frac{£525{,}000}{£600{,}000} = £175{,}000.$$

The amount to be shown in a year's profit and loss account will be the appropriate portion of the attributable profit/loss by reference to work done to date, less any profit already taken up in prior years.

4.0 BALANCE SHEET

A contract which is not yet completed will be shown under current assets as work in progress.

The amount included should be:

Cost of work to date (whether certified or not)	£
+ Profit taken to date (SSAP 9)	£
or	
Deduct any loss shown	£( )
− Cash received to date	£( )
= Work in progress valuation	£

The cost of materials unused, value of plant on site should be shown as assets.

5.0 LONG-TERM CONTRACTS—WORK IN PROGRESS AND SSAP 9

(a) If the outcome of a contract cannot be reasonably assessed before the conclusion then it is cautious or prudent not to take up any profit on the work certified to date.

(b) If it is anticipated that there will be a loss on a contract *as a whole* then provision should be made *for the whole of the loss* as it is recognised.

(c) With regard to the calculation of the profit, the following should be noted:

(i) Where the outcome can be assessed with reasonable *certainty* then profit should be taken, i.e. the whole contract must be considered. A contractor may complete phase one of the contract successfully and the profit he has made on this point should not be taken unless he is certain the rest of the contract can be successfully completed without making any loss.

(ii) Rectification work must be anticipated and provision made for calculating attributable profit.

(iii) Cost increases such as likely increases in raw material prices, wage rates, salaries and other overhead costs, must be taken into account, so far as these are not covered by the terms of the contract.

(d) Calculation of the attributable profit is performed by subtracting from the sales value of the contract:

(i) total cost to date;

(ii) total estimated further cost to complete;

(iii) future costs of rectification and guaranteed work.

In addition, in estimating future costs, the likely increases in wages and salaries, raw material prices and other overhead costs must be considered in so far as these are not recoverable.

(e) The amount to be reflected in the current year's profit and loss account will be the appropriate portion of the above (d) total profit on the work done to date, less any profit already taken up in prior years.

(f) The method used for taking up profit needs to be consistently applied.

6.0 CONTRACT COSTING SUMMARY

STEP 1 EXPENDITURE INCURRED

Debit the contract with the expenditure incurred to date: classify the expenditure into:

(a) materials

(b) labour

(c) other.

STEP 2 ASSETS NOT FULLY USED

Credit the contract with assets, e.g. materials, plant etc., which have not been fully utilised and carry forward these balances. *The assets carried forward will, of course, appear in the balance sheet.*

STEP 3 ACCRUALS AND PREPAYMENTS

At the end of a period there are invariably some payments due, which will not be paid until the next period. To give a complete picture of the expenditure incurred to date, the accruals must be debited to the contract and the amount carried forward as a credit balance in the contract account.

Payments made in advance should be credited to the contract account and carried forward as a debit balance in the contract account.

These balances—accruals and prepayments—should also be reflected in the balance sheet.

STEP 4 CALCULATION OF THE COST OF WORK TO DATE

(a) Expenditure incurred to date (step 1)

(b) *add* accruals (step 3)

(c) *less* repayments (step 3)

(d) *less* assets not fully used (step 2), e.g. stock of raw materials, plant at net tra value.

STEP 5 COST OF WORK CERTIFIED

(a) Cost of work to date (step 4)

(b) *less* cost of work not yet certified.

STEP 6 CASH RECEIVED

(a) Value of work certified to date

(b) *less* retention.

STEP 7 CALCULATION OF NOTIONAL PROFIT/LOSS

(a) Value of work certified

(b) *less* cost of work certified (step 2)

= notional profit/loss.

STEP 8 PROFIT/LOSS TO BE TAKEN TO THE PROFIT AND LOSS ACCOUNT

(a) *Early stage of the contract:*

$$\tfrac{2}{3}\text{ Notional profit} \times \frac{\text{Cash received}}{\text{Value of work certified}}$$

(b) *Contract at an advanced stage:*

$$\text{Notional profit} \times \frac{\text{Value of work certified}}{\text{Contract price}}$$

(c) *Loss:* the total loss expected on completion should be written off as a period cost (if the value of work certified is less than the cost of work certified).

STEP 9 JOURNAL ENTRIES

(a) *Cash received*

Cash	debited
Contractee	credited

(b) *Profit taken to the profit and loss account*

Contract account	debited
Profit and loss account	credited

(c) *Loss taken to the profit and loss account*

Profit and loss account	debited
Contract account	credited

STEP 10 BALANCE SHEET

Work in Progress/Contract Account—No.		£
Cost of work to date	(step 1)	
Add: Profit	(step 8)	
Deduct: Loss	(step 8)	
Less: Cash received	(step 6)	

The cost of materials unused and value of plant on site should be shown as assets.

Illustration 3

H Ltd are public works contractors and have been successful in securing a contract for building a large swimming pool and sports arena at a price of £275,000. Work commenced on 1st July 19_7 and the contract is due to be completed in 18 months from that date.

By December 19_7, most of the preliminary excavation and piling have been completed, and the expenditure relating to the contract was as follows:

Value of plant sent to the site		£125,000
Stores sent from depot		320
Materials purchased:	cement	4,600
	reinforcing rods	9,200
	sand and ballast	2,720
	fuel oil for bulldozers	2,970
Wages paid		13,660
Wages accrued		520
National Insurance		1,800
Insurance		400
Miscellaneous expenses and overhead		30,200

The last certificate for work done was dated 15th December 19_7, and the total amount certified under the contract to that date was £80,000. The cost of work from that date to the end of the year was estimated at £7,000. Payment on the certificate is subject to 15 per cent retention, and all money due has been received.

At 31st December 19_7, the valuation put upon the plant was £106,000 and materials on site amounted to £1,750.

You are required to show:

(a) the contract account;

(b) the contractee's account,

and to show as part of your answer the amount of profit you consider might be fairly taken on the contract, and how you have calculated it.

Suggested answer

(a) *Contract account*

H LTD: Contract No. ……

	£		£
Materials			
Stores	320	Materials c/f	1,750
Cement	4,600	Work in progress c/f	
Reinforcing rods	9,200	(*see* Note 2)	85,544
Sand and ballast	2,720	Plant less depreciation	
Fuel oil	2,970	(*see* Note 3)	106,000
Wages: Paid	13,660		
Accrued c/f	520		
National Insurance	1,800		
Insurance	400		
Miscellaneous expenses	30,200		
Plant at cost	125,000		
	191,390		
Profit and loss account (*see* Note 1)	1,904		
	£193,294		£193,294
Materials b/f	1,750	Wages b/f	520
Plant b/f	106,000		
WIP b/f	85,544		

(b) *Contractee's account*

31.12._7	Cash in respect of Certificates 1–5	£80,000	
	Less: Retention	£(12,000)	£68,000

NOTE 1

CALCULATION OF PROFIT

	£	£
(a) *Cost of work to date*		191,390
Less: Materials	1,750	
Plant	106,000	(107,750)
		£83,640

	£
(b) *Cost of work certified*	
Cost of work to date	83,640
Less: Cost of work not yet certified	(7,000)
	£76,640

CASH RECEIVED

	£
(c) Value of work certified	80,000
Retention 15 per cent	12,000
	£68,000

NOTIONAL PROFIT

	£
Value of work certified	80,000
Cost of work certified	76,640
	£3,360

PROFIT AND LOSS ACCOUNT

$$\tfrac{2}{3} \times £3{,}360 \times \frac{£68{,}000}{£80{,}000} = £1{,}904$$

NOTE 2

WORK IN PROGRESS

	£
Cost of work to date	83,640
Profit	1,904
	£85,544

NOTE 3

	£
Plant sent to site	125,000
Valuation as at 31.12._7	(106,000)
	£19,000

NOTE

	£
Work in progress (as above (a))	85,544
Less: Contractor's account (cash received)	(68,000)
	£17,544

7.0 EXAMPLE

Contract No. Sandra 731

	£000
Contract price £12,000,000	
Valuation of work certified by architects	11,000
Cash received	9,900
WIP at 1st June Y1	6,700
Costs incurred during the year:	
Materials	1,050
Labour	975
Other expenses	775
Plant and equipment:	
Net book value 1st June Y1	700
Net book value 31st May Y2	175
Purchases during the year	125
Cost of work not yet certified	800

Agreed retention rate is 10 per cent of the value of work certified by the architects. The contract is nearing completion and the on-site manager estimates that costs of £400,000, additional to those tabulated above, will be required in order to complete the contract. He also considers that plant and equipment on site will be worthless by the time the contract is completed. The opening work in progress shown above includes an estimated profit of £1,150,000. The directors of the company propose to incorporate into the company's profit and loss account for the year ended 31st May Y2 the following amount of profit—£2,400,000.

You are required, making whatever calculation you consider necessary, to explain whether you agree with the directors' proposed profit.

Suggested answer

The proposal to include £2,400,000 profit in this year's profit and loss account is incorrect:

(a) The amount to be shown in year ended 30th May Y2 profit and loss account should be the total profit to date by reference to the work done to date, less any profits already taken. A profit of £1,150,000 has already been taken in previous years' accounts.

(b) *Calculation of attributable profit*

			£000
Work in progress at the beginning less profit £6,700 − 1,150		=	5,550
Add: Cost incurred during the year £1,050 + 975 + 775		=	2,800
	£000		
Plant and equipment	700		
Plant and equipment New	125		
	825		
Less: Net book value	175		650
Total cost of work to date			9,000
Cost of work not yet certified			(800)
Cost of work certified			£8,200

NOTIONAL PROFIT

	£000
Value of work certified	11,000
Cost of work certified	8,200
	£2,800

PROFIT TO BE INCLUDED THIS YEAR

		£000
$£2{,}800 \times \dfrac{\text{Value of work certified}}{\text{Contract price}} = £2{,}800 \times \dfrac{£11{,}000}{£12{,}000}$	=	2,567
Less: Profit taken to date		1,150
Profit and loss account Y2		£1,417

OR

	£000	£000
Contract price		12,000
Cost to date	9,000	
Estimated completion costs	600	9,600
Total estimated profit		£2,400

		£000
$£2{,}400 \times \dfrac{£11{,}000}{£12{,}000}$	=	2,200
Less: Profit taken to date		1,150
		£1,050

Note: The method used for calculating such profits needs to be applied consistently.

CHAPTER ELEVEN

Methods of Product Costing III – Process

1.0 INTRODUCTION

In mass production industries output consists of uniform products. The products being homogeneous it is assumed that the same mix of materials, labour and overhead is chargeable to each unit of product produced. The expenditure incurred in the manufacturing process is charged to departments or processes through which products flow. It may not be possible, practicable or economical to identify cost incurred with units of products. The cost of a fully completed unit is, therefore, an average cost.

2.0 PROCESS COSTING SYSTEMS

Industries using process costing may be broadly classified as follows:

2.1 Industries producing a single homogeneous product

The costs incurred in one process are transferred to another as the completed units are transferred. Examples of single-product industries which use process costing are sugar, gas, water, ice, paper, rubber, tea, Portland cement etc.

2.2 Industries producing different products in one and the same process

The characteristic of the manufacturing process is that one product is produced at a time. For example, most fruits and vegetables are seasonal in nature and canneries will generally process one for a period, to be followed by another.

Again, costs incurred in one process are transferred to another as the completed units are transferred.

2.3 Industries producing a single homogeneous product in one process

The products using the same basic raw material require different manufacturing operations. For example, frozen meat, canned meat, salt beef etc.

3.0 COMPARISON OF JOB COSTING AND PROCESS COSTING

Job costing and process costing are compared in Table 4.

Table 4. COMPARISON OF JOB COSTING AND PROCESS COSTING

Job costing	*Process costing*
1 Accumulation of costs to jobs.	1 Accumulation of costs to processes.
2 Manufactured to customers' specifications. Each job has its own characteristics which cause it to differ.	2 Products consist of like units, identical manufacturing specifications.
3 Amount of work involved in identifying costs with jobs is immense.	3 No effort is made to identify costs incurred with individual units of product.
4 Costs are identified directly with each job.	4 Product cost is an average cost. The cost of a complete unit is determined by dividing the total cost of a period by the total units produced during the period.
5 Since costs are identified with job the value of uncompleted jobs is easy to obtain.	5 The problem of process costing is the problem of work in progress.

4.0 MAJOR PROBLEMS ASSOCIATED WITH PROCESS COSTING

(a) Accounting treatment of losses.

(b) Valuation of work in progress at the beginning and end of a period.

(c) Costing of joint and by-products.

5.0 PROCESS COSTING—UNIT COST CALCULATION

Due to the inherent nature of production operations, the work on a unit of product has to be done in several processes. As output from one process is transferred to another for further processing, costs incurred up to that stage in terms of materials, labour and overhead are also transferred.

The cost of a complete unit in a simple manufacturing process is calculated by dividing the total cost of a period by the number of units produced during the period.

5.1 Single and multi-process production

Illustration 1

It is assumed that all units introduced are completed at the end of the process.

PROCESS ACCOUNT—SINGLE-PROCESS PRODUCTION

Process A

Output (units)		*Amount (£)*	*Output (units)*		*Amount (£)*
50,000	Raw materials	100,000	50,000	Transferred out	200,000
	Labour	50,000			
	Overhead	50,000			
		200,000			200,000

Calculation of the average or unit cost:

$$\frac{\text{Total cost incurred}}{\text{Number of units produced}} = \frac{£200{,}000}{50{,}000} = £4.00.$$

Unit cost calculation is not so simple when there are work in progress and/or losses.

PROCESS ACCOUNT—MULTI-PROCESS PRODUCTION

If we assume that the entire output of process A is transferred to another process, B, for further processing, the output of process A is treated as raw material of process B. Therefore, the material, labour and overhead costs incurred in process A lose their identity in process B. The £200,000 is treated as the transferred-in cost or the raw material cost of process B.

Process B

Output (units)		*Amount (£)*	*Output (units)*		*Amount (£)*
50,000	Raw material cost or transferred-in cost from process A	200,000	50,000	Fully completed and transferred to packed stock	400,000
	Labour	100,000			
	Overhead	100,000			
		400,000			400,000

Average cost per unit: $\frac{£400,000}{50,000} = £8.00$

6.0 ACCOUNTING FOR LOSSES

In order to calculate the average cost per unit, the cost department has to reconcile the input to a process with output from it. For various reasons the output from a process is found to be less than the input. The loss must be analysed to determine the factors causing it.

6.1 Possible causes

(a) *Waste.* In certain types of processes material physically disappears on account of evaporation or shrinkage, or the output may be in the form of a residue which has no value.

(b) *Scrap.* This is a kind of material residue from certain types of manufacturing processes. Scrap is usually insignificant in quantity and the sales value is relatively low. For example the timber industry produces sawdust and trimmings, the leather industry pieces and cuttings.

(c) *Spoiled work.* The output of a process which does not meet quality standards is sold as seconds or in bulk without further processing.

(d) *Defective units.* These are the output of a process which does not meet quality standards but can be brought back to normal standards by rectification or rework.

6.2 Normal loss

Uncontrollable or normal loss

Theoretically, losses in processes may be eliminated completely but in practice it may not be economical to do so because the cost incurred in reducing losses may be greater than the costs of spoilage.

Normal or uncontrollable spoilage is treated as a part of the cost of producing the good units because the production of a specified number of good units necessitates the process of a larger number of units.

Normal spoilage is expected and allowed for in planning.

The treatment of normal loss is really treatment by neglect. The cost incurred will be borne by expected output. The sales value of the expected loss is either treated as other income or credited to the process account.

Average cost per unit without work in progress

$$\text{Average cost per unit} = \frac{\text{Cost incurred } \textit{less} \text{ Sales value of normal loss}}{\text{Units introduced } \textit{less} \text{ Expected or normal loss}}$$

Refer to Illustration 1.

$$\text{Process A: } \frac{£100{,}000 - £500}{20{,}000 - 2{,}000} = £5.5278;$$

$$\text{Process B: } \frac{£245{,}028 - £475}{19{,}000 - 950} = £13.5486.$$

Illustration 2

NORMAL AND ABNORMAL LOSSES AND ABNORMAL GAINS WITH NO OPENING OR CLOSING WORK IN PROGRESS

RA & RR manufacturing company produces a single product, Joslin, which passes through two processes before completion and transfer to the finished goods store. During July, data relating to this product were as shown:

	Process one	*Process two*
Input		
Basic raw materials		
20,000 units	£40,000	–
Direct materials added in process	10,000	£20,000
Conversion cost	50,000	120,000
Output	*Units*	*Units*
Normal loss in process of input	10%	5%
All scrap has a scrap value per unit of	£0.25	£0.50
Good units produced	19,000	17,900

There was no stock at the start or at the end of either process.

PROCESS ACCOUNT

Process One

Input (units)		*Amount (£)*	*Output (units)*		*Amount (£)*
20,000	Basic raw material	40,000	2,000	Normal loss (2,000 at £0.25)	500
–	Additional material	10,000	19,000	Good units transferred to process two at £5.5278	105,028
	Conversion cost	50,000			
1,000	Abnormal gain 1,000 × £5.5278	5,528		Cost per expected unit $\frac{£100,000 - £500}{\text{expected 18,000 units}}$ = £5.5278	
		105,528			105,528

NORMAL LOSS ACCOUNT

Process One

Input (units)		*Amount (£)*	*Output (units)*		*Amount (£)*
2,000	Process 1 Account	500	1,000	Sales value of actual scrap 1,000 at £0.25	250
			1,000	Abnormal gain	250
2,000		500	2,000		500

ABNORMAL GAIN ACCOUNT

Process One

Input (units)		*Amount (£)*	*Output (units)*		*Amount (£)*
1,000	Normal loss account	250	1,000	Process account	5,528
–	Profit and loss account	5,278			
1,000		5,528	1,000		5,528

PROCESS ACCOUNT

Process Two

Input (units)		*Amount (£)*	*Output (units)*		*Amount (£)*
19,000	Process one	105,028	950	Normal loss 5% 950 at £0.50	475
–	Additional materials	20,000	17,900	Units fully completed at £13.5486	242,520
–	Conversion cost	120,000	150	Abnormal loss at £13.5486	2,033
				Cost per expected unit $\frac{£245{,}028 - £475}{(19{,}000 - 950) \text{ units}}$ = £13.5486	
19,000		245,028	19,000		245,028

NORMAL LOSS ACCOUNT

Process Two

Input (units)		*Amount (£)*	*Output (units)*		*Amount (£)*
950	Process account	475	1,100	Sales value of actual scrap 1,100 at £0.50 (Debit cash/ debtors)	550
150	Abnormal gain	75			
1,100		550	1,100		550

ABNORMAL LOSS ACCOUNT

Process Two

Input (units)		*Amount (£)*	*Output (units)*		*Amount (£)*
150	Process account	2,033	150	Normal loss account	75
			–	Profit and loss account	1,958
150		2,033	150		2,033

7.0 AVERAGE COST PER UNIT WITH WORK IN PROGRESS AT THE END

7.1 Illustrations of unit cost calculation with work in progress

The calculation of the cost per unit is not quite straightforward when there are uncompleted units on hand at the beginning and/or at the end of the period.

Illustration 3—Process A

Units	*Units*
Opening work in progress	nil
Units introduced this period	50,000
Units finished	40,000
Units uncompleted	10,000
Costs incurred	£
Materials	100,000
Labour	67,500
Overhead	67,500

Note: Technical estimate of the work in progress:

Materials 100 per cent completed.
Labour and overhead 50 per cent completed.

The work in progress at the end of the period complicates the unit cost calculation. The first step therefore is to make a technical estimate of the degree of completion of work in progress. Unlike fully completed units it has not received all the materials, labour and overhead required to complete it; it cannot, therefore, be taken as consisting of fully completed units for the purpose of determining the average cost per unit.

The work in progress must be expressed in relation to the finished units; in terms of elements of cost as our purpose is to calculate the average cost per unit. For example, 1,000 partly completed units on which 50 per cent of the work has been completed are equivalent to 500 completed units in terms of materials, labour and overhead.

In terms of complete units unfinished, output is expressed as *whole, equivalent,* or *effective* units.

There are six steps in the calculation of the equivalent units and the calculation of cost per unit, as follows:

STEP 1 IDENTIFY THE PROBLEM

Prepare the process account and reconcile unit columns.

PROCESS A

Process account

Input (units)		*Amount (£)*	*Output (units)*		*Amount (£)*
50,000	Raw materials	100,000	40,000	Completed	?
	Labour	67,500			
	Overhead	67,500	10,000	Work in progress carried forward	?
50,000			50,000		

Note: The problem is the valuation of work done, i.e. calculation of the average cost.

STEP 2 CONVERT PRODUCTION INTO EQUIVALENT UNITS (AT THIS STAGE IGNORE COST)
Statement of production in terms of equivalent units

Units			*Equivalent units*		
In	*Out*		*Materials*	*Labour*	*Overhead*
nil	nil	Work in progress b/f	nil	nil	nil
50,000					
	40,000	Completed	40,000	40,000	40,000
	10,000	Work in progress c/f			
		100% materials	10,000	–	–
		50% labour and overhead		5,000	5,000
50,000	50,000		50,000	45,000	45,000

STEP 3 COST CHARGED TO THE PROCESS

	Total	*Materials*	*Labour*	*Overhead*
Work in progress b/f	nil	nil	nil	nil
Incurred during the current period	£200,000	£100,000	£67,500	£67,500
	£200,000	£100,000	£67,500	£67,500

STEP 4 COST PER EQUIVALENT UNIT

	Total	*Material*	*Labour*	*Overhead*
Cost to be accounted for—step 3	£200,000	£100,000	£67,500	£67,500
Equivalent units produced—step 2	–	50,000	45,000	45,000
Cost per equivalent unit		£2.00	£1.50	£1.50

STEP 5 EVALUATION

(a) Work introduced and completed.

(b) Work in progress uncompleted at the end of the current period.

STATEMENT OF EVALUATION

	Equivalent units		
	Materials	*Labour*	*Overhead*
Step 2 (Refer)			
Work in progress b/f	nil	nil	nil
Work introduced and completed	40,000	40,000	40,000
Work in progress c/f	10,000	5,000	5,000
Step 4 (Refer)			
Cost per unit	£2.00	£1.50	£1.50
	£	£	£
Step 5 Evaluation			
Work in progress b/f	nil	nil	nil
Work completed during the period	80,000	60,000	60,000
Work in progress c/f	20,000	7,500	7,500

STEP 6 THE PROCESS ACCOUNT IN ITS FINAL FORM

Process A

Units In		*Amount (£)*	*Units Out*		*Amount (£)*
nil	Work in progress b/f	nil	nil	Work in progress b/f	nil
50,000	Raw materials	100,000	40,000	Completed units Transferred out	200,000
	Labour	67,500	10,000	Work in progress c/f Refer Step 5	35,000
	Overhead	67,500			
		235,000			235,000
10,000	WIP b/f	35,000			

Illustration 4—Work in progress at various stages of completion

The following data relate to process A for period one.

Units	*Units*
Work in progress b/f	nil
Units started	50,000
Units completed	30,000
Work in progress c/f	20,000

The degree of completion of the WIP c/f was:

Material		100%
Labour and overhead	Batch 1	50% of the units were 50% completed
	Batch 2	20% of the units were 30% completed
	Batch 3	30% of the units were 40% completed

Costs: materials £150,000; labour £77,200; overhead £38,600.

Required: In step-by-step fashion, prepare a production cost report showing cost of goods completed and cost of work in progress carried forward.

THE STEPS REQUIRED

Step 1 Identify the problem (reconciliation)
Step 2 Statement of production
Step 3 Costs charged to the process
Step 4 Cost per equivalent unit
Step 5 Statement of evaluation
Step 6 The process account.

STEP 2 STATEMENT OF PRODUCTION

Input (units)	*Output (units)*		*Equivalent units*		
			Materials	*Labour*	*Overhead*
–	–	Work in progress b/f	–	–	–
50,000	30,000	Units started and completed	30,000	30,000	30,000
		Work in progress c/f			
	10,000	50% Batch 1—50%	10,000	5,000	5,000
	4,000	20% Batch 2—30%	4,000	1,200	1,200
	6,000	30% Batch 3—40%	6,000	2,400	2,400
			50,000	38,600	38,600

STEP 3 COSTS CHARGED TO THE PROCESS

	Total	*Materials*	*Labour*	*Overhead*
Costs brought forward (work in progress b/f)	nil	nil	nil	nil
Cost incurred this period	£265,000	£150,000	£77,200	£38,600
	£265,800	£150,000	£77,200	£38,600

STEP 4 COST PER EQUIVALENT UNIT

	Total	*Materials*	*Labour*	*Overhead*
Cost—Step 3		£150,000	£77,200	£38,600
Equivalent units produced—Step 2		50,000	38,600	38,600
Cost per unit	£6.00	£3.00	£2.00	£1.00

STEP 5 (STEPS 2 AND 4) STATEMENT OF EVALUATION

Statement of Evaluation

	Total	*Materials*	*Labour*	*Overhead*
Work in progress b/f	nil	nil	nil	nil
Units completed:	£180,000			
30,000 × £3.00		£90,000		
30,000 × £2.00			£60,000	
30,000 × £1.00				£30,000
Work in progress:				
Batch 1	45,000			
10,000 × £3.00		30,000		
5,000 × £2.00			10,000	
5,000 × £1.00				5,000
Batch 2	15,600			
4,000 × £3.00		12,000		
1,200 × £2.00			2,400	
1,200 × £1.00				1,200
Batch 3	25,200			
6,000 × £3.00		18,000		
2,400 × £2.00			4,800	
2,400 × £1.00				2,400
Total	£265,800	£150,000	£77,200	£38,600

STEPS 1 AND 6 THE PROCESS ACCOUNT

Process account

Input (units)		*Amount (£)*	*Output (units)*		*Amount (£)*
nil	Work in progress b/f	nil	nil	Work in progress b/f	nil
50,000	Units started	150,000	30,000	Units completed	180,000
	Labour	77,200	10,000	Work in progress batch 1	45,000
	Overhead	38,600	4,000	Work in progress batch 2	15,600
			6,000	Work in progress batch 3	25,200
				Refer to Step 5	
50,000		265,800	50,000		265,800
10,000	Work in progress b/f				
	Batch 1—50%	45,000			
	Batch 2—30%	15,600			
	Batch 3—40%	25,200			

8.0 NORMAL LOSS AND WORK IN PROGRESS AT THE END

The practical treatment in accounting for normal loss is *treatment by neglect.* The cost incurred will be borne by expected output. The sales value of normal spoilage is credited to the process account.

Illustration 5

During period one the input to process A of basic raw material was 2,000 units at a cost of £4.50 per unit. Labour and overhead incurred during the period was £20,000. At the end of the period 1,400 units have been fully completed, 400 units are in process and only 50% are completed as to labour and overhead; 200 units have been spoiled. Normal loss is expected to occur at the beginning of the process or during the process.

STATEMENT OF PRODUCTION

Reconciliation			*Material*	*Conversion cost*
In (units)	*Out (units)*		*(units)*	*(units)*
nil	nil	Work in progress b/f	nil	nil
	200	Normal loss—neglect	–	–
2,000	1,400	Units completed	1,400	1,400
	–	Abnormal loss	–	–
	400	Work in progress c/f	400	200
2,000	2,000		1,800	1,600

STATEMENT OF COST

	Total	*Material*	*Conversion cost*
Cost brought forward	–	nil	nil
Cost incurred during period	£30,000	£9,000	£20,000
Total	£30,000	£9,000	£20,000

	Total	*Material*	*Conversion cost*
Cost per equivalent unit	£17.50	£5.00	£12.50

STATEMENT OF EVALUATION

	Total	*Material*	*Conversion cost*
Work in progress b/f	nil	nil	nil
Normal loss	–	–	–
Units completed	£24,500		
1,400 × £5.00		£7,000	
1,400 × £12.50			£17,500
Abnormal loss	–	–	–
Work in progress c/f	4,500		
400 × £5.00		2,000	
200 × £12.50			2,500
Total	£29,000	£9,000	£20,000

PROCESS ACCOUNT

Input (units)		*Amount (£)*	*Output (units)*		*Amount (£)*
2,000	Raw materials	9,000	200	Normal loss	–
	Conversion cost	20,000	1,400	Units completed	24,500
				Abnormal loss	–
			400	Work in progress c/f	4,500
2,000		£29,000	2,000		£29,000

9.0 AVERAGE COST PER UNIT WITH GAINS AND LOSSES AND WORK IN PROGRESS AT THE END

Illustration 6

The manufacture of product Jade by the RA & DJ processing company is completed by means of two consecutive processes. The data shown below are for the month of July, year 7.

During July the input to process one of basic raw material was 10,000 units at £2.00 per unit. Further materials were added during the processing as shown below. There was no opening work in process. Loss occurs at the beginning of a process.

DATA FOR JULY

	Process one Abnormal loss	Process two Abnormal gain
Expected/normal loss as a percentage of input	10%	5%
Good output in units	8,000	6,800
Work in process carried forward—units (50% completed as to labour and overhead)	800	1,000
Scrap value per unit	£0.20	£0.50
Direct materials added in process	£27,000	£24,000
Conversion cost	£24,000	£48,000

Note: Follow the six steps.

PROCESS ONE (NOTE SIX STEPS)

STEP 2 STATEMENT OF PRODUCTION

Process one

Reconciliation					
Input (units)	*Output (units)*		*Basic material (units)*	*Additional material (units)*	*Conversion cost (units)*
–	–	Work in progress b/f	–	–	–
10,000	1,000	Normal loss (10% input)	–	–	–
	8,000	Units transferred to process 2	8,000	8,000	8,000
	800	Work in process c/f	800	800	400
	200	Abnormal loss	200	200	200
10,000	10,000		9,000	9,000	8,600

STEP 3 STATEMENT OF COST

	Total	*Basic material*	*Additional material*	*Conversion cost*
Cost brought forward	–	–	–	–
Cost incurred during period		£20,000	£27,000	£24,000
Less: Sales value of normal scrap (1,000 × £0.20)		(200)		
	£70,800	£19,800	£27,000	£24,000

STEP 4 COST PER EQUIVALENT UNIT

	Total	*Basic material*	*Additional material*	*Conversion cost*
Cost	£70,800	£19,800	£27,000	£24,000
Equivalent units	–	9,000	9,000	8,600
Cost per equivalent unit	£7.991	£2.20	£3.00	£2.791

STEP 5 STATEMENT OF EVALUATION

	Total	*Basic material*	*Additional material*	*Conversion cost*
Work in progress b/f	–	–	–	–
Normal loss	–	–	–	–
Units transferred to process 2	£63,926			
8,000 × £2.20		£17,600		
8,000 × £3.00			£24,000	
8,000 × £2.791				£22,326
Abnormal loss	1,598			
200 × £2.20		440		
200 × £3.00			600	
200 × £2.791				558
Work in progress c/f	5,276			
800 × £2.20		1,760		
800 × £3.00			2,400	
400 × £2.791				1,116
	£70,800	£19,800	£27,000	£24,000

STEPS 1 AND 6

Process account—Process one

Input (units)		*Amount (£)*	*Output (units)*		*Amount (£)*
–	Work in progress b/f	–	–	Work in progress b/f	–
10,000	Basic raw material	£20,000	1,000	Normal loss	£200
–	Additional material	27,000	8,000	Transferred to process 2	63,926
–	Conversion cost	24,000	200	Abnormal loss	1,598
			800	Work in progress c/f	5,276
10,000		£71,000	10,000		£71,000

Process one—Normal loss account

Input (units)		*Amount (£)*	*Output (units)*		*Amount (£)*
1,000	Process account	£200		Actual scrap—sales value of 1200 units at £0.20	£240
200	Transferred to the abnormal loss account (balancing figure)	40			
1,200		£240	1,200		£240

Process one—Abnormal loss account

Input (units)		*Amount (£)*	*Output (units)*		*Amount (£)*
200	Process account	£1,598	200	Normal loss A/c Profit and loss A/c	£40 1,558
200		£1,598	200		£1,598

STEP 2

Statement of production: process two

Reconciliation					
Input (units)	*Output (units)*		*Transferred in cost (units)*	*Additional material (units)*	*Conversion cost (units)*
–	–	Work in progress b/f	–	–	–
	400	Normal loss (5%)	–	–	–
8,000	6,800	Transferred from process one and completed	6,800	6,800	6,800
	1,000	Work in progress c/f	1,000	1,000	500
	nil	Abnormal loss	nil	nil	nil
8,000	8,200				
	(200)	Abnormal gain (unexpected increase in output)	(200)	(200)	(200)
8,000	8,000		7,600	7,600	7,100

STEP 3 STATEMENT OF COST

	Total	*Transferred in cost*	*Additional material*	*Conversion cost*
Cost b/f	–	–	–	–
Cost incurred during period	£135,926	£63,926	£24,000	£48,000
Sales value of normal loss (400 × £0.50)	(200)	(200)		
	£135,726	£63,726	£24,000	£48,000

STEP 4 COST PER EQUIVALENT UNIT

	Total	*Transferred in cost*	*Additional material*	*Conversion cost*
Cost		£63,726	£24,000	£48,000
Equivalent units		7,600	7,600	7,100
Cost per whole unit	£18.3039	£8.3850	£3.1579	£6.7610

STEP 5 STATEMENT OF EVALUATION

	Total	*Transferred in cost*	*Additional material*	*Conversion cost*
Work in progress b/f	–	–	–	–
Normal loss	–	–	–	–
Work fully completed	£124,464			
6,800 × £8.3550		£57,018		
6,800 × £3.1579			£21,474	
6,800 × £6.7610				£45,972
Abnormal loss		–	–	–
Work in progress c/f	14,923			
1,000 × £8.3550		8,355		
1,000 × £3.1579			3,158	
500 × £6.7610				3,380
Abnormal gain	(3,661)			
200 × £8.3550		(1,677)		
200 × £3.1579			(632)	
200 × £6.7610				(1,352)
	£135,726	£63,726	£24,000	£48,000

PROCESS TWO STEPS 1 AND 6

Process two account

Input (units)		*Amount (£)*	*Output (units)*		*Amount (£)*
–	Work in progress b/f	–	–	Work in progress b/f	–
8,000	Transferred from process one	£63,926	400	Normal loss 5%	£200
–	Additional material	24,000	6,800	Work fully completed	124,464
	Conversion cost	48,000	–	Abnormal loss	–
200	Abnormal gain	3,661	1,000	Work in progress c/f	14,923
8,200		£139,587	8,200		£139,587

Process two—Normal loss account

Input (units)		*Amount (£)*	*Output (units)*		*Amount (£)*
400	Process account	200	200	Sales value of total scrap—*actual scrap* (200 × £0.50) cash or other debtors debited	100
			200	Transferred to abnormal gain account	100
400		£200	400		£200

Process two—Abnormal gain account

Input (units)		*Amount (£)*	*Output (units)*		*Amount (£)*
200	Normal loss account	100	200	Process account	3,661
–	Profit and loss account	3,561			
200		£3,661	200		£3,661

10.0 AVERAGE COST PER UNIT WITH WORK IN PROGRESS AT THE BEGINNING

10.1 Process with opening work in progress

In the previous illustrations the processes had closing work in progress stock. These stocks become the opening stock work in progress of the next period.

When there is opening work in progress, the output completed will be grouped into three batches:

Batch 1 Opening work in progress, which was partly completed at the end of the last period or partly processed in the current period (work in progress b/f).

Batch 2 Units that were introduced and completed within the current period.

Batch 3 Units that were introduced during the current period but were not fully completed (work in progress c/f).

Cost per unit calculation

Calculations of the cost per unit become even more complicated when there is opening work in progress.

10.2 Choice of method of accounting for opening work in progress

There are two methods to choose from:

(a) average method,

(b) first in first out method.

Each has its advantages and disadvantages. The one widely used in industry is the average method, because it is the simpler of the two.

Rules of the game

(a) Remember that these two are methods of valuing the opening work in progress.

(b) *Use FIFO* if the value of the opening work in progress is one *lump sum figure* and the *stage of completion is given.* For example, opening work in progress 2,000 units; £30,400; stage of completion 100 per cent materials, 50 per cent labour and overhead: FIFO is the only one possible.

(c) *Use average* if the opening work in progress value is given in terms of materials, labour and overhead but the stage of completion is *not* given. For example, opening work in progress 2,000 units; materials £24,000; labour £3,200; overhead £3,200. The stage of completion is not given—average is the only method possible.

(d) *Your choice—FIFO or average:* if the degree of completion and the value in terms of materials, labour and overhead of the opening work in progress are given then you have a choice, for example:

Opening work in progress		2,000 units
Cost: Materials	£24,000	
Labour	3,200	
Overhead	3,200	
Degree of completion		
Materials	100 per cent	
Labour and overhead	50 per cent	

(e) If the question suggests a method then it must be followed.

10.3 Average method

The opening work in progress is treated as a part of current production. This method ignores the fact that these units were partly completed in the previous period. The cost of the opening work in progress is added to the cost incurred in the current period and the average cost is calculated.

The opening work in progress *loses* its identity.

Illustration 7—Average method

The following information relates to process A:

Units			
Opening work in progress	2,000		
Units produced during the period	16,000		
Units completed during the period	14,800		
Work in progress at the end	3,200		
Stage of completion	*Material*	*Labour and Overhead*	
Opening work in progress	100%	50%	
Closing work in progress	100%	25%	
Costs	*Material*	*Labour*	*Overhead*
Opening work in progress	£24,000	£3,200	£3,200
Costs incurred during the current period	£192,000	£63,680	£63,680

All materials were introduced at the start of the process while labour and overhead were incurred uniformly throughout the process.

STEP 1 CONSIDER THE PHYSICAL FLOW OF UNITS. IN OTHER WORDS ACCOUNT FOR THE INPUT TO THE PROCESS

The opening work in progress does not form a part of the input during the current period.

Input	Units introduced during the period	16,000	
Output	Units completed		14,800
	Less: Opening work in progress		2,000
	Units introduced and completed during the current period		12,800
	Work in progress c/f		3,200
			16,000

STEP 2 STATEMENT OF PRODUCTION

Reconciliation			*Equivalent units*		
Input	*Output*		*Material*	*Labour*	*Overhead*
2,000	Identity is lost	Work in progress b/f	Loses its identity		
16,000	14,800	Units completed	14,800	14,800	14,800
	3,200	Work in progress c/f 25%	3,200	800	800
18,000	18,000		18,000	15,600	15,600

STEP 3 STATEMENT OF COST

	Total	*Material*	*Labour*	*Overhead*
Cost b/f (i.e. work in progress b/f)	£30,400	£24,000	£3,200	£3,200
Cost incurred this period	319,360	192,000	63,680	63,680
	£349,760	£216,000	£66,880	£66,880

STEP 4 COST PER EQUIVALENT UNIT

	Total	*Material*	*Labour*	*Overhead*
Cost (step 3)	£349,760	£216,000	£66,880	£66,880
Equivalent units (step 2)	–	18,000	15,600	15,600
Cost per equivalent unit	£20.5744	£12.00	£4.2872	£4.2872

STEP 5 STATEMENT OF EVALUATION

	Total	Material	Labour	Overhead
Work in progress b/f	–	–	–	–
Units completed	£304,500			
14,800 × £12.00		£177,600		
14,800 × £4.2872			£63,450	
14,800 × £4.2872				£63,450
Work in progress c/f	45,260			
3,200 × £12.00		38,400		
800 × £4.2872			3,430	
800 × £4.2872				3,430
Total	£349,760	£216,000	£66,880	£66,880

Process account (steps 1 and 6)

Input (units)		*Amount (£)*	*Output (units)*		*Amount (£)*
2,000	Work in progress b/f	£30,400	–	Work in progress b/f	–
16,000	Materials	192,000	14,800	Units completed	£304,500
	Labour	63,680			
	Overhead	63,680	3,200	Work in progress c/f	45,260
18,000		£349,760	18,000		£349,760

10.4 First in first out method

The principle of first in first out means that the work brought forward uncompleted from last period (opening work in progress) is completed first, before work is started on the current period's input. This method therefore treats the opening work in progress as if it were a separate batch; in other words, opening work in progress *keeps* its identity.

The cost of output completed in a period is worked out in three parts:

(a) The cost incurred during the current period to complete the work in progress brought forward.

(b) The cost of units started and completed in the current period.

(c) The cost of work started but not completed (WIP c/f) in the current period.

Illustration 8—First in first out
Assume the data used to illustrate the average method (Illustration 7).

Note: Assume work in progress brought forward was 100 per cent completed in terms of materials and 50 per cent in terms of labour and overhead.

STEP 1 STOCK RECONCILIATION (REFER TO AVERAGE METHOD)

STEP 2 STATEMENT OF PRODUCTION

Reconciliation			*Statement of equivalent units*		
In (units)	*Out (units)*		*Materials*	*Labour*	*Overhead*
2,000	2,000	Work in progress b/f 50% completed, labour and overhead; 100% completed, materials	–	1,000	1,000
16,000	12,800	Input this period	12,800	12,800	12,800
	3,200	Work in progress c/f 25%	3,200	800	800
18,000	18,000		16,000	14,600	14,600

STEP 3 STATEMENT OF COST

	Total	*Material*	*Labour*	*Overhead*
Cost of work in progress b/f	—	—	—	—
Cost incurred this period	£319,360	£192,000	£63,680	£63,680
	£319,360	£192,000	£63,680	£63,680

STEP 4 COST PER EQUIVALENT UNIT

	Total	*Material*	*Labour*	*Overhead*
Cost (step 3)	£319,360	£192,000	£63,680	£63,680
Units (step 2)	–	16,000	14,600	14,600
Cost per equivalent unit	£20.7232	£12.00	£4.3616	£4.3616

STEP 5 STATEMENT OF EVALUATION

		Statement of evaluation		
	Total	*Material*	*Labour*	*Overhead*
Opening work in progress	£8,722	–	–	–
Materials		–	–	–
Labour 1,000 × £4.3616			£4,361	
Overhead 1,000 × £4.3616				£4,361
Input completed during period	265,258			
Materials 12,800 × £12.00		£153,600		
Labour 12,800 × £4.3616			55,829	
Overhead 12,800 × £4.3616				55,829
Work in progress carried forward	45,380			
Materials 3,200 × £12.00		38,400		
Labour 800 × £4.3616			3,490	
Overhead 800 × £4.3616				3,490
	£319,360	£192,000	£63,680	£63,680

STEP 6

Progress account

Input (units)		*Amount (£)*	*Output (units)*		*Amount (£)*
2,000	Work in progress b/f	£30,400	2,000	Work in progress b/f £30,400 + £8,722	£39,122
16,000	Materials	192,000	12,800	Input completed	265,258
	Labour	63,680			
	Overhead	63,680	3,200	Work in progress	45,380
18,000		£349,760	18,000		£349,760

11.0 ABNORMAL LOSSES WITH OPENING AND CLOSING WORK IN PROGRESS

Illustration 9—FIFO and average methods

The manufacture of product K, by the James Milford Manufacturing Company, is completed by means of four successive processes. The work in progress for process two for period 7 is being prepared and there are given below the debit items of that account.

WORK IN PROGRESS BROUGHT FORWARD:	1,000 units at £2,600
This comprises the following costs:	
Transferred from process one	£1,400
Direct materials	£640
Direct wages	£208
Production overhead	£352

The stage reached in process two was as follows:

Direct materials	100 per cent
Direct wages and overhead	50 per cent

INPUT DURING PERIOD 7

Transferred from process one:	10,500 units at £21,000
Direct materials	£7,120
Direct wages	£3,600
Production overhead	£7,264

The following information is available:

(a) Normal loss in process for a month was 1,000 units.

(b) The stage reached in process 2 was as follows:

	Scrapped during period 7	*Stock in progress at the end of period 7*
Number of units	1,200	1,200
Materials added in process	90%	60%
Direct wages and overhead	60%	50%

(c) Sales value of units scrapped was £0.50 per unit.
The value received from these units considered to be normal loss was regarded as a reduction in the cost of the input from process one.

(d) All completed units have been transferred to process three.

Note: Should the FIFO or the average method be used? Look at the opening work in progress. If the degree of completion and the detailed values are both given, you may use either.

First in first out method

STEP 2 STATEMENT OF PRODUCTION

Reconciliation						
Input (units)	*Output (units)*		*Transferred in cost (units)*	*Materials added (units)*	*Labour (units)*	*Overhead (units)*
1,000	1,000	Work in progress b/f	–	–	500	500
	1,000	Normal loss	–	–	–	–
10,500	8,100	Units started and completed during this period	8,100	8,100	8,100	8,100
	200	Abnormal loss	200	180	120	120
	1,200	Work in progress c/f	1,200	720	600	600
11,500	11,500		9,500	9,000	9,320	9,320

STEP 3 STATEMENT OF COST

	Total	*Transferred in cost*	*Materials added*	*Labour*	*Overhead*
	£	£	£	£	£
Work in progress b/f (cost b/f—ignore)	–	–	–	–	–
Cost incurred during period	38,984	21,000	7,120	3,600	7,264
Sales value of normal loss (1,000 × £0.50)	(500)	(500)	–	–	–
	£38,484	£20,500	£7,120	£3,600	£7,264

STEP 4 COST PER EQUIVALENT UNIT

	Total	*Transferred in cost*	*Materials added*	*Labour*	*Overhead*
Cost incurred	£38,484	£20,500	£7,120	£3,600	£7,264
Equivalent units	–	9,500	9,000	9,320	9,320
Cost of equivalent unit	£4.1147	£2.1579	£0.7911	£0.3863	£0.7794

STEP 5 STATEMENT OF EVALUATION (FIFO)

	Total	*Transferred in cost*	*Materials added*	*Labour*	*Overhead*
Work in progress b/f	£583				
500 × £0.3863		–	–	£193	–
500 × £0.7794					£390
Units started and completed during period	33,329				
8,100 × £2.1579		£17,479			
8,100 × £0.7911			£6,408		
8,100 × £0.3863				3,129	
8,100 × £0.7794					6,313
Abnormal loss	713				
200 × £2.1579		432			
180 × £0.7911			142		
120 × £0.3863				46	
120 × £0.7794					93
Work in progress c/f	3,859				
1,200 × £2.1579		2,589			
720 × £0.7911			570		
600 × £0.3863				232	
600 × £0.7794					468
	£38,484	£20,500	£7,120	£3,600	£7,264

STEPS 1 AND 6 PROCESS ACCOUNT (FIFO)

Input (units)		*Amount (£)*	*Output (units)*		*Amount (£)*
1,000	Work in progress b/f	£2,600	1,000	Work in progress b/f (2,600 + 583)	£3,183
10,500	Process one	21,000	1,000	Normal loss at £50	500
	Direct materials added	7,120	8,100	Input completed during period	33,329
	Direct labour	3,600	200	Abnormal loss	713
	Overhead	7,264	1,200	Work in progress c/f	3,859
11,500		£41,584	11,500		£41,584

Process—Normal loss account

Input (units)		*Amount (£)*	*Output (units)*		*Amount (£)*
1,000	Process account	500	1,200	Sales value of *actual* scrap (1,200 at £50)	600
200	Abnormal loss	100			
1,200		£600	1,200		£600

Process—Abnormal loss account

Input (units)		*Amount (£)*	*Output (units)*		*Amount (£)*
200	Process account	713	200	Normal loss account	100
				Profit and loss account	613
200		£713	200		£713

Average method

STEP 2 STATEMENT OF PRODUCTION

Reconciliation *Input (units)*	*Output (units)*		*Transferred in cost (units)*	*Materials added (units)*	*Labour (units)*	*Overhead (units)*
1,000	–	Work in progress b/f	–	–	–	–
	1,000	Normal loss	–	–	–	–
10,500	9,100	Units completed during the period	9,100	9,100	9,100	9,100
	200	Abnormal loss	200	180	120	120
	1,200	Work in progress c/f	1,200	720	600	600
11,500	11,500		10,500	10,000	9,820	9,820

STEP 3 STATEMENT OF COST

	Total	*Transferred in cost*	*Materials added*	*Labour*	*Overhead*
Work in progress b/f (cost brought forward)	£2,600	£1,400	£640	£208	£352
Cost incurred during period	38,984	21,000	7,120	3,600	7,264
Sales value of normal scrap	(500)	(500)			
	£41,084	£21,900	£7,760	£3,808	£7,616

STEP 4 COST PER EQUIVALENT UNIT

	Total	*Transferred in cost*	*Materials added*	*Labour*	*Overhead*
Cost incurred	£41,084	£21,900	£7,760	£3,808	£7,616
Equivalent units	–	10,500	10,000	9,820	9,820
Cost per equivalent unit	£4.0251	£2.0857	£0.776	£0.3878	£0.7756

STEP 5 STATEMENT OF EVALUATION (AVERAGE)

	Total	*Transferred in cost*	*Materials added*	*Labour*	*Overhead*
Work in progress b/f					
Units completed	£36,629				
9,100 × £2.0857		£18,980			
9,100 × £0.776			£7,062		
9,100 × £0.3878				£3,529	
9,100 × £0.7756					£7,058
Abnormal loss	696				
200 × £2.0857		417			
180 × £0.776			140		
120 × £0.3878				46	
120 × £0.7756					93
Work in progress c/f	3,759				
1,200 × £2.0857		2,503			
720 × £0.776			558		
600 × £0.3878				233	
600 × £0.7756					465
Total	£41,084	£21,900	£7,760	£3,808	£7,616

STEPS 1 and 6 PROCESS ACCOUNT (AVERAGE)

Input (units)		*Amount (£)*	*Output (units)*		*Amount (£)*
1,000	Work in progress b/f	2,600	1,000	Work in progress b/f	–
10,500	Transferred from process 1	21,000		Normal loss	500
			9,100	Units completed	36,629
	Direct materials added	7,120			
	Direct labour	3,600	200	Abnormal loss	696
	Overhead	7,264	1,200	Work in progress c/f	3,759
11,500		£41,584	11,500		£41,584

Normal loss account

Input (units)		*Amount (£)*	*Output (units)*		*Amount (£)*
1,000	Process account	500	1,200	Sales value of actual scrap (cash debtors) at £0.50	600
200	Abnormal scrap	100			
1,200		£600	1,200		£600

Abnormal loss account

Input (units)		*Amount (£)*	*Output (units)*		*Amount (£)*
200	Process account	696	200	Normal loss account	100
			–	Profit and loss A/c	596
200		£696	200		£696

12.0 AVERAGE COST PER UNIT WITH (A) WORK IN PROGRESS—START, (B) WORK IN PROGRESS—END, (C) ABNORMAL GAIN

Illustration 10

David Manufacturing Company produced three products, Deva, Rod and Sena, by a number of processes. Process four is the last process in which they are jointly processed. The following information is obtained in respect to process four for period 7.

Transfer from process three 20,000 units at £9,200.

Transfer to further processing 18,200 units.

Direct materials added in process four £15,000.

Direct labour incurred in process four £20,000.

Production overhead incurred in process four £40,000.

Units scrapped in process four £1,400.

Scrap value per unit £0.50.

Opening stock 3,200 units—comprising the following costs:

Transferred from process three	£1,680
Materials added process four	£600
Labour	£800
Overhead	£1,600

Closing stock (work in progress c/f)		3,600 units
Completed as to:	materials	80 per cent
	labour	50 per cent
	overhead	40 per cent.

Normal (expected) loss: 9 per cent of input.

STEP 2 STATEMENT OF PRODUCTION

Reconciliation						
Input (units)	*Output (units)*		*Transferred in cost (units)*	*Materials added (units)*	*Labour (units)*	*Overhead (units)*
3,200	–	Work in progress b/f	–	–	–	–
	1,800	Normal loss (9% of 20,000)	–	–	–	–
	18,200	Units completed	18,200	18,200	18,200	18,200
20,000	–	Abnormal loss	–	–	–	–
	3,600	Work in progress c/f	3,600	2,880	1,800	1,440
	23,600		21,800	21,080	20,000	19,640
	(400)	Abnormal gain	(400)	(400)	(400)	(400)
23,200	23,200		21,400	20,680	19,600	19,240

STEP 3 STATEMENT OF COST

	Total	Transferred in cost	Materials added	Labour	Overhead
Work in progress b/f	£4,680	£1,680	£600	£800	£1,600
Cost incurred this period	84,200	9,200	15,000	20,000	40,000
	£88,880	£10,880	£15,600	£20,800	£41,600
Sales value of normal scrap (1,800 × £0.50)	(900)	(900)	–	–	–
	£87,980	£9,980	£15,600	£20,800	£41,600

STEP 4 COST PER EQUIVALENT UNIT

	Total	Transferred in cost	Materials added	Labour	Overhead
Cost incurred	£87,980	£9,980	£15,600	£20,800	£41,600
Equivalent units	–	21,400	20,680	19,600	19,240
Cost per equivalent unit	£4.4442	£0.4664	£0.7544	£1.0612	£2.1622

STEP 5 STATEMENT OF EVALUATION (AVERAGE METHOD)

	Total	Transferred in cost	Materials added	Labour	Overhead
Work in progress b/f	–	–	–	–	–
Units completed	£80,884				
18,200 × £0.4664		£8,488			
18,200 × £0.7544			£13,730		
18,200 × £1.0612				£19,314	
18,200 × £2.1622					£39,352
Abnormal loss	–	–	–	–	–
Work in progress c/f	8,874				
3,600 × £0.4664		1,679			
2,880 × £0.7544			2,172		
1,800 × £1.0612				1,910	
1,440 × £2.1622					3,113
Less: Abnormal gain	(1,778)				
400 × £0.4664		(187)			
400 × £0.7544			(302		
400 × £1.0612				(424)	
400 × £2.1622					(865)
	£87,980	£9,980	£15,600	£20,800	£41,600

(Steps 1 and 6) Process account—average method

Input (units)		*Amount (£)*	*Output (units)*		*Amount (£)*
3,200	Work in progress b/f	£4,680	–	Work in progress b/f	–
			1,800	Normal loss	900
20,000	Process three	9,200			
			18,200	Output completed	80,884
	Materials added	15,000			
	Labour	20,000	–	Abnormal loss	–
	Overhead	40,000	3,600	Work in progress c/f	8,874
23,200		88,880	23,600		90,658
400	Abnormal gain	1,778	–		–
23,600		£90,658	23,600		£90,658

Normal loss account

Input (units)		*Amount (£)*	*Output (units)*		*Amount (£)*
1,800	Process account	£900	1,400	Sales value of actual scrap (1,400 at £0.50) (cash/debtors)	700
			400	Abnormal gain	200
1,800		£900	1,800		900

Abnormal gain account

Input (units)		*Amount (£)*	*Output (units)*		*Amount (£)*
400	Normal loss account	£200	400	Process account	£1,778
–	Profit and loss account	1,578			
400		£1,778	400		£1,778

13.0 EXAMINATION TECHNIQUES

In the study of process costing questions, the student often *ignores* the purpose of the exercise, i.e. the calculation of the unit cost. By and large the unit cost is an average cost.

Questions on process costing can be broadly divided into 3 groups:

(a) You are required to prepare accounts for each of the processes I, II and III without works in progress opening and/or closing. In this type of question you are expected to account for abnormal gains and/or losses:
Open the 3 accounts for each process: process account
normal loss account
abnormal loss/gain account

(b) You are required to prepare accounts for two processes with work in progress carried forward:
Follow 6 steps.

(c) You are required to prepare accounts for one or more processes with opening WIP and closing WIP:
Use 6 steps and follow either FIFO or average.

13.1 Unit cost calculation without work in progress

(a) The calculation is quite straightforward if the question *does not involve work in progress*:

COST

The average cost per unit is calculated thus:	
Materials, labour and overhead	£x
Less: Sales value of the expected/normal loss	(£x)
Total cost to be accounted for	£x

PRODUCTION

Units introduced during the period input	= units
Less: Expected/normal loss	= (units)
Expected number of whole units	= units

UNIT COST

$$\text{Average cost} = \frac{\text{Total cost to be accounted for}}{\text{Expected number of units}}$$

(b) Open three separate accounts for each process:

(i) Process account—process one
(ii) Normal loss account—process one
(iii) Abnormal loss/abnormal gain account—process one.

13.2 Unit cost calculation with work in progress

The calculation of the cost per unit is not quite straightforward when there are uncompleted units on hand at the beginning and/or at the end of an accounting period. These questions can be solved very easily by following a uniform step-by-step method.

STEP 1 THE PROCESS ACCOUNTS—THREE SEPARATE ACCOUNTS

Reconciliation of input (units) with output (units). Make allowances for normal losses.

STEP 2 STATEMENT OF PRODUCTION

(a) If there is *opening WIP*, use either FIFO or average method.

(b) If there is *no opening WIP*, the preparation of the statement is quite straightforward.

STEP 3 STATEMENT OF COST

Note: If there is opening WIP, then:
FIFO: ignore cost brought forward.
Average: include cost brought forward.
Make allowances for the sales value of normal/expected loss.

STEP 4 COST PER WHOLE OR EQUIVALENT UNIT

i.e. the average cost per unit.

STEP 5 STATEMENT OF EVALUATION

STEP 6 COMPLETE THE PROCESS ACCOUNTS

(a) process account

(b) normal loss account

(c) abnormal gain/loss account.

13.3 Conclusion

The step approach may not be the fastest way, but once it is understood, you will develop confidence and be able to answer any question on process costing. Once you master the technique and only then, should you use short cuts.

CHAPTER TWELVE

Methods of Product Costing IV – Joint Products and By-Products

1.0 JOINT PRODUCTS

Joint products are products manufactured simultaneously, from the same raw materials. None of the products can be treated as the main product, since the products have significant relative sales value, for example:

Industry	*Raw material*	*Products*
Tea	Tea	Grade 1; grade 2; etc.
Dairy products	Milk	Cream, skim milk, butter, ice cream, etc.
Fishing	Raw fish	Fresh fish, salt fish, canned fish, fish oil, etc.
Oil refining	Crude oil	Gasoline, kerosene, naphtha, benzene, etc.

The raw material which produces several products may go through several manufacturing processes. Up to the stage of production, known as the split-off point, the individual products cannot be identified. The costs incurred up to this point of manufacture are termed joint costs.

2.0 PROBLEMS IN JOINT PRODUCT COSTING

A general picture of the problems is given by Fig. 10.

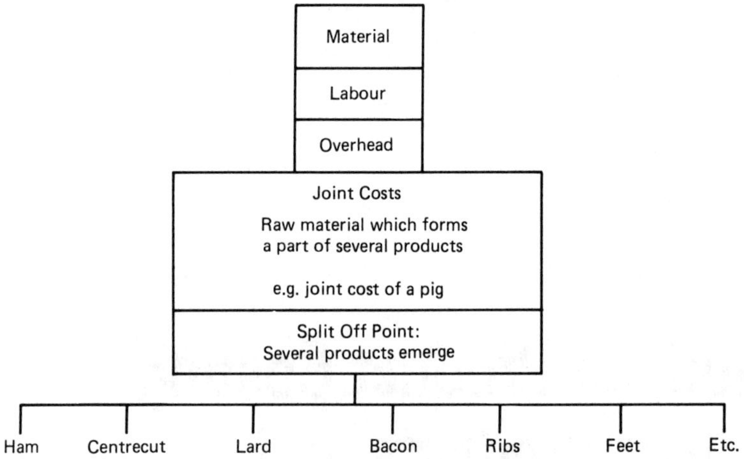

Fig. 10. *Example of joint product costing.*

2.1 Cost allocation

The problem here is how to apportion the costs incurred up to the split-off point equitably between the individual products. *See* **3.0** below. (Costs incurred after the split-off point can, of course, be identified with separate products in the usual way.)

2.2 Decision making

This problem consists of whether to process the product further or sell at the split-off point (*see* **4.0** below).

3.0 COST ALLOCATION

Generally speaking, three basic approaches are commonly used:

(a) physical unit or quantitative method, such as weight or volume;

(b) relative sales value basis—market value at the split-off point;

(c) relative sales value basis—hypothetical market value.

3.1 Joint cost apportionment on the basis of physical measures of the product

The joint cost is apportioned to the various products on the basis of some suitable physical coefficient contained in the products. For example, the distribution of the joint cost may be made in proportion to the raw materials in each product.

Illustration 1

Let us assume that 20,000 barrels of crude oil were processed from which the quantity of each product after allowing for a normal loss of 400 barrels was:

Product	*Quantity (barrels)*
Fuel oil	10,000
Gasoline	5,000
Kerosene	2,000
Benzene	1,000
Lubricating oil	600
Miscellaneous	1,000
Output	19,600
Normal loss	400
Input	20,000
Joint cost of £156,800.	

JOINT COST APPORTIONMENT

Product	*Net output (barrels)*	*Basis of joint cost apportionment*	*Cost apportioned*
Fuel oil	10,000	$\frac{£156,800}{19,600} \times 10,000$	£80,000
Gasoline	5,000	$\frac{£156,800}{19,600} \times 5,000$	40,000
Kerosene	2,000	$\frac{£156,800}{19,600} \times 2,000$	16,000
Benzene	1,000	$\frac{£156,800}{19,600} \times 1,000$	8,000
Lubricating oil	600	$\frac{£156,800}{19,600} \times 600$	4,800
Miscellaneous	1,000	$\frac{£156,800}{19,600} \times 1,000$	8,000
	19,600		£156,800

The physical unit method of apportionment is not always useful or practicable or may have no relationship to the sales value of products produced. If the joint cost of a tonne of tea were assigned on the basis of raw material contained in the products, the best-quality tea would show fabulous profits and lower grades would consistently show losses.

If the output cannot be expressed in terms of the same physical unit this method of apportionment of joint cost cannot be used, unless some common denominator is found.

3.2 Joint cost apportionment on the basis of market value at the split-off point

This method takes into account both the selling price of the products produced at the split-off point and the quantities produced.

Illustration 2

Let us assume that four joint products are produced at a joint cost of £70,000. The quantities produced are:

Product	*Output (lb)*	*Final selling price per lb*
CH	20,000	£4
AN	10,000	£6
DA	5,000	£10
NA	4,000	£20
Loss	(10,000)	
Input	50,000	

JOINT COST APPORTIONMENT

Product	*Units produced and sold (lb)*	*Selling price per unit (£)*	*Total sales value (£)*	*Basis of joint cost apportionment (£)*	*Cost apportioned (£)*
CH	20,000	4	80,000	$\frac{70{,}000}{280{,}000} \times 80{,}000$	20,000
AN	10,000	6	60,000	$\frac{70{,}000}{280{,}000} \times 60{,}000$	15,000
DA	6,000	10	60,000	$\frac{70{,}000}{280{,}000} \times 60{,}000$	15,000
NA	4,000	20	80,000	$\frac{70{,}000}{280{,}000} \times 80{,}000$	20,000
			£280,000		£70,000

3.3 Joint cost apportionment on the basis of a hypothetical market value

This method is suitable for the apportionment of joint cost in cases where after the split-off point the products are not saleable. They do not have a market value at the split-off point. In such cases a hypothetical market value at the split-off point is used. This is calculated as: final market value (i.e. after further processing), less cost incurred after the split-off point.

Illustration 3

1	2	3	4	5	6
Product	*Output (lb)*	*Final market value per lb*	*Processing cost per lb after split-off point*	*Hypothetical market value per lb* (4 – 3)	*Joint cost* (£)
Grade one	20,000	£5	£1.00	£4.00	–
Grade two	40,000	£4	£0.70	£3.30	–
Grade three	60,000	£3	£0.50	£2.50	–
Grade four	80,000	£2	£0.20	£1.00	–
Grade five	50,000	£1	£0.10		–
	250,000				206,800

The method of apportioning is exactly as in Illustrations 1 and 2 above, using the hypothetical market value (column 5 × column 2) as the basis of calculation.

Illustration 4—Joint products: comprehensive illustration

Rod South Ltd produces 3 products, A, B and C, by the operation of a process. The costs for a period are as follows:

Input	Materials	650 tons at £20 per ton
	Labour	£5,000
	Overheads	£6,000
Output	300 tons of product A	
	200 tons of product B	
	100 tons of product C	
	50 tons of expected loss.	

Product A is sold at a price of £50 per ton.

Product B is passed to a second process, in which labour costs are £10 per ton of input and overheads is at 200 per cent on labour. The output is 190 tons of product M which is sold at £120 per ton.

Product C is passed to another process in which labour costs are £4 per ton and overhead is again at 200 per cent on labour. The output is 85 tons of product S which is sold at £250 per ton.

You are required to:

(a) Apportion the costs incurred prior to the split-off point.

(b) Present figures to management to show the profitability of operating the processes. All process losses should be regarded as normal.

(a) ALLOCATION OF JOINT COST

METHOD 1 PHYSICAL MEASURE (SUCH AS WEIGHT OR VOLUME)

Joint cost:	materials	£13,000
	labour	5,000
	overhead	6,000
		24,000

Product	Production (tons)	Cost (£)	Weighting	Cost assigned (£)
A	300		$\frac{300}{600}$ × £24,000	12,000
B	200		$\frac{200}{600}$ × £24,000	8,000
C	100		$\frac{100}{600}$ × £24,000	4,000
	600	24,000		24,000

METHOD 2 HYPOTHETICAL MARKET VALUE

Product	A	B	C
Final market value	£50	£120	£250
Additional cost incurred:			
Labour	–	10	4
Overhead	–	20	8
Hypothetical market value per unit	£50	£90	£238
Units produced tons	300	200	100
Hypothetical market value	£15,000	£18,000	£23,800
Joint costs £24,000 =	£6,338	£7,605	£10,057

(b) OPERATING STATEMENT

Period

Product	Total	A	B	C
Sales units	–	300	190	85
Selling price per unit	–	£50.00	£120.00	£250.00
Sales	£59,050	£15,000	£22,800	£21,250
Joint costs (method 2)	£24,000	£6,338	£7,605	£10,057
Additional costs				
Labour				
£10 × 200	£2,000	–	£2,000	–
£4 × 100	£400	–	–	£400
Overhead—200 per cent of direct labour	£4,800	–	£4,000	£800
Total cost of goods sold	£31,200	£6,338	£13,605	£11,257
Gross profit	£27,850	£8,662	£9,195	£9,993

4.0 JOINT PRODUCTS AND MANAGERIAL DECISIONS

The cost incurred up to the split-off point, regardless of the various methods of apportionment to the individual products, is an inherent result of the manufacturing process. The aim should be to reduce these costs or at least to keep them at a reasonable level.

The decision to process a joint product further after the split-off point is *not* determined by:

(a) the size of the total joint cost;

(b) the joint cost apportioned to the product in question.

It *is* determined by:

(a) production facilities available for further processing;

(b) additional facilities required for further processing;

(c) additional income from further processing. The relevant costs are the additional costs as compared with additional income.

Illustration 5

RA & RB Company produced three joint products at a joint cost of £450,000:

Product	*Output (units)*
KE	200,000
TE	200,000
YA	100,000

The company is faced with the decision whether to sell the products at the split-off point to other processors. If the company selects this alternative the sales value per unit would be:

KE £2.50 TE £2.00 YA £0.50

The company has the facilities to further process the three products and sell them as follows:

Product	*Selling price per unit*	*Additional processing costs*
KE	£4.00	£200,000
TE	3.00	100,000
YA	1.00	75,000

The decision whether to further process or to sell the products at the split-off point should not be made on a total cost/revenue basis. Joint costs are not relevant for this decision. The inclusion of joint costs will yield inconsistent results.

JOINT COST ALLOCATED ON THE BASIS OF WEIGHT

Income statement

Product	*Total*	*KE*	*TE*	*YA*
Sales (units)		200,000	200,000	100,000
Selling price per unit		£4.00	£3.00	£1.00
Sales value	£1,500,000	£800,000	£600,000	£100,000
Joint costs	450,000	180,000	180,000	90,000
Further processing costs	375,000	200,000	100,000	75,000
Profit (loss)	£675,000	£420,000	£320,000	£(65,000)

JOINT COST ALLOCATED ON THE BASIS OF THE MARKET VALUE AT THE SPLIT-OFF POINT

Income statement

Product	Total	KE	TE	YA
Sales (units)	–	200,000	200,000	100,000
Selling price per unit	–	£4.00	£3.00	£1.00
Sales value	£1,500,000	£800,000	£600,000	£100,000
Joint costs (*see* Note)	450,000	236,842	189,474	23,684
Further processing costs	375,000	200,000	100,000	75,000
Profit (loss)	£675,000	£363,158	£310,526	£1,316

Note Joint cost allocation
Market value of the products at the split-off point

	Market value	*Joint cost allocation*
KE	200,000 × £2.50 = £500,000	$\frac{£500,000}{£950,000}$ × £450,000 = £236,842
TE	200,000 × £2.00 = £400,000	$\frac{£500,000}{£950,000}$ × £400,000 = £189,474
YA	100,000 × £0.50 = £50,000	$\frac{£500,000}{£950,000}$ × £50,000 = £23,684
		£450,000

The two methods of joint cost allocation have given inconsistent results. The weight or volume method shows a loss of £65,000 for product YA, whereas the relative sales value method shows a profit of £1,316. The apparent profitability of the individual products depends on the method selected for allocating the cost incurred up to the split-off point. Any method is largely arbitrary because KE cannot be obtained without obtaining YA and vice versa.

In deciding whether to process further or sell at the split-off point, the joint costs are *irrelevant*. The approach that will yield valid results is to *compare the additional costs* incurred after the split-off point *with additional income.*

Product	KE	TE	YA
Sales (units)	200,000	200,000	100,000
Selling price after further processing	£4.00	£3.00	£1.00
Selling price at the split-off point	£2.50	£2.00	£0.50
Difference in selling prices	£1.50	£1.00	£0.50
Additional cost per unit	£1.00	£0.50	£0.75
Profit (loss) per unit	£0.50	£0.50	(£0.25)

In summary, as long as the additional revenue is *greater* than additional costs, further processing is justified, i.e. product YA should not be processed further but should be sold at £0.50.

Income statement

Product	Total	KE	TE	YA
Sales (units)		200,000	200,000	100,000
Selling price per unit		£4.00	£3.00	£0.50
Sales value	£1,450,000	£800,000	£600,000	£50,000
Joint costs	450,000	Same for each alternative		
Additional costs	300,000	200,000	100,000	–
Profit (loss)	£700,000			

It must be noted that the allocation of joint costs to products may *not* serve a useful purpose. The aim should be to *reduce* these costs or at least to keep them at a reasonable level. The *only* reliable measure of product profitability is the contribution the products make towards joint costs.

Example 1

You are the cost accountant of RA & DJ manufacturing company. The company produces from a single raw material four different products RB, RD, RJ and RS. The production director is considering proposals to discontinue certain work at present done on these products. You are requested by the board of directors to submit the following information, on the basis of which a decision could be made:

(a) a profit and loss statement under present conditions;

(b) an assessment of the change in the profit and loss statement, given in answer to (a), if the proposals being considered were adopted;

(c) any recommendations you consider you should put forward arising out of the assessment.

The following data apply:

The cost of the basic raw material was £167,500 and the initial processing costs amounted to a further £320,500. The products are produced simultaneously. Product RJ is produced without further processing. The other three products undergo further processing before being sold. It is the company's policy to apportion the joint cost on a suitable sales value basis.

The output, sales and additional processing costs were as follows:

Product	*Output (units)*	*Sales (£)*	*Additional processing costs (£)*
RB	2,000,000	480,000	100,000
RD	448,625	145,000	80,000
RJ	25,000	20,000	–
RS	45,000	150,000	5,000

The proposal being considered by the production director is to sell the products to other processors immediately after the split-off point. The additional processing costs of products RB, RD and RS would either no longer be incurred or be charged to an alternative use. The prices per unit to be obtained from the other processes would be:

RB	£0.16
RD	£0.20
RJ	£0.80
RS	£2.50

Answer guide

(a) *Profit and loss statement under the present conditions*

Product	Total	RB	RD	RJ	RS
Sales—units	–	2,000,000	448,625	25,000	45,000
Sales—value	£795,000	£480,000	£145,000	£20,000	£150,000
Joint costs (*see* Note)	488,000	304,000	52,000	16,000	116,000
Additional costs	185,000	100,000	80,000	–	5,000
Profit (loss)	£122,000	£76,000	£13,000	£4,000	£29,000

Note: The joint cost is apportioned on the basis of sales value less *further processing costs.*

	Total	RB	RD	RJ	RS
Sales value	£795,000	£480,000	£145,000	£20,000	£150,000
Additional costs	£(185,000)	£(100,000)	£(80,000)	–	£(5,000)
Market value at the split-off point	£610,000	£380,000	£65,000	£20,000	£145,000
Joint cost					
$\frac{£488,000}{£610,000} \times £380,000$	–	£304,000	–	–	–
$\frac{£488,000}{£610,000} \times £65,000$	–	–	£52,000	–	–
$\frac{£488,000}{£610,000} \times £20,000$	–	–	–	£16,000	–
$\frac{£488,000}{£610,000} \times £145,000$	–	–	–	–	£116,000

(b) *Profit and loss statement, products sold at split-off point*

Product	Total	RB	RD	RJ	RS
Sales—units		2,000,000	448,625	25,000	45,000
Selling price per unit		£0.16	£0.20	£0.80	£2.50
Sales value (note 2)	£542,225	£320,000	£89,725	£20,000	£112,500
Joint cost	488,000				
Profit (loss)	£54,225				

Profit under present conditions (a)	£122,000
Profit if the products are sold at the split-off point	54,225
Profit reduced by	£67,775

(c) *Recommendations*
In deciding whether to further process or sell at the split-off point the joint costs are not relevant. The increase in sales value after further processing should be compared with the additional costs incurred, as follows:

Product	Total	RB	RD	RJ	RS
Sales value after further processing	£795,000	£480,000	£145,000	£20,000	£150,000
Sales value at the split-off point	542,225	320,000	89,725	20,000	112,500
Difference	252,775	160,000	55,275	nil	37,500
Further processing costs	185,000	100,000	80,000	nil	5,000
Profit (loss)	£67,775	£60,000	£(24,725)	nil	£32,500

From the above statement it follows that products RB and RS should be further processed and product RD should be sold at the split-off point without further processing.

If this can be done, the position will be as follows:

Product	Total	RB	RD	RJ	RS
Sales value	£739,725	£480,000	£89,725	£20,000	£150,000
Further processing costs	105,000	100,000	nil	nil	5,000
Contribution towards joint costs	634,725	380,000	89,725	20,000	145,000
Joint costs	488,000	–	–	–	–
	£146,725				

5.0 BY-PRODUCTS

These are saleable products *incidentally* produced in addition to the main product, for example:

Industry	*Main product*	*By-products*
Fishing	Raw fish	Fish offal (oil and fertiliser)
Dairy	Butter and cheese	Buttermilk
Soap	Soap	Glycerine
Gas	Gas	Coke, tar and ammonia
Meat packing	Dressed meat	Hides and trimmings, edible fats
Coke	Coke	Ammonia, coal tar, benzene and gas
Flour milling	High-grade flour	Low-grade flour, milk feed, bran

5.1 Classification

By-products are sometimes classified into two groups:

(a) by-products requiring no further processing and sold in their original form;

(b) by-products requiring further processing after separation from the main product.

5.2 Methods of accounting for by-products

Accounting for by-products may be by non-cost methods (**5.3**) or by cost methods (**5.4**).

5.3 Non-cost methods

The non-cost methods make no attempt to apportion the joint cost to by-products. Alternatives are:

(a) by-product income treated as other income or additional income;

(b) by-product income deducted from the cost of goods sold;

(c) by-product income deducted from the cost of production;

(d) net realisable value deducted from cost of production.

Each of these four methods is shown in the following illustration.

Illustration 6

	Main product	*By-product*
Opening stock (units)	nil	nil
Production (units)	50,000	10,000
Closing stock (units)	5,000	2,000
Cost of production	£800,000	–
Cost of sales	£720,000	–
Sales value per unit	£30	£2.50
Further processing cost per unit	–	£0.50

INCOME FROM BY-PRODUCT SALES

Gross sales value (8,000 at £2.50)	20,000
Less: Further processing costs (8,000 at £0.50)	(4,000)
Net income from by-product sales	£16,000

NET REALISABLE VALUE

Gross sales value (10,000 at £2.50)	25,000
Less: Further processing cost (10,000 at £0.50)	5,000
Net realisable value	£20,000

(a) *By-product income as other or additional income*

Sales—main product (45,000 at £30)			£1,350,000
	Units	*£*	
Opening stock	nil	nil	
Production	50,000	800,000	
Closing stock	5,000	80,000	
Cost of sales	45,000	720,000	720,000
Gross profit			£630,000
Other income/additional income			
Revenue from sales of by-product			16,000
Profit			£646,000

(b) *By-product income deducted from the cost of goods sold*

Sales—main product (45,000 at £30)			£1,350,000
	Units	£	
Opening stock	nil	nil	
Production	50,000	800,000	
Closing stock	5,000	80,000	
Cost of goods sold	45,000	720,000	
Less: Sales value of by-product		(16,000)	704,000
Gross profit			£646,000

(c) *By-product income deducted from the cost of production*

Sales—main product (45,000 at £30)			£1,350,000
	Units	£	
Opening stock	nil	nil	
Production	50,000	800,000	
Less: Sales value of by-product	–	16,000	
	50,000	784,000	
Closing stock $\frac{£784,000}{£50,000} \times 5,000$	(5,000)	(78,400)	
Cost of goods sold	£45,000	£705,600	£705,600
Profit			£644,400

(d) *Net realisable value deducted from cost of production*

Sales—main product (45,000 at £30)			£1,350,000
	Units	£	
Opening stock	nil	nil	
Production	50,000	800,000	
Net realisable value of by-product (*see* Note 2)	–	20,000	
	50,000	780,000	
Closing stock $\frac{£780,000}{£50,000} \times 5,000$	(5,000)	(78,000)	
Cost of sales	£45,000	£702,000	£702,000
Profit			£648,000

The best method conceptually is (d), where the expected sales value less costs of disposal is deducted from the total cost of production of the main product. This method is identical to the accounting treatment of scrap.

Since the sales values of by-products are not significant, no harm is done by using any of the non-cost methods of valuation.

5.4 Cost methods

(a) Replacement cost method (opportunity cost method)
When the by-products resulting from the manufacturing process are utilised by the company for some other purpose, the cost which would have been incurred had the by-product been purchased from sources outside is treated as the cost of the by-product and is credited to the main product. For example, this method is common in the cotton spinning industry. The cotton waste resulting in the manufacture of fine yarn is utilised in the cotton mill for manufacturing lower quality yarn. The cost of fine yarn is reduced by the purchasing price of cotton waste produced.

(b) Standard cost method
A predetermined price is used to cost by-products. The cost of by-products so determined is credited to the main product.

Illustration 6—Joint products/by-products
M Ltd, a manufacturing company, makes two products, MD and NG, by processing materials in department 1. Product MD is processed further in department 2 and product NG in department 3.

For a given period, the following transactions are recorded:

	Department 1	*Department 2*	*Department 3*
Materials issued (lb)	200,000	–	–
Cost of materials	£200,000		
Conversion cost	£100,000		
Output: product MD	150,000		
product NG	50,000		
Transferred to department 2		150,000	
Transferred to department 3			50,000
Further processing costs:			
Materials	–	£20,000	£5,000
Labour	–	£40,000	£10,000
Overhead	–	£40,000	£10,000

Product MD sells for £6.00 per pound.
Product NG sells for £2.00 per pound.

You are required to:

(a) Prepare a statement assuming that products MD and NG are joint products and that 50,000 units of MD and 5,000 of NG were fully completed and on hand at the end of the period.

(b) Prepare a statement assuming that product NG was to be treated as a by-product with the net realisable value credited to the main product MD (cost Method 3: Reverse Cost/Market Value Method), with a gross profit of 20 per cent on MD.

Suggested answer

INCOME STATEMENT (1)

Product	Total	MD	NG
Sales (lb) (1)	–	100,000	45,000
Selling price per lb	–	£6.00	£2.00
Sales value	£690,000	£600,000	£90,000
Joint costs—production (dept 1) (Note 1)	300,000	274,286	25,714
Further processing cost	125,000	100,000	25,000
Total cost of production	425,000	374,286	50,714
Less: Stock carried forward (Note 2)	(129,832)	(124,760)	(5,072)
Cost of goods sold (2)	295,168	249,526	45,642
Gross profit (1 – 2)	£394,832	£350,474	£44,358

NOTE 1 APPORTIONMENT OF JOINT COST

Product	*Output (lb)*	*Price per lb*	*Total market value*	*Further processing costs*	*Hypothetical market value*
MD	150,000	£6	£900,000	£100,000	£800,000
NG	50,000	£2	£100,000	£25,000	£75,000

The joint cost of £300,000 is apportioned on the basis of the hypothetical market value of products produced:

$$\text{Product MD} \quad \frac{£300,000}{£875,000} \times £800,000 = \underline{\underline{£274,286}}.$$

$$\text{Product NG} \quad \frac{£300,000}{£875,000} \times £75,000 = \underline{\underline{£25,714}}.$$

NOTE 2 CLOSING STOCK VALUATION

Product	MD	NG
Total cost of production	£374,286	£50,714
Units produced (lb)	150,000	50,000
Cost per unit	£2.4952	£1.0143
Closing stock (lb)	50,000	5,000
Value of stock carried forward	£124,760	£5,072

INCOME STATEMENT (2)

	Main product	*By-product*
Joint cost: department 1	£300,000	–
Further processing costs: department 2	100,000	–
Total production costs	400,000	
Sales value—by-product (500,000 × £2.00)	–	£100,000
Less: Estimated gross profit (20 per cent)		(20,000)
		80,000
Less: Cost after the split-off point: department 3		(25,000)
		55,000
Value of by-product to be credited to the main product	(55,000)	–
Net cost of production	345,000	–
Closing stock 50,000 lb $\frac{£345,000}{£150,000} \times 50,000$	(115,000)	–
Cost of goods sold	230,000	–
Sales value	600,000	–
Gross profit	£370,000	–

Example 2

P Ltd pıoduces two joint products MD and KG through processing two materials M and K. In addition, a by-product RD is produced. Of the combined weight of input of M and K, 55 per cent becomes MD and 30 per cent KG; 10 per cent RD and 5 per cent lost.

The waste has no selling value. The net realisable value of RD is regarded as a reduction in the costs of MD and KG and is treated in the accounts accordingly.

It is estimated that to finish RD after the initial processing costs £0.20 per lb.

After the initial processing MD is transferred to process 2 and KG to process 3. In both processes it is estimated that 5 per cent of input will be lost, with a scrap value of £0.15 per lb.

Costs of initial processing are apportioned to products in proportion to their gross sales values.

From the following information prepare the process accounts. It can be assumed that materials are introduced at the beginning of the process, that opening and closing work in process is 50 per cent complete and that the costs are charged out on a first in first out basis.

		lb	£
Opening work in progress:			
Process 2		100,000	27,000
Process 3		60,000	7,500
Material issues:			
Material M		600,000	60,000
Material K		400,000	90,000
Conversion costs:			
Initial processing			50,000
Process 2			102,550
Process 3			28,000
Closing work in progress:			
Process 2		120,000	
Process 3		40,000	
Selling prices:			
Main product	MD = £2.00		
Main product	KG = £1.50		
By-product	RD = £0.50		

Answer guide

Initial processing department

Input (lb)		*Amount (£)*	*Output (lb)*		*Amount (£)*
–	Opening work in progress	–	50,000	Normal loss: 5% of input £0.15	7,500
600,000	Material M	60,000	550,000	Transferred to process 2: 55% (Note 2)	115,323
400,000	Material K	90,000	300,000	Transferred to process 3: 30% (Note 2)	47,177
–	Conversion costs	50,000	100,000	By-product RD (Note 1)	30,000
			–	Closing work in progress	–
1,000,000		200,000	1,000,000		200,000

NOTE 1 NET REALISABLE VALUE OF BY-PRODUCT

Gross sales value (100,000 lb at £0.50)	£50,000
Less: Further additional costs incurred (100,000 lb at £0.20)	20,000
Net realisable value of by-product	£30,000

NOTE 2 INITIAL PROCESSING COST APPORTIONMENT ON THE BASIS OF GROSS SALES VALUES

Initial processing cost	£200,000
Less: Sales value of normal scrap	(7,500)
Less: Net realisable value of by-product produced (Note 1)	(30,000)
Joint cost	£162,500

Product	*Output (lb)*	*Selling price per lb*	*Sales value*	*Joint costs*
MD	550,000	£2.00	£1,100,000	£115,323
KG	300,000	£1.50	£450,000	£47,177
			£1,550,000	£162,500

Process 2

Input (lb)		*Amount (£)*	*Output (lb)*		*Amount (£)*
			27,500	Normal loss (5% at £0.15)	4,125
100,000	Work in progress b/f	27,000	100,000	Work in progress completed (Note 3)	37,005
550,000	Transferred from initial processing	115,323	402,500	Input completed	166,200
–	Conversion costs	102,550	–	Abnormal loss	–
–	Abnormal gain	–	120,000	Work in progress c/f	37,543
650,000		244,873	650,000		244,873

NOTE 3 WORK IN PROGRESS B/F

Cost of work in progress b/f	£27,000
Add: Cost incurred during period	10,005
	£37,005

Process 2: Statement of production

Reconciliation			*Transferred in cost*	*Conversion cost*
In (lb)	*Out (lb)*		*(lb)*	*(lb)*
	27,500	Normal loss	–	–
100,000	100,000	Work in progress b/f	–	50,000
550,000	402,500	Input completed	402,500	402,500
–	–	Abnormal loss	–	–
	120,000	Work in progress c/f	120,000	60,000
650,000	650,000		522,500	512,500

Statement of cost

	Total	*Transferred in cost*	*Conversion cost*
Cost b/f opening work in progress (*Note*—FIFO)	–	–	–
Cost incurred	£217,873	£115,323	£102,550
Less: Sales value of scrap	(4,125)	(4,125)	–
	£213,748	£111,198	£102,550

Cost per equivalent unit

	Total	*Transferred in cost*	*Conversion cost*
Cost incurred	£213,748	£111,198	£102,550
Equivalent units produced	–	522,500	512,500
Cost per equivalent unit	£0.4129	£0.2128	£0.2001

Statement of evaluation

	Total	*Transferred in cost*	*Conversion cost*
	£	£	£
Work in progress b/f			
50,000 at £0.2001	10,005	–	10,005
Input completed during the period	166,200		
402,500 at £0.2128		85,660	
402,500 at £0.2001			80,540
Abnormal loss	–	–	–
Work in progress c/f	37,543		
120,000 at £0.2128		25,538	
60,000 at £0.2001			12,005
	£213,748	£111,198	£102,550

Process 3

Input (lb)		*Amount (£)*	*Output (lb)*		*Amount (£)*
60,000	Work in progress b/f	7,500	15,000	Normal loss 5% (150,000 at £0.15)	2,250
300,000	Transferred from initial processing	47,117	60,000	Work in progress b/f (*see* Note 4)	10,347
	Conversion cost	28,000	245,000	Input completed	61,825
			–	Abnormal loss	–
			40,000	Work in progress c/f	8,195
360,000		82,617	360,000		82,617

NOTE 4 WORK IN PROGRESS BROUGHT FORWARD

Cost of work in progress b/f	£7,500
Add: Cost incurred during the period	2,847
	£10,347

Process 3: Statement of production

Reconciliation				
Input (lb)	*Output (lb)*		*Transferred in cost*	*Conversion cost*
60,000	60,000	Work in progress b/f	–	30,000
	15,000	Normal loss	–	–
300,000	245,000	Input during the current period completed	245,000	245,000
	–	Abnormal loss	–	–
	40,000	Work in progress c/f	40,000	20,000
360,000	360,000		285,000	295,000

Statement of cost

	Total	*Transferred in cost*	*Conversion cost*
Cost b/f (Work in progress b/f) (Note: FIFO)	–	–	–
Cost incurred during the period	£75,117	£47,117	£28,000
Less sales value of normal scrap (15,000 at £0.15)	(2,250)	(2,250)	–
	£72,867	£44,867	£28,000

Cost per equivalent unit

	Total	*Transferred in cost*	*Conversion cost*
Cost incurred	£72,867	£44,867	£28,000
Equivalent units produced	–	285,000	295,000
Cost per equivalent unit	£0.2523	£0.1574	£0.0949

Statement of evaluation

	Total	*Transferred in cost*	*Conversion cost*
Work in progress b/f			
30,000 at £0.0949	£2,847	–	£2,847
Input completed	61,825		
245,000 at £0.1574		£38,570	
245,000 at £0.0949			23,255
Abnormal loss	–	–	–
Work in progress c/f	8,195		
40,000 at £0.1574		6,297	
20,000 at £0.0949			1,898
	£72,862	£44,867	£28,000

CHAPTER THIRTEEN

Techniques and Systems of Product Costing and Income Determination

1.0 TECHNIQUES OF PRODUCT COSTING AND INCOME DETERMINATION

1.1 Classification of techniques of product costing

Generally speaking there are two main product costing techniques:

(a) absorption costing,

(b) marginal costing (*see* Fig. 11).

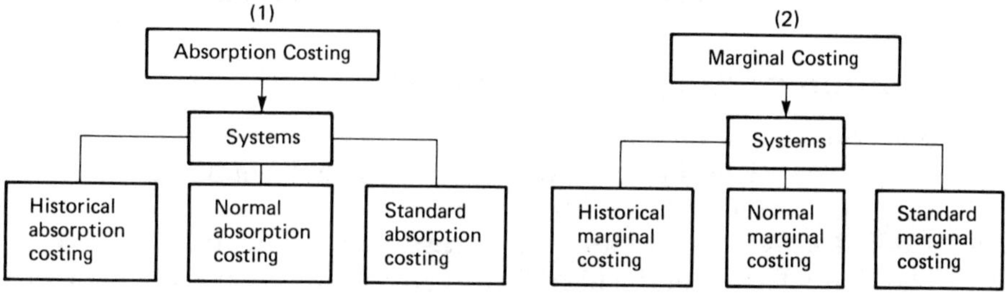

Fig. 11. *Product costing techniques.*

The essential differences between the two techniques are shown in Figs 12 and 13, which give the cost flow with absorption and marginal costing. Note how in absorption costing the fixed production overhead is taken to product cost and included in stock. In marginal costing all fixed production overhead is written off as a period cost.

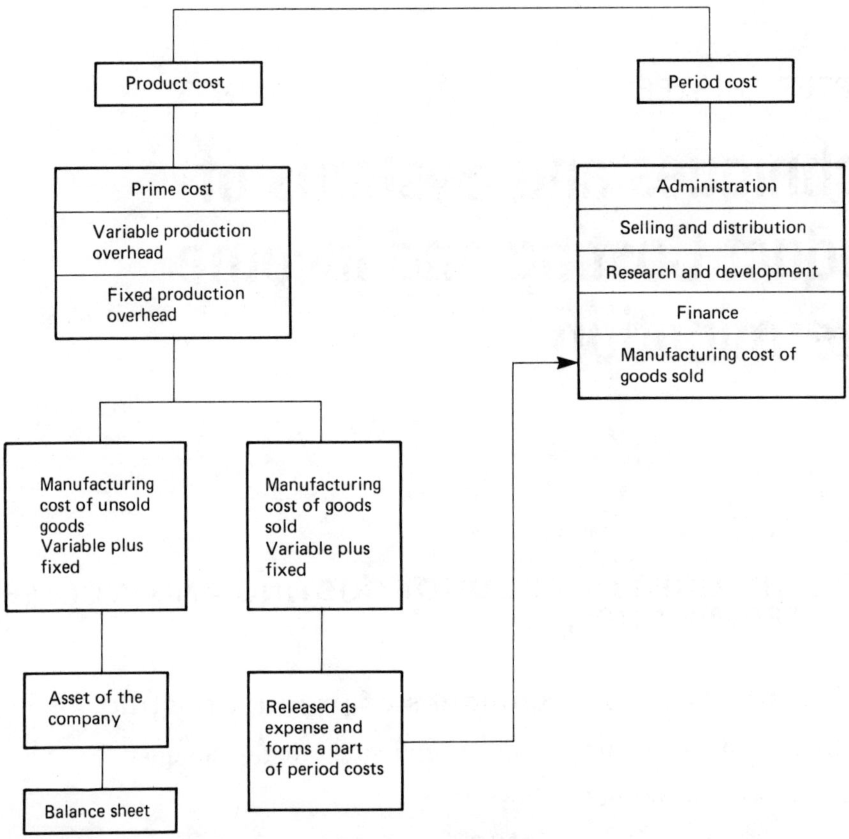

Fig. 12. *Cost flow with absorption costing.*

2.0 COST FLOW WITH ABSORPTION COSTING

2.1 Absorption costing—product cost

All production costs are treated as product costs. These expenses are held as assets of the company until sold. They become expenses only when the unit of product, to which the production costs are linked, is sold.

The most noteworthy aspect of absorption costing is the treatment of fixed factory overhead. The characteristic of the fixed factory overhead is that it does not vary with levels of output but is rather a period cost. Examples are rent, depreciation, insurance. The one thing these costs have in common is that they are joint costs and are therefore extremely difficult to trace to the units of product. For identifying manufacturing overhead with products a predetermined overhead expenditure is related to a level of activity and an absorption rate is calculated by dividing the predetermined expenditure by the expected level of activity. This rate is referred to as the overhead absorption rate and is used to apply overhead to cost units as they are produced.

2.2 Absorption costing—period cost

Selling and distribution, administration, research and development and financial costs are relatively independent of the production function. These costs are not treated as product costs. It is an accounting convention that these costs are written off in the period.

Production cost of goods sold is also treated as a period cost because it does not form part of the assets of the company any more.

Illustration 1

Joslin & Rod Manufacturing Company makes a single product. During the first quarter of year 4, 250,000 units were produced. The cost of this production was:

Materials	£150,000
Labour	50,000
Variable factory overhead	50,000
Fixed factory overhead	100,000
Variable selling, administration and other	50,000
Fixed selling, administration and other	100,000

During the first quarter of year 4 200,000 units of product were sold at £5 per unit.

PRODUCT COST (ALL PRODUCTION COSTS)

Materials	£150,000
Labour	50,000
Variable factory overhead	50,000
Fixed factory overhead	100,000
If unsold—an asset of the company	£350,000

PERIOD COST

(a) Manufacturing cost of goods sold

$$\frac{£350{,}000}{250{,}000 \text{ units}} \times 200{,}000 \text{ units} = £280{,}000$$

(b) Non-production cost (variable and fixed) = £150,000

£430,000

ASSET OF THE COMPANY—CLOSING STOCK

Manufacturing cost of products in stock	
Cost of goods manufactured	£350,000
Less: Manufacturing cost of goods sold	280,000
Closing stock	£70,000

CLOSING STOCK REPRESENTS

Direct materials	£30,000
Direct labour	10,000
Variable factory overhead	10,000
Fixed factory overhead	20,000
	£70,000

Fixed production costs which are incurred in respect of a definite period of time are linked to products and are released when the product is sold. Unsold units in addition to £50,000 of variable costs which vary with production are charged with £20,000 of fixed costs to be carried forward to a future period. The central issue is the timing for the release of the fixed manufacturing expenses.

3.0 COST FLOW WITH MARGINAL COSTING

See Fig. 13.

3.1 Marginal costing—product cost

Marginal costing assigns only the variable production costs to the product. It defines the product cost as the *total variable costs* to produce the product.

3.2 Marginal costing—period cost

All non-production costs are treated as period costs:

(a) variable manufacturing cost of goods sold;

(b) fixed manufacturing costs are not treated as product costs;

(c) selling, distribution, administration, research and development and financial costs.

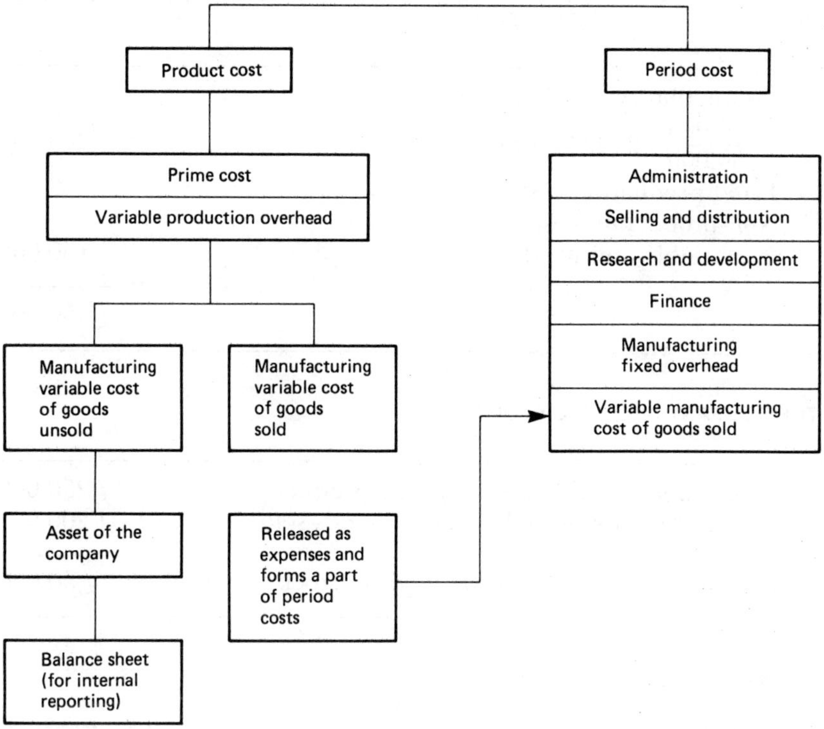

Fig. 13. *Cost flow with marginal costing.*

Illustration 2

The given data are as in Illustration 1.

PRODUCT COST

Materials	£150,000
Labour	50,000
Variable overhead	50,000
Variable cost of production if unsold— an asset of the company	£250,000

PERIOD COST

(a)	Production *variable* cost of goods sold: $\frac{£250,000}{£250,000} \times 200,000$ units	= £200,000
(b)	Fixed production costs	= 100,000
(c)	Non-production costs (variable and fixed)	= 150,000
		£450,000

ASSET OF THE COMPANY—CLOSING STOCK

Production variable cost of goods produced	£250,000
Less: Production variable cost of goods sold	£200,000
Production variable cost of goods in stock	£50,000

CLOSING STOCK REPRESENTS

Materials	£30,000
Labour	10,000
Variable production overhead	10,000
	£50,000

4.0 FUNDAMENTAL DIFFERENCES BETWEEN ABSORPTION AND MARGINAL COSTING

There are fundamental differences between absorption and marginal costing as techniques of product costing and income determination, as follows.

4.1 Cost timing

What is the *proper time* to treat manufacturing fixed costs as expenses:

(a) at the time of incurrence (marginal), or

(b) at the time the units to which they are allocated are sold (absorption)?

4.2 Cost classification

The absorption costing approach to product costing and income determination follows a *functional* cost classification. Costs are seldom classified according to their variability, although such a classification is possible. Hence an absorption costing statement of income would have the following layout. Marginal costing approach to product costing and income determination classifies costs according to their variability.

4.3 Fundamental differences—comprehensive illustrations

Illustration 3

ICMA Ltd produces a single product which is bottled and placed in cases. The normal level of operations, on which the production fixed overhead is based, is 60,000 cases per month.

Data for the last three months were as follows:

Month	1	2	3
Production (units)	70,000	50,000	60,000
Sales (units)	60,000	50,000	65,000
Per case:			
Selling price		£50	
Production cost:			
direct materials		5	
direct labour		10	
variable overhead		5	

Fixed production overhead: budgeted: £180,000 per month
actual: £175,000 per month

Actual selling and administration overhead (per month):
fixed £655,000 and
variable 10 per cent of sales value.

Required:

(a) Prepare profit and loss statements for the three months based on a system of:

(i) absorption costing,

(ii) marginal costing.

(b) Reconcile and comment on the difference in the profit figures you report for (i) and (ii) in (a).

Suggested answer
(a) (i) *Profit and loss statement—normal absorption costing*

Period/month			One	Two	Three
Opening stock (units)			Nil	10,000	10,000
Production (units)			70,000	50,000	60,000
Closing stock (units)			(10,000)	(10,000)	(5,000)
Sales (units)			60,000	50,000	65,000
			£000	*£000*	*£000*
Sales at £50 per unit		(1)	3,000	2,500	3,250
Opening stock (Note 1)	at £23 per unit		nil	230	230
Production	at £23 per unit		1,610	1,150	1,380
Closing stock	at £23 per unit		(230)	(230)	(115)
Manufacturing cost of goods sold		(2)	1,380	1,150	1,495
Trading profit (1 − 2)		(3)	1,620	1,350	1,755
(Under-)/over-absorption of fixed production overhead (Note 2)		(4)	35	(25)	5
Gross profit (3 +/− 4)		(5)	1,655	1,325	1,760
Variable selling (10% of sales)		(6)	300	250	325
Fixed selling and administration		(7)	655	655	655
Net profit/(loss) (5 − 6 + 7)		(8)	700	420	780

(ii) *Profit and loss statement—normal marginal costing*

Period/month			One	Two	Three
Opening stock (units)			nil	10,000	10,000
Production (units)			70,000	50,000	60,000
Closing stock (units)			(10,000)	(10,000)	(5,000)
Sales (units)			60,000	50,000	65,000
			£000	*£000*	*£000*
Sales		(1)	3,000	2,500	3,250
Opening stock (Note 1)	at £20 per unit		nil	200	200
Production	at £20 per unit		1,400	1,000	1,200
Closing stock	at £20 per unit		(200)	(200)	(100)
Variable production cost of sales		(2)	1,200	1,000	1,300

Period/month		One	Two	Three
Gross contribution (1 − 2)	(3)	1,800	1,500	1,950
Non-production variable costs (10% of sales)	(4)	300	250	325
Contribution towards fixed costs (3 − 4)	(5)	1,500	1,250	1,625
Fixed costs:				
Production	(6)	175	175	175
Administration, selling and distribution	(7)	655	655	655
Net profit (loss) (5 − 6 + 7)	(8)	670	420	795

NOTE 1 COST PER UNIT FOR STOCK VALUATION PURPOSES UNDER NORMAL COSTING

	Absorption	*Marginal*
Direct materials	£5	£5
Direct labour	10	10
Variable overhead	5	5
Fixed overhead*	3	–
	£23	£20

*Predetermined fixed production overhead absorption rate under normal absorption costing:

$$\frac{\text{Budgeted overhead}}{\text{Budgeted output}} = \frac{£180,000}{60,000} = £3.00 \text{ per unit.}$$

NOTE 2 OVER-/UNDER-ABSORBED FIXED OVERHEAD

Period/month	*Actual*	*Absorbed*	*Over-/(under)-absorbed*
One	175,000	70,000 × £3 = £210,000	35,000
Two	175,000	50,000 × £3 = £150,000	(25,000)
Three	175,000	60,000 × £3 = £180,000	5,000

(b) *Comments on the results shown by the two methods*

(i) *Production exceeds sales (period 1)*

Where production is greater than sales, absorption costing gives a net profit greater than marginal costing (period 1). This is because some of the manufacturing fixed overhead remains in stock under absorption costing. Fixed manufacturing expenses under marginal costing are treated as period costs.

	Absorption (£000)	*Marginal (£000)*	*Difference (£000)*
Opening stock	nil	nil	nil
Closing stock:			
10,000 × £23	230		
10,000 × £20		200	30
Difference			30

(ii) *Sales equal production (period 2)*
Where sales equal production, both techniques of production costing and income determination yield the same profit (period 2).

	Absorption (£000)	*Marginal (£000)*	*Difference (£000)*
Opening stock:			
10,000 × £23	230		
10,000 × £20		200	(30)
Closing stock:			
10,000 × £23	230		
10,000 × £20		(200)	(30)
Difference			nil

(iii) *Sales exceed production (period 3)*
When sales exceed production, marginal costing net profits are greater than absorption costing (period 3).

	Absorption (£000)	*Marginal (£000)*	*Difference (£000)*
Opening stock:			
10,000 × £23	230		
10,000 × £20		200	(30)
Closing stock:			
5,000 × £23	115		
5,000 × £20		100	15
Difference			(15)

Absorption costing matches fixed costs included in stock brought forward from the previous period plus the current period's manufacturing costs against sales, whereas marginal costing matches only current manufacturing fixed costs against sales.
(iv) Under absorption costing fixed production costs are identified with products, to be released when the products are sold. Under marginal costing fixed production costs are released in the period and are not applied to products.

(v) *Stock valuation*
Absorption costing—Variable plus fixed cost of production = £23 per unit.
Marginal costing—Variable cost of production = £20 per unit.

(vi) Where production fluctuates and sales remain constant, marginal costing gives a constant profit because net profit is not affected by stock changes. Absorption costing under the same circumstances gives a fluctuating net profit.

Illustration 4

The given data are as in Illustration 3.
You are required to:

(a) Prepare profit and loss statements for the three months based on a system of:

(i) absorption costing,
(ii) marginal costing.

(b) Reconcile profit figures you report for (i) and (ii) in (a).

Note 1 Unit cost for stock valuation purposes under historical product costing:

Period/month	One	Two	Three
Fixed overhead (actual)	£175,000	£175,000	£175,000
Production (actual)	70,000	50,000	60,000
Per unit	£2.50	£3.50	£2.9166
Variable cost per unit	£20.00	£20.00	£20.00
Cost per unit	£22.50	£23.50	£22.9166

Note 2 Production fixed overhead

Period/month	*Actual*	*Absorbed*	*Over/under*
One	£175,000	70,000 × £2.50 = £175,000	nil
Two	£175,000	50,000 × £3.50 = £175,000	nil
Three	£175,000	60,000 × £2.9166 = £175,000	nil

Suggested answer

(a) (i) *Profit and loss statement—historical absorption costing*

Period/month					One	Two	Three
Opening stock (units)					nil	10,000	10,000
Production (units)					70,000	50,000	60,000
Closing stock (units)					(10,000)	(10,000)	(5,000)
Sales (units)					60,000	50,000	65,000
					£000	*£000*	*£000*
Sales				(1)	3,000	2,500	3,250
		Period					
	1	2	3				
Opening stock (Note 1)	–	£22.50	£23.50		nil	225	235
Production	£22.50	£23.50	£22.9166		1,575	1,175	1,375
Closing stock	£22.50	£23.50	£22.9166		(225)	(235)	(115)
Production cost of sales				(2)	1,350	1,165	1,495
Over-/(under-)absorption (Note 2)				(3)	nil	nil	nil
Gross profit (1 − 2)				(4)	1,650	1,335	1,755
Variable selling				(5)	300	250	325
Fixed administration and selling				(6)	655	655	655
Profit (loss) (4 − (5 + 6))				(7)	695	430	775

(ii) *Profit and loss statement—historical marginal costing*

Period	One	Two	Three
Opening stock (units)	nil	10,000	10,000
Production (units)	70,000	50,000	60,000
Closing stock (units)	(10,000)	(10,000)	(5,000)
Sales (units)	60,000	50,000	65,000

Period		One	Two	Three
		£000	*£000*	*£000*
Sales at £50 per unit	(1)	3,000	2,500	3,250
Opening stock at £20 per unit		nil	200	200
Production at £20 per unit		1,400	1,000	1,200
Closing stock at £20 per unit		(200)	(200)	(100)
Variable production Cost of sales	(2)	1,200	1,000	1,300
Gross contribution (1 − 2)	(3)	1,800	1,500	1,950
Selling variable costs	(4)	300	250	325
Contribution towards fixed costs (3 − 4)	(5)	1,500	1,250	1,625
Fixed costs production		175	175	175
Administration and selling		655	655	655
Profit (loss)		670	420	795

(b) *Reconciliation of net profit*

Period	One	Two	Three
	£000	*£000*	*£000*
Absorption	695	430	775
Marginal	670	420	795
Difference	25	10	(20)
Opening stock	*£000*	*£000*	*£000*
Absorption	nil	10,000 × £22.50 = 225	10,000 × £23.50 = 235
Marginal	nil	10,000 × £20.00 = 200	10,000 × £20.00 = 200
Difference (A)	nil	(25)	(35)
Closing stock			
Absorption	10,000 × £22.50 = 225	10,000 × £23.50 = 235	5,000 × £22.9166 = 115
Marginal	10,000 × £20.00 = 200	10,000 × £20.00 = 200	5,000 × £20.00 = 100
Difference (B)	25	35	15
Net difference (B − A)	£25	£10	£(20)

CHAPTER FOURTEEN

Cost Classification

1.0 INTRODUCTION

Cost classification may be defined as the process of grouping costs according to their common characteristics. There are a number of ways of classifying costs, but they may be classified broadly according to three criteria (Fig. 14):

(a) nature;

(b) function;

(c) behaviour.

The method of classification to be used depends upon the purpose.

2.0 PURPOSES OF CLASSIFYING COSTS

The principal aims of cost classification are:

(a) product costing for stock valuation and income determination;

(b) planning;

(c) control;

(d) decision making.

Classifications may also be required for other purposes. It is the responsibility of the cost accountant to provide information in the form in which it is required by management.

3.0 THREE MAJOR POINTS CONCERNING COST CLASSIFICATION

3.1 Period of time

The period of time selected affects the applicability of the classification. For example, rent payable under a long lease, or under non-cancellable leases of equipment, will be incurred whether the factory or the machine is operated eight hours or sixteen hours a day. It is essential to remember that these costs are alterable. In the long run the cost pattern can be changed, for example by not renewing the lease. In the short run, however, once committed, there is little opportunity to change costs.

3.2 Relevant range

This is the span of activity over which the cost behaviour can reasonably be expected to remain valid. Outside this range the costs must be reassessed.

3.3 Relevance

When is a cost relevant? When is a cost irrelevant? Decision makers are concerned with things they can affect. To make efficient and effective decisions management requires data which directly relate to the alternatives being considered. Historical costs are useful only in predicting future costs. Management also requires relevant expected future costs.

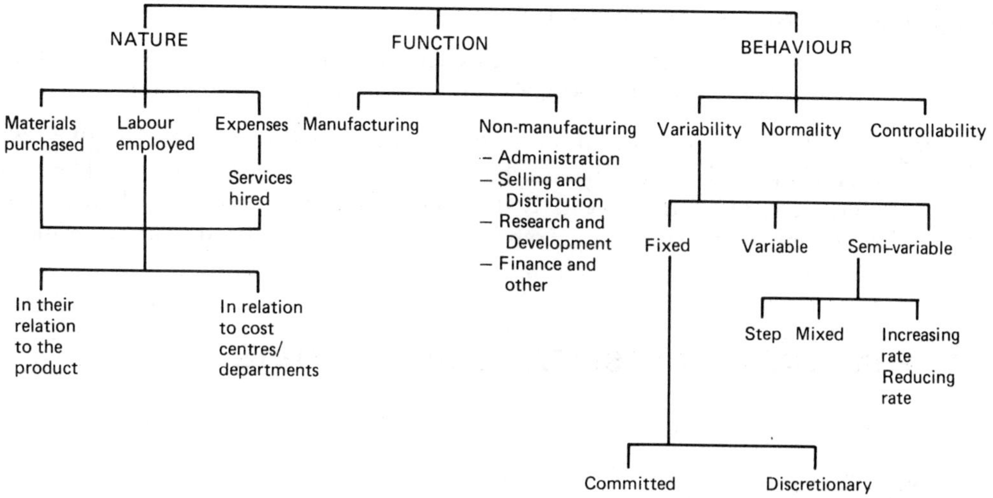

Fig. 14. *Classification of costs (grouping costs according to their common characteristics).*

4.0 NATURAL CLASSIFICATION OF COSTS

The broad groups into which costs may be classified according to their nature are:

(a) materials,

(b) labour,

(c) expenses.

This basic classification may be expanded further as appropriate for a given object.

4.1 Costs in relation to the product

These may be divided as follows:

(a) *Direct costs*. These are costs which can be identified with cost units. They are direct materials, direct labour and direct expenses.

(b) *Indirect costs*. These consist of costs which cannot be identified with cost units—they are the aggregate of indirect materials, indirect labour and indirect expenses.

(c) *Prime cost*. This is the aggregate of direct materials, direct labour and direct expenses (i.e. which can be identified with products).

(d) *Overhead*. Costs which cannot be identified directly with products are termed overheads; i.e. all costs excluding prime costs are overheads.

4.2 Costs in relation to cost centres/departments

On such a basis, costs break down into:

(a) *direct costs:* materials, labour and expenses which can be identified with and allocated to cost centres, salaries and wages, depreciation; and

(b) *indirect costs:* materials, labour and expenses which cannot be identified with cost centres, but which can be apportioned to cost centres. The main characteristic of these costs is that they are joint costs—they benefit more than one cost centre; e.g. rent and rates, depreciation and insurance of buildings, lighting and heating.

5.0 FUNCTIONAL CLASSIFICATION OF COSTS

This classification of costs is made on the basis of the functions they perform:

(a) manufacturing costs;

(b) administration costs;

(c) selling and distribution costs;

(d) research and development costs;

(e) finance and other costs.

A few examples of expenses under each of these headings are given below:

MANUFACTURE	ADMINISTRATION	SELLING AND DISTRIBUTION
Direct material Direct labour Indirect salaries/wages Management salaries Depreciation of plant and machinery Rent, rates, light and heat Repairs and maintenance of plant, machinery and factory buildings Insurance	Salaries and wages Legal expenses Repairs and maintenance of office buildings and equipment Stationery Insurance	Salaries and wages Advertising Debt collection Servicing Containers Packing Transport Warehousing Insurance

RESEARCH AND DEVELOPMENT	FINANCE AND OTHER
Wages and salaries of research and testing staff, materials and facilities used in laboratories and research departments, payments to outside research organisations	Bank charges Long term loans – interest Donations

6.0 BEHAVIOURAL CLASSIFICATION OF COSTS

It is absolutely essential in cost accounting to separate variable and non-variable costs for planning, control and decision making. Some costs are unaffected by variations in the level of activity; they are incurred in relation to time. Others vary with activity, while others still may be partly fixed and partly variable. By and large, it is the level of activity which assists in classifying costs according to their variability.

6.1 Fixed costs

These are defined as costs which tend to be *unaffected* by variations in the volume of output (*see* Fig. 15). Fixed costs are therefore known as period costs.

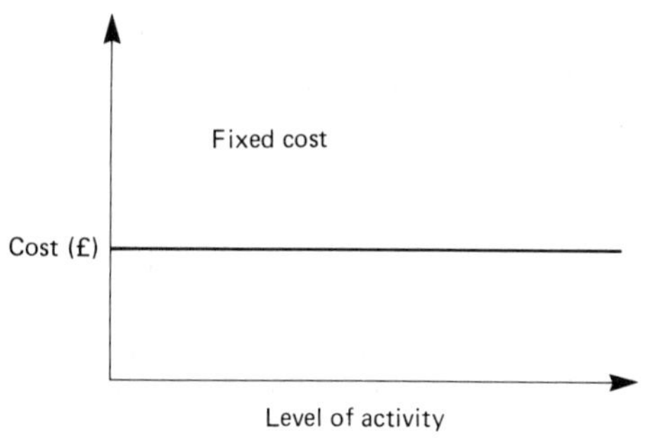

Fig. 15. *Basic graph of fixed cost.*

(a) Characteristics of fixed costs

(i) Costs are fixed only in relation to a start period during which no changes in capacity occur (Fig. 16). Note that the costs in year 3 are greater than in year 1 or 2 because the level of output in year 3 is greater.

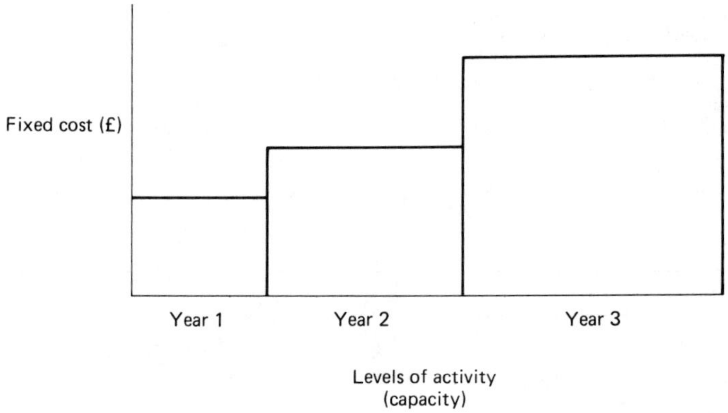

Fig. 16. *Graph of fixed cost for separate periods.*

(ii) Fixed cost per unit varies with level of output.

	Year 1	*Year 2*	*Year 3*
Fixed cost	£50,000	£75,000	£150,000
Volume of output (units)	50,000	80,000	200,000
Fixed cost per unit	£1.00	£0.9375	£0.750

(iii) By and large, fixed costs are uncontrollable—in the sense that they are not influenced by the action of a departmental head. However, somebody in the organisation must be responsible for authorising them.

(b) Types of fixed costs

(i) COMMITTED FIXED COSTS

These are affected essentially by long-run needs, e.g. depreciation of plant and equipment, rent and rates, insurance, salaries of important personnel. These are the standing fixed costs, costs that continue to be incurred when the activity level is zero and cannot be reduced without an adverse influence on the company.

(ii) DISCRETIONARY FIXED COSTS

These may not have any relation to level of activity. Examples are donations, advertising and sales promotion, research and development etc. The characteristics of these are that they could be reduced in difficult times and increased in favourable times. By and large the level of these costs is decided by top management from period to period and they are therefore short-term fixed costs in comparison with committed fixed costs.

(c) Implications of fixed costs for management

Fixed costs therefore have two major implications for management:

(i) planning is important;
(ii) it is important to keep capacity fully utilised.

6.2 Variable costs

These are costs which tend to vary directly with variations in the volume of output. Although the amount of variable cost varies in total, the variable cost per unit tends to remain constant at all levels of activity (Fig. 17).

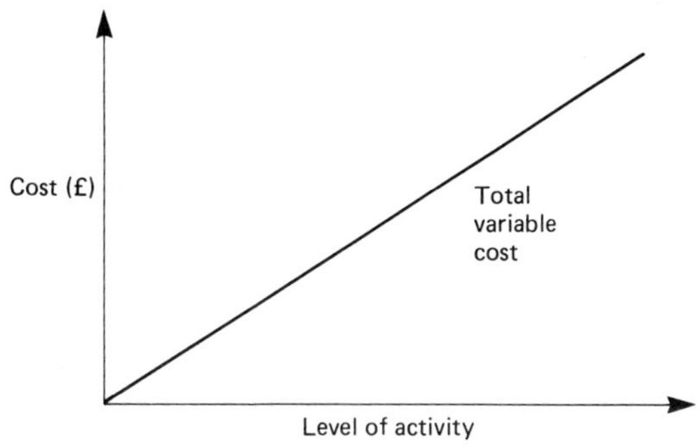

Fig. 17. *Basic graph of variable cost.*

6.3 Semi-variable costs

A cost which is partly fixed and partly variable is described as semi-variable. The cost changes with the level of activity but not in direct proportion.

Semi-variable costs could be grouped into four main classes:

(a) Stairstep cost

The relationship between the cost and the level of output is neither linear nor curvilinear but takes the form of steps (Fig. 18). An example of such a cost is canteen

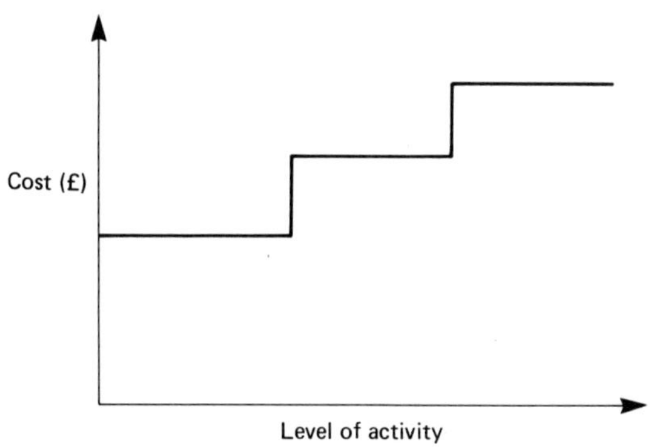

Fig. 18. *Graph of semi-variable cost (stairstep cost).*

cost, where an additional assistant is required when the labour force reaches the 40 per cent level of factory activity and a further two assistants when 70 per cent activity is reached. Supervisors' salaries often tend to behave in the same way. One supervisor for every 10 men; two for 15 men, three for 20 men and a manager for every three supervisors.

(b) Costs which increase at a decreasing rate (Fig. 19)
For example, assume that an outside printing service charges

£20 for the first 1,000 time sheets
£15 for the next 1,000 time sheets
£12 for the next 1,000 time sheets
£10 for the next 1,000 time sheets
£8 for the next 1,000 time sheets.

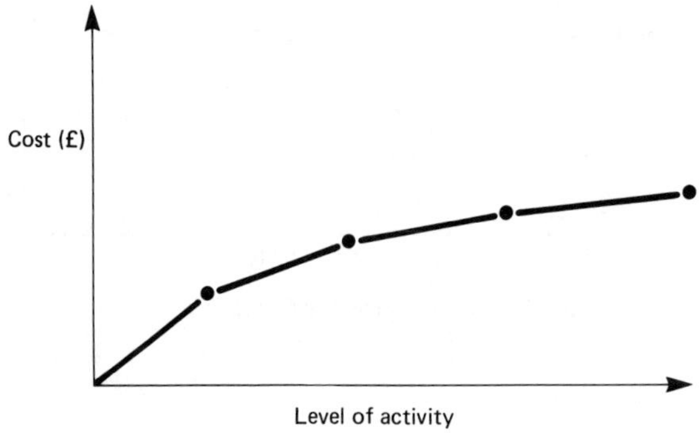

Fig. 19. *Graph of cost increasing at decreasing rate.*

(c) Costs which increase at an increasing rate (Fig. 20)
For example, carriage services per ton:

£20 for the first 20 tons
£35 for the next 20 tons
£50 for the next 20 tons

No extra charge until the service reaches 100 tons, then £55 per ton for all subsequent tonnage.

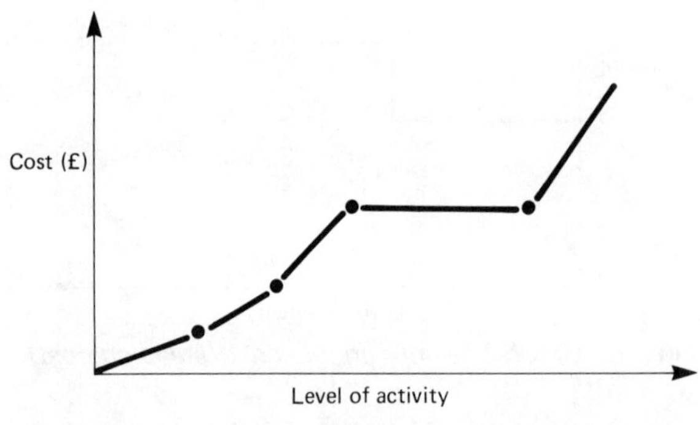

Fig. 20. *Graph of cost increasing at increasing rate.*

(d) Partly fixed, partly variable costs

Salesmen's remuneration is an example of such a cost (Fig. 21). There is a fixed salary up to a certain level of orders received, plus commission at a fixed percentage after that level has been reached. Heat, light and telephone are also semi-variable costs (Fig. 22).

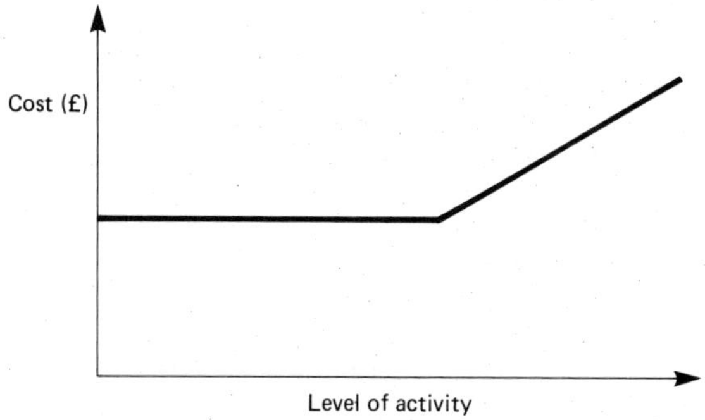

Fig. 21. *Graph of salesmen's remuneration (semi-variable cost).*

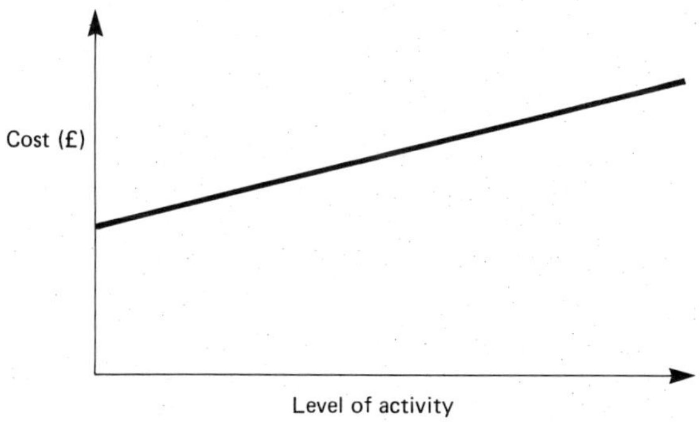

Fig. 22. *Graph of heat, light and telephone costs (semi-variable).*

6.4 Illustration

Work through the following illustration to check your understanding of this chapter so far.

Illustration 1

There are given below for the months of June, July and August, 19_5 the costs and production of a department making a single product. The efficiency of the department has been consistent during the three months.

Year	*Prime cost*	*Production overhead*	*Total cost*	*Production (units)*
19_5				
June	£141,750	£139,860	£281,610	31,500
July	202,500	164,160	366,660	45,000
August	189,000	158,760	347,760	42,000

You are required to:

(a) analyse the above costs according to their behaviour;

(b) use the information provided to compile the cost under the same headings given above for the month of September when 50,000 units were produced.

Suggested answer

(a) (i) *Prime cost*

The prime cost is the variable costs of production. Comparison of the monthly figures given shows a consistent cost per unit of £4.50 which may reasonably be adopted for September:

	June	*July*	*August*
Prime cost	£141,750	£202,500	£189,000
Output (units)	31,500	45,000	42,000
Prime cost per unit	£4.50	£4.50	£4.50

(a) (ii) *Production overhead*

Calculation of the production overhead cost per unit gives us:

Month	*Cost*	*Output*	*Cost per unit*
June	£139,860	£31,500	£4.44
July	164,160	45,000	£3.65

Therefore the overhead costs are partly fixed and partly variable. The fixed and variable costs are separated in the following manner:

	Units		*Cost*
Highest level of activity (July)	45,000		£164,160
Lowest level of activity (June)	31,500		139,860
Difference	13,500		24,300
Variable cost per unit	$\frac{£24,300}{£13,500}$	=	£1.80

The "fixed" element is £83,160, as shown below:

	June	*July*	*August*
Level of activity (units)	31,500	45,000	42,000
Production overhead	£139,860	£164,160	£158,760
Variable cost per unit: £1.80			
∴ Variable cost at these activity levels	£56,700	£81,000	£75,600
Fixed cost	£83,160	£83,160	£83,160

(b) *Costs for September 19_5*

	Output	*Cost per unit*
Units	50,000	–
Prime cost (50,000 × £4.50)	£225,000	£4.50
Variable production overhead (50,000 × £1.80)	90,000	1.80
Variable cost of production	315,000	6.30
Fixed cost of production	83,160	1.66
Total cost of production	£398,160	£7.96

7.0 CLASSIFICATION ACCORDING TO NORMALITY

According to their normality costs could be grouped into two main classes:

7.1 Normal cost

This cost is normally incurred at a given level of output in the condition in which that level of output is normally attained. For example, if overtime is planned and worked, either regularly or during certain periods, then the additional cost incurred is a normal cost of production. But if overtime had to be worked to complete an order by a specified date then the cost of the overtime is not a normal cost.

7.2 Abnormal cost

This is a cost *not* normally incurred at a given level of output in the conditions in which that level of output is normally attained. For example, test marketing of a new product is abnormal in relation to the period in which it is incurred. A company using public transport facilities may have to incur additional costs during a period of strike by the public transport employees. During a bad patch a company may decide to retain its labour force until such time as it recovers. The cost of retaining the extra employees is an abnormal cost.

7.3 Conclusion

Costs, then, are classified either as normal or abnormal in relation to the level of activity attained and the conditions in which that output is usually attained.

8.0 CLASSIFICATION ACCORDING TO CONTROLLABILITY

Costs may be either controllable or non-controllable:

(a) *Controllable cost:* one which is influenced by the action of a given member of an undertaking.

(b) *Non-controllable cost:* one which is not influenced by the action of a given member of an undertaking.

In distinguishing between the two it is necessary to bear four points in mind:

(a) Controllability of a cost is determined only in relation to a *stated* member of an undertaking. Somebody in the organisation must be responsible for every cost. For example, a departmental manager who uses plant facilities may not be able to control rent, rates and insurance of the building; but these may be controllable by the building services manager who may have been assigned the responsibility for choosing building facilities.

(b) When controllability of a cost is referred to, it is used in relation to the incurrence of the cost and not to its use.

(c) Cost must also be related to a period of time. In the long run all costs are controllable. On the other hand, in the short periods very few costs may be controllable.

(d) Usually there are only a few costs which can be made the sole responsibility of one person.

9.0 EXAMPLES

Example 1—Cost classification in relation to the product

The profit and loss account of RB Ltd is shown below for the year 31st December 19_7:

Sales revenue		£270,000
Direct materials	£40,000	
Direct labour	80,000	
Overheads (all fixed)	60,000	180,000
Net profit		£90,000

RB makes three products—Standard, Super and Deluxe. In order to provide more information to management the profit and loss account may be recast in terms of the products, i.e. *a cost and revenue classification in relation to the product*:

	Total	*Standard*	*Super*	*Deluxe*
Sales revenue	£270,000	£70,000	£150,000	£50,000
Direct materials	£40,000	£10,000	£22,000	£8,000
Direct labour	80,000	20,000	40,000	20,000
Overheads	60,000	6,000	30,000	24,000
Profit (loss)	£90,000	£34,000	£58,000	£(2,000)

The income statement provides better information: we see that the Standard and Super make profits while Deluxe makes a loss. Thus we have a guide for action—should we eliminate the Deluxe model?

From the manner in which the data is presented one might agree that by dropping the Deluxe model the company would save £2,000. Should we do so?

Answer guide

A cost classification according to behaviour is helpful in answering this question:

	Total	*Standard*	*Super*	*Deluxe*
Sales revenue	£270,000	£70,000	£150,000	£50,000
Direct materials	40,000	10,000	22,000	8,000
Direct labour	80,000	20,000	40,000	20,000
Variable cost of sales	£120,000	£30,000	£62,000	£28,000
Difference between the sales value and variable cost of sales	150,000	40,000	88,000	22,000
Overheads	60,000			
	£90,000			

If the Deluxe model is eliminated:

	Total	*Standard*	*Super*
Sales revenue	£220,000	£70,000	£150,000
Direct materials	32,000	10,000	22,000
Direct labour	60,000	20,000	40,000
Variable cost of sales	£92,000	£30,000	£62,000
Difference between the sales value and the variable cost of sales	128,000	40,000	88,000
Overhead	60,000		
	£68,000		

To eliminate the Deluxe model would in fact involve a reduction of profit of £22,000 and not a saving of £2,000.

Example 2—Cost behaviour patterns

(This should be attempted before checking the answer.)

State whether the following items (a) to (p) are:

(i) variable costs;
(ii) committed fixed costs;
(iii) discretionary fixed costs;
(iv) mixed costs; or
(v) step costs.

(a) Plant and machinery—straight-line depreciation.
(b) Plant and machinery—depreciation charge based on machine hour basis.
(c) Cost of raw materials consumed.
(d) Advertising costs.
(e) Rent and rates.
(f) Heating and lighting.
(g) Research and development costs.
(h) Salesmen's total compensation, including salaries and commission.
(j) Repair and maintenance costs.
(k) Consultancy fees.
(l) Donations.
(m) Training costs.
(n) Supervisors' salaries. A new supervisor is engaged for every fifteen workers employed.
(p) Electricity bill—a flat charge, plus a variable cost after a certain number of units is consumed.

Suggested answer

(a)	(ii)	(h)	(iv)
(b)	(i)	(j)	(iv)
(c)	(i)	(k)	(iii)
(d)	(iii)	(l)	(iii)
(e)	(ii)	(m)	(iii)
(f)	(iv)	(n)	(v)
(g)	(iii)	(p)	(iv)

Example 3

(a) What are the non-volume factors which cause costs to vary?

(b) What factors must management consider in the year-to-year planning of fixed costs?

Suggested answer

(a) *Non-volume factors*

(i) changes in the product specifications;
(ii) changes in raw materials used;
(iii) changes in the method of manufacture;
(iv) changes in plant and machinery;
(v) changes in working conditions;
(vi) changes in working hours;
(vii) changes in price paid for cost factors;
(viii) changes in management policy towards costs.

(b) *Fixed cost planning*

(i) the prices of cost factors;
(ii) the level of activity planned;
(iii) possible organisational changes;
(iv) possible changes in plant facilities.

Example 4

The graphs in Fig. 23(a) to (k) reflect the pattern of certain production cost items in a manufacturing company in a year. The horizontal axes represent the volume of production or the level of activity, while the vertical axes of the graphs represent the total cost. The zero point is at the intersection of the two axes.

Select the graph that matches the production cost items numbered (i) to (x) below. A graph may be used more than once.

(i) *Depreciation of equipment*—when charged on a straight-line basis.

(ii) *Depreciation of equipment*—where the amount of depreciation charged is based on a machine-hour basis.

(iii) *Cost of raw materials consumed.*

(iv) *Rates on a factory building donated by the local authority*, where the agreement calls for a payment of £50,000 per annum unless 400,000 direct labour hours are worked, in which case no rates need to be paid.

(v) *Rates on a factory building donated by the local authority*, where it has been agreed that a payment of £50,000 must be made, less £50 for each direct labour hour worked in excess of 400,000 direct labour hours, but with a minimum payment of £5,000.

(vi) *Royalty*—£0.50 per unit produced with a maximum charge of £10,000 per annum.

(vii) *Water rate, which is computed as follows:*
First 5,000,000 gallons or less: a flat charge of £1,000.
Next 100,000 gallons: £0.001 per gallon consumed.
Next 100,000 gallons: £0.002 per gallon consumed.
Next 100,000 gallons: £0.003 per gallon consumed.
All subsequent units: £0.004 per gallon consumed.

(viii) *Supervisor cost*—where there is one supervisor for every ten men or less, and one foreman for every three supervisors, and when each man represents 35 hours of production, thus:
Hours under 350, one supervisor;
Hours 351–700, two supervisors;
Hours 701–1,050, three supervisors, plus one foreman
etc.

(ix) *Outside service*
£0.50 for the first 20,000 units.
£0.40 for the next 20,000 units.
£0.30 for all subsequent units.

(x) *Carriage service*
£10 per ton for the first 10,000 tons.
£20 per ton for the next 10,000 tons.
£30 per ton for the next 10,000 tons.

No extra charge until the service reaches 50,000 tons, then £32 per ton for all subsequent tonnage.

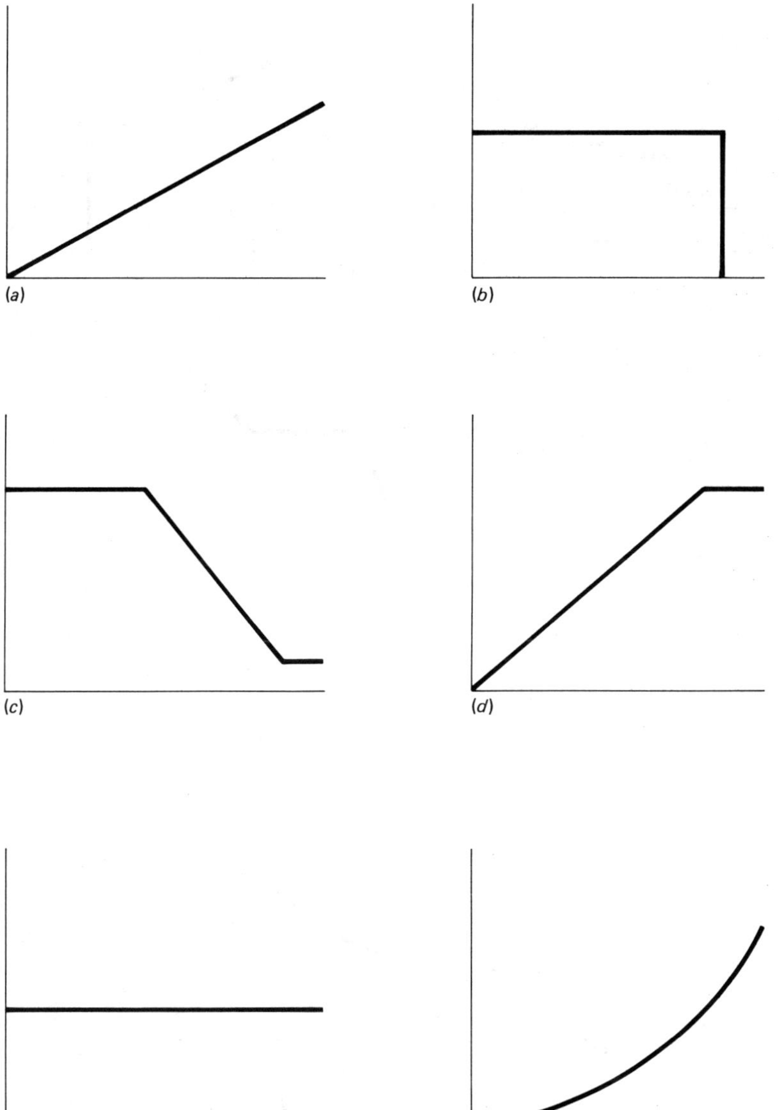

Fig. 23. *Graphs for Example 4.*

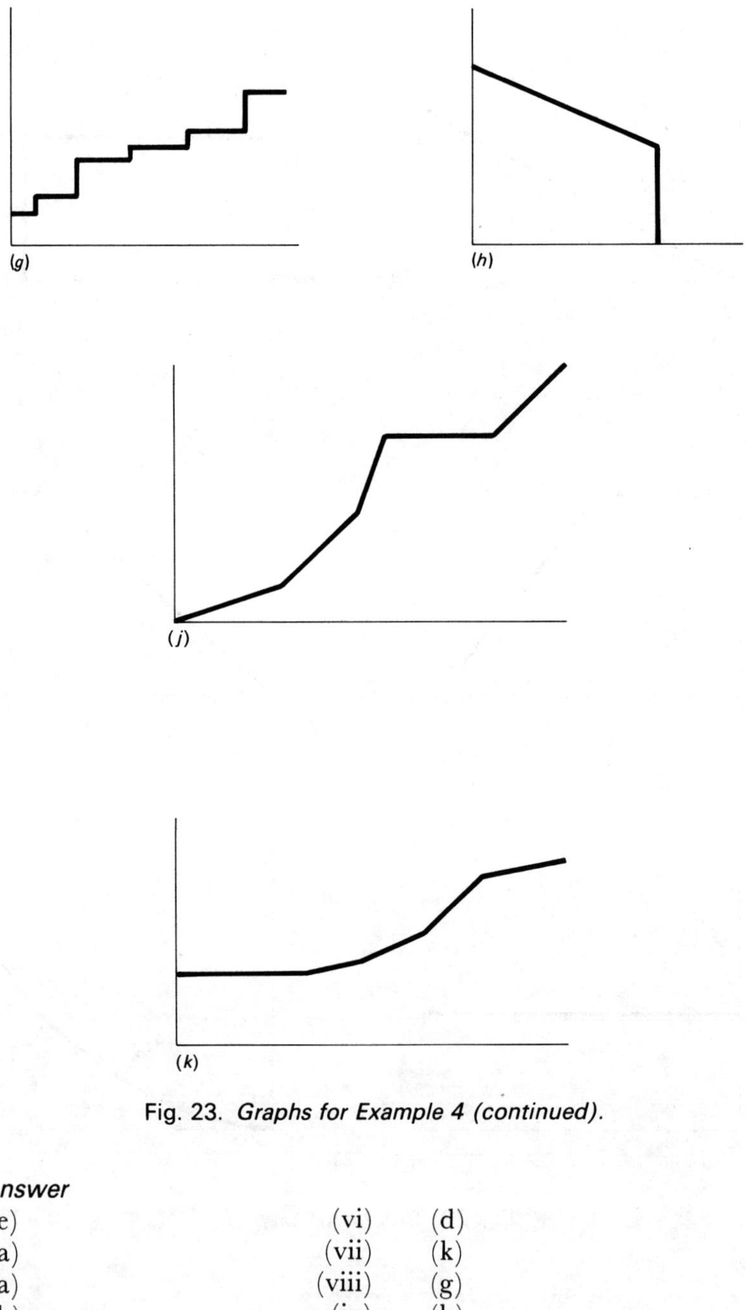

Fig. 23. *Graphs for Example 4 (continued).*

Suggested answer

(i)	(e)	(vi)	(d)
(ii)	(a)	(vii)	(k)
(iii)	(a)	(viii)	(g)
(iv)	(b)	(ix)	(h)
(v)	(c)	(x)	(j).

CHAPTER FIFTEEN

Cost – Volume – Profit Analysis

1.0 PLANNING AND DECISION MAKING

1.1 Planning

Planning is a basic function of management. It is the function by which managers decide:

(a) what goals are to be accomplished;

(b) how they are to be reached.

Planning gives the manager a warning of *possible future crises* and by planning he avoids the need to take sudden decisions.

1.2 The concept of profit and the Golden Rule

Where costs can be classified as fixed and variable, cost prediction becomes extremely easy, as the following illustration shows:

Illustration 1

Fixed costs	
Production	£4,000
Selling and administration	£6,000
Variable costs per unit:	
Production	£10
Selling	£2

Total cost at varying levels of activity can be easily determined:

Level of activity (units)	1,000	4,000	5,000
Variable costs at £12 per unit	£12,000	£48,000	£60,000
Fixed costs (£4,000 + £6,000)	£10,000	£10,000	£10,000
Total cost	£22,000	£58,000	£70,000

It also tells us that by deducting total variable costs from total sales value it gives a *fund* towards fixed costs and profit.

The Golden Rule is: *To maximise profit, you must maximise total contribution.*

Level of activity (units)	1,000	4,000	5,000
Sales value at £30 per unit	£30,000	£120,000	£150,000
Variable production costs at £10 per unit	10,000	40,000	50,000
Gross contribution	20,000	80,000	100,000
Selling variable costs at £2 per unit	2,000	8,000	10,000
Total contribution (*fund*) towards fixed costs	18,000	72,000	90,000
Fixed costs: Production	4,000	4,000	4,000
Selling and administration	6,000	6,000	6,000
Profit (loss)	£8,000	£62,000	£80,000

1.3 Cost–volume–profit (CVP) analysis

The study of the interrelationships of sales, costs and profit is usually called cost–volume–profit analysis (CVP analysis). This approach draws the attention of managers to important problems and leads the way to their solution.

(a) What happens if planned sales are not achieved?

- (i) What will be the impact of different selling prices on net profit?
- (ii) What will be the impact of different sales volumes on net profit?
- (iii) What will be the impact on volume and on profit if prices are changed?

(b) What if costs change?

- (i) What will be the impact of an increase in variable cost on net profit?
- (ii) What will be the impact of an increase in fixed costs on net profit?

2.0 ILLUSTRATIVE PROBLEM

Illustration 2

Using the following assumptions,

sales units	600,000
selling price per unit	£20
marginal cost per unit	£10
fixed costs	£3,000,000
contribution per unit	£10

what will be the impact on profit if the following occur?

(a) Increase in price by 10 per cent; decrease in price by 10 per cent.

(b) Increase in volume by 10 per cent; decrease in volume by 10 per cent.

(c) (i) Increase in price by 10 per cent; decrease in volume by 10 per cent.

(ii) Decrease in price by 10 per cent; increase in volume by 10 per cent.

(d) Variable costs increase by 10 per cent; variable costs decrease by 10 per cent.

(e) Fixed costs increase by 10 per cent; fixed costs decrease by 10 per cent.

(f) (i) Selling price increase 10 per cent
Volume decrease 10 per cent
Variable cost increase 10 per cent
Fixed cost increase 10 per cent

(ii) Selling price decrease 10 per cent
Volume increase 10 per cent
Variable cost decrease 10 per cent
Fixed cost decrease 10 per cent.

Suggested answer

(a) *Impact of price changes on net profit*

	Price increase	*Normal*	*Price decrease*
Change in price	10%	Normal	10%
Units	600,000	600,000	600,000
Contribution per unit	£12	£10	£8
Fund	£7,200,000	£6,000,000	£4,800,000
Fixed cost	3,000,000	3,000,000	3,000,000
Profit	£4,200,000	£3,000,000	£1,800,000

Contribution per unit:

Contribution per unit, normal	£10	£10
Due to price increase 10 per cent	2	
Due to price decrease		(2)
	£12	£8

The illustration shows that with a 10 per cent increase in price, profit increases by 40 per cent and a 10 per cent decrease in price results in a fall in profit by 40 per cent.

(b) *Impact of volume changes on net profit*

	Volume increase 10%	*Normal*	*Volume decrease 10%*
Units	660,000	600,000	540,000
Contribution per unit	£10	£10	£10
Fund	£6,600,000	£6,000,000	£5,400,000
Fixed cost	£3,000,000	£3,000,000	£3,000,000
Profit	£3,600,000	£3,000,000	£2,400,000

Contribution per unit remains constant.

The illustration shows that with a 10 per cent increase in volume, profit increases by 20 per cent and a 10 per cent decrease in price results in a 20 per cent fall in profits.

(c) *Impact of price and volume changes on net profit*

	Price increase 10% Volume decrease 10%	*Normal*	*Price decrease 10% Volume increase 10%*
Units	540,000	600,000	660,000
Contribution per unit	£12	£10	£8
Fund	£6,480,000	£6,000,000	£5,280,000
Fixed cost	3,000,000	3,000,000	3,000,000
Profit	£3,480,000	£3,000,000	£2,280,000

Contribution per unit increases.

The illustration shows that:

(i) The price increase compensates the decrease in volume.

(ii) The volume increase does not compensate the reduction in price.

(d) *Impact of variable cost changes on net profit*

	Variable cost increase 10%	*Normal*	*Variable cost decrease 10%*
Units	600,000	600,000	600,000
Contribution per unit	£9	£10	£11
Fund	£5,400,000	£6,000,000	£6,600,000
Fixed cost	£3,000,000	£3,000,000	£3,000,000
Profit	£2,400,000	£3,000,000	£3,600,000

Contribution per unit:

Contribution per unit, normal	£10	£10
Change in the variable cost per unit		
increase 10%	(1)	
decrease 10%		1
	£9	£11

Owing to the increase in variable cost, contribution per unit is reduced. The illustration shows that a 10 per cent increase in variable costs results in a 20 per cent reduction in profit and a 10 per cent decrease in variable costs increases profit by 20 per cent.

(e) *Impact of fixed cost changes on net profit*

	Fixed cost increase	*Normal*	*Fixed cost decrease*
Units	600,000	600,000	600,000
Contribution per unit (no change)	£10	£10	£10
Fund	£6,000,000	£6,000,000	£6,000,000
Fixed cost	£3,300,000	£3,000,000	£2,700,000
Profit	£2,700,000	£3,000,000	£3,300,000

The illustration shows that a 10 per cent decrease in fixed costs increases profit by 10 per cent and a 10 per cent increase in fixed costs reduces profits by 10 per cent. Contribution per unit, volume and the fund remain unaltered.

(f) *Impact of changes in price, variable cost, fixed cost, and volume on net profit*

	Selling price increase 10% *Volume decrease 10%* *Variable cost increase 10%* *Fixed cost increase 10%*	*Normal*	*Selling price decrease 10%* *Volume increase 10%* *Variable cost decrease 10%* *Fixed cost decrease 10%*
Units	5,400,000	600,000	660,000
Contribution per unit	£11	£10	£9
Fund	£5,940,000	£6,000,000	£5,940,000
Fixed cost	£3,300,000	£3,000,000	£2,700,000
Profit	£2,640,000	£3,000,000	£3,240,000

Contribution per unit:

Contribution per unit, normal		£10	£10
Selling price	increase	2 +	
	decrease		(2)
Variable cost	increase	(1)	
	decrease		1 +
		£11	£9

3.0 CONTRIBUTION APPROACH TO COST–VOLUME–PROFIT ANALYSIS

Cost–volume–profit is the relationship of four variables:

Sales (volume)

Sales (price)

Variable costs (marginal cost)

Fixed costs.

The study of these four factors helps management in planning and decision making.

Let us study the effects on the company of changes in these variables singly and in combination.

3.1 Single-product situation

Illustration 3

Sena & RB of London sold 30,000 units of its product at £50 per unit. Marginal costs are £30 per unit (£20 production and £10 other). Fixed costs are incurred uniformly throughout the year and amount to £400,000. There are no beginning and ending stocks.

Required:

(a) What is the net profit of the company?

(b) What is meant by "contribution"?

(c) The term "break-even" implies that point at which the company *neither* makes a profit *nor* suffers a loss.

What is:

(i) The company's break-even point in units?

(ii) The company's break-even point in sales value?

(iii) If the material costs are 50 per cent of variable costs of production and if the cost of materials increase by 50 per cent how many units are required to break even?

(iv) "When the *fund* equals fixed costs the company breaks even." Do you agree?

(d) *Margin of safety*
The margin of safety figure indicates how much sales may decrease before the company will suffer a loss. Total sales less sales value at break-even point is the margin of safety.

(i) How is such a figure determined, in (a) units, (b) sales value?

(ii) "Profit equals the margin of safety." Do you agree?

(e) *Profit–volume ratio and variable cost ratio*

(i) What is the variable cost percentage of the company?

(ii) What is the profit–volume (P/V) ratio of the company?

(iii) What effect would a 10 per cent increase in selling price have on the profit–volume ratio?

(iv) What percentage increase in selling price is needed to offset a 10 per cent increase in variable costs?

(f) *Consider each case separately*
What are the net profit, break-even point, margin of safety and P/V ratio, if:

(i) volume sold increases by 25 per cent;

(ii) volume sold decreases by 25 per cent;

(iii) selling price increases by 10 per cent;

(iv) selling price decreases by 10 per cent;

(v) variable costs increase by 10 per cent;

(vi) variable costs decrease by 10 per cent;

(vii) fixed costs increase by 20 per cent;

(viii) fixed costs decrease by 20 per cent.

(g) *Consider each case separately*
What are the net profit, break-even point, margin of safety and P/V ratio, if:

(i) selling price increases by 10 per cent with a volume reduction of 20 per cent;

(ii) selling price decreases by 10 per cent with a volume increase of 20 per cent;

(iii) selling price decreases by 10 per cent, volume increases by 20 per cent and fixed costs increase by 20 per cent;

(iv) selling price increases by 10 per cent, marginal cost increases by 10 per cent, volume decreases by 20 per cent and fixed costs decrease by 10 per cent.

(h) *The volume and the fund necessary to offset changes*
The desired fund would be:

$$\text{Fixed cost} + \text{Desired profit.}$$

The desired volume would be:

$$\frac{\text{Desired fund}}{\text{Contribution per unit}}$$

(i) Selling price reduced by 10 per cent, marginal cost increased by 10 per cent and fixed costs decreased by 10 per cent.

(ii) Selling price increased by 20 per cent, marginal cost increased by 10 per cent and fixed costs increased by 25 per cent.

(iii) In (i) and (ii) what would be the volume necessary to make a profit of:

(1) £400,000?
(2) £100,000?
(3) £25,000?

Suggested answer

Selling price per unit	£50
Marginal costs—production	20
Gross contribution	30
Other variable costs	10
∴ Net contribution	£20

(a) *Profit of the company*

Fund (£20 × 30,000 units)	£600,000
Fixed costs	£400,000
Net profit	£200,000

(b) *What is meant by contribution?*

(i) Gross contribution = Sales value less variable cost of production.

(ii) Net contribution = Sales value less total marginal cost *or* Gross contribution less other variable costs.

(c) *Single-product situation*

(i) *Break-even points in units:*

$$\frac{\text{Fixed cost}}{\text{Contribution per unit}} = \frac{£400{,}000}{£20} = 20{,}000 \text{ units.}$$

(ii) *Sales value at break-even point:*

$$\frac{\text{Fixed cost}}{\text{Contribution per unit}} \times \text{Sales price per unit}$$

$$\frac{£40{,}000}{£20} \times £50 = £1{,}000{,}000.$$

(iii) *Break-even point—increase in the cost of material*

Variable cost of production		£20	
50% of cost of materials		£10	
Increase in cost (50% of £10)		£5	
Selling price per unit			£50
Marginal cost of production	£20		
Increase in the cost of materials	5		25
Other variable costs			10
Net contribution per unit			£15

New break-even point $\left(\dfrac{£400,000}{£15}\right)$ = 26,667 units

(iv) When the fund equals fixed costs the company breaks even—yes. Proof:

Volume	*Net contribution per unit*	*Fund*	*Fixed cost*	*Profit*
26,667	£15	£400,000	£400,000	nil

(d) *Margin of safety—single-product situation*

(i) (a) *Units*

Total sales (volume)	£30,000
Break-even point (units)	20,000
Margin of safety	£10,000

(b) *Sales value*

Total sales value (£50 × 30,000)	£1,500,000
Break-even point	1,000,000
Margin of safety	£500,000

(ii) Profit equals the margin of safety—yes. Proof:

	Units	*Value*
Total sales	30,000	£1,500,000
Break-even point	20,000	1,000,000

Excess		
Margin of safety	10,000	500,000
Less: Marginal cost of the excess (10,000 × £30)		300,000
Profit		£200,000

Note
Break-even point: the company recovers fixed costs. The contribution made by the excess (total sales less break-even point) is all profit, i.e. the margin of safety.

(e) *Profit–volume ratio and variable cost ratio*

(i) *Variable cost ratio* =

	Selling price	*Variable cost*	*Contribution*
Per unit	£50	£30	£30

$\frac{£30}{£50} \times 100 = \underline{\underline{60}}$ per cent.

(ii) *Profit–volume ratio* $= \frac{C}{S} \times 100$

$\frac{£20}{£50} \times 100 = \underline{\underline{40}}$ per cent.

(iii) *10 per cent increase in selling price:*

Per unit	*Selling price*	*Marginal cost*	*Contribution*
Per unit	£50	£30	£20
Increase	5	–	5
	£55	£30	£25

Effect: $\frac{£25}{£55} \times 100 = 45.45$ per cent = 45.45 per cent

P/V ratio: Which is an increase of: = $\underline{\underline{5.45}}$ per cent

(iv) *Percentage increase in selling price to offset a 10 per cent increase in variable cost:*

	SP 1	*Marginal cost*	*Contribution*	*P/V*
Normal	£50	£30	£20	40%
Increase	–	3	17	34%
Increase in the SP to offset the decrease in the P/V to 17%:				
	£55	£33	£22	40%

Required: A 10 per cent increase in the selling price.

Suggested answer (continued)

		1	2	3	4	5	6	7	8 and 9		10 and 11		12
					(2 − 3)	(1 × 4)		(5 − 6)	8	9	10	11	($\frac{4}{2}$ × 100)
									(6 ÷ 4)	(8 × 2)	(1 − 8)	(10 × 2)	
									Break-even point		Margin of safety		
	Case	*Volume (units)*	*SP per unit*	*MC per unit*	*Contribution per unit*	*Fund*	*Fixed cost*	*Profit loss*	*Units*	*Sales value*	*Units*	*Sales value*	*P/V ratio*
(f)	*Normal*	30,000	£50	£30	£20	£600,000	£400,000	£200,000	20,000	£1,000,000	10,000	£500,000	£40.00
	(i)	37,500	50	30	20	750,000	400,000	350,000	20,000	1,000,000	17,500	875,000	40.00
	(ii)	22,500	50	30	20	450,000	400,000	50,000	20,000	1,000,000	2,500	125,000	40.00
	(iii)	30,000	55	30	25	750,000	400,000	350,000	16,000	880,000	14,000	770,000	45.45
	(iv)	30,000	45	30	15	450,000	400,000	50,000	26,667	1,200,000	3,333	150,000	33.33
	(v)	30,000	50	33	17	510,000	400,000	110,000	23,529	1,176,450	6,471	323,550	34.00
	(vi)	30,000	50	27	23	690,000	400,000	290,000	17,391	869,550	12,609	630,450	46.00
	(vii)	30,000	50	30	20	600,000	480,000	120,000	24,000	1,200,000	6,000	300,000	40.00
	(viii)	30,000	50	30	20	600,000	320,000	280,000	16,000	800,000	14,000	700,000	40.00
(g)	*Normal*	30,000	£50	£30	£20	£600,000	£400,000	£200,000	20,000	£1,000,000	10,000	£500,000	£40.00
	(i)	24,000	55	30	25	600,000	400,000	200,000	16,000	880,000	8,000	440,000	45.45
	(ii)	36,000	45	30	15	540,000	400,000	140,000	26,667	1,200,000	9,333	419,985	33.33
	(iii)	36,000	45	30	15	540,000	480,000	60,000	32,000	1,440,000	4,000	180,000	33.33
	(iv)	24,000	55	33	22	528,000	360,000	168,000	16,364	736,380	7,636	343,620	40.00

Suggested answer (continued)

(h) (i) and (ii)

			Normal	*SP reduced by 10%* *MC increased by 10%* *Fixed cost* *decreased by 10%*	*SP increased by 20%* *MC increased by 10%* *Fixed cost* *increased by 25%*
				I (*see* note)	*II*
SP	(1)		£50	£45	£60
MC	(2)		£30	£33	£33
Contribution	(3)	(1 − 2)	£20	£12	£27
Volume	(4)		30,000	30,000	30,000
(Note: Volume assumed constant.)					
Fund	(5)	(4 × 3)	£600,000	£360,000	£810,000
Fixed cost	(6)		400,000	360,000	500,000
Profit	(7)	(5 − 6)	200,000	nil	310,000

Note: *To offset the change in I above* (company breaks even)

The fund required = Fixed cost + Profit
= £360,000 + £200,000
= £560,000

Volume required $= \dfrac{£560,000}{£12}$
= 46,667 units

(iii) *Volume required in (i) and (ii) above*

				I	*II*
	Contribution per unit	(1)		£12	£27
	Fixed cost	(2)		£360,000	£500,000
(1)	*Profit required*	(3)		£400,000	£400,000
	Fund required	(4)	(2 + 3)	£760,000	£900,000
	Volume required	(5)	(4 ÷ 1)	63,333 units	33,333 units
(2)	*Profit required*	(6)		£100,000	£100,000
	Fund required	(7)	(2 + 6)	£460,000	£600,000
	Volume required	(8)	(7 ÷ 1)	38,333 units	22,222 units
(3)	*Profit required*	(9)		£25,000	£25,000
	Fund required	(10)	(2 + 9)	£385,000	£525,000
	Volume required	(11)	(10 ÷ 1)	32,083 units	19,444 units

3.2 Multi-product situation

The last illustration assumed that Sena & RB of London produced and sold only one product.

Let us assume that the company makes and sells a number of products, i.e. that there is a sales mix.

Illustration 4

Sena & RB of London sold three products, RA, DJ and RN. The selling prices, costs and sales volume are shown in Exhibit One.

EXHIBIT ONE

Product		RA	DJ	RN
Selling price per unit		£2.50	£4.00	£10.00
Marginal cost per unit		1.50	2.00	4.00
Contribution per unit		£1.00	£2.00	£6.00
Sales volume (units)		80,000	30,000	15,000
Fixed costs (annum)	£150,000			

Sena & RB of London—Income statement

	RA	DJ	RN	Total
Sales (units)	80,000	30,000	15,000	–
Sales (value)	£200,000	£120,000	£150,000	£470,000
Less: Marginal cost	120,000	60,000	60,000	240,000
Contribution—fund	£80,000	£60,000	£90,000	£230,000
Sales as a percentage of total sales (A)	42.55%	25.53%	31.92%	100%
Profit–volume ratio (B)	40%	50%	60%	48.936%
Contribution of each product per pound of sales revenue (A × B)	17.02%	12.77%	19.15%	48.936%

Note

Product RA: $\frac{£80{,}000}{470{,}000} \times 100 = 17.02$ *per cent.*

BREAK-EVEN POINT

For the company with a sales mix of RA £200,000, DJ £120,000 and RN £150,000 the break-even point is

(i) $\dfrac{\text{Total fixed cost}}{\text{Total contribution}} \times \text{Total sales}$

$$= \frac{\pounds 150{,}000}{\pounds 230{,}000} \times \pounds 470{,}000$$
$$= \pounds 306{,}523.$$

or

(ii) $\dfrac{\text{Fixed cost}}{\text{P/V ratio}} = \dfrac{\text{Fixed cost}}{\text{C/S}}$

$$= \frac{\pounds 150{,}000}{48.936\%} \times 100$$
$$= \pounds 306{,}523.$$

MARGIN OF SAFETY

Total sales less Sales value at break-even point
= £470,000 − £306,523 = £163,477.

PRODUCT PROFITABILITY

Multiplying each product's percentage share of total sales by its P/V ratio gives the total contribution per pound of sales for each product.

Although product RN does not have the highest P/V ratio, it has the highest contribution per pound of sales revenue at 19.15 per cent. DJ has a higher P/V ratio, but the volume is not sufficient to be more profitable than RA, which has a lower P/V ratio but a larger volume. *Other things being equal, a higher profit–volume ratio product is always preferred to a lower P/V ratio product but one must not forget the volume consideration*, e.g.

Product	RA	DJ
P/V ratio	40%	50%
Sales value	£200,000	£120,000
Contribution towards the fund	£80,000	£60,000

If management had the choice of selling an additional 10,000 units of either RA or DJ, it would be foolish not to select the one with the higher profit–volume ratio.

ADDITIONAL INCOME STATEMENT ON 10,000 UNITS

Product	RA	DJ
Sales (units)	10,000	10,000
Selling price per unit	£2.50	£4
Sales value	£25,000	£40,000
P/V ratio	40%	50%
Additional contribution	£10,000	£20,000

4.0 CONTRIBUTION AND KEY FACTORS (FIRMS OPERATING AT PRACTICAL CAPACITY, i.e. FULLY UTILISING AVAILABLE RESOURCES)

4.1 The Rule

In order to maximise profit, maximise total contribution. If product Super has a contribution per unit of £10 and product Standard one of £5 per unit, Super is more profitable than Standard. But it may not be so if we consider the volume sold. Supposing the company sold 10,000 units of Super and 25,000 units of Standard, then the product that makes the largest total contribution to profit is the Standard product.

Super = £10 × 10,000 = £100,000
Standard = £5 × 25,000 = £125,000.

The point is that the company must maximise total contribution.

Illustration 5
Let us assume that RA & RB Manufacturing Company has the choice of one of the products RA, RB and RJ:

Product	RA	RB	RJ
Sales value per unit	£50	£62	£16
Marginal cost	30	30	10
Contribution per unit	20	32	6
Profit–volume ratio (C/S)	40%	51.6%	37.5%

Product RB has the highest profit–volume ratio, but it does not follow that it is the product that must be sold to make maximum profit. To make maximum profit, if the products are in competition with each other the company must produce and sell the product which gives the company the largest *fund* and not the one which gives the highest contribution per unit or the one which has the highest P/V ratio.

Illustration 6
Let us assume that the company has the choice of either selling:

24,000 units of RA *or*
7,500 units of RB *or*
60,000 units of RJ

Product	RA	RB	RJ
Expected sales (units)	24,000	7,500	60,000
Contribution per unit	£20	£32	£6
Total contribution (fund)	£480,000	£240,000	£360,000

The illustration shows that the most profitable product is RA, then RJ, and the least profitable product is RB, which gave the highest P/V ratio. Low contribution per unit and a larger turnover may be better than large contribution per unit and small turnover.

4.2 Limitations

In a multi-product situation when the firm is operating at practical capacity, decisions often have to be made as to which product should be dropped, i.e. to determine the best mix.

In practice there may be limitations to the manufacture and sale of the most profitable product. For example, the company may have a monopoly in the market for its products but may not be able to obtain a material which forms part of the products in sufficient quantity to satisfy demand. Therefore the raw material becomes the key factor.

4.3 The key or limiting factor and the Golden Rule

A key or limiting factor is any economic resource that restricts or limits the production or sale of a company's products. The Golden Rule is:

> Where there is a limiting factor, to maximise profit select the product which gives the highest contribution per unit of the limiting factor.

4.4 Relationship between contribution and limiting factor

Illustration 7

Assume that product RA takes 4 hours, RB 8 hours and RJ 1 hour to produce. The company has a capacity of 240,000 direct labour hours. The products are made in competition with each other. Which one should the company push?

Product	RA	RB	RJ
(1) Contribution per unit (Refer to Illustration 4)	£20	£32	£6
Limiting factor: *Direct labour hours*			
(2) Direct labour hours per unit	4	8	1
(3) Profitability in terms of the limiting factor (1 ÷ 2)	£5	£4	£6
(4) *Choice*—most profitable product	Second	Third	First
Proof			
(5) Assuming the company concentrates on one product and uses the available capacity to make and sell the one product	240,000 hours	240,000 hours	240,000 hours
(6) Production/Sales units (5 ÷ 2)	60,000 units	30,000 units	240,000 units
(7) Fund (6 × 1)	£1,200,000	£960,000	£1,440,000

The choice would be product RJ because it contributes the most per unit of the limiting factor—*see* line 3 (Golden Rule).

4.5 Examples of limiting factors

(a) Labour hours—(quantity)

(b) Labour grade—(quality)

(c) Machine hours—(manufacturing capacity)

(d) Raw materials

(e) Bought out component

(f) Financial resources

4.6 More than one limiting factor

In real life limiting factors are to be found in every direction. In the short term it may not be possible to increase production capacity and/or obtain the necessary production personnel and/or the required grade of material, etc. In situations where there are more than two limiting factors the company may find that no single product can be selected as the most profitable one. So if RJ is the most profitable product in terms of direct labour hours, RA in terms of direct materials and RB in terms of financial resources, which product should the company push? No categorical answer can be given. All that we could say is that the company in such circumstances should manufacture all three products in certain specific proportions. These complicated problems are resolved by linear programming techniques.

Illustration 8

Assume data as in previous illustration 7.

In addition, market research has shown that the demand for the products is:

Product	RA	24,000 units
	RB	12,000 units
	RJ	60,000 units.

The most profitable sales and production mix would be:

60,000 units of RJ at 1 hour per unit	=	60,000 hours
24,000 units of RA at 4 hours per unit	=	96,000 hours
		156,000
Available		240,000 hours
Difference to make RB (84,000 ÷ 8 = 10,500 units)		84,000 hours

4.7 Limitations: limiting factor

The purpose of identifying the limiting factor is to indicate the most profitable course of action when there are alternative courses.

Once the limiting factor is identified the analyst assumes that conditions will remain unchanged not only over the relevant range of output but also over a *definite* period of time. If these assumptions *remain valid during the short period* then contribution in terms of the limiting factor is a valuable technique in determining company profit.

During periods of constant economic change, the technique loses much of its importance, for the period may be too short to identify the limiting factor. Therefore unless the limiting factor can be identified and will hold good for some length of time (where the time lag is long enough, and conditions remain constant) it would be better for a company to produce and sell the products which give the greatest total contribution.

Illustration 9

Bourne View Manufacturing Company produces three independent products, RB, RS and RJ. The selling prices, costs and other relevant data follow:

Product	RB	RS	RJ
Selling price per unit	£60	£100	£125
Direct materials	20	25	40
Direct labour	20	15	25
Variable overhead	10	15	10
Materials used per unit	20 lb	25 lb	40 lb
Direct labour (hours)	4	3	5
Machine hours per unit	2	3	1
Expected demand	20,000	20,000	20,000

(a) Should the company produce and sell all three products if adequate resources are available?

(b) How much of each product should be produced if capacity is limited to 200,000 direct labour hours?

(c) How much of each product should be produced if only 1,500,000 lb of material are available?

(d) How much of each product should be produced if only 100,000 machine hours are available?

Suggested answer

(a) If a product gives contribution it will be profitable to make and sell that product. The contribution made by the product will increase the fund.

Product	Total	RB	RS	RJ
Selling price per unit	–	£60	£100	£125
Marginal cost per unit	–	50	55	75
Contribution per unit	–	10	45	50
Expected demand	–	20,000	20,000	20,000
Contribution	–	£200,000	£900,000	£1,000,000
Fund	£2,100,000	–	–	–

Product	RB	RS	RJ
Contribution per unit	£10	£45	£50
Direct labour hours per unit	4	3	5
Pounds of materials per unit	20	25	40
Machine hours per unit	2	3	1
Contribution per unit of the limiting factor			
Per direct labour hour	£2.50	£15.00	£10.00
Per lb of material	£0.50	£1.80	£1.25
Per machine hour	£5.00	£15.00	£50.00
Choice: products in terms of profitability			
Limiting factor:			
Direct labour hours	Third	First	Second
Materials	Third	First	Second
Machine hours	Third	Second	First

(b) If capacity is limited to 200,000 direct labour hours, the company should produce:

			Use of the scarce resource
(i)	Product RS	20,000 × 3	60,000 hours
(ii)	Product RJ	20,000 × 5	100,000 hours
	Balance		40,000 hours
			200,000 hours

(iii) Product RB $\frac{40{,}000}{4 \text{ hours per unit}}$ = 10,000 units

Summary:

RS	= 20,000 units	=	60,000 hours
RJ	= 20,000 units	=	100,000 hours
RB	= 10,000 units	=	40,000 hours
			200,000 hours

(c) If capacity is limited to 1,500,000 lb of direct materials, the company should produce:

		Use of the scarce resource
(i) Product RS	20,000 × 25	500,000 lb
(ii) Product RJ	20,000 × 40	800,000 lb
		1,300,000 lb
(iii) Product RB	10,000 × 20	200,000 lb
		1,500,000 lb

(d) If capacity is limited to 100,000 machine hours, the company should produce:

		Use of the scarce resource
(i) Product RJ	20,000 × 1	20,000 hours
(ii) Product RS	20,000 × 3	60,000 hours
(iii) Product RB	10,000 × 2	20,000 hours
		100,000 hours

Example 1

"IT NEVER RAINS BUT IT POURS!"

During a management meeting this morning (which was attempting to reschedule the firm's limited production facilities to accommodate a newly won export order from Japan), the senior engineering foreman interrupted the deliberations and announced that one of the automatic finishing lathes had broken down, and after a cursory inspection the fault appeared to be serious.

"It never rains—but it pours!" said the managing director, watching the departing works engineer and foreman. "Just as orders were picking up after the recession. Well we can't afford to lose an order—any order—but it now looks as though we can't meet our commitments. We had better adjourn until tomorrow when we will have more information to go on."

Now, later on the same day, the works engineer informs you that the machine will be out of order for two months, and that the maximum available machine hours on the remaining automatic finishing lathes will be 3,500 hours.

He also says that the managing director wants to know:

(a) which products/orders you would recommend we should produce,

(b) what will be the cost of this breakdown.

You are required to prepare that information. Costs, revenues and production requirements during the period were:

	Product			*Special order*	*Japan export order*
	A	*B*	*C*		
Production required during the next two months (units)	750	250	250	75	100
Time on automatic finishing lathe (hours/unit)	2	4	5	4	5
Sales value (£/unit)	25	40	30	40	50
Variable costs (£/unit)	7	9	4	7	15
Fixed costs (£/unit)	12	18	23	27	27
Profit (£/unit)	6	13	3	6	8

(30 minutes)

Suggested answer

	Product			*Special order*	*Japan export order*
	A	*B*	*C*		
Sales value per unit	£25	£40	£30	£40	£50
Marginal cost per unit	£7	£9	£4	£7	£15
Contribution per unit	£18	£31	£26	£33	£35
Limiting factor:					
Finishing lathes					
Machine hours per unit	2	4	5	4	5
Contribution per machine hour	£9	£7.75	£5.20	£8.25	£7
in order of profitability	1	3	5	2	4

(a) *Production target next two months*

Automatic finishing lathe: available hours = 3,500

(i)	Product A	= 750 × 2 =	1,500 machine hours
(ii)	Special order	= 75 × 4 =	300 machine hours
(iii)	Product B	= 250 × 4 =	1,000 machine hours
(iv)	Japan export order	= 100 × 5 =	500 machine hours
			3,300
(v)	Product C (least profitable)	= 40 × 5 =	200 left
			3,500 machine hours

(b) *The cost of the breakdown*

		Total	Product A	Product B	Product C	Special order	Japan export order
Without the breakdown							
Sales (units)	(1)		750	250	250	75	100
Contribution per unit	(2)		£18	£31	£26	£33	£35
Fund	(3) (1 × 2)	£33,725	£13,500	£7,750	£6,500	£2,475	£3,500
With the breakdown							
Sales (units)	(4)	–	750	250	40	75	100
Contribution per unit	(5)	–	£18	£31	£26	£33	£35
Fund	(6) (4 × 5)	£28,265	£13,500	£7,750	£1,040	£2,475	£3,500
Summary		£	£	£	£	£	£
Without breakdown		33,725	13,500	7,750	6,500	2,475	3,500
With breakdown		28,265	13,500	7,750	1,040	2,475	3,500
Difference		(5,460)	nil	nil	(5,460)	nil	nil

Example 2

A company manufacturing four products is preparing plans for year 8. The engineering department has estimated that machine shop A's capacity will be 40,000 hours and it will not be possible to manufacture all requirements for products MDN, JA, RD and MP.

The company can choose between the alternative courses of action given below to obtain the products in excess of normal production capacity:

(a) to buy entirely from outside suppliers

(b) to buy from outside suppliers and/or use a partial second shift.

The data given below are for the year 8:

Estimated cost per unit	*MDN*	*JA*	*RD*	*MP*
Variable costs				
Direct materials	£20	£15	£13	£25
Direct wages	3	4	11	20
Direct expenses	5	10	5	30
Fixed overhead	25	15	13	25
Total cost of production	£53	£44	£42	£100
Requirements in units	4,000	7,000	3,000	5,600

Direct expenses relate to the use of the machine shop A which costs £5 per machine hour to operate. Fixed production overhead is absorbed as a percentage of direct materials.

Quotations obtained from outside suppliers indicate a willingness to manufacture all or any part of the total requirements at the following prices, each delivered to the factory:

Product	*Price*
MDN	£30.50
JA	£31.00
RD	£25.00
MP	£87.00

Second-shift operations would increase direct wages costs by 25 per cent over the normal shift and fixed overhead by £300 for each 1,000 (or part thereof) second-shift hours worked.

Identify:

(a) Which components, and in what quantities, should be manufactured in the 40,000 hours available in machine shop A.

(b) Whether it would be profitable for the company to introduce a second shift instead of buying from outside.

(40 minutes)

Suggested answer

	Product			
	MDN	*JA*	*RD*	*MP*
Selling price per unit (In the absence of a selling price, accept the outside price.)	£ 30.50	£ 31.00	£ 25.00	£ 87.00
Marginal cost per unit	28.00	29.00	29.00	75.00
Contribution per unit	2.50	2.00	(4.00)	12.00
Limiting factor: Machine shop A (Direct expenses cost £5 per machine hour.)	1 hour	2 hours	1 hour	6 hours
Contribution per machine hour	£2.50	£1.00	£(4.00)	£2.00
Product profitability	One	Three	Buy outside. Outside price is cheaper than company's marginal cost.	Two

(a) *Product mix*

Available hours, shop A: 40,000

Product	MDN	4,000 × 1	= 4,000 hours
Product	MP	5,600 × 6	= 33,600 hours
			37,600 hours
	Balance		2,400 hours
			40,000 hours
Product	JA	1,200 × 2 hours	= 2,400 units

Summary: Product mix (most profitable mix)

		Hours	*Units*
Product	MDN	4,000	4,000
Product	MP	33,600	5,600
Product	JA	2,400	1,200

(b) *Whether to introduce second shift or buy outside*

(i) Product RD should be bought outside as its variable manufacturing cost is greater than the outside price.

(ii) Product JA:

Balance of requirement units

Units required	7,000
Less: Production	1,200
Difference	5,800

(1)

Contribution per unit		£2.00
Due to the second shift		
Wages increase: 25%		(1.00)
	Contribution	£1.00

Total fund or saving if the second shift is introduced:

5,800 × £1	=	£5,800
Additional fixed costs $£300 \times \frac{5,800 \times 2}{1,000}$	=	3,600
(to nearest 1,000)		
Advantage gained by making		£2,200

(2)

	Make (second shift)	*Buy (outside)*
Product	JA	JA
Quantity (units)	5,800	5,800
Cost per unit £31.00	–	£179,800
Variable cost per unit:		
Materials £15.00	£87,000	–
Labour £4.00	23,200	–
Labour premium 25% × £4 = £1.00	5,800	–
Direct expenses £10.00	58,000	–
Additional fixed expenses (refer to note)	3,600	–
	£177,600	£179,800

Advantage gained by making: £2,200.

Note: Additional fixed costs:

5,800 × 2 hours per unit	=	*11,600 hours*
£300 per 1,000 hours or part thereof: fixed costs	=	$\frac{12{,}000 \text{ hours}}{1{,}000 \text{ hours}} \times £300$
	= *£3,600*	

Example 3

Joslin Manufacturing Company produces three products, Kalu, Sudu, Podi. The marginal costs and the selling prices are:

	Kalu	*Sudu*	*Podi*
Direct materials	£30	£20	£50
Direct labour: Dept 1	10 hours	16 hours	20 hours
Dept 2	8 hours	6 hours	10 hours
Variable overhead	£10	£12	£15
Selling price	£124	£122	£195

The company is restricted to a 40-hour working week. The hourly rates of pay are department 1, £2.00 and department 2, £3.00. The company plans its production operations in relation to the 4-week periods which are used for accounting purposes. The labour force expected to be available for each of the first two periods of the forthcoming year are:

	Department 1	*Department 2*
Period 1	77	50
Period 2	107	50

However, no guarantee is given to them that their services will necessarily be required and only time spent on production is paid for.

The sales manager has estimated demand for period 1 to be 300 of each product, increasing by 20 per cent cumulative per period throughout the year. Stock changes are insignificant.

Prepare the most profitable production plan for the company to pursue for each of the two periods in question.

(50 minutes)

Suggested answer

PRODUCTION PLAN FOR PERIOD 1 (LIMITING FACTOR DEPARTMENT 1)

Profitability in terms of the limiting factor: produce in order—Kalu, Podi and then Sudu.

Production budget

Kalu	300 units × 10	=	3,000 hours
Podi	300 units × 20	=	6,000 hours
Sudu	137 units × 16	=	2,200 hours
Available capacity in department 1			11,200 hours

PRODUCTION PLAN FOR PERIOD 2 (LIMITING FACTOR DEPARTMENT 2)

Profitability in terms of the limiting factor: produce in order—Sudu, Podi and Kalu.

Production budget

Sudu	360 units × 6	=	2,160 hours
Podi	360 units × 10	=	3,600 hours
Kalu	280 units × 8	=	2,240 hours
Available capacity in department 2			8,000 hours

	Product		
	Kalu	*Sudu*	*Podi*
Direct materials	£30	£20	£50
Direct labour: Dept 1	20	32	40
Dept 2	24	18	30
Variable overhead	10	12	15
Total variable cost	£84	£82	£135
Selling price	124	122	195
Contribution per unit	£40	£40	£60
DL hours per unit: Dept 1	10 hours	16 hours	20 hours
Dept 2	8 hours	6 hours	10 hours
Contribution per hour: Dept 1	£4.0	£2.500	£3.0
Dept 2	£5.0	£6.667	£6.0
Product profitability: Dept 1	One	Three	Two
Dept 2	Three	One	Two

Department	Dept 1 (hours)	Dept 2 (hours)
Period 1		
Capacity available	11,200	8,000
Capacity required	13,800	7,200
Department 1 is the limiting factor in period 1		
Period 2		
Capacity available	17,120	8,000
Capacity required	16,560	8,640
Department 2 is the limiting factor in period 2		

NOTE 1 DIRECT LABOUR—AVAILABLE CAPACITY

	Dept 1 (hours)	*Dept 2 (hours)*
Period 1		
77 × 160	11,200	
50 × 160		8,000
Period 2		
107 × 160	17,120	
50 × 160		8,000

NOTE 2 DIRECT LABOUR—CAPACITY REQUIRED, PERIOD 1

	Product	*Dept 1 (hours per unit)*	*Dept 2 (hours per unit)*	*Dept 1 (hours)*	*Dept 2 (hours)*
Output:	Kalu = 300	10	8	3,000	2,400
	Sudu = 300	16	6	4,800	1,800
	Podi = 300	20	10	6,000	3,000
				13,800	7,200

Direct labour—capacity required, period 2

	Product	*Dept 1 (hours per unit)*	*Dept 2 (hours per unit)*	*Dept 1 (hours)*	*Dept 2 (hours)*
Output:	Kalu = 360	10	8	3,600	2,880
	Sudu = 360	16	6	5,760	2,160
	Podi = 360	20	10	7,200	3,600
				16,560	8,640

5.0 BREAK-EVEN CHART AND COST–VOLUME–PROFIT ANALYSIS

5.1 Underlying assumptions

(a) It is assumed that the behaviours of costs and revenues are always determined with reasonable accuracy.

(b) By and large all costs can be classified as fixed or variable.

(c) Variable costs change at a linear rate.

(d) Fixed costs do not change in the relevant range.

(e) Selling prices are to be left unchanged as sales volume increases.

(f) It is assumed that the firm continues to sell a single product, or the given sales mix will be unchanged as volume changes over the relevant range.

(g) Stocks are kept either constant or at zero level. Therefore it is assumed that production equals sales.

(h) The period of time selected is short and it is assumed that time value of money is not significant.

(i) It is assumed that the manufacturing facilities anticipated for the purpose of the analysis do not change.

(j) Prices of cost factors are to be unchanged.

(k) The most important assumption of all is that volume is the only factor affecting costs.

Therefore, the break-even chart, the profit–volume graph and the cost–volume profit–analysis must be used with great care. One must be aware of the limitations associated with the above assumptions.

5.2 The break-even chart—two formats

The study of cost–volume–profit is often done by *break-even analysis*—finding the production level at which a product or firm makes no profit and no loss. The break-even point can either be calculated algebraically or arrived at graphically.

Study Fig. 24. Costs are divided into two parts: *fixed costs*, represented by a line parallel with the horizontal axis because they do not vary with production levels, and variable costs, which do.

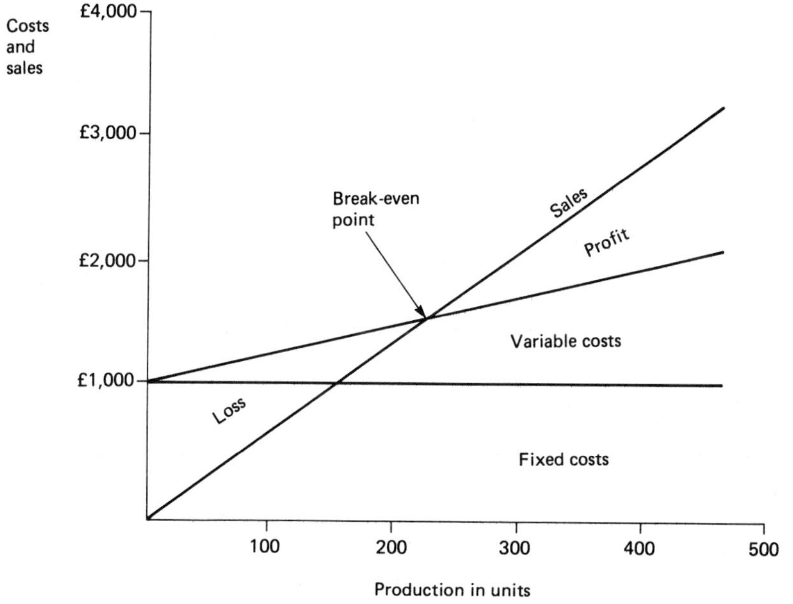

Fig. 24. *Break-even chart.*

Sales are plotted on the same chart, and the point at which the sales line crosses the total cost line is the break-even point. Above this production level a profit is made, while below it there is a loss.

An alternative format for the break-even chart is presented in Fig. 25. The only difference between this chart and Fig. 24 is that the variable cost line is entered before the fixed costs so that it starts at the origin. This layout is technically superior because it is more logical for the variable cost line to begin at the origin, so displaying more clearly the variable costs incurred at each level of production.

5.3 The margin of safety

The term "margin of safety" is used to describe the extent to which the budgeted sales level exceeds the break-even sales level.

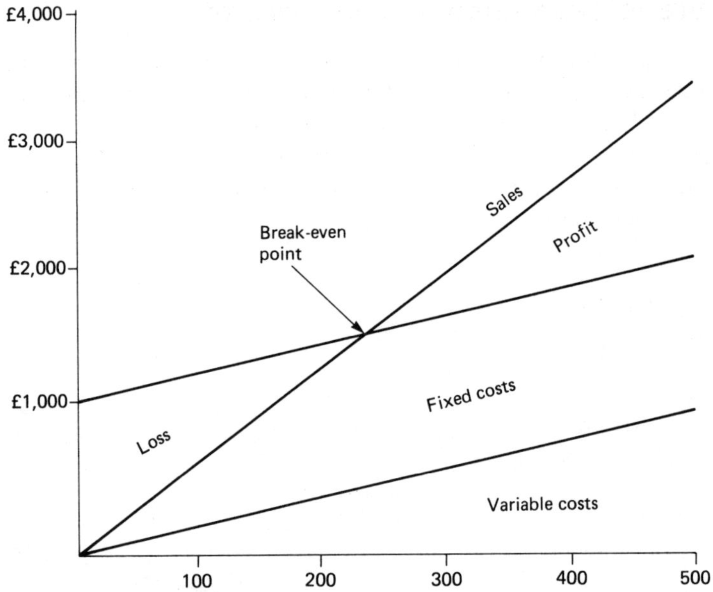

Fig. 25. *Break-even chart, alternative form.*

5.4 The profit–volume graph

The profit–volume graph is a variant on the break-even chart. It relates contribution to sales revenue and demonstrates more clearly than the break-even chart the relationships between sales, variable costs, fixed costs and profit or loss at different levels of activity.

Study Fig. 26. The horizontal axis indicates various levels of sales. Contribution at each level is indicated by the oblique line. In Fig. 26 the contribution generated by sales of £2,000 is shown to be required to cover fixed costs. Above this level there is a profit.

Illustration—Profit–volume graph for individual products

The data are as follows:

Product	*Sales volume (units)*	*Sales value (£)*	*Marginal cost (£)*	*Fund (£)*	*P/V ratio (%)*
R	10,000	50,000	20,000	30,000	60
B	20,000	120,000	80,000	40,000	33
S	20,000	100,000	20,000	80,000	80
P	10,000	30,000	20,000	10,000	33
		Fund		160,000	
		Fixed costs		60,000	
		Profit		100,000	

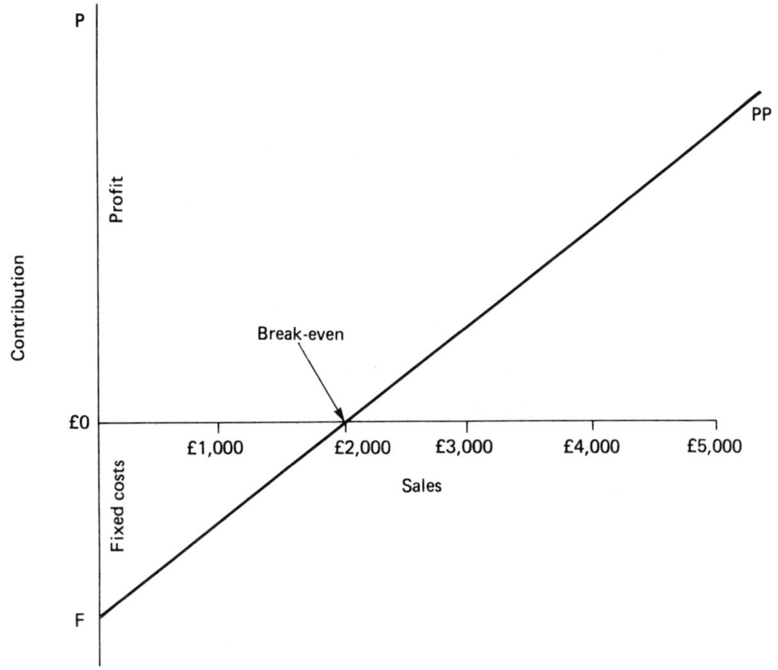

Fig. 26. *Profit–volume graph.*

To construct the profit–volume graph (Fig. 26), the profit path of all products is first drawn starting from fixed costs £60,000 below the sales lines and ending £100,000 above the sales line at a sales volume of £300,000. The products are shown on the graph in order of profitability, starting with product S which has the highest profit–volume ratio (80 per cent). The profit path shows that the product contributes £80,000 at a sales volume of £100,000 (horizontal axis). Product R (60 per cent P/V ratio) is then drawn, starting from £100,000 sales value (product S) ending at £150,000 of sales. Note the £150,000 point on the sales line is a cumulative sales total of products S and R. The contribution made by product R is added to the contribution made by product S. At a combined total of £150,000 sales the two products have contributed £110,000 towards fixed costs and profit. In drawing the profit path of individual products, cumulative totals are used:

Products in order of profitability	*Sales value*	*Cumulative sales value*	*Contribution*	*Cumulative contribution*
S	£100,000	£100,000	£80,000	£80,000
R	50,000	150,000	30,000	110,000
B	120,000	270,000	40,000	150,000
P	30,000	300,000	10,000	160,000

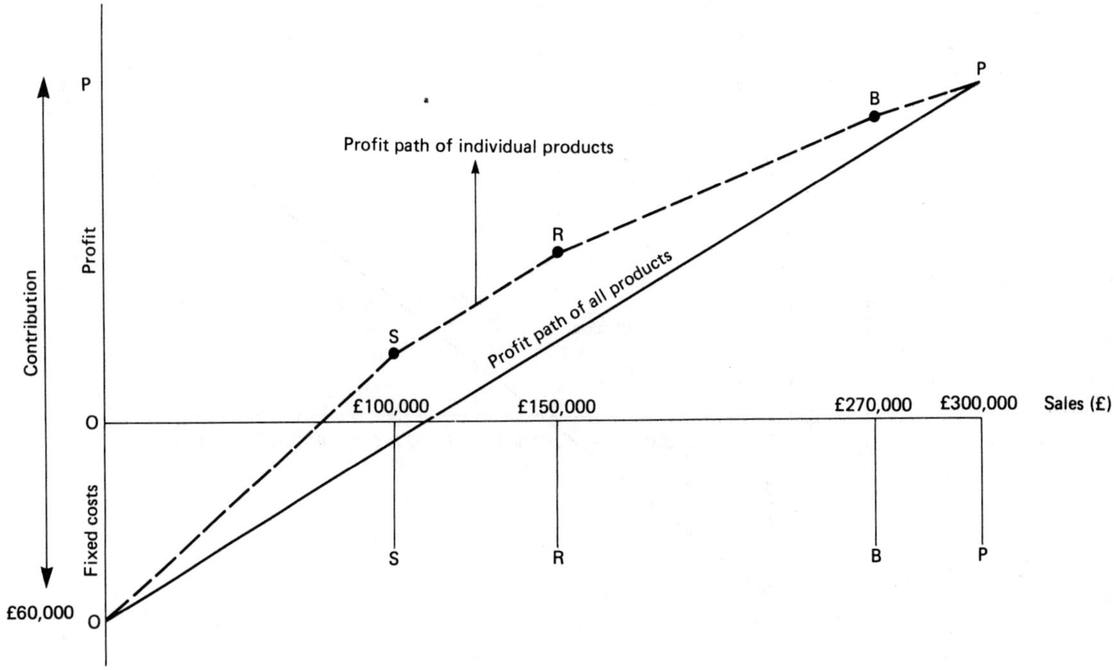

Fig. 27. *Profit–volume graph for individual products. Note: sales value less marginal cost equals fund towards fixed cost and profit.*

CHAPTER SIXTEEN

Contribution Approach to Short-Term Decision Making

1.0 INTRODUCTION

The first step in decision making is planning. Planning gives the manager a warning of possible future crisis situations. It is the function by which managers decide:

(a) what *goals* are to be set; and

(b) how they are going to be accomplished.

1.1 Two unique characteristics in short-term decisions

(a) These decisions involve obtaining the maximum possible from existing resources or facilities.

(b) The time span is so short that one assumes that the time value of money is not significant. In other words £1 now is worth £1 in 6 months' time.

1.2 The accountant's role

The primary role of the accountant in the decision-making process is to act in the capacity of an expert on cost analysis and to ensure that *all* relevant information is passed to the manager responsible for making the decision.

Thus the accountant

(a) is a collector and reporter of information;

(b) is a technical expert in cost analysis;

(c) provides the manager with relevant:

(i) qualitative information

(ii) quantitative information.

1.3 Relevant information—fundamental principles

(a) Any factor that remains the same whatever course of action is selected is irrelevant.

Joint costs incurred up to the split-off point are not relevant in deciding whether to further process a product.

Supposing a company has 20,000 units of a product in stock unsold for the last 5 years. Cost per unit 5 years ago was £2. It is an asset of the company and is valued at £40,000. An overseas company has offered to purchase this product at £0.50 per unit.

In stock	20,000 units at £2	= £40,000
Offer	20,000 units at £0.50	= £10,000

If these units cannot be otherwise sold then it is an error on the part of the manager to treat £40,000 as a cost. Regardless of what one does the cost of these 20,000 units will always be £40,000. It is a historical fact. Therefore the cost of £40,000 is not a relevant cost.

Again, in deciding whether to take your car to work or use public transport: road tax, insurance and depreciation are irrelevant because these costs will normally be the same whether you drive the car or not.

(b) The function of decision making is to select a course of action for the future. To be relevant a cost must meet three criteria:

(i) it is not a historical cost;

(ii) it is an expected future cost;

(iii) the cost differs between alternatives.

1.4 Role of fixed costs in short-term decision making

Are fixed costs relevant to short-term decision making? Do not jump to conclusions—study the facts of the situation.

Illustration 1

A company has capacity to produce 50,000 units of a product. Owing to a recession the firm is operating at 50 per cent capacity. The variable cost of the product is £10 and the fixed cost is £5. The chairman of an overseas company has offered to buy 10,000 units of the product for £120,000. Should this offer be accepted even though it is below full cost?

What are the relevant costs? The relevant costs are those costs which are affected by the decision to accept or reject the offer, i.e. the variable manufacturing costs of £10 per unit.

Fixed costs are irrelevant—they are not affected by this decision. They remain the same. Regardless of the amount, fixed overhead is *not* relevant. If we include fixed costs the offer may be rejected, thereby losing £2 per unit contribution towards fixed costs and profit. In other words, by not accepting the order when there is spare capacity, the company would lose £2 × 10,000 units = £20,000. How much of fixed costs are charged or absorbed by units of products is not relevant to this decision because total fixed costs remain unchanged.

1.5 Are all variable costs relevant and all fixed costs irrelevant?

(a) Sometimes fixed costs are affected by a decision and variable costs are not. In Illustration 1, the overseas visitor may be willing to purchase the 10,000 units in the UK and make his own arrangements regarding shipment. This would save the company shipping expenses. Therefore if these costs are variable costs then they are not relevant to this decision.

(b) As far as fixed costs are concerned, one could say that they are relevant if and when they are expected to be altered. If the acceptance of the order increases fixed costs by £5,000, then £5,000 is a relevant fixed cost in deciding whether to accept or reject the offer. The relevance of costs depends on the purpose in hand.

Often students make wrong conclusions in the examination room by assuming that fixed costs are not relevant because they remain fixed regardless of one's action.

Illustration 2

R & D Limited manufacture a product sold in the home market. For the last two years the company has been operating below practical capacity.

An overseas visitor to London is very much interested in the product and has offered to buy the excess capacity for the next ten years at a fixed price of £5.50 per unit. The managing director was convinced that the offer was profitable since the company's fixed costs will be spread over a greater number of units. The company was operating at 50 per cent of its normal capacity.

The company's income statement for the year just ended:

Sales (units)	20,000
Unit price	£10
Sales	£200,000
Marginal cost of production (£6 per unit)	120,000
Contribution	80,000
Fixed costs	40,000
Profit	£40,000

	Cost per unit	
	Capacity utilisation 50% before	*Capacity utilisation 100% after*
Marginal cost	£6	£6
Fixed cost $\frac{£40,000}{£20,000}$	2	
$\frac{£40,000}{£40,000}$	–	1
	£8	£7

Beware of unit costs. How fixed costs (£40,000) are allocated among products is not relevant to the decision because the total fixed costs have remained constant.

The offer is £5.50 per unit, i.e. £0.50 below marginal cost, but is compensated by a decrease in fixed cost per unit of £1.00. One would expect net profit to increase by £0.50 × 20,000 units.

If the offer is accepted:

	Regular business	*Additional business*	*Combined operations*
Sales (units)	20,000	20,000	–
Selling price	£10	£5.50	–
Sales value	£200,000	£110,000	£310,000
Marginal cost: £6 × 20,000	120,000	–	120,000
£6 × 20,000	–	120,000	120,000
Contribution	80,000	(10,000)	70,000
Fixed costs (apportioned)	(20,000)	(20,000)	(40,000)
Net profit	£60,000	£(30,000)	£30,000

Through the acceptance of the offer and the increase of capacity, the net income of the company has dropped by £10,000. The spreading of total fixed costs over a greater number of units will not alter the amount (£40,000) of fixed costs. The fixed costs per unit have fallen from £2 to £1 but this is not relevant to the decision because the total fixed costs are not affected.

2.0 ADDING A NEW PRODUCT

Illustration 3

You are the sales director of the Edith Manufacturing Company. The results of last year's trading were submitted to you by the accountant and show:

Sales	£200,000
Less: Marginal cost of sales	100,000
Contribution	100,000
Less: Fixed costs	75,000
Net profit	£25,000

You have conducted a study of the profit potential of two new products; the manufacture of *one* can be undertaken without incurring additional fixed costs. The following tabulation shows estimated selling prices and costs directly associated with these new products:

	Product	
	Pat	*Pad*
Selling price per unit	£40	£50
Variable cost of manufacturing	£10	£10
Other variable costs	£20	£10
Available capacity can produce	20,000 units	6,000 units

Market research indicates that these units may be sold at the expected selling prices. Which product should be added?

PROJECTED INCOME STATEMENT—FOR NEXT YEAR

	Pat	*Pad*
Sales: 20,000 × £40	£800,000	
6,000 × £50		£300,000
Less: Marginal cost: 20,000 × £30	600,000	
6,000 × £20		120,000
(Fund) net contribution	£200,000	£180,000

Product Pat has the largest fund, £20,000 more than Pad. This is the most profitable product. However, if these products are sold in new markets and additional fixed selling and distribution costs are incurred then these have to be deducted before a final decision is made. Let us assume the products require additional fixed selling and distribution expenditure of £40,000 for Pat and £30,000 for Pad.

	Pat	*Pad*
Net contribution	£200,000	£180,000
Less: Additional fixed cost	40,000	30,000
Product contribution	£160,000	£150,000

On the basis of quantitative information, product Pad should be rejected in favour of product Pat.

Fixed manufacturing costs are not relevant for this decision. Additional fixed selling and distribution expenses are relevant in addition to the variable costs.

If the costs of the two new products are estimated on a total cost basis, then part of the fixed manufacturing costs would have to be apportioned to the two new products:

	Pat	*Pad*
Sales	£800,000	£300,000
Less: Marginal cost of sales	600,000	120,000
Net contribution	200,000	180,000
Less: Additional fixed costs	40,000	30,000
Apportioned joint fixed costs	25,000	25,000
Profit (loss)	£135,000	£125,000

Note: The existing product would now have to carry only £25,000 fixed manufacturing overhead and would appear to be more profitable.

If management decides to apportion the joint fixed costs between the existing products and the new product (Pat or Pad) it will lower the cost per unit of all products, especially the existing products. But how the joint fixed cost of £75,000 is apportioned to products has no significance for decisions to produce the new product because there is no change in the total joint fixed cost.

3.0 PRODUCT DELETION

Illustration 4

Assume that the RA & RB Manufacturing Company produces and sells three products: RA, RB and RJ. The income statement at the end of period 7 appears below:

	RA	*RB*	*RJ*	*Total*
Sales (units)	1,000	2,400	3,200	–
Sales value per unit	£80	£48	£40	–
Marginal cost per unit	£48	£24	£16	–
Contribution—fund	£32,000	£57,600	£76,800	£166,400
Fixed costs				
Separable	£25,000	£10,000	£20,000	£55,000
Joint	£10,000	£24,000	£32,000	£66,000
(allocated on volume basis)				
Net profit	£(3,000)	£23,600	£24,800	£45,400

Management is considering dropping product RA because it believes that it has reduced profits by £3,000. Management believes that by an intensive sales campaign of £50,000 per annum it could drop product RA and sell 2,000 additional units of product RB.

The company would save the separable fixed costs if product RA is dropped. Would you advise the company to do this?

Suggested answer

IF CHANGES WERE MADE AS SUGGESTED

	RA	*RB*	*RJ*	*Total*
Sales (units)	–	4,400	3,200	–
Contribution per unit	–	£24	£24	–
Total contribution	–	£105,600	£76,800	£182,400
Separable fixed costs	–	10,000	20,000	30,000
Advertising	–	50,000	–	50,000
Joint fixed costs	–	24,000	32,000	56,000
Joint fixed costs apportioned to RA	10,000	–	–	10,000
	£(10,000)	£21,600	£24,800	£36,400

It is better to leave things as they are. The adoption of the proposal would lead to a drop in profits of £45,400 – £36,400 = £9,000.

If the company can produce a new product, RS, an overseas customer has offered to buy 2,000 units per annum for the next five years at £50 per unit.

Cost estimate—product RS

Selling price	£50
Variable costs	25
Additional fixed costs	nil
Separable fixed costs	25,000

The company is working at full capacity and if the offer is accepted it would have to drop one of the existing products. Management is considering dropping product RA and making RS. Would this increase overall company profits?

	Product RA	*New product RS*	*Difference*
Sales (units)	1,000	2,000	
Contribution per unit	£32	£25	
Total contribution	£32,000	£50,000	£18,000
Separable fixed costs	£25,000	£25,000	
Net income	£7,000	£25,000	£18,000

Joint fixed costs are not relevant to this decision.

If RA, RB and RJ are *independent* products, it would be profitable for the company to accept the overseas customer's offer as it would increase net profit by £18,000.

Example Addition or deletion of departments

RA & RB Company owns a department store. It sells three major lines of their products in three departments. Income statements for the three departments and for the total firm are as follows:

	Total (£000)	*Department One Furniture (£000)*	*Department Two Menswear (£000)*	*Department Three Do-It-Yourself (£000)*
Sales	9,200	4,000	3,200	2,000
Marginal cost	6,240	3,200	2,240	800
Contribution	2,960	800	960	1,200
Fixed cost:				
Separable	1,200	600	400	200
Discretionary	720	120	200	400
Committed	520	120	200	200
Total fixed cost	2,440	840	800	800
Profit (loss)	520	(40)	160	400

Separable fixed costs could be avoided by not operating a department. Management is considering whether to:

(a) Continue the furniture department or discontinue the furniture department.

(b) Drop the furniture department and use the space to extend the do-it-yourself department. This would increase sales of the do-it-yourself department by £200,000 with the unit cost structure remaining constant. The company would be able to avoid not only the separable fixed costs but also the discretionary fixed costs incurred in the furniture department, but would have an increase of £20,000 in the separable fixed costs in the do-it-yourself department.

Suggested answer (a)

	Drop Furniture (Menswear and Do-It-Yourself) (£000)	*Keep Furniture (all three depts) (£000)*	*Difference (£000)*
Sales	5,200	9,200	4,000
Marginal cost	3,040	6,240	3,200
Contribution	2,160	2,960	800
Fixed cost:			
Separable	600	1,200	600
Discretionary	600	720	120
Committed	520	520	nil
	440	520	80

Do not drop the furniture department if the vacated space and other facilities are to remain idle.

Suggested answer (b)

DROP FURNITURE—EXTEND DO-IT-YOURSELF

		Drop furniture—extend DIY			
	Keep all three depts:		*Do-It-Yourself*		*Menswear*
	Total (£000)	*Total (£000)*	*Normal (£000)*	*Extension (£000)*	*Normal (£000)*
Sales	9,200	5,400	2,000	200	3,200
Marginal cost	6,240	3,180	800	140	2,240
Contribution	2,960	2,220	1,200	60	960
Fixed costs:					
Separable	1,200	620	200	20	400
Discretionary	720	600	400	–	200
Committed	520	520	–	–	–
Profit (loss)	520	480			

Summary (this *emphasises* the importance of obtaining the maximum contribution towards the fixed costs):

	Furniture (£000)	*Extend DIY (£000)*	*Difference (£000)*
Sales	4,000	200	3,800
Marginal cost	3,200	140	3,060
Contribution	800	60	740
Fixed costs:			
Separable	600	20	580
Discretionary	120	–	120
Committed	–	–	–
Profit (loss)	80	40	40

The analysis shows that it would be better for the company to leave things alone.

4.0 DECISION ON METHODS OF MANUFACTURE

In problems involving decisions on methods of manufacturing the cost analysis is quite simple. The method already in use can be compared with the alternatives. Costs which are common may be ignored. The marginal cost of the product as produced under each method should be ascertained. The method which gives the largest contribution should be selected. Thus if a new method saves 4 direct labour hours per unit, and the labour cost is £2.00 per hour, by introducing this method the company would save £8 per unit. If the estimated output is 1,000 units the saving is £8,000.

Against this any additional costs incurred should be set off.

4.1 Practical difficulty

The saving calculated above may not be a real saving unless there is a reduction in the direct labour force, or the 4,000 hours saved (4 hours per unit × 1,000) is used to do other productive work.

If there is no reduction in the labour force or in its use, then the above remains an accounting exercise and the proposed method will not increase profits as expected.

4.2 Limiting factor

In deciding upon the method of manufacture, the method which yields the greatest contribution per limiting factor is the most profitable.

Illustration 5

Sena of London produces a single product using hand labour. A decision now has to be made whether to continue with hand labour or introduce machine type A, or machine type B.

Choice	*Hand labour*	*Machine type A*	*Machine type B*
Number of units per:			
Man hour	10	20	15
Machine hour	–	40	60
Direct materials per unit (lb)	10	10	10
Marginal cost under each alternative per unit	£25	£15	£30
Selling price	£50	£50	£50
Contribution per unit	£25	£35	£20
Contribution per man hour	£250	£700	£300
Contribution per machine hour	–	£1,400	£1,200
		Most profitable method	
Contribution per unit	£25	£35	£20

Choice	*Hand labour*	*Machine type A*	*Machine type B*
Contribution per unit of product	£25	£35	£20
Contribution per man hour	£250	£700	£300
Contribution per machine hour	–	£1,400	£1,200
Contribution per lb of material	£2.5	£3.5	£2.0
Choice of methods:			
With *no limiting* factors	Second	First	Third
With limiting factors:			
Man hours	Third	First	Second
Machine hours	–	First	Second
Direct materials	Second	First	Third

4.3 Single shift; overtime; second shift

Most companies operate a single shift of eight hours per day, for five days of the week or forty hours per week. Often overtime is worked temporarily to meet sudden or planned demand (Easter and Christmas).

If a company finds that it has to work overtime because of annual increases in demands, it has a choice:

(a) increase capacity by purchasing new machinery (*see* Illustration 6);

(b) add a second shift (*see* Illustration 7); or

(c) introduce overtime regularly throughout the year.

Illustration 6: Increase capacity—purchase new machinery
Sena of London, a company manufacturing hairdressing accessories, shows the following results for the year ending 31st December, year 7:

Product	*S*	*E*	*N*	*A*
Annual production (units)	80,000	20,000	100,000	60,000
Selling price per unit	£5.00	£7.50	£10.00	£15.00
Direct materials per unit	1.00	2.00	1.75	4.50
Direct labour per unit	1.25	1.50	3.00	4.50
Variable overhead per unit	0.75	1.50	2.00	2.50
Fixed overhead per unit	1.25	1.50	3.00	4.50
Profit (loss) per unit	0.75	1.00	0.25	(1.00)

Production capacity in year 8 is such that output can be increased by 80,000 units over that in year 7 (no output can be reduced). The 80,000 units can be of one product or a combination of products. No product can be increased by more than 80,000 units over the year 7 level. Total fixed costs, variable costs per unit and selling prices in year 8 will be the same as in year 7.

(a) Which output or outputs should be increased to maximise profit in year 8?

(b) Demand for the firm's product is such that production can be increased further by 200,000 units in addition to the anticipated increase of 80,000. To make this increase possible, management is considering the purchase of new plant specially for the manufacture of product E (the variable operating costs of the new plant in year 8 will be the same as for the existing plant).

Subject to use of this new capacity for increased production of product E, the planned deployment of existing capacity will be the same as in year 7.

It is anticipated that in year 8 direct materials and direct labour costs of all products will increase by 10 per cent, that selling prices will remain unchanged and that additional fixed costs attributable to the new plant will total £90,000 per annum.

You are required:

(i) to calculate which output or outputs should be increased in year 8 in order to fully absorb production capacity and maximise profit, on the assumption that all goods produced can be sold at the stated prices?

(ii) to calculate how many additional units of product E will have to be sold in year 8 at the price stated in order to ensure that the overall results will be £100,000 more than those for year 7?

Suggested answer (a)

NOTE 1 CONTRIBUTION PER UNIT

	S	*E*	*N*	*A*
Selling price	£5.00	£7.50	£10.00	£15.00
Marginal cost	£3.00	£5.00	£6.75	£11.50
Contribution	£2.00	£2.50	£3.25	£3.50

NOTE 2 FIXED COSTS

No. of units sold/produced	80,000	20,000	100,000	60,000
Fixed cost per unit	£1.25	£1.50	£3.00	£4.50
Total fixed costs	£100,000	£30,000	£300,000	£270,000

Total fixed cost = £700,000.

Year 7—income statement:

	Total (£000)	*S*	*E*	*N*	*A*
Sales (units)		80,000	20,000	100,000	60,000
Contribution per unit		£2.00	£2.50	£3.25	£3.50
Total contribution		£160,000	£50,000	£325,000	£210,000
Fund	745	–	–	–	–
Fixed cost	700				
	45				

The answer to question (a), which output should be increased, is: given that an increase of 80,000 units of one product or a combination of products is possible in year 8, product A should be produced, since this offers the greatest contribution per unit of product (Note 1).

Suggested answer (b)

Income statement before increase in capacity of E:

	Total	*S*	*E*	*N*	*A*
Sales (units)	–	80,000	20,000	100,000	140,000
Contribution per unit		£1.775	£2.150	£2.775	£2.600
Total contribution		£142,000	£43,000	£277,500	£364,000
Total fund	£826,500				
Fixed cost	700,000				
Net profit	£126,500				

ADDITIONAL PROFIT REQUIRED

Net profit for year 8 before the sale of additional units of E	£126,500
Net profit for year 7	45,000
Difference	81,500
Profit needed from new plant	100,000
Additional profit required	£18,500

The additional units of product E should contribute towards additional fixed costs of £90,000 plus a profit of £18,500.

TOTAL ADDITIONAL FUND REQUIRED

Fixed cost	£90,000
Additional profit	18,500
	£108,500

Contribution per unit of E (Note 3) £2.150

Number of additional units of E $\frac{£108{,}500}{£2.150} = 50{,}465$ units

NOTE 3 CONTRIBUTION PER UNIT—WITH MATERIALS AND LABOUR COST INCREASE OF 10 PER CENT

Product	*S*	*E*	*N*	*A*
Original contribution per unit (*see* above)	£2.00	£2.50	£3.25	£3.50
Less: Increase in material cost	(0.10)	(0.20)	(0.175)	(0.45)
Less: Increase in labour cost	(0.125)	(0.15)	(0.30)	(0.45)
Contribution per unit	£1.775	£2.150	£2.775	£2.60

Illustration 7

Sena of London produces an amplifier, the selling price of which is £100 and the standard cost £70, made up as follows:

Direct materials	£40
Direct labour	10
Variable overhead	4
Fixed overhead	16

The factory, located in Montreux, Switzerland, is producing 200,000 amplifiers per year, this output representing 100 per cent capacity at single-shift working.

Demand for the amplifier is in excess of production and Harry Neasden, the marketing manager, considers that an increase of 50 per cent in the quantity sold could be achieved during the forthcoming year.

A second shift has been proposed. This would increase production capacity to 360,000 units per annum and would attract additional fixed overhead of £1,900,000. A shift work premium of 20 per cent would be payable to the direct labour force engaged on the second shift, but if production were increased to 300,000 units per annum then the whole of the direct materials used would qualify for a large user discount of 10 per cent.

Required:
To inform the directors

(a) whether it would be profitable for the company to add the second shift in order to meet the increase in demand;

(b) the minimum annual increase in production/sales to justify the addition of the second shift.

Suggested answer

NOTE CONTRIBUTION PER UNIT:

	Selling price	*Direct materials*	*Direct labour*	*Variable overhead*	*Contribution per unit*
Before shift	£100	£40	£10	£4	£46
After shift	100	36	12	4	48

(a) Second shift—expected sales increase 100,000 units. Additional income if second shift is introduced is:

Contribution	
100,000 × 48	£4,800,000
Fixed costs	1,900,000
	£2,900,000
Add: Large user discount on the original production of 200,000 units (200,000 × 4)	800,000
	£3,700,000

(b) Minimum annual increase in production/sales to justify the addition of the second shift.

At least the increase in fixed costs must be recovered.

Increase in fixed costs—£1,900,000.

Contribution per unit:

Selling price	£100	
Less: Materials	40	(10 per cent user discount production has to reach 300,000 units)
Labour	12	
Variable overhead	4	
	£44	

Number of units required to recover fixed costs:

$$\frac{£1,900,000}{£44} = 43,182 \text{ units.}$$

Proof		£
Additional units 43,182 × £44	=	1,900,000
Additional fixed costs	=	1,900,000
Difference		nil

5.0 MAKE-OR-BUY DECISIONS

Companies are often faced with the problem of deciding whether to make or buy a component. The accountant is the technical expert in cost analysis. He has to collect, analyse and report relevant information to the manager. The manager, armed with this information, will evaluate each of the relevant factors and make a decision on which alternative has the largest net advantage. The accountant's role and responsibility is therefore manifold:

(a) He is the technical expert in cost analysis.

(b) He is the collector and reporter of information.

(c) He ensures that the manager is guided by relevant information.

(d) He tries to quantify as much information as possible.

(e) He provides qualitative information.

5.1 The key (quantitative) factor

In quantitative terms, it is possible to distinguish between three sets of circumstances each of which may provide the key factor in the decision to make or buy:

(a) capacity is available to produce: there is idle capacity which cannot be put to any other use (*see* Illustration 8).

(b) capacity is available to produce, but could be put to an alternative use, e.g. renting or producing another product: make or buy (*see* Illustration 9).

(c) Production facilities are limited in relation to the sales demand made on them. To satisfy demand it is necessary to buy outside (*see* Illustration 11).

5.2 Where there is idle capacity

The choice here is not whether to make or buy; rather, it is how best to use the idle facilities. It will be profitable for a company in this situation to make *if* the variable manufacturing cost is lower than the outside price. This is on the assumption that additional fixed costs will not be incurred and that facilities are available.

Illustration 8

TOTAL COST OF MAKING 50,000 UNITS OF PART PRINCE 154

Variable cost of production	£150,000
Fixed costs (apportioned)	150,000
Total cost	£300,000
Cost per unit (£300,000 ÷ 50,000)	£6.00

Another manufacturer offers to sell the same part for £4. Should the company make or buy the part? The *key question* is whether the variable manufacturing cost is lower than the outside price. The £3 fixed overhead apportioned to the part is not relevant to this decision. The £150,000 apportioned to the product will continue regardless of the decision whether to make or buy.

	Make		*Buy*
Marginal cost	£150,000		–
Outside price	–	50,000 × £4 =	£200,000
Fixed cost	150,000		120,000
Total cost	£300,000		£350,000

The company should make.

The illustration highlights the relevance of variable costs and irrelevance of the fixed costs of £150,000. In the next illustration, however, fixed costs *are* relevant in a make-or-buy decision.

Illustration 8A—Relevance of fixed costs (I)

TOTAL COST OF MAKING 50,000 UNITS OF PART PRINCE 154

Variable cost of production	£150,000
Separable fixed costs	50,000
Joint fixed costs (apportioned)	100,000
Total cost	£300,000
Cost per unit (£300,000 ÷ 50,000)	£6.00

Supposing the same manufacturer as in Illustration 8 offers to sell the part to the company for £3.50. Should the company make or buy outside? You may assume that if the part is bought outside then the company will be able to save the separable fixed costs of £50,000.

COST COMPARISON

	Make	*Buy*
Variable cost of production	£150,000	–
Purchase (£3.50 × 50,000)	–	£175,000
Separable fixed costs	50,000	–
Joint fixed costs	–	–
	£200,000	£175,000
Cost per unit	£4.00	£3.50

The separable fixed costs which can be avoided (£50,000) are relevant. If the company makes the part then the cost per unit is £4.00, including separable fixed cost. By making, the company is losing £25,000. In other words, fixed costs which can be avoided in the future are relevant.

Illustration 8B—Relevance of fixed costs (II)

Freeman International has decided to introduce a new product, Emile. The estimated demand for the product is 100,000 units. Because of available capacity no additional fixed costs will be incurred to produce the product. However, £200,000 of company fixed costs will be allocated to the product in its first year. Emile requires a component part called KF. Freeman International requests assistance from its management accountant in arriving at a decision on whether to manufacture the part KF (facilities available) or buy it from a supplier who is prepared to supply the company with its needs.

The management accountant, using the estimated production and sales forecast, has developed the following costs:

COST PER UNIT OF EMILE

Direct materials	£6.00
Direct labour	4.00
Overhead $\frac{£200,000}{100,000 \text{ units}}$	2.00
	12.00
Part KF (variable cost to make)	4.00
	£16.00

The bought-out price of the *part* would be £5.

(a) Should the company make or buy the part? The company should make the part. The Golden Rule is:

If the marginal cost is less than the outside price—make it.

£5 − £4 = £1.00 contribution. £1.00 × 100,000 = £100,000 towards the fund if the part is manufactured.

(b) Instead of 100,000 units of the product, latest sales estimates show sales volume at 250,000 units. At this new volume, additional equipment has to be purchased to produce KF. The equipment if purchased will have a capacity of producing 350,000 units of KF per annum. The cost of this equipment and its maintenance costs per annum at a level of output of 250,000 units would be £400,000. Under these circumstances should Freeman International make or buy the part KF?

	Make	*Buy*
Variable cost: £4 × 250,000	£1,000,000	–
250,000 × £5	–	£1,250,000
Additional fixed costs	400,000	–
	£1,400,000	£1,250,000

At a volume of 250,000 units of Emile (which requires 250,000 units of KF), Freeman International should buy the part:

Cost of buying	£1,250,000
Cost of making	1,400,000
Buying KF will save	£150,000

Note *The additional fixed cost is relevant to the decision.*

5.3 Capacity available but could be put to alternative use

What can be done with the facilities if the component is bought out?

If the facilities *remain idle* then it will be profitable for the company to make if the variable cost of production is lower than the outside price. This does not hold true if the facilities can be put to alternative use. If the facilities released can be put to some other use or rented, the alternatives should be considered.

Illustration 9

The income statement of Sena of London appears below for the year which has just ended. The company manufactures one product in the finishing department, parts for which are made in the KF department.

Income statement for year ended 31st December, year 6

	KF parts department	*Finishing department*	*Total*
Sales (units)	–	–	500,000
Selling price per unit	–	–	£180
	(£000)	(£000)	(£000)
Sales value	–	–	90,000
Variable costs—production			
£10 × 500,000	5,000		
£30 × 500,000		15,000	
Other variable costs	–	2,500	
Total variable costs	5,000	17,500	22,500
Contribution	–	–	67,500
Identifiable fixed costs	5,000	20,000	25,000
Joint fixed costs	5,000	20,000	25,000
Operating income	–	–	17,500

(a) The company has located a supplier who is willing to manufacture next year's supply of 800,000 parts for £13 each.

What would be the effect on operating income if the company purchased rather than made the parts? Assume that the identifiable fixed costs allocated to department KF parts would have been avoided.

(b) The company could have purchased the parts for £13 each and used the facilities in the KF parts department for the manufacture of a new product, Nimal. The direct materials and direct labour per unit of the product are £10 and £15 respectively. The variable overhead per unit is £5.00. The selling price would have been £50.00. It proposes to do this as market conditions are so favourable that it can sell 500,000 units of Nimal. The fixed costs (identifiable and joint) would have continued. *What would operating income have been if the company bought the necessary parts and made and sold the new product Nimal?*

Suggested answer

(a)	*Make*	*Buy*
Units required	800,000	800,000
Purchase cost 800,000 × £13		£10,400,000
Variable costs 800,000 × £10	£8,000,000	
Identifiable fixed costs	5,000,000	
	£13,000,000	£10,400,000

Even if the facilities used to manufacture the parts *were to become idle*, it would be better for the company to purchase the parts outside, as it would increase net income by £2,600,000.

(b) Operating statement year 7 if the company does not purchase outside part KF:

	Part KF department	*Finishing department*	*Total*
Sales (units)	–	–	800,000
Selling price	–	–	£180
	(£000)	(£000)	(£000)
Sales value	–	–	144,000
Variable costs—production			
£10 × 800,000	8,000	–	
£30 × 800,000	–	24,000	
Other variable costs: £5.00 × 800,000	–	4,000	
Total variable costs	8,000	28,000	36,000
Contribution—fund	–	–	108,000
Identifiable fixed costs	5,000	20,000	25,000
Joint fixed costs	5,000	20,000	25,000
Operating income	–	–	58,000

Make and buy—Operating statement, year 7
The company could have purchased the part for £13.00 each and used the vacated space (part department) to produce and sell Nimal.

	Produce Nimal	*Finishing department*	*Total*
Sales units	500,000	800,000	–
Selling price	£50	£180	–
	(£000)	(£000)	(£000)
Sales value	25,000	144,000	169,000
Purchase cost: £13 × 800,000	–	10,400	10,400
Make: £30 × 50,000	15,000	–	15,000
£30 × 800,000		24,000	24,000
£5 × 800,000		4,000	4,000
Fund	10,000	105,600	115,600
Identifiable fixed costs	5,000	20,000	25,000
Joint fixed costs	–	–	25,000
Net income	–	–	65,000

In sum:

Product Nimal		
Selling price per unit		£50
Less: Marginal costs		30
Net contribution per unit		£20
Volume (units)		500,000
Fund		£10,000,000
Less: Cost of parts KF		
Make £10 × 800,000	=	£8,000,000
Buy £13 × 800,000	=	10,400,000
Excess cost of outside purchase		(2,400,000)
Advantage of making product Nimal		£7,600,000

The fixed costs of the company are not relevant to the make-or-buy decision, although they must be recovered before the company makes a profit.

5.4 Production facilities are limited in relation to the sales demand made on them. To satisfy demand it is necessary to buy outside

Illustration 10

RB & RJ Limited produces three products, R, B and P. The company is operating at practical capacity. The sales manager is considering adding a new product, Gowell. This product can be developed in space now used to manufacture the standard product R with only minor alterations. It is estimated that Gowell would produce £800,000 in revenue, has a contribution margin ratio of 25 per cent and identifiable fixed costs of £60,000.

A supplier offers to supply product R for £25.

As far as can be seen, the sales outlook is such that the plant could operate at full capacity.

The managing director wanted to know whether the company should purchase product R outside and manufacture product Gowell.

Suggested answer

The following income statements are for the three products and for the company:

RB & RJ LIMITED

Income statement for the period ended 31st December, year 9

Product	*R*	*B*	*P*	*Total*
Sales (units)	20,000	50,000	80,000	–
Selling price per unit	£20	£50	£80	
	(£000)	(£000)	(£000)	(£000)
Sales value	400	2,500	6,400	9,300
Variable cost	300	500	1,600	2,400
Contribution	100	2,000	4,800	6,900
Identifiable fixed costs	50	500	800	1,350
Contribution after charging separable fixed costs	50	1,500	4,000	5,550
Joint fixed costs	–	–	–	2,550
Net profit				3,000

Income statement if product Gowell is produced and R bought out

Sales of product Gowell			£800,000
Marginal cost (75 per cent × 800,000)			600,000
Contribution			200,000
Increased identifiable fixed costs		£10,000	10,000
Contribution after charging separable fixed costs			190,000
Less:			
Additional costs incurred in purchasing product R:			
Outside price	£25 per unit		
Marginal cost to produce	£15		
	£10 × 200,000		(200,000)
Net loss to the company if R is bought outside and Gowell is manufactured			£(10,000)

Illustration 10A

The board of directors of Colombo Pleasure Products Ltd requests the assistance of its management accountant in arriving at a decision on whether to continue manufacturing a certain part of an assembly or to buy it from an outside supplier who has been quoting a price of £2.70 per unit.

The company's annual requirement is 80,000 units and the cost of producing the 80,000 units last year was:

Direct materials	£80,000
Direct labour	120,000
Plant depreciation	10,000
Plant insurance	2,000
Plant maintenance contract	3,000
General fixed costs apportioned to this production	10,000
Other	5,000

The following unit cost increases are anticipated for the forthcoming year if the company continues to manufacture the part:

Direct materials	10%
Direct labour	20%
Plant insurance	5%
Maintenance contract	10%

If it is decided to discontinue production, the machinery used to make the parts could be sold and its book value would be realised.

If the part is purchased, the following costs will be incurred in addition to the basic price charged by the supplier:

Freight	£0.50 per unit
Inspection and storage	£10,000
Insurance	£1,000
Other	£1,400

Suggested answer

IF THE PART IS MANUFACTURED

Annual requirement (units)	80,000
Materials (£80,000 + 10%)	£88,000
Direct labour (£120,000 + 20%)	144,000
Depreciation	10,000
Other	5,000
Insurance (£2,000 + 5%)	2,100
Maintenance contract (£3,000 + 10%)	3,300
Manufacturing costs	£252,400

IF THE PART IS PURCHASED OUTSIDE

Invoice price (80,000 × £2.70)	£216,000
Freight (80,000 × £0.50)	40,000
Inspection and storage	10,000
Insurance	1,000
Other	1,400
Total cost if purchased	£268,400
If manufactured	(252,400)
If part is manufactured company saves	£16,000

(These figures exclude apportioned fixed costs incurred whether manufactured or bought.)

5.5 Make or buy—qualitative factors

Qualitative factors to be considered in addition to a cost analysis to arrive at a sound make-or-buy decision are as follows:

(a) Capacity usage
Will the company continue to have excess capacity? If the part is not being manufactured, would a greater effort be made to utilise excess capacity in other production?

(b) Quality considerations

(i) *Buy outside:* the desired quality cannot be produced within. Outside specialists are doing the job and it is cheaper for the company to buy outside rather than employ its own specialists.

(ii) *Make it:* the desired quality cannot be purchased.

(c) Abnormal idle time
Would the decision to buy outside upset present production schedules and result in an abnormal idle time within the department?

(d) Supplier(s)

(i) The company may *have to make* if the quantity needed is not attractive to outside suppliers.

(ii) Will delivery by outsider be dependable? Are there any dangers of bottlenecks due to non-delivery?

(iii) What is the supplier's reputation among his customers as to meeting delivery dates?

(iv) Is the supplier financially stable?

(v) Would the purchase requirements and price be fixed by contract?

(vi) Are the supplier's production facilities adequate to meet the company's demand?

(vii) Should the company rely solely on one supplier or in order to avoid interruptions should the work be distributed to two or more suppliers? How would this affect price?

(e) Extra costs
Are there any extra costs entailed in buying parts which are not expressed in monetary terms, i.e. ordering and receiving costs, freight, inspection and quality control?

(f) Human relations
There are human-relations aspects of, and costs associated with, possible employee redundancies. A decision to buy, resulting in reducing the company's labour force, may bring protests from the unions and affect productivity. If the decision is to make rather than buying this may help in labour relations, but must be weighed against possible additional costs and loss of supplier's goodwill—for the supplier may also be a customer of the company.

6.0 SELLING PRICE DECISIONS—THE ROLE OF COSTS IN PRODUCT PRICING

6.1 Full cost pricing

In the long run a company should recover its total cost or go out of business. The following formulae express the full cost-based price:

(a) Selling price per unit =

$$\frac{\text{Total cost} + \text{Desired net profit}}{\text{Total quantity}}$$

(b) Selling price per unit =

$$\frac{\text{Total cost} + \text{Desired rate of return} \times \text{Capital employed}}{\text{Total quantity}}$$

The selling price is then adjusted to suit competitive conditions.

Illustration 11

Assume that a company has budgeted production of 500,000 units requiring the following costs:

COST OF PRODUCTION BUDGET

Direct materials	£100,000
Direct labour	200,000
Variable factory overhead	50,000
Fixed factory overhead	150,000
Selling and distribution (fixed)	100,000
Administration and other (fixed)	100,000
Total cost	£700,000
Desired net profit	600,000
Capital employed	3,000,000
Expected rate of return	20%

SELLING PRICE PER UNIT

(a) $\frac{£700{,}000 + £600{,}000}{500{,}000} = £2.60$

(b) $\frac{£700{,}000 + (£3{,}000{,}000 \times 20\%/100)}{500{,}000}$

$= \frac{£700{,}000 + £600{,}000}{500{,}000} = £2.60$

PROBLEM OF APPORTIONING FIXED COST TO PRODUCTS

To determine the full cost of a product the fixed costs have to be apportioned over a specific number of units. In the previous example the fixed costs were £350,000.

Factory	£150,000
Selling and distribution	100,000
Administration and other	100,000
	£350,000

The fixed costs per unit are $\frac{£350{,}000}{500{,}000} = £0.70$.

If the company's level of activity increased to 700,000 or dropped to 250,000 units then the per-unit fixed costs would drop to $\frac{£350{,}000}{700{,}000} = £5$ or increase to $\frac{£350{,}000}{250{,}000} = £1.40$.

The marginal cost per unit will remain the same regardless of the level of output.

SELLING PRICES AT VARIOUS LEVELS OF ACTIVITY

Number of units	250,000	500,000	700,000
Variable cost	£175,000	£350,000	£490,000
Fixed cost	350,000	350,000	350,000
Total cost	525,000	700,000	840,000
Target mark-up: 85.7% of cost	450,000	600,000	720,000
Sales value	975,000	1,300,000	1,560,000
Selling price per unit	£3.90	£2.60	£2.2286
Variable cost per unit	0.70	0.70	0.70
Fixed costs per unit	1.40	0.70	0.50
Total cost per unit	2.10	1.40	1.20

The cost per unit at 250,000 units is £2.10, whereas at 700,000 units it is £1.20. This is because the fixed costs are spread over a greater number of units.

Illustration 12
South Western Company has been operating at 50 per cent capacity. North Eastern Company has requested South Western to produce 5,000 units of their product and would pay £150 per unit. The company's variable costs per unit will be £160. The fixed costs of the company amount to £150,000. The managing director thinks that the offer should be accepted. Although it results in a loss of £10 per unit on the variable costs, he argues that it will gain £15 by spreading fixed costs.

No matter how the fixed costs are spread among units of products, it is not relevant to the decision. The total fixed costs will be £150,000. The regular sales had a current volume of 5,000 units and a net profit of £50,000.

Sales 5,000 × £200	£1,000,000
Variable costs 5,000 × £160	800,000
Fixed costs	150,000
Net profit	£50,000

Suggested answer

If the offer is accepted at £150, the new business will alter the income statement as follows:

	Present	*New*	*Total*
Units	5,000	5,000	10,000
Selling price per unit	£200	£150	–
Variable costs per unit	£160	£160	–
Sales value	£1,000,000	£750,000	£1,750,000
Variable costs	800,000	800,000	1,600,000
Fixed costs	150,000	–	150,000
Profit (loss)	£50,000	£(50,000)	nil

If the fixed costs are spread on a fifty–fifty basis it will alter the income statement but the company's profit will still be nil.

Alternative answer

	Present sales	*Order*	*Total*
Units	5,000	5,000	10,000
Variable costs per unit	£160	£160	–
Selling price per unit	£200	£150	–
Sales value	£1,000,000	£750,000	£1,750,000
Variable costs	800,000	800,000	1,600,000
Fixed costs	75,000	75,000	150,000
Profit (loss)	£125,000	£(125,000)	nil

If the company accepts the order, the company will lose at the rate of £10 per unit on additional sales if the selling price is fixed at £150 per unit.

6.2 Contribution approach

Illustration 13

Assume the cost behaviour pattern as in the previous illustration. Assume further that North Eastern Company offers £170 per unit for the 5,000 units that have an ordinary target price of £200. Should the offer be accepted?

	Full cost pricing	*Contribution approach*
Selling price per unit	£170	£170
Marginal cost per unit	160	160
Fixed cost per unit $\frac{£150,000}{10,000}$	15	–
Total cost per unit	175	160
Apparent decrease in net profit	(5)	–
Contribution	–	10

If the decision maker uses full cost pricing, the offer is definitely unattractive because the price of £170 does not cover the total cost. Under the contribution approach he sees a short-term advantage of £10 per unit (5,000 × £10 = £50,000) from accepting the offer at £170 per unit. It is assumed that the company's fixed costs will not be affected by the acceptance of the offer.

But there are long-run effects to consider. Will the acceptance of the offer affect the long-run pricing policy of the company? If the offer is rejected on these grounds it is, in effect, willing to forgo £10 per unit now in order to protect its long-run market position.

Illustration 14

P. C. Gray and Company has prepared the following budgeted figures for the current year:

Sales (10,000 units at £20)	£200,000
Prime cost (10,000 at £3.00)	30,000
Variable factory overhead (10,000 × £1.00)	10,000
Fixed production costs	50,000
Selling and distribution variable costs (10,000 × £1.00)	10,000
Fixed selling and distribution and administration	40,000
Net profit	£60,000

The area sales manager had asked the sales director for permission to sell 5,000 additional units for £7 per unit. The sales director refused, on the grounds that the price was below full cost. What is the effect of this decision? You may assume that the company is working below capacity.

Suggested answer

FULL COST OF THE PRODUCT

Prime cost	£3
Variable overhead	1
Selling and other	1
	5
Fixed costs per unit: $\frac{50,000+40,000}{10,000}$	9
Full cost	£14

CONTRIBUTION APPROACH

Selling price	£7
Marginal cost	5
Contribution	£2

Total contribution (5,000 × £2) £10,000.

The decision made by the sales director has resulted in reducing the company's profit by an amount of the lost contribution.

By not accepting the order, in the short run profit will be reduced by £10,000. The income forgone represents the amount the company is willing to invest now in order to protect its long-run market advantage.

What would happen to the company if the order affected its current market, i.e. that all products had to be sold at £7?

INCOME STATEMENT

Sales (15,000 units at £7 per unit)		£105,000
Prime cost (15,000 at £3)	£450,000	
Variable factory overhead (15,000 × £1)	15,000	
Selling and distribution variable cost (15,000 × £1)	15,000	75,000
Net contribution		30,000
Fixed costs: Production		50,000
Selling, distribution and administration		40,000
Net loss for the year		£(60,000)

It is therefore essential that consideration should be given to the effect of special order pricing on regular sales.

6.3 Merits of the contribution approach—pricing

(a) The contribution approach to pricing decisions provides refined information since it classifies costs according to their behaviour. It does not mix costs which vary with levels of output with costs which do not. The absorption costing approach may not be that helpful in price fixing since it provides pricing formulae expressed as a percentage of total absorption costs rather than, say, variable costs.

(b) The contribution approach to pricing is often criticised on the grounds that it leads to under-pricing and that therefore full cost pricing, which includes full costs, is a better guide to long-run pricing decisions. This argument has weaknesses:

(i) As long as volume is variable, even under full costing, there is no single unit cost that may be used as a guide to pricing.

(ii) Other factors such as consumer demand and competitor behaviour may influence pricing decisions to such an extent that they often overshadow costs as price-influencing factors.

(iii) Dumping—the practice of selling below full cost in selected areas—is another version of the contribution approach to pricing.

7.0 OPERATION VERSUS PLANT SHUT-DOWN

Companies are often faced with the problem of whether to close down temporarily a part of the plant during periods of low demand.

7.1 How long should operations be continued?

As long as products contribute towards *fixed expenses*, a company seems to be better off than if the plant were shut down.

7.2 Size of fund

The fund required to continue production is the difference between the following:

(a) fixed costs at normal operations,

(b) fixed costs when plant is shut down.

7.3 Arguments against shut-down

(a) If the company continues operation, expenses that would be incurred with the closing down of the plant will be saved; e.g. an increase in factory security.

(b) Continued operation means saving the expenses that will otherwise be incurred if the plant is reopened again at a later stage.

(c) A shut-down for a short period of time will not eliminate all costs. Rent, rates, depreciation and insurance will have to be incurred during the shut-down period.

(d) If the factory is shut down, this will affect not only morale but also its market standing if it cannot meet consumer demand.

Illustration 15

Lanka Manufacturing Company is considering temporarily closing down a division due to an unexpected fall in demand. On the basis of the following information you are required by the board of directors to prepare a statement in such a way as to show clearly whether or not it is advisable to close down the division temporarily.

Production capacity	50%	70%	90%	100%
Units	50,000	70,000	90,000	100,000
Prime cost	£210,000	£294,000	£378,000	£420,000
Production overhead	200,000	240,000	290,000	300,000
Other overhead	90,000	102,000	114,000	120,000

The division is operating at 60 per cent capacity with a turnover of £515,000. If it is decided to close the division temporarily, it is estimated that:

(a) expenses that would be incurred with the closing down of the division would amount to £60,000;

(b) present fixed costs would be reduced by £54,000 per annum;

(c) plant maintenance during shut-down would be £10,000 per annum;

(d) on reopening, the cost of overhauling plant, training and engagement of new personnel would be £30,000.

It is expected that in about twelve months time it may be possible to work at 80 per cent capacity.

Suggested answer

NOTE 1 CALCULATION OF VARIABLE OVERHEAD PER UNIT AND FIXED COST

Capacity	*Production costs*	*Other costs*	*Total cost*
Low (50,000 units, 50%)	£200,000	£90,000	£290,000
High (100,000 units, 100%)	300,000	120,000	420,000
Difference (50,000 units, 50%): variable cost	£100,000	£30,000	£130,000

Variable cost per unit: $\frac{£130,000}{50,000 \text{ units}} = £2.60$ per unit.

At 70 per cent level of activity:

Production overhead	£240,000
Other overhead	102,000
Total overhead	342,000
Less: Variable overhead (70,000 × £2.60)	182,000
Fixed cost	£160,000

Proof: At 100 per cent level of activity:

Production overhead	£300,000
Other overhead	120,000
	420,000
Less: Variable cost (100,000 × £2.60)	260,000
Fixed cost	£160,000

NOTE 2 ESTIMATED COST OF THE SHUT-DOWN (FOR A YEAR)

Closing down		£60,000
Reopening costs		30,000
Plant maintenance		10,000
		100,000
Present fixed costs	£160,000	
Less: Reduction	(54,000)	106,000
Cost of shut-down		£206,000

NOTE 3 IF OPERATIONS CONTINUE

Sales value	£515,000
Less: Prime cost (60,000 at £4.20 per unit)	252,000
Variable overhead (60,000 × £2.60 per unit)	156,000
Contribution	107,000
Fixed costs	160,000
Loss	£(53,000)

As long as products contribute towards fixed costs a shut-down is ruled out. In addition, the fixed costs of continuing operations (£160,000) are £46,000 less than the cost of closing down.

If the fixed costs of closing down the division for a period of one year had been £150,000 then the fund required to remain in operation would have been the difference between the following:

Fixed cost at normal operation	£160,000
Fixed cost when plant is shut down	150,000
Difference	£10,000

Minimum fund required to continue operations is £10,000 (*see* **7.2**).

Alternative solution

	Continue operations	*Shut down*	*Difference*
Cost:			
Prime cost	£252,000	nil	£(252,000)
Variable overhead	156,000	nil	(156,000)
Fixed overhead	160,000	£106,000	(54,000)
Closing down	–	60,000	60,000
Reopening	–	30,000	30,000
Plant maintenance	–	10,000	10,000
	568,000	206,000	(362,000)
Sales value	515,000	–	515,000
Net loss	£(53,000)	£(206,000)	£153,000

CHAPTER SEVENTEEN

Differential Costing for Short-Term Decision Making

1.0 INTRODUCTION AND DEFINITIONS

Differential cost may be defined as the difference between total cost at one level of activity and total cost at another level of activity.

If an increase in the level of activity is anticipated then differential costs may be termed incremental costs.

If a decrease in the level of activity is anticipated then the differential costs may be termed avoidable costs, e.g. the differential cost or the avoidable costs of a decrease in production is the difference between the cost of producing the present high output and that of the expected lower output.

Relevant costs are future differential costs, i.e. those which will be different under each alternative.

2.0 THE ROLE OF FIXED COSTS

If the decrease or increase in the level of activity affects fixed costs then these costs should be considered differential costs. It is generally accepted that if the plant has excess capacity then new or additional volume may be accepted if the selling price is greater than variable costs. In such a situation, fixed costs are not relevant if they remain fixed at an increased level of output. But if they are incurred because of the increased level of activity then they are certainly variable. Once incurred, if they are committed fixed costs, they become a permanent feature and the company may find that it has capacity far in excess of requirements.

The following illustration has been prepared so as to place particular emphasis on the role of fixed costs.

Illustration 1

Sena of London operates at 100 per cent of normal capacity. At this volume it produces 50,000 units of a product.

Income statement

Sales (50,000 units at £10 each)	£500,000
Prime cost (£5 per unit)	250,000
	250,000
Variable production overhead (£1 per unit)	50,000
	200,000
Fixed production overhead	100,000
Factory profit	£100,000

The marketing director reports that an overseas customer has offered to pay £7.50 per unit for an additional 20,000 units. To produce the additional order fixed costs would increase by £25,000. Would you advise the company to accept the order?

DIFFERENTIAL COST STATEMENT—METHOD 1

	Present business	*With additional business*	*Difference*
Sales	£500,000	£650,000	£150,000
Prime cost	250,000	350,000	100,000
Variable production overhead	50,000	70,000	20,000
Fixed production overhead	100,000	125,000	25,000
Factory profit	£100,000	£105,000	£5,000

DIFFERENTIAL COST STATEMENT—METHOD 2

	Present	*Additional*	*Total*
Sales	£500,000	£150,000	£650,000
Prime cost	250,000	100,000	350,000
Variable production overhead	50,000	20,000	70,000
Fixed production overhead	100,000	25,000	125,000
Factory profit	£100,000	£5,000	£105,000

TRADITIONAL STATEMENT FOR ADDITIONAL BUSINESS

Sales (20,000 units at £7.50)	£150,000
Prime cost (20,000 at £5)	100,000
Variable production overhead (20,000 at £1)	20,000
Joint fixed production overhead (using a predetermined rate of absorption: $\frac{£100,000}{50,000}=£2$) (20,000 at £2)	40,000
Separable fixed costs	25,000
Loss on additional business	(£35,000)

The traditional cost statement for additional business would cause management to *reject* the offer.

Management may also not accept the offer because as computed under the traditional method (absorption costing) the price offered per unit is less than the total cost per unit and also because it is less than the current selling price of £10 per unit:

Price offered—per unit		£7.50
Cost per unit	£	
Prime cost	5.00	
Variable production overhead	1.00	
Joint fixed costs	2.00	
Separable fixed costs $\left(\frac{£25,000}{20,000}\right)$	1.25	9.25
Loss per unit		£(1.75)

In the differential cost statements (methods 1 and 2) the additional business has been charged with *differential cost only*. It should be noted that the reason for the differential profit is that *the regular sales were not affected by the acceptance of additional business*. If the acceptance of additional business caused the price to be reduced to £7.50 per unit on all sales then the result would be a loss of £20,000 for the company:

REVISED INCOME STATEMENT—ALL SALES AT £7.50

Sales (70,000 units at £7.50)	£525,000
Variable costs (70,000 at £6)	420,000
Joint fixed production costs	100,000
Separable fixed production costs	25,000
Loss	£(20,000)

3.0 THE ROLE OF VARIABLE COSTS

In differential cost studies, if the plant is not operating at practical capacity owing to lack of orders, variable costs usually represent the differential cost whether they are incremental or avoidable. The term refers to those costs that will change. It is often assumed that the variable cost per unit will remain constant regardless of the level of activity.

One may question the validity of the above assumption. What if the variable cost per unit does not remain constant at various levels of activity? An increased level of activity may cause the variable cost per unit to change for a variety of reasons. Examples are:

(a) at a higher level of output material cost per unit may be reduced by bulk buying at lower prices;

(b) direct labour cost per unit may increase as a result of overtime working if there is a labour shortage;

(c) greater spoilage and waste with increased production.

The illustration that follows puts particular emphasis on the role of variable costs:

Illustration 2

The following are assumed:
Sena of London produces 40,000 units operating at 50 per cent capacity.

Production fixed costs	£20,000
Other fixed costs	£40,000
Variable cost per unit:	
Direct material	£3.00
Direct labour	2.00
Variable overhead	1.00
	£6.00

Selling price per unit: £10.

An overseas customer offers to buy increased quantities during the forthcoming year at the following prices:

10,000 units at £9
20,000 units at £8
30,000 units at £7
40,000 units at £6

If the offer is accepted then the variable cost per unit is expected to change as follows:

First 10,000 units	Would cause a drop in the material cost per unit due to large-scale purchases.
Next 10,000 units	A *further* reduction in the material cost per unit but an increase in direct wages.
Next 10,000 units	Would involve some overtime and so variable overhead per unit would increase.
Next 10,000 units	A further reduction in material cost per unit, and increased labour cost per unit and variable cost per unit.

SUMMARY OF EXPECTED CHANGES

Units	1st 10,000	2nd 10,000	3rd 10,000	4th 10,000
Material per unit	(5%)	(5%)	–	(5%)
Labour per unit	–	5% +	–	5% +
Variable overhead per unit	–	–	5% +	5% +

VARIABLE COST PER UNIT AT VARIOUS LEVELS OF ACTIVITY

	Normal (£)	*Additional 10,000*	*Additional 20,000*	*Additional 30,000*	*Additional 40,000*
Direct material	3.00	2.85	2.7075	2.7075	2.572
Direct labour	2.00	2.00	2.1000	2.1000	2.205
Direct expenses	1.00	1.00	1.0000	1.0500	1.1025
Variable cost per unit	6.00	5.85	5.8075	5.8575	5.8795

DIFFERENTIAL COST STATEMENT

	Normal 40,000	*Additional 10,000*	*Additional 20,000*	*Additional 30,000*	*Additional 40,000*
Sales value per unit	£10	£9.00	£8.00	£7.00	£6.00
Variable cost per unit	6	5.85	5.8075	5.8575	5.8795
Contribution per unit	£4	£3.15	£2.1925	£1.1425	£0.1205
Fund	160,000	31,500	43,850	34,275	4,820

It would be most profitable to accept the additional order for 20,000 units at £8.00 per unit.

Notes

The following points must be borne in mind:

(a) Differential costs due to an increase in the level of activity may be termed incremental costs.

(b) Differential costs due to a decrease in the level of activity may be termed avoidable costs.

(c) The term fixed costs is sometimes misleading. If fixed costs are incurred for additional business which will not be continued then the additional fixed costs may be treated as variable costs. If the additional fixed costs become committed fixed costs, they should be treated as fixed costs.

(d) In a differential cost statement, costs allocated to the additional business are costs which can be identified directly with additional business.

(e) Under-utilised capacity costs or fixed costs which are ordinarily incurred are not charged to additional business. How joint fixed costs are spread among units is not relevant to the decision because the total fixed costs are unaffected. This is true despite the fact that joint fixed costs per unit have fallen in Illustration 1 from

$$\frac{£100{,}000}{50{,}000} = £2.00 \text{ per unit} \quad \text{to} \quad \frac{£100{,}000}{70{,}000} = £1.44 \text{ per unit.}$$

(f) Regarding product pricing and the differential cost approach, we have assumed in Illustration 2 that an additional 20,000 units could be sold at £8.00 and regular sales are unaffected. This is true only if:

(i) separate markets exist for the product

(ii) price differences can be made between buyers.

(g) In the differential cost statement the additional business has been charged with differential cost only. For decision-making purposes differential cost analysis has a distinct advantage.

(h) Full cost must be covered in the long run. If not then the company will face financial difficulties. Differential cost analysis is useful only for incremental orders *or in determining avoidable costs. For example, assume:*

Normal capacity	*50,000 units*
Production/sales	*25,000 units*
Selling price per unit	*£30*
Marginal cost per unit	*£20*
Fixed costs	*£200,000.*

An additional order for 20,000 units can be obtained at £22 per unit.

If the company accepts the additional order then it will reduce losses or increase profits because the additional order will contribute £40,000 towards fixed costs (£2 × 20,000 units). However, *if this leads to the acceptance of all sales at £22 without a reduction in variable cost per unit or in fixed cost per unit to compensate then the company will be making a loss of* £110,000.

Contribution (£2 × 45,000 units)	*£90,000*
Fixed costs	*200,000*
Loss	*£(110,000)*

In the short run, using differential costs the company may increase its profits but in the long run products have to recover their full cost.

It must be kept in mind that overall company objectives are usually long-run objectives. In making short-term decisions one must consider their long-term implications.

4.0 EQUIPMENT REPLACEMENT DECISIONS AND DIFFERENTIAL COSTS

4.1 Irrelevant value of old equipment

In problems involving the replacement of equipment and similar matters it is essential to realise that the book value of existing (old) equipment is *irrelevant*. It is a past or a historical cost. The company has incurred it and in replacement decisions it is not relevant.

4.2 Relevant future costs

Relevant costs for decision making are the expected future costs of

(a) continuing with the present machinery,

(b) replacing it with new.

The decision depends upon the difference between these two costs and hence is a differential costing problem.

Illustration 3

In this illustration the following are assumed:

Original cost of the machine	£100,000
Provision for depreciation	£50,000
Useful life left	5 years
Annual operating cost	£35,000
Scrap value—now	£10,000
Scrap value—5 years	nil

A new machine is available:

Cost	£60,000
Life	5 years
Scrap value	nil
Operating costs per annum	£20,000

If the asset is replaced then the company would increase net income as follows:

Cost of the new machine	£60,000
Less: Disposable value of old machine	10,000
Net outlay now	£50,000

Operating expenses—old	£35,000
Operating expenses—new	20,000
Saving per annum	£15,000

5 years together:

Savings (£15,000 × 5 years)	£75,000
Less: Investment (depreciation)	50,000
Net income	£25,000

4.3 Further relevant items

Apart from the book value of old equipment, five items which need to be considered in equipment replacement decisions are:

(a) *Disposable value of old equipment* (£10,000). This is considered to be relevant because it is an expected future inflow that differs between various alternatives. In the example the disposable value of the old equipment now is £10,000 and in 5 years is nil.

(b) *Cost of new equipment* (£60,000). A relevant cost, being an expected future outflow that will differ between alternatives.

(c) *Loss or gain on disposal* (£40,000). This is a combination of the book value (irrelevant cost) and scrap value (relevant inflow). It *is not relevant* in the context of which alternative is the best.

(d) *Disposable value of new equipment* (nil). This is a relevant inflow of cash.

(e) *Net outlay* (£60,000 − £10,000 = £50,000).
The investment involved in the purchase of the new equipment *now* requires an outlay of £50,000 (£60,000 − £10,000). Regardless of where the company obtains this money, it has a cost. If the company has liquid cash which it can invest, instead of buying the equipment, the company is sacrificing investment income by buying the equipment. If the company borrows money it will have to pay interest.
Therefore the decision maker should add *a notional cost for using £50,000 in buying equipment.*

Notional costs do not involve actual cash outlay and are not reflected in income determination, but in making comparisons and in decision making the inclusion of imputed costs is important.

Illustration 4

Sena of London has acquired a machine for £25,000 with a life of 4 years. At the end of its useful life the machine is worth £1,000, but its disposable value now is £10,000. Annual output 10,000 units.

Its estimated operating costs are (4 years together):

Direct materials	£100,000
Direct labour	200,000
Variable production overhead 50 per cent of direct labour	100,000
Fixed manufacturing overhead	50,000
Repairs—estimated	5,000
Machine depreciation	24,000
Selling and other	44,000
Total cost	£523,000

Neville Colombo, a machine salesman, has offered a superior new machine which would cost £30,000 and has the same potential output. However, the salesman claims that it has certain cost savings. Its estimated operating costs are (4 years together):

Direct materials	£100,000
Direct labour	£150,000
Variable production overhead 50 per cent of direct labour	£75,000
Fixed manufacturing overhead	£55,000
Repairs	£3,000
Machine depreciation	£30,000
Selling and other costs	£44,000

The general manager countered this argument by saying that the company has to retain the old machine to recover the investment of £25,000.

The alternative is that of keeping the old machine or buying the new one.

DIFFERENTIAL COST STATEMENT

	Old machine 4 years together 1	*New machine 4 years together 2*	*Difference 3 (2−1)*
Output in units	40,000	40,000	nil
Cost:			
Materials	£100,000	£100,000	nil
Labour	200,000	150,000	£50,000
Variable production overhead	100,000	75,000	25,000
Fixed production overhead	50,000	55,000	(5,000)
Disposable value of old equipment	(1,000)	(10,000)	9,000
Repairs	5,000	3,000	2,000
Machine depreciation (Note (b))	nil	30,000	(30,000)
Selling and other costs	44,000	44,000	nil
Total cost	£498,000	£447,000	£51,000

Notes

(a) *Direct material costs and selling and other costs are irrelevant because they are common in both alternatives.*

(b) *The original cost of the old machine is not relevant to the decision. Since the company has invested £25,000 not so long ago it may try to keep using it to recover the investment. The differential cost statement demonstrates that the original investment in the light of current conditions was unwise. Probably that was the best of the alternatives then, and what is incurred is a sunk cost. What is relevant now is, what can be done about it? Should we replace it or keep it? To put it in another way, the question management has to answer now is whether or not the company will be better off by buying the new machine.*

(c) *The new machine, if bought, will reduce costs by £51,000 over a period of 4 years, or £12,750 per annum, on an investment of £20,000 (i.e. about 64 per cent return). If the additional revenue/cost saving is greater than the additional investment, it will be profitable for a company to incur the additional investment. This is based on the assumption that the return on this investment is acceptable. Regardless of the cost of the original investment, it will be advantageous to make the investment.*

5.0 CONTINUED OPERATION VERSUS TEMPORARY SHUT-DOWN

Differential cost studies may be applied to the problem of whether to continue operation or have a temporary plant shut-down.

Illustration 5
Due to an economic recession Sena of London is considering the closure of one of its factories for a temporary period. The following information is available:

Normal plant capacity	100,000 units
Fixed cost—at present	£200,000
Fixed cost if plant is shut down	£75,000
Expenses that would be incurred with the closing down	£15,000
Plant maintenance during shut-down	£10,000
On reopening—overhauling plant, training and other costs would be	£10,000
Variable cost per unit	£8.00
Reduced selling price per unit	£10.40
Estimated sales and volume (units)	50,000

DIFFERENTIAL COST STATEMENT

	Continue operation	*Shut-down*	*Difference*
Sales (units)	50,000	–	–
Sales price per unit	£10.40		
Marginal cost per unit	£8.00		
Contribution per unit	£2.40		
Fund	£120,000	nil	£120,000
Fixed costs	200,000	£75,000	125,000
Other expenses	–	15,000	(15,000)
Plant maintenance	–	10,000	(10,000)
Reopening costs	–	10,000	(10,000)
Profit (loss)	£(80,000)	£(110,000)	£30,000

If the factory is closed down, the loss due to fixed costs would be £110,000, whereas if it operates at 50 per cent of its normal capacity then the loss will be only £80,000.

CHAPTER EIGHTEEN

Standard Costing – An Introduction to Concepts

1.0 INTRODUCTION

1.1 Comparison between standard costing and historical costing

In our work so far, we have covered only those costing systems which record, as a matter of history, actual costs incurred in making a product or providing a service. Although there is a place for such costing systems, they suffer from the important drawback that they do not provide information in a convenient form for cost *control*, as opposed to cost *recording*.

The costing method employed by the majority of well-organised concerns is *standard costing*, in which a *standard cost* for each product or operation is worked out in advance. Actual costs incurred are then compared with these standard costs and the variations between standard and actual are analysed and summarised to provide really detailed information for management to form the basis of corrective action where actual costs exceed standard.

2.0 STANDARD COSTING SYSTEMS

2.1 Definition

Standard costing is the preparation of standard costs and their use to classify the financial results of a business, particularly by the measurement of variations of actual costs from standard costs and the analysis of the causes of the variations for the purpose of maintaining maximum efficiency by executive action.

2.2 Principles (plan) of a standard costing system

(a) *Set up standard costs for each product based on technical specifications.* These are summarised in a standard cost card (*see* Illustration 1 below). The following items are included:

materials: specification, quantities, prices

labour: grade, times, rates

production variable overhead: times, rates

production fixed overhead: times, rates

For a product passing through a number of operations, the standard product cost card must specify the standard cost at each stage.

(b) *Record actual costs.* Actual costs are calculated for each period, analysed over the departments incurring the costs.

(c) *Record actual output.*

(d) *Calculate the standard cost of actual output* in terms of materials, labour and overhead.

(e) *Compare actual costs with standard cost of actual production.*

(f) *Analyse variances*

(i) by factors

(ii) by causes

(g) *Report results* to management.

(h) *Take corrective action* whenever the variances reported show this to be necessary.

(i) *Effectiveness:* To be effective the system needs to be *understood* and *respected* by the *managers* it is *designed to help* in controlling the costs for which they are held responsible.

Illustration 1—Principles of standard costing
(The reader should follow the steps.)

(a) *Standard cost card* *Product:* RB 747 *Quantity:* one pound

	Standard quantities	*Standard prices*	*Standard cost*
Raw materials	10 lb	£2	£20
Direct labour	5 hours	4	20
Variable production overhead	5 hours	1	5
Fixed production overhead	5 hours	3	15
			£60

(b) *Actual costs*—period

Raw materials purchased and used:	
600 lb at £3 per lb	£1,800
Direct labour: 300 hours	1,500
Variable production overhead	300
Fixed production overhead	700

(c) *Record actual output:* RB 747—50 units.

(d) *Calculate the standard cost of actual output*

		Standard quantities	*Standard prices*	*Standard cost*
Raw materials: 50 × 10 lb	=	500 lb	£2	£1,000
Direct labour: 50 × 5	=	250 hours	4	1,000
Variable production overhead: 50 × 5	=	250 hours	1	250
Fixed production overhead: 50 × 5	=	250 hours	3	750
				£3,000

(e) *Comparison*

Expense	*Actual cost*	*Standard cost of actual output*	*Cost variance*
Raw materials	600 lb at £3 =£1,800	50 units at 10 lb per unit=500 lb 500 lb at £2=£1,000	£800 adverse
Direct labour	300 hours at £5=£1,500	50 units at 5 hours per unit=250 hours 250 hours at £4=£1,000	£500 adverse
Variable overhead	£300	50 units at 5 hours per unit=250 hours 250 hours at £1=£250	£50 adverse
Fixed overhead	£700	50 units at 5 hours per unit=250 hours 250 hours at £3=£750	£50 favourable
Total	£4,300	£3,000	£(1,300)

(f) *Variance analysis by causes*
A standard costing system would normally report:

(i) in which departments of a company cost variances had occurred;

(ii) which items of expenses differed from the standard cost of actual production;

(iii) causes of the variances for corrective action.

3.0 TYPES OF STANDARDS

Figure 28 depicts the relationship between the standard types.

3.1 Introduction

The *standard* is an *exact measure* of what should take place if performance is efficient, in terms of

(a) quantities,

(b) prices.

To be effective all the people involved must be prepared to make it work. Standard costing is not just an accounting exercise. The accountant's function is largely that of providing relevant information to management. The ultimate value of the system lies in the *action* of the managers to take steps to achieve the targets set. It is generally accepted that managers should be involved in setting these standards, and that, while standards should reflect a high degree of efficiency, they should be achievable and be seen to be achievable by responsible managers. The system, to be effective, needs managers' participation, respect and understanding. The system is designed to help managers in controlling costs for which they are held responsible.

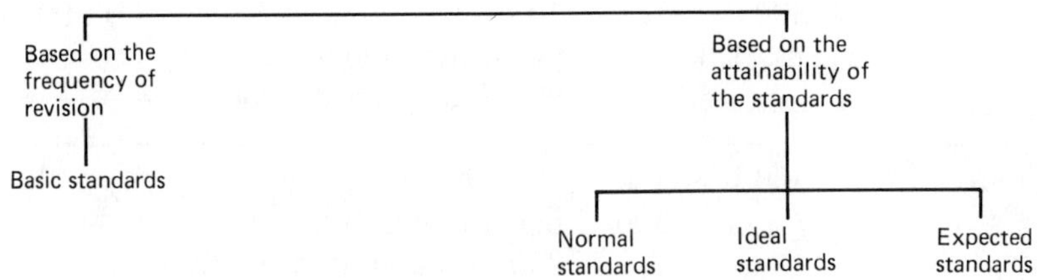

Fig. 28. *Different types of standards.*

3.2 Basic standards

These are standards based on basic conditions or circumstances. They are rarely used in practice.

Such standards, prepared for some base year, remain unchanged for a long period of time unless the production operations are changed.

Illustration 2

Base year: the year 1 is taken as the base year.
Average labour rate per hour: £2.00.
Average material cost per unit: £3.00.
These figures are then used to represent a 100 per cent for comparison with later years.

CURRENT YEAR: YEAR 5

Average labour rate per hour: £3.50.
Average material cost per unit: £6.00.

COMPARISON

	Base year	*Current year*
Labour rate	£2.00 (100%)	£3.00
Material cost per lb	£3.00 (100%)	£6.00

In comparison with the base year the labour rate per hour is 150 per cent and material cost per lb is 200 per cent.

As stated above, basic standards are infrequently used. The principle used in the basic standard is similar to that used in the cost of living price index.

3.3 Normal standards

Costs which are predetermined to be applied over a period of a complete business cycle are termed normal standards. The standard therefore represents the average conditions to be expected throughout the whole of the business cycle. Normal standards are not frequently used for product costing purposes as most of the deviations would be beyond the control of management. The concept of a normal standard is by and large theoretical.

3.4 Ideal standards

Such a standard reflects the ideal combination of factors:

(a) the best plant and equipment layout;

(b) the best possible prices for materials, labour and overhead;

(c) a high degree of efficiency in the utilisation of resources.

Ideal standards are really targets to be aimed for rather than goals to be achieved. They are distant aims, extremely desirable targets but rarely attainable goals. In a narrow sense such standards are engineering standards, e.g. if the waste of direct materials was at an absolute minimum, machinery never broke down, no time was lost, and if the labour force produced the maximum output they are capable of producing during a specific period of time.

3.5 Expected standards

These are currently attainable standards. The important aspect of the expected standard is that it is *related* to the current conditions—conditions the company expects to prevail over a relatively short period of time, e.g. a year. Further, it allows for normal losses, that is, direct material standards include allowances for normal wastage, direct labour standards include allowance for normal idle time and do not expect the direct labour force to work at maximum efficiency all the time. The standards are therefore not as tight as the ideal standards and not as far removed from present conditions as the normal and the basic standards.

3.6 Selecting the type of standard

The management of a company must give thought to the following points:

(a) Which type of standard will be most useful for product costing purposes?

(b) Which type of standard will be most useful for control purposes?

(c) Standards measure managers' efficiency. It is most likely, unless the managers agree to the standards set and get involved in setting them, that these standards set by the accountants' departments will not be treated as fair and reasonable standards by managers whose activity they measure.

Expected standards (**3.5**) are those most likely to meet the requirements of the average business cost control system.

CHAPTER NINETEEN

Variance Analysis I – Direct Materials

1.0 INTRODUCTION

At the centre of the standard cost system is the standard cost card. The card contains details of the standard quantities and standard prices to produce a cost unit (a single product or a batch).

1.1 Basic standard cost card

Illustration 1

STANDARD COST CARD Product: JAD 1. Unit: 100 lb

Direct materials	*Standard quantity*	*Standard price*	*Standard cost*
Type A	40 lb	£1	£40
B	40 lb	2	80
C	45 lb	3	135
Input: Total materials	125 lb		255
Less: Normal loss	(25 lb)		
Output total materials	100 lb		£255

Two factors must be considered in determining material cost standards:

(a) the quantity of materials to be used (*see* **2.0**);

(b) the prices of materials (*see* **3.0**).

2.0 QUANTITY OF MATERIALS TO BE USED

The quantity of materials to be used is based upon determination of the following:

2.1 Kind and quality specifications

The prices and quantities depend upon the kind and quality of the materials. Therefore, prior to the determination of quantities, specifications should be determined for the kind and quality of each raw material.

2.2 Allowance for waste, shrinkage and scrap

In the process of manufacture, if there is a loss in materials then allowance is normally made for it. It must be borne in mind that the allowance should reflect only those losses considered unavoidable, normal or uncontrollable under the conditions assumed when setting the quantity standards. In the illustration above, 20 per cent of input is treated as an uncontrollable loss.

3.0 PRICES OF MATERIALS

Material price standards are normally based on expected prices for the period. In most companies the setting of price standards is the responsibility of the purchasing department. The purchasing manager may set price standards on a variety of bases. Examples are:

(a) Prices agreed upon in long-term purchase contracts.

(b) Use of statistical forecasting.

(c) Arbitrary estimates based upon expense in the type of business.

(d) Average of prices paid on the recent purchases.

He may also take into account the price advantages to be gained by determining the economic batch size, method of delivery, credit terms, and cost of storage.

4.0 BASIC VARIANCE ANALYSIS

4.1 Definitions

The following definitions are used:

(a) Direct material cost variance (total variance)
"The *difference* between the *standard cost* of *materials specified* and the *actual cost* of *materials used*." (ICMA.)

In the analysis of the total/cost variance:

(b) Material price variance

"The proportion of the material cost variance which is due to the difference between the standard price specified and the actual price paid." (ICMA.)

(c) Material usage variance

The proportion of the material cost variance which is due to the difference between the standard quantity specified and the actual quantity used.

Illustration 2

The following data are given for a product:

Standards per unit of product:

		SQ × SP	=	standard cost
Material A	lb	2 × £2	=	£4.00
Material B	lb	3 × £1	=	£3.00
				£7.00

Actual details for a given financial period:

Direct materials	*Purchased*	*Used*
Type A	200,000 = £500,000	180,000
Type B	300,000 = £300,000	300,000
Actual output in units	90,000	

There were no stocks of raw materials or work in progress at the beginning of the period and no work in progress at its end.

You are required to calculate the following variances:

(a) Direct materials cost;

(b) Direct materials price;

(c) Direct materials usage.

Note: Material Price Variance—see Chapter 3, ***3.10****. Price variance is the difference between actual price paid and the standard price specified.*

Material type A: Purchases are greater than usage. The price variance may be calculated

on purchases: 200,000 × £(2.50 − 2.00) = £100,000, or

on usage: 180,000 × £(2.50 − 2.00) = £90,000.

The isolation of material price variance at the time of purchase is convenient for stock recording purposes since it simplifies the records by enabling them to be maintained at standard price. This method has one major problem, since raw-material stocks will not be at actual prices paid for the materials.

Material type B: Purchases equal issues. The price variance is the same whether it is based on issues or on purchases.

Suggested answer

Type	Quantity used actual price	Quantity used SP		Standard cost of actual output	Cost variance	Analysis	
						Price	Usage
Type A	1	2	3	4	5 (4–1)	6 (2–1)	7 (4–3)
Price variance on quantity used	180,000 × £2.50 = £450,000	180,000 × £2 = £360,000	–	90,000 × 2 = 180,000 × £2 = £360,000	£(90,000)	£(90,000)	nil
Type A	AQ bought × AP	Actual quantity bought × SP	Actual quantity used × SP	Standard cost of actual output	Cost variance	Price	Usage
	1	2	3	4	5 (6+7)	6 (2–1)	7 (4–3)
Price variance on quantity bought	200,000 × £2.50 = £500,000	200,000 × £2 = £400,000	180,000 × £2 = £360,000	90,000 × 2 × 180,000 × £2 = £360,000	£(100,000)	£(100,000)	nil
Type B	300,000 × £1 = £300,000	300,000 × £1 = £300,000		90,000 × 3 = 270,000 × £1 = £270,000	£(30,000)	nil	£(30,000)

4.2 Allowances for normal losses while materials are in process

An allowance is normally made in determining standard quantities. The allowances for the expected or normal loss should reflect only those losses which are uncontrollable under the conditions assumed when standards were set. The inclusion of an allowance for normal losses assists to highlight any abnormal or controllable losses in process.

Illustration 3

Rod Reis chemical company recently adopted a standard cost system. A complete study of all operations of equipment and production facilities and a revaluation of materials costs and labour rates preceded the installation. The standard cost card for one of the products shows the following materials standards:

	Batch 100 lb *Std quantity*	*Std price*	*Std cost*
Department 1	(lb)	(£ per lb)	(£)
Material A	50	5	250
Material B	40	2	80
Department 2			
Material C	30	1	30
Material D	30	2	60
	150		420
Standard shrinkage $33\frac{1}{3}$	(50)		–
	100		420

Actual results for the period

830 lb of raw materials used as follows:

300 lb of material A at £6	£1,800
250 lb of material B at £3	750
100 lb of material C at £1	100
180 lb of material D at £1.50	270
830	

Actual output of finished product = five batches.

Calculate:

(a) material cost variance;
(b) material price variance;
(c) material usage variance.

Suggested answer

Department	*Actual cost*		*Actual quantity used at standard price*		*Standard cost of production*		*Cost variance*	*Variance analysis by causes*	
								Price	*Usage*
	1		*2*		*3*		*4* (*3–1*)	*5* (*2–1*)	*6* (*3–2*)
Dept 1									
Material A	300 × £6 =	£1,800	300 × £5 =	£1,500	5 × 50 × £5 =	£1,250	£(550)	£(300)	£(250)
Material B	250 × £3 =	£750	250 × £2 =	500	5 × 40 × £2 =	400	(350)	(250)	(100)
		£2,550		£2,000		£1,650	£(900)	£(550)	£(350)
Dept 2									
Material C	100 × £1 =	£100	100 × £1 =	£100	5 × 30 × £1	£150	£50 +	nil	£50 +
Material D	180 × £1.50 =	270	180 × £2 =	360	5 × 30 × £2 =	300	30 +	90 +	(60)
		£370		£460		£450	£80 +	£90	£(10)
Total (depts 1 + 2)		£2,920		£2,460		£2,100	£(820)	£(460)	£(360)

4.3 Standard cost of actual output

If all the units introduced at the beginning are fully completed at the end of each period no problem arises. If at the end of the period there are partly completed units, these will have to be expressed in terms of whole or equivalent units in order to calculate the standard cost of *actual output*.

Note: Actual output may consist of two parts:

(a) Fully completed units;

(b) Partly completed units (WIP).

Illustration 4

Product RBX is produced from three types of raw materials, R, B and P.

Materials	*Standard quantity (lb)*	*Standard price per lb*	*Standard cost*
R	1	£2	£2
B	3	£3	£9
P	2	£4	£8
			£19

DATA FOR PERIOD 1:

Production:	Completed units of RBX		5,000
	Work in progress incorporating raw materials 50% R and B (Material P is added at the end of the process)		500
		lb	*Price per lb*
Materials used:	Material R	5,600	£2
	Material B	17,000	£3
	Material P	10,000	£5

STATEMENT OF PRODUCTION—(WHOLE/EQUIVALENT UNITS)

Input	*Output*	*R*	*B*	*P*
5,500	5,000 fully completed	5,000	5,000	5,000
	500 work in progress c/f	250	250	–
5,500	5,500	5,250	5,250	5,000

Suggested answer

Material type	*Actual cost*	*Actual quantity used at standard price*	*Standard cost of actual production*	*Total variance*	*Variance analysis*	
					Price	*Usage*
	1	*2*	*3*	*4* (*3–1*)	*5* (*2–1*)	*6* (*3–2*)
R	5,600 lb × £2 = £11,200	5,600 × £2 = £11,200	5,250 × 1 lb 5,250 × £2 = £10,500	(£700)	nil	350 lb excess usage × £2 = £700
B	17,000 lb × £3 = £51,000	17,000 × £3 = £51,000	5,250 × 3 lb 15,750 lb × £3 = £47,250	(£3,750)	nil	1,250 lb excess usage × £3 = £3,750
P	10,000 lb × £5 = £50,000	10,000 × £4 = £40,000	5,000 × 2 lb 10,000 × £4 = £40,000	(£10,000)	(£10,000)	nil
Total	£112,200	£102,200	£97,750	(£14,450)	(£10,000)	(£4,450)

* Refer to statement of production.

Calculate:

(a) materials cost variance;

(b) materials price variance;

(c) material usage variance.

Suggested answer—see p. 360

5.0 RAW MATERIAL USAGE VARIANCE—MIX AND YIELD

5.1 Further analysis of usage variance

The material usage variance is the result of using more or less material on production than was predetermined. It may be further analysed by causes into the following:

(a) Material mix variance
If the actual mixture does not comply with the standard mixture a mix variance results.

(b) Material yield variance
For example, in the manufacture of canning fruits the yields may vary with the mixture.
Note: In order to highlight the mix and yield variances, prices of raw materials have been ignored.

5.2 Material mix variance

Illustration 5
To isolate the material mix variance, the actual quantity must be compared with the actual quantity expressed in standard proportions, i.e. whether the quantities actually used conform to the standard formula.

The standard quantity to produce five units of product is:

2 lb of material R
3 lb of material J
1 lb of material P.

To produce 500 units of a finished product, the raw material standard quantities are:

	Standard quantities specified
Material R (lb)	200
Material J (lb)	300
Material P (lb)	100
	600
Less normal loss	(100)
Good output	500

Actual data	*Period 1*	*Period 2*	*Period 3*
Actual quantity produced	2,000 units	2,000 units	2,000 units
Actual quantity of materials	*(lb)*	*(lb)*	*(lb)*
used: Material R	800	1,000	1,000
Material J	1,200	1,000	1,000
Material P	400	400	700

VARIANCE ANALYSIS

Raw material	*Actual quantity used (lb)*	*Actual quantity expressed in standard proportions (lb)*	*Mix variance (lb)*
	1	*2*	*3* (*2*−*1*)
Period 1			
R	800	$\frac{200}{600} \times 2{,}400 =$ 800	nil
J	1,200	$\frac{300}{600} \times 2{,}400 =$ 1,200	nil
P	400	$\frac{100}{600} \times 2{,}400 =$ 400	nil
Total	2,400		nil
Period 2			
R	1,000	$\frac{200}{600} \times 2{,}400 =$ 800	(200)
J	1,000	$\frac{300}{600} \times 2{,}400 =$ 1,200	200
P	400	$\frac{100}{600} \times 2{,}400 =$ 400	nil
Total	2,400	2,400	nil
Period 3			
R	1,000	$\frac{200}{600} \times 2{,}700 =$ 900	(100)
J	1,000	$\frac{200}{600} \times 2{,}700 =$ 1,350	350
P	700	$\frac{100}{600} \times 2{,}700 =$ 450	(250)
Total	2,700	2,700	nil

5.3 Material yield variance

Illustration 6

Material yield variance is the difference between the standard yield specified and actual yield obtained.

Standard cost information to produce 100 lb of product Bop is as follows:

Direct materials (lb):	Ingredient M	40
	Ingredient D	40
	Ingredient N	40
		120
	Normal loss	(20)
	Good output	100 lb

ACTUAL DATA

During period 1 the output of Bop was 5,000 lb, the input materials being:

2,680 lb material M
2,000 lb material D
3,000 lb material N

Note: In order to highlight the mix and yield variances prices of raw materials have been ignored.

Suggested answer

Material type	*Actual quantity used (lb)*	*Actual quantity expressed in standard proportion (lb)*	*Standard quantity in actual output (lb)*	*Material usage variance (lb)*	*Variance analysis Mix (lb)*	*Variance analysis Yield (lb)*
	1	*2*	*3*	*4* (*3–1*)	*5* (*2–1*)	*6* (*3–2*)
M	2,680	$\frac{40}{120} \times 7{,}680 = 2{,}560$	$5{,}000 \times \frac{40}{100} = 2{,}000$	(680)	(120)	(560)
D	2,000	$\frac{40}{120} \times 7{,}680 = 2{,}560$	$5{,}000 \times \frac{40}{100} = 2{,}000$	nil	560	(560)
N	3,000	$\frac{40}{120} \times 7{,}680 = 2{,}560$	$5{,}000 \times \frac{40}{100} = 2{,}000$	(1,000)	(440)	(560)
	7,680	7,680	6,000	1,680	nil	1,680

Comprehensive illustration 7

Rod is a garden fertiliser produced by mixing three chemicals, R, O and D, in proportions 5, 3 and 2 respectively. The standard prices of the chemicals are R £2.00 per lb, O £3.00 per lb and D £4.00 per lb. The normal yield from the mixing process is 80 per cent, the loss being due to evaporation and removal of residual chemicals of no value which arise during the process.

During period one the output of Rod was 80,000 lb, the input materials being

45,000 lb of R which costs £2 per lb
30,000 lb of O which costs £3 per lb
21,000 lb of D which costs £5 per lb
96,000 lb

STANDARD COST CARD Product: Rod Unit: 80 lb

Raw material	*Standard quantity (lb)*	*Standard price (£)*	*Standard cost (£)*
R	50	2	100
O	30	3	90
D	20	4	80
Input	100		270
Normal loss (20%)	(20)		–
Good output (80%)	80		270

Required:
Calculate and present the material cost variances.

Suggested answer—see p. 365

6.0 EXAMPLE

DN Products Limited produces a facing tile with a standard size of 4 inches × 3 inches × ½ inch. The standard product mix for making 5,000 square feet of tiles (or 60,000 tiles), after allowing for normal breakage, is as follows:

Raw material	*Standard quantity (lb)*	*Standard price per lb (£)*	*Standard cost (£)*
R	1,000	0.60	600
A	400	2.00	800
P	600	0.50	300
	2,000		1,700

Suggested answer

	Actual cost	Actual quantity used at standard prices	Actual quantity used in standard proportion at standard prices	Standard cost of actual output	Cost variance (£)	Cost variance: Price (£)	Cost variance: Usage (£)	Usage: Mix (£)	Usage: Yield (£)
	1	*2*	*3*	*4*	*5* (*4–1*)	*6* (*2–1*)	*7* (*4–2*)	*8* (*3–2*)	*9* (*4–3*)
R	45,000 × £2	45,000 × £2	$\frac{50}{100}$ × 96,000 = 48,000	80,000 × $\frac{50}{80}$ =			5,000 × £2	3,000 + × £2	2,000 + × £2
	= £90,000	= £90,000	48,000 × £2 = £96,000	50,000 × £2 = £100,000	£10,000 +	nil	= £10,000 +	= £6,000 +	= £4,000 +
O	30,000 × £3	30,000 × £3	$\frac{30}{100}$ × 96,000 =	80,000 × $\frac{30}{80}$ =				1,200 × £3	1,200 + × £3
	= £90,000	= £90,000	28,800 × £3 = £86,400	30,000 × £3 = £90,000	nil	nil	nil	= £(3,600)	= £3,600 +
D	21,000 × £5	21,000 × £4	$\frac{20}{100}$ × 96,000 = 19,200	80,000 × $\frac{20}{80}$ =			(1,000 × £4)	(1,800 × £4)	800 × £4
	= £105,000	£84,000	= 19,200 × £4 = £76,800	20,000 × £4 = £80,000	£(25,000)	£(21,000)	= £(4,000)	= £(7,200)	£3,200 +
Total	£285,000	£264,000	£259,200	£270,000	£(15,000)	£(21,000)	£6,000 +	(£4,800)	£10,800 +

During a recent production run 864,000 tiles from 15 mixes were produced. The following raw materials were used:

Raw material	*Quantity*	*Price per lb*
R	18,000	£0.40
A	5,000	£2.00
P	9,000	£0.60

Raw materials were taken into stock at actual prices and issued at standard prices. (Material price variance was calculated at the time of issue.)

Calculate and present the material price, mix and yield variances.

(40 minutes)

Suggested answer

NOTE 1 ACTUAL QUANTITY USED (lb)

R	18,000
A	5,000
P	9,000
	32,000 lb

NOTE 2 ACTUAL QUANTITY EXPRESSED IN STANDARD PROPORTIONS (*see Note 3*)

R $32{,}000 \times \frac{1{,}000}{2{,}000} = 16{,}000$ lb

A $32{,}000 \times \frac{400}{2{,}000} = 6{,}400$ lb

P $32{,}000 \times \frac{600}{2{,}000} = 9{,}600$ lb

32,000 lb

NOTE 3 STANDARD PROPORTIONS

Either: 1,000 lb of R, 400 of A and 600 of P

or: 10 of R, 4 of A and 6 of P.

NOTE 4

(a) A batch of 5,000 square feet of tiles = 60,000 tiles.

(b) The actual output of 864,000 tiles ÷ 60,000 tiles expresses the actual output in terms of batches, i.e. 14.40 batches.

(c) *Standard cost of actual output*—14.4 batches.

The standard product mix for making one batch after allowing for normal losses is:

R	1,000 lb
A	400
P	600

The standard mix to produce 14.4 batches is:

R	1,000 × 14.4 = 14,400 lb
A	400 × 14.4 = 5,760 lb
P	600 × 14.4 = 8,640 lb

Standard cost of actual output

R	14,400 × £0.60 = £8,640
A	5,760 × £2.00 = £11,520
P	8,640 × £0.50 = £4,320
	£24,480

NOTE 5

The actual mix of 15 mixes is not relevant.

Raw material	*Actual cost*	*Actual quantity used at standard prices*	*Actual quantity expressed in standard proportions*	*Standard cost of actual output* (Note 4: 14.4 batches)	*Total/cost variance*
	1	*2*	*3* (Note 2)	*4*	*5 (4 − 1)*
R	18,000 × £0.40 = £7,200	18,000 × £0.60 = £10,800	16,000 × £0.60 = £9,600	14.40 × 1,000 = 14,400 × £0.60 = £8,640	£1,440+
A	5,000 × £2.00 = £10,000	5,000 × £2.00 = £10,000	6,400 × £2.00 = £12,800	14.40 × 400 = 5,760 × £2.00 = £11,520	£1,520+
P	9,000 × £0.60 = £5,400	9,000 × £0.50 = £4,500	9,600 × £0.50 = £4,800	14.40 × 600 = 8,640 × £50 = £4,320	£(1,080)
Total	£22,600	£25,300	£27,200	£24,480	£1,880+

VARIANCE ANALYSIS

Raw material	*Total variance*	*Price*	*Usage*	*Usage variance*	
				Mix	*Yield*
		6 (2−1)	*7 (4−2)*	*8 (3−2)*	*9 (4−3)*
R	£1,440+	3,600+	(14,400 − 18,000 × £0.60) (£2,160)	(£1,200)	(960)
A	£1,520+	nil	(5,760 − 5,000 × £2.00) £1,520+	£2,800+	£(1,280)
P	£(1,080)	(900)	(8,640 − 9,000 × £0.50) (£180)	£300+	£(480)
Total	£1,880+	£2,700+	£(820)	£1,900+	£(2,720)

CHAPTER TWENTY

Variance Analysis II – Direct Labour

1.0 INTRODUCTION

As in the case of direct materials, *two* factors must be considered in determining labour cost standards:

(a) the labour time or quantity standard;

(b) the labour rate standard.

1.1 Prior conditions

Prior conditions to setting standard costs for direct labour are:

(a) *The general working conditions* that affect the efficiency and effectiveness must be looked into; for example

   (i) conditions of plant and machinery;

   (ii) plant layout;

   (iii) instructions, planning of work and control of work flow;

   (iv) the right quality and quantity of materials and internal transport.

(b) *Fundamental information*

   (i) the production operations necessary;

   (ii) the grade or grades of labour required;

   (iii) wage payment plans.

1.2 Direct labour time (quantity) standards

The labour time standard is one against which actual performance is measured. To set ideal time standards would be self-defeating, as the actual would most likely be greater than the standard and over a period of time the workers would regard the standard as having no real meaning. The direct labour time standards should therefore be based upon current attainable standards—attainable by conscientious effort—and include only the elements that can be influenced and controlled by the worker. Waiting, breakdown and setting up are normally treated as production overhead and not treated as direct labour.

(a) Methods of setting labour time standards

Examples of methods are:

(i) *Average of past performance.* This is taken from the cost sheets from the preceding periods. This method may be used if a similar operation has been performed in the past in precisely the same way.

Even if one accepts average past performance, which is not scientifically predetermined, as standards, care must be taken that past inefficiencies are not reflected in the future standards.

(ii) *Advanced estimates based upon experimental test runs.* Where an operation has not been performed before in exactly the same manner, an advance estimate will have to be made.

(iii) *Scientific methods.* Time standards based on scientific methods are usually set by work study practitioners (industrial engineers).

An essential first step is to make absolutely sure that the *method of work* is the best that is available and practicable in the light of the task to be performed.

The next step is *work measurement*, a technique which determines the times required for the performance of specific tasks.

The standards are set by the industrial engineering department based on observations made on a worker or a group in actual working conditions. Allowances are made for personal needs, delays beyond the control of the employee, fatigue, etc.

(b) Work measurement

Work measurement involves:

(i) listing the movements required to perform the operation;

(ii) timing these movements with a stopwatch over a period of time;

(iii) examining the data recorded;

(iv) setting times for the movements, which will reflect a realistic standard of performance;

(v) making time allowances in setting standards for fatigue, unavoidable delays and personal needs;

(vi) issuing the time standards.

1.3 Direct labour rate standards

Direct labour rate standards are based on rates:

(a) agreed between the company and the unions representing the workforce;

(b) agreed between the employee and the personnel department at the time of hiring;

(c) which may include fringe benefits;

(d) which in many companies consist of *departmental direct labour hour rates*, each of these being established to cover all the direct employees in a cost centre, even though the actual wages of employees differ for various reasons.

Illustration 1—Departmental standard direct labour hour rate

			Cost centre
(a)	Number of employees:		10
(b)	Rate per hour:	5 are paid	£2.00
		2 are paid	£2.50 due to seniority
		3 are paid	£2.75 due to seniority
		10 employees	
(c)	Productive hours per employee per week		32
(d)	Working weeks per annum		45
(e)	Productive hours per annum per employee ((c) × (d)): 32 × 45		1,440
(f)	Hours payable per employee: 40 × 52		= 2,080
(g)	Estimated wages per annum:	5 × £2.00 × 2,080	= £20,800
		2 × £2.50 × 2,080	= £10,400
		3 × £2.50 × 1,080	= £15,600
		Total wages	£46,800
(h)	Total productive hours: 10 × 1,440		= 14,400
(i)	Departmental standard direct labour hour rate		$= \frac{£46,800}{14,400} = £3.25$ per hour.

2.0 DIRECT LABOUR COST VARIANCE

2.1 Definitions

The difference between the standard direct labour cost of actual output and the actual direct wages paid is termed the direct labour cost variance. It may be analysed into three components, as follows:

(a) Direct labour rate variance

This is defined as that portion of the direct labour cost variance which is due to the difference between the *standard rate of pay* specified and the *actual rate* paid.

(b) Direct labour efficiency variance

This consists of that portion of the direct labour cost variance which is due to the difference between the *standard labour hours specified* for actual output and the *actual labour hours worked.*

(c) Direct labour idle time variance

This is defined as that portion of the direct labour cost variance which is due to the difference between the actual *hours paid* and the actual *hours worked.*

Illustration 2

ACCA Ltd manufactures two different types of component in *two production departments*, a press shop and a fitting department.

The budgeted production and standard labour costs for period 8 were:

	Dept One	*Dept Two*
Budgeted production:		
Component A	6,000 units	5,000 units
Component B	8,000 units	9,000 units
Standard labour cost per unit:		
Component A	£3	£8
Component B	£6	£6
Standard wage rate per hour	£3	£4

Actual results for period 8 were:

	Dept One	*Dept Two*
Production:		
Component A	4,000 units	6,000 units
Component B	7,800 units	8,600 units
Gross wages paid to direct workers	£60,000	£90,000

Throughout period 8 there were 135 direct workers employed in department one and 145 in department two. All employees in both departments attended and were paid for a 40-hour week in each of the four weeks in period 8. However, during the final week in the fitting department each employee was idle for 5 hours, the result of poor machine maintenance.

Required:
Calculate and present the direct wage variances for period 8.

Suggested answer

NOTE 1 STANDARD COST CARD

	Component A			Component B		
	SH	SR	SC	SH	SR	SC
Dept One	1	£3	£3	2	£3	£6
Dept Two	2	£4	£8	1.5	£4	£6
Standard direct labour cost			£11			£12

DIRECT LABOUR COST VARIANCE ANALYSIS—*see* p. 374

Illustration 3—Departmental rate

ICMA Limited manufactures a single product in department RX. There are 250 employees earning a standard wage rate of £2.00 per hour. The company operates a 40-hour week, without any overtime, and the standard performance for the department for one hour is 500 units. During a period of four weeks, the actual output of the department was 79,000 units, all of which was transferred to packed stock store. Due to a machine breakdown ten hours of idle time were incurred. 50 employees were actually paid at the rate of £3.00 per hour; 75 employees were paid at £1.75 per hour and the remainder were paid at the standard rate.

Calculate and present the labour cost variances.

Suggested answer

NOTE 1 PRELIMINARY CALCULATIONS

(a) One departmental hour = 250 standard hours.

(b) Standard performance for one departmental hour is 500 units.

(c) Standard hours per unit:
250 standard hours = 500 units
30 standard minutes = one unit.

LABOUR COST VARIANCES—*see* p. 375

3.0 LABOUR MIX VARIANCE

Deviation due to the changed composition of the working team or gang on a particular job. It must be noted that only that part of the rate of pay variance due to the changed composition of the gang can be calculated unless particulars of the standard performance of the substitute gang is given.

Illustration 4

ACCA Limited manufactures one standard product. A team of workers engaged in the production of the single product is made up as follows (p. 376):

DIRECT LABOUR COST VARIANCE ANALYSIS

Department	*Actual wages paid*	*Actual hours paid at standard rate*	*Actual hours worked at standard rate*	*Standard cost of actual output*	*Labour cost variance*	*Analysis*		
						Rate	*Idle time*	*Efficiency*
	1	*2*	*3*	*4*	*5* (*4 − 1*)	*6* (*2 − 1*)	*7* (*3 − 2*)	*8* (*4 − 3*)
One	135 × 40 × 4 × actual rate = £60,000	135 × 40 × 4 = 21,600 × £3 = £64,800	21,600 × £3 = £64,800	A = 4,000 × 1 = 4,000 B = 7,800 × 2 = 15,600 Total standard hours = 19,600 × £3 = £58,800	£(1,200)	£4,800 +	nil	£(6,000)
Two	145 × 40 × 4 × actual rate = £90,000	145 × 40 × 4 = 23,200 × £4 = £92,800	145 × 40 × 3 = 17,400 hours 145 × 35 × 1 = 5,075 hours Total hours = 22,475 × £4 = £89,990	A = 6,000 × 2 = 12,000 B = 8,600 × 1.5 = 12,900 Total standard hours = 24,900 × £4 = £99,600	£9,600 +	£2,800 +	£(2,810)	£9,610 +

LABOUR COST VARIANCES

Cost centre	Actual wages paid	Actual hours paid at standard rate	Actual hours worked at standard rate	Standard cost of actual output	Cost/ total variance	Variance analysis		
						Rate	*Idle time*	*Efficiency*
	1	*2*	*3*	*4*	*5* (*4*−*1*)	*6* (*2*−*1*)	*7* (*3*−*2*)	*8* (*4*−*3*)
	50 × 160 hours: 8,000 × £3.00	250 men × 160 hours:	250 × 150 hours:	79,000 × ½ hours:				
	= £24,000	40,000 × £2.00	37,500 × £2.00	39,500 standard hours of production × £2.00 per hour			2,500 hours idle × £2.00	2,000 hours efficient × £2.00
	75 × 160 hours: 12,000 × £1.75 = £21,000	= £80,000	= £75,000	= £79,000	(£6,000)	(£5,000)	(£5,000)	£4,000 +
	125 × 160 hours: = 20,000 × £2.00 = £40,000							
	£85,000	£80,000	£75,000	£79,000	(£6,000)	(£5,000)	(£5,000)	£4,000 +

STANDARD GANG

Grade	*No. of workers*	*Hourly wage rate depending upon merit rating*	*Standard rates*
A	8	£3.00–£4.00	£3.50
B	7	£2.00–£3.00	£2.50
C	5	£1.00–£2.00	£1.50

The standard hourly wage rates used for product costing and control purposes are grade A £3.50, grade B £2.50, grade C £1.50.

In a working week of 40 hours the team is expected to produce 200 units of the product. During a period of four weeks, it was necessary to change the gang composition owing to sickness and the team during that period (4 weeks) consisted of:

ACTUAL GANG

Grade	*No. of workers*	*Hourly wage rate*
A	9	£4.00
B	7	£3.00
C	4	£2.00

During the 4-week period 10 hours were lost due to a power failure. The output of the team for the 4-week period was 1,000 units.

PRELIMINARY CALCULATIONS

(i) *Standard cost of the standard gang per hour*

Grade	A	B	C
Number	8	7	5
Standard hourly rate per grade	£3.50	£2.50	£1.50
	£28.00	£17.50	£7.50
Standard cost of the standard gang per hour	£53.00		

(ii) *Standard cost of the actual gang per hour*

Grade	A	B	C
Number	9	7	4
Standard rate per hour	£3.50	£2.50	£1.50
	£31.50	£17.50	£6.00
Standard cost of the actual gang per hour	£55.00		

(iii) *Actual cost of the actual gang per hour*

Grade		A	B	C
Number		9	7	4
Actual rate per hour		£4.00	£3.00	£2.00
		£36.00	£21.00	£8.00
Actual rate of the actual gang per hour	£65.00			

4.0 TWO COMPREHENSIVE EXAMPLES

Example 1

RJ Limited produces a single product. Established standard costs for unit of product are:

	Ref.	*Standard quantity (lb)*	*Standard price per lb*	*Standard cost (£)*
Direct materials	MP	10	£2.00	20.00
	RS	20	£3.00	60.00
Direct labour				
Grade	A	10	£3.00	15.00
Grade	B	5	£2.00	10.00

Actual data for the month of April

Stocks in hand at 1st April

Direct materials	MP	50,000 lb	£3.00 (at actual price)
	RS	100,000 lb	£3.00 (at standard price)
Finished goods		10,000 units	

There were no work-in-progress stocks at either the beginning or the end of the month.

Purchases of raw materials

MP	100,000 lb	£250,000
RS	200,000 lb	£400,000

Cost centre/ grade	Actual wages paid	Actual hours paid at the standard rate of the actual gang	Actual hours paid at the standard rate of the standard gang	Actual hours worked at the standard rate of the standard gang	Standard cost of actual output	Cost variance	Variance analysis			
							Rate of pay	Gang composition	Idle time	Efficiency
	1	2	3	4	5	6 (5 − 1)	7 (2 − 1)	8 (2 − 3)	9 (4 − 3)	10 (5 − 4)
	160 × £65	160 × £55	160 × £53	150 × £53	$\frac{40}{200} \times 1{,}000$ 200 × £53					
	£10,400	£8,800	£8,480	£7,950	£10,600	£200 +	£(1,600)	£(320)	£(530)	£2,650

Issues of raw materials

MP	120,000 lb
RS	240,000 lb

Direct wages

	Hours paid	*Hours worked*	*Rate per hour*
Grade A	120,000	110,000	£2.50
Grade B	60,000	45,000	£2.50

Production during April

10,000 units

Note
Stocks of MP are priced on an actual cost FIFO basis.
Stocks of raw material RS are kept at standard cost.

You are required to produce a working paper calculating and analysing the variances which you consider should be incorporated into the operating statement for April.

DIRECT MATERIALS and DIRECT LABOUR—*see* pp. 380–1

Example 2

Suresh-Ipoh Malaysia International—a manufacturing company—produces a single product in department 28.

The standard labour force of the department consists of:

Grade	*Number of employees*	*Rate per hour*
1	500	£5.00
2	400	£4.00

During July the company experienced a shortage of certain grades of labour. In department 28 the actual labour force was:

Grade	*Number of employees*	*Rate per hour*
1	350	£4.00
	150	£6.00
2	250	£5.00
	150	£6.00

DIRECT MATERIALS

Type	Actual cost of purchases	Actual quantity bought at standard price	Actual quantity used at standard price	Standard cost of actual output	Cost variance	Variance analysis	
						Price	*Usage*
	1	*2*	*3*	*4*	*5* (*6*+*7*)	*6* (*2*−*1*)	*7* (*4*−*3*)
RS	200,000 × £2	200,000 × £3	240,000 × £3	10,000 × 20 = 200,000 × £3		£1 × 200,000 Favourable	40,000 × £3
	£400,000	£600,000	£720,000	£600,000	£80,000	£200,000	(£120,000)
	Actual cost of actual quantity issued (FIFO)	*Actual quantity issued at standard price*		*Standard cost of actual output*			
	1	*2*	*3*	*4*	*5* (*4*−*1*)	*6* (*2*−*1*)	*7* (*4*−*3*)
MP	50,000 × £3 = £150,000 70,000 × £2.50 = £175,000	120,000 × £2	–	10,000 × 10 = 100,000 × £2		£1 × 50,000 £0.50 × 70,000	20,000 × £2.00
	£325,000	£240,000	–	£200,000	(£125,000)	(£85,000)	(£40,000)

DIRECT LABOUR

Grade	Actual wages paid	Actual hours paid at standard rate	Actual hours worked at standard rate	Standard cost of actual output	Total/ cost variance	Variance analysis		
						Rate	Idle time	Efficiency
	1	*2*	*3*	*4*	*5* (*4 − 1*)	*6* (*2 − 1*)	*7* (*3 − 2*)	*8* (*4 − 3*)
A	100,000 × £2.50	120,000 × £3	110,000 × £3	10,000 × 10 = 100,000 × £3		120,000 × £0.50	(10,000 × £3.00)	(10,000 × £3.00)
	£300,000	£360,000	£330,000	£300,000	nil	£60,000	(£30,000)	(£30,000)
B	60,000 × £2.50	60,000 × £2	45,000 × £2	10,000 × 5 = 50,000 × £2.00		60,000 × £0.50	15,000 × £2.00	5,000 × £2.00
	£150,000	£120,000	£90,000	£100,000	(£50,000)	(£30,000)	(£30,000)	£10,000

The standard performance for the department is 100 units per hour. An 8-hour day is in operation and there were 4 working weeks of 5 days each in July. Actual production during the month was 12,000 units. A breakdown of a key machine resulted in 10 hours of lost production.

You are required from the above data given for July to:

(a) calculate the direct wages variances;

(b) analyse this variance in terms of:

(i) wage rates,

(ii) labour efficiency,

(iii) idle time.

Suggested answer

NOTE 1 STANDARD COST CARD Batch: 100 units

	Standard quantity (hours)	*Standard rate (£)*	*Standard cost (£)*
Grade 1	500	5	2,000
Grade 2	400	4	1,600
			3,600

NOTE 2

Where the department works *one* hour, 500 hours of grade 1 labour and 400 hours of grade 2 labour hours are produced.

One departmental hour = 900 standard hours

A batch of 100 units requires one departmental hour or 900 standard hours.

NOTE 3

Actual output 12,000 = 120 batches.

PERIOD/MONTH JULY: DIRECT LABOUR COST VARIANCE ANALYSIS: DEPARTMENT 28

Grade	Actual cost	Actual hours paid at standard rate	Actual hours worked at standard rate	Refer notes (1–3) Standard cost of actual output	Total/cost variance	Analysis		
						Rate	Idle time	Efficiency
	1	2	3	4	5 (4 − 1)	6 (2 − 1)	7 (3 − 2)	8 (4 − 3)
1	350 × 160 × £4 = £224,000 150 × 160 × £4 = £144,000	350 × 160 × £5 = £280,000 150 × 160 × £5 = £120,000	350 × 150 × £5 = £262,500 150 × 150 × £5 = £112,500	120 × 500 × £5 = £300,000				
Total 1	£368,000	£400,000	£375,000	£300,000	£(68,000)	£32,000		£(75,000)
2	250 × 160 × £5 = £200,000 150 × 160 × £6 = £144,000	250 × 160 × £4 = £160,000 150 × 160 × £4 = £96,000	250 × 150 × £4 = £150,000 150 × 150 × £4 = £90,000	120 × 400 × £4				
Total 2	£344,000	£256,000	£240,000	£192,000	£(152,000)	£(88,000)	£(16,000)	£(48,000)
Total 1 and 2	£712,000	£656,000	£615,000	£492,000	£(220,000)	£(56,000)	£(41,000)	£(123,000)

CHAPTER TWENTY-ONE

Variance Analysis III – Manufacturing Overhead

1.0 CLASSIFICATION OF OVERHEAD COSTS

All manufacturing overhead costs do not follow the same pattern. Some vary with changes in the level of output since they are closely related to the production operations; these are *variable* costs. Some costs vary in response to changes in volume, but not in direct proportion, and are referred to as *semi-variable* costs. Certain costs do not change with changes in volume over a wide range of activity. They are more related to time than to output; these are termed *period* or *fixed* costs.

1.1 Predetermined overhead rates for product costing

These involve:

(a) determination of budgeted overhead costs

(b) planned level of activity expressed in standard hours.

The formula for the standard overhead rate is:

$$\frac{\text{Budgeted overhead for the period}}{\text{Level of activity planned expressed in standard hours}} = \text{Rate per standard hour.}$$

1.2 Choice of single or departmental predetermined rates of absorption

(a) Predetermined single (plant-wide) overhead rate

This may be used:

(i) where only one product is manufactured;

(ii) where all producing departments contribute in uniform proportions to the fabrication of every product.

If a single (plant-wide) rate is used the budgeted overhead for the period for the entire plant is divided by the planned level of activity to determine the overhead rate of absorption.

(b) Predetermined departmental overhead rates

Note: You are advised to revise Chapter 7 to ensure a complete understanding of the topic.

These require:

(i) Departmentalisation of costs—primary distribution.

(ii) The apportionment of service department costs to producing departments—secondary distribution.

(iii) Predetermining the level of output departmentally in standard hours.

1.3 Separation of fixed and variable overhead costs

The budgeted overhead or *numerator* of the formula may be classified according to its behaviour into two broad classes: fixed costs and variable costs. They reflect the planned expenditure at a predetermined level of activity.

The *denominator* of the formula *must* be a single level of activity within the relevant range. The predetermined level of activity may be linked with one of the following activity levels:

(a) practical plant/departmental capacity;

(b) production budget requirements—expected level of activity;

2:0 OVERHEAD COST VARIANCE

The overhead cost variance is the difference between the actual overhead cost incurred and the standard cost of overhead absorbed in the actual output.

Overhead variances may be computed separately for fixed and variable overhead.

2.1 Required information

In order to analyse the overhead variance in detail, six items of information are necessary:

(a) budgeted overhead for the period;

(b) budgeted level of activity expressed in standard hours;

(c) predetermined overhead rate of absorption per standard hour;

(d) actual output achieved during the period (standard hours produced during the period);

(e) actual number of direct labour hours worked;

(f) actual overhead for the period.

3.0 VARIABLE OVERHEAD VARIANCES

3.1 Definitions

Variable overhead cost/total variance
This is the difference between the actual cost and the standard cost of actual output.

Variable overhead spending variance
This consists of that portion of the variable overhead cost variance which is due to the difference between the actual cost incurred and the budget based on actual hours worked (flexible budget).

Variable overhead efficiency variance
This is that portion of the variable overhead cost variance which is due to the difference between the budget based on actual hours worked (flexible budget) and the standard cost of actual output.

Illustration 1: Variance analysis—variable overhead
RA and RB Ltd established the following standards for variable factory overhead. Budgeted output 40,000 units at 3 standard hours per unit.

Variable factory overhead	£48,000	
Standard direct labour hours	120,000	
Variable overhead rate per standard hour		£0.40.
Variable overhead rate per unit (3 × £0.40)		£1.20.

ADDITIONAL INFORMATION CONCERNING ONE MONTH'S OPERATIONS

Actual variable costs incurred	£54,000	
Actual output (units)	50,000	
Actual hours worked	140,000	
Variable overhead cost variance:		
Actual overhead		£54,000
Overhead absorbed = 150,000 × £0.40		£60,000
(50,000 units × 3 standard hours	= 150,000	
Overhead rate per standard hour	= £0.40)	
Overhead cost variance	£6,000F	

WORKING PAPER—ANALYSIS OF VARIABLE OVERHEAD VARIANCE

Cost centre	*Actual*	*Budget based on actual direct labour hours worked (actual hours worked at the standard rate)*	*Standard cost of actual output*	*Total/cost variance*	*Variance analysis*	
					Spending	*Efficiency*
	1	*2*	*3*	*4* (*3*−*1*)	*5* (*2*−*1*)	*6* (*3*−*2*)
	£54,000	140,000 × £0.40 = £56,000	50,000 × 3 = 150,000 standard hours at £0.40	£6,000F	2,000F	4,000F
	£54,000	£56,000	£60,000	£6,000F	£2,000F	£4,000F

Note: the analysis of the variable cost variance into spending and efficiency is similar to the analysis of direct labour cost variance into rate and efficiency variances.

4.0 FIXED OVERHEAD VARIANCES

4.1 Definitions

Fixed overhead cost variance—total variance
This is the difference between the fixed overhead incurred and the fixed overhead absorbed.

The total fixed overhead variance can be further analysed by causes:

Fixed overhead expenditure variance
That portion of the fixed overhead cost variance which is due to the difference between the fixed overhead incurred and the budgeted fixed overhead.

Fixed overhead volume variance
That portion of the fixed overhead cost variance which is due to the difference between budgeted standard hours and the standard labour hours specified for the production achieved. Volume variance may be analysed into efficiency, capacity and calendar.

Fixed overhead efficiency variance
That portion of the fixed overhead volume variance which is due to the difference between the actual hours worked during the period and the standard hours specified for the output achieved during the period.

Fixed overhead capacity variance
That portion of the fixed overhead volume variance which is due to the difference between the budgeted capacity expressed in standard hours and actual hours worked during the period.

Fixed overhead calendar variance
That portion of the fixed overhead volume variance which is due to the difference between the number of working days in the budget period expressed in hours (i.e. the budgeted hours) and the actual number of working days in the period to which the budget is applied expressed in hours.

4.2 Variance analysis—fixed overhead—basic variance analysis

An example is given in the following illustration.

Illustration 2
DIAS Company produces a range of products. Normal activity (practical plant capacity) for a period is 100,000 standard direct labour hours. Budgeted fixed factory overhead is £300,000. For product costing purposes the overhead rate of absorption is £3.00 per standard direct labour hour.

Compute the fixed factory cost variance and analyse the total variance by causes into expenditure and volume under each of the following independent conditions. Indicate whether the variances are favourable or unfavourable.

WORKING PAPER

Case	Actual cost	Budget	Standard cost of actual output	Cost/total variance	Variance analysis (A = adverse F = favourable) Expenditure	Volume
	1	2	3	4 (3–1)	5 (2–1)	6 (3–2)
(a)	£300,000	£300,000 / 100,000	100,000 × £3.00 = £300,000	nil	nil	nil
(b)	£250,000	£300,000 / 100,000	100,000 × £3.00 = £300,000	£50,000F	£50,000F	nil
(c)	£350,000	£300,000 / 100,000	100,000 × £3.00 = £300,000	£50,000A	£50,000A	nil
(d)	£300,000	£300,000 / 100,000	120,000 × £3.00 = £360,000	£60,000F	nil	20,000 × £3.00 £60,000F
(e)	£300,000	£300,000 / 100,000	80,000 × £3.00 = £240,000	£60,000A	nil	20,000 × £3.00 £60,000A
(f)	£250,000	£300,000 / 100,000	120,000 × £3.00 = £360,000	£110,000F	£50,000F	£60,000F
(g)	£350,000	£300,000 / 100,000	80,000 × £3.00 = £240,000	£110,000A	£50,000A	£60,000A
(h)	£350,000	£300,000 / 100,000	120,000 × £3.00 = 360,000	£10,000F	£50,000A	£60,000F
(i)	£250,000	£300,000 / 100,000	80,000 × £3.00 = £240,000	£10,000A	£50,000F	£60,000A
(j)	£240,000	£300,000 / 100,000	80,000 × £3.00 = £240,000	nil	£60,000F	£60,000A

(a) Actual level of activity was 100,000 standard hours and actual fixed costs were £300,000.

(b) Actual level of activity was 100,000 standard hours and the actual fixed costs were £250,000.

(c) Actual level of activity was 100,000 standard hours and actual fixed costs were £350,000.

(d) Actual level of activity was 120,000 standard hours and actual fixed costs were £300,000.

(e) Actual level of activity was 80,000 standard hours and actual fixed costs were £300,000.

(f) Actual level of activity was 120,000 standard hours and actual fixed costs were £250,000.

(g) Actual level of activity was 80,000 standard hours and actual fixed costs were £350,000.

(h) Actual level of activity was 120,000 standard hours and actual fixed costs were £350,000.

(i) Actual level of activity was 80,000 standard hours and actual fixed costs were £250,000.

(j) Actual level of activity was 80,000 standard hours and actual fixed costs were £240,000.

4.3 Product costing versus control

Illustration 3

FLEXIBLE BUDGET SUMMARY MANUFACTURING OVERHEAD DEPARTMENT: MACHINE SHOP

	Production budget	*Practical plant capacity*	*Maximum capacity*
Level of activity (capacity in hours)	20,000	30,000	40,000
Variable overhead	£40,000	£60,000	£80,000
Fixed overhead	60,000	60,000	60,000
Total	£100,000	£120,000	£140,000
Overhead rates of absorption	£5.00	£4.00	£3.50
Variable overhead rate	£2.00	£2.00	£2.00
Fixed overhead rate	£3.00	£2.00	£1.50

For product costing purposes the budgeted costs for a single level of activity must be used. If the production budget is used for product costing purposes the standard overhead rate is therefore £5.00, reflecting a rate of £3.00 per hour for the fixed costs and £2.00 per hour for the variable costs. It must be noted that the overhead rate of £5.00 includes the cost of underutilised capacity.

For control purposes it would be better to use either the practical or maximum capacity so that underutilised capacity may be reported to management.

CALCULATION OF OVERHEAD COST VARIANCES WITH THE AID OF GRAPHS

DATA

Budgeted expenditure:	Fixed	£60,000
	Variable	£40,000
Budgeted level of activity:		20,000 standard hours.
Overhead rates:	Fixed	£3.00 per standard hour
	Variable	£2.00 per standard hour

ACTUAL RESULTS

Overhead incurred:	Fixed	£80,000
	Variable	£70,000
Standard hours produced		30,000

(a) *Variable overhead* (Fig. 29(a))
The budget and recovery line (absorbed line) slopes upwards at the rate of £2.00 per standard direct labour hour. At this rate the budget and the standard cost of actual output is £60,000 (£2.00 × 30,000). The actual cost incurred is £70,000. The total variance £10,000 unfavourable.

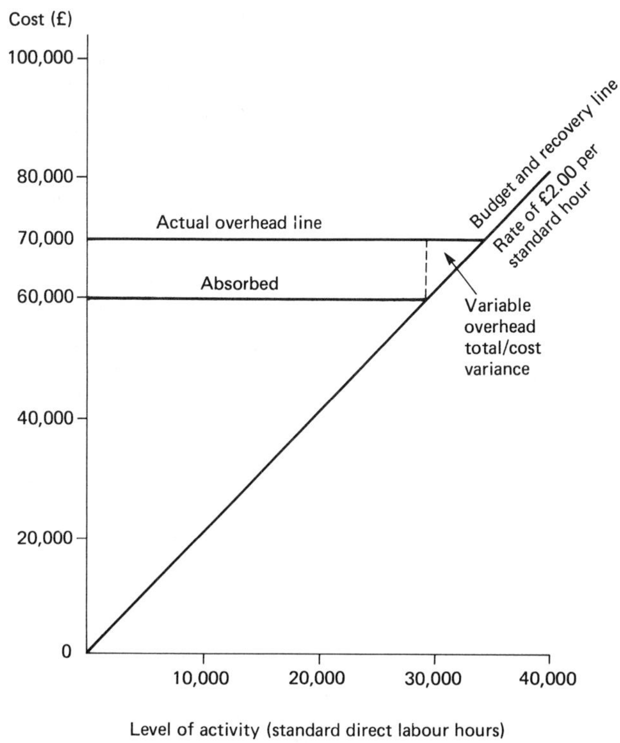

Fig. 29(a). *Variable overhead.*

(b) *Fixed overhead* (Fig. 29(b))
The budget line for fixed overhead is a straight line, on the assumption that the fixed costs remain constant over that range of output. The recovery (absorbed) line slopes upwards at the rate of £3.00 per standard direct labour hour produced. The predetermined rate is used to cost production, regardless of the level of activity actually attained and the actual expenditure incurred.

The fixed overhead cost variance can be read from the graph. It is the difference between £80,000 (actual expenditure incurred) and £90,000 (the standard cost of actual output, 30,000 standard hours at £3.00 per hour). The total/cost variance is £10,000 favourable.

The fixed overhead expenditure variance can be read from the graph, i.e. it is the difference between £60,000 (budgeted fixed overhead) and £80,000 (actual fixed overhead incurred). The expenditure variance is £20,000 unfavourable.

The fixed overhead volume variance can be read from the graph. It is the difference between the budgeted level of activity (20,000 standard direct labour hours) and the actual output expressed in standard hours (30,000). The volume variance is 10,000 standard hours or 10,000 × £3.00 per standard hours = £30,000 favourable.

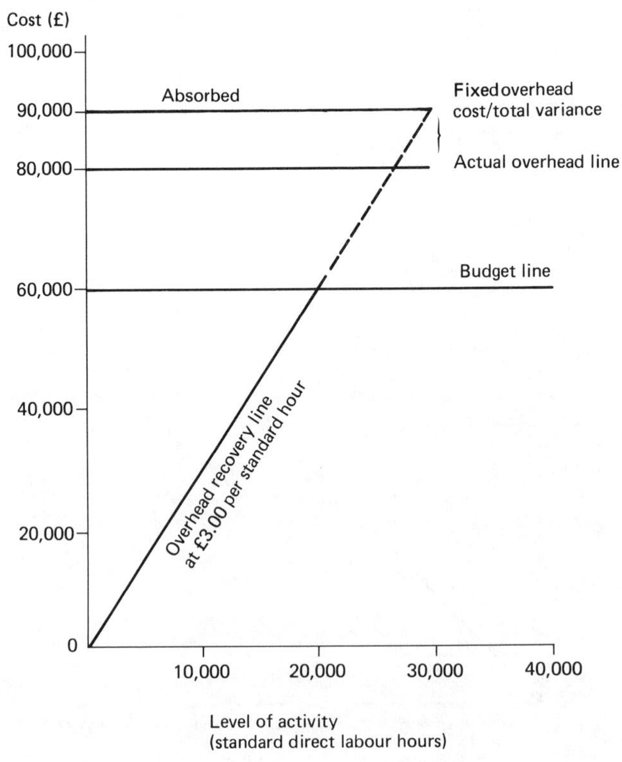

Fig. 29(b). *Fixed overhead.*

5.0 COMPREHENSIVE ILLUSTRATION

Ramsu Limited, a manufacturing company, has developed a standard costing system. The following information is available for period 6:

	Overhead Budget	Actual
Fixed		
Rent and rates, heat and light	£20,000	£22,000
Insurance	2,000	2,500
Supervision	6,000	8,000
Depreciation	4,000	4,000
	£32,000	£36,500
Variable		
Material handling	£3,000	£2,500
Supplies	6,000	5,000
Maintenance	6,000	8,000
Fuel	3,000	2,500
Power, heat and light	4,000	3,000
	£22,000	£21,000
Budgeted hours (standard hours)	20,000	–
Working days	20	20

During period six 18,000 actual hours were worked and 22,000 standard hours of output were produced.

You are required to calculate and present:

(a) standard fixed overhead rate per standard hour;

(b) standard variable overhead rate per standard hour;

(c) variable overhead cost variance and an analysis by causes;

(d) fixed overhead cost variance and an analysis by causes.

Suggested answer

OVERHEAD RATES OF ABSORPTION

(a) *Standard fixed overhead rate per standard hour*

$$\frac{£32{,}000}{20{,}000} = \underline{\underline{£1.60.}}$$

(b) *Standard variable overhead rate per standard hour*

$$\frac{£22{,}000}{20{,}000} = \underline{\underline{£1.10.}}$$

NOTE 1 COMBINED OVERHEAD RATE OF ABSORPTION

$$\frac{£32{,}000 + £22{,}000}{20{,}000} = \underline{\underline{£2.70.}}$$

(c) *Variable overhead variance analysis*

Dept	*Actual*	*Budget based on actual direct labour hours worked*	*Standard cost of actual output*	*Total variance*	*Variance analysis*	
					Spending	*Efficiency*
	1	*2*	*3*	*4* (*3*−*1*)	*5* (*2*−*1*)	*6* (*3*−*2*)
	£21,000	18,000 × £1.10	22,000 × £1.10	£3,200 favourable	£1,200 adverse	Favourable 4,000 hours at £1.10
	£21,000	£19,800	£24,200	£3,200F	£1,200A	£4,400F

(d) *Fixed overhead variance analysis*

					Variance analysis			
							Volume	
Actual	*Budget*	*Budget based on actual direct labour hours worked at standard rate*	*Standard cost of actual output*	*Total variance*	*Expenditure*	*Volume*	*Efficiency*	*Capacity*
1	2	*3*	*4*	*5* (*4* − *1*)	6 (2 − *1*)	*7* (*4* − 2)	*8* (*4* − *3*)	*9* (*3* − 2)
£36,500	$\frac{£32{,}000}{20{,}000} = £1.60$	18,000 × £1.60	2,200 × £1.60	£1,300 adverse	£4,500 adverse	2,000 hours favourable at £1.60	4,000 hours efficiency £1.60	2,000 adverse £1.60
£36,500	£32,000	£28,800	£35,200	£1,300A	£4,500A	£3,200F	£6,400F	£3,200A

Note 2 *Fixed overhead capacity variance* This is the difference between the actual hours worked and the budget expressed in terms of actual number of working days during the budget period.

Actual hours worked in 20 days		18,000
Budget expressed in terms of actual number of days worked during the period	1,000 × 20 =	20,000 hours
	Capacity variance	2,000 hours

Note 3 *Budgeted hours per day* $\frac{20{,}000}{20} = 1{,}000.$

6.0 EXAMPLES

Example 1

The following information relates to the activities in period number six of a production department in a manufacturing company.

Activity level in standard direct labour hours, budgeted	*Budgeted overhead allowance*
(hours)	(£)
12,000	60,000
28,000	108,000
40,000	144,000

The combined predetermined overhead rate for the department is £3.80 per standard hour.

For period six the following actual data are available:

	Actual activity level		*Actual overhead incurred*
Standard hours	26,000	Fixed	£26,000
Actual hours	30,000	Variable	80,000
			£106,000

You are required to calculate:

(a) the budgeted fixed cost;

(b) the level of activity on which the standard overhead rate has been fixed;

(c) cost variances for both variable and fixed.

Suggested answer

(a) *Budgeted fixed costs (high and low method)*
The difference between the highest and lowest levels of activity and the difference of the corresponding costs are worked out, and the fixed and variable costs are separated in the following manner:

Highest level of activity (hours)	40,000	Corresponding cost	£144,000
Lowest level of activity (hours)	12,000	Corresponding cost	£60,000
Difference	28,000		£84,000

Variable cost per standard direct labour hour:

$$\frac{£84{,}000}{28{,}000}$$

Level of activity (hours)	12,000	28,000	40,000
Total cost	£60,000	£108,000	£144,000
Variable cost at £3.00 per standard hour	£36,000	£84,000	£120,000
Fixed cost	£24,000	£24,000	£24,000

(b) *Level of activity on which the standard overhead rate has been fixed*

Predetermined rate of absorption	£3.80
Less: Variable overhead rate per standard hour	£3.00
Therefore the fixed overhead rate	£0.80

Total fixed overhead budgeted £24,000 divided by the fixed overhead rate would give us the budgeted level of activity:

$$\frac{£24{,}000}{£0.80} = 30{,}000 \text{ standard direct labour hours}$$

ANALYSIS OF THE COST VARIANCE

(a)	*Expenditure variance*	= £7,667 adverse
	Actual cost	£32,000
	Budget ($\frac{1}{12}$ £292,000)	£24,333
(b)	*Volume variance*	£5,667 favourable
	Budget ($\frac{1}{12}$)	= £24,333
	Standard cost of actual output	£30,000
	or	
	Budgeted hours $\frac{1}{12} \times 584{,}000$	= 48,666
	Standard hours recovered	= 60,000
	Volume variance (hours)	11,334 at £0.50
		= £5,667

ANALYSIS OF THE VOLUME VARIANCE

(a)	*Efficiency variance*	£5,000 favourable
	Actual hours worked	50,000
	Standard hours produced (15,000 × 4)	60,000
	Efficiency variance	10,000
	or 10,000 × £0.50	= £5,000
(b)	*Capacity variance*	£4,200 adverse
	Actual hours worked (24 days)	50,000
	Budget expressed in terms of actual working days:	
	$\frac{584{,}000}{240} \times 24$ capacity variance	= 58,400
		8,400
	at £0.50 per hour	£4,200
	Calendar variance:	£4,867 favourable.
	Budget for 20 working days ($\frac{1}{12}$)	48,666
	Revised budget 24 working days	58,400
	Calendar variance	9,734
	at £0.50 per hour	£4,867

SUMMARY

Fixed overhead cost variance		£2,000 adverse
Expenditure variance	£7,667 adverse	
Volume variance	£5,667 favourable	
	£2,000 adverse	

VOLUME VARIANCE—SUMMARY

	In hours	*Rate per hour*	*Cost*
Volume variance	11,334	£0.50	£5,667
Analysis			
Efficiency	10,000	£0.50	£5,000
Capacity	(8,400)	£0.50	£(4,200)
Calendar	9,734	£0.50	£4,867
	11,334	£0.50	£5,667

FIXED OVERHEAD VARIANCE ANALYSIS

Actual cost	*Original budget*	*Standard cost of actual output*	*Total/cost variance*	*Basic variance analysis*	
				Expenditure	*Volume*
1	2	*3*	*4* (*3*−*1*)	*5* (*2*−*1*)	*6* (*3*−*2*)
£32,000	$\frac{1/12 \times 292{,}000}{1/12 \times 584{,}000}$	15,000 × 4 = 60,000 standard hours at £0.50	£2,000 adverse	£7,667 adverse	(60,000 − 48,660) = 11,334 hours at £0.50 = £5,667 favourable
£32,000	£24,333	£30,000	£2,000A	£7,667A	£5,667F

Note: A = *adverse;* F = *favourable.*

ANALYSIS OF THE VOLUME VARIANCE

Volume variance	*Standard hours produced*	*Actual hours worked*	*Original budget expressed in terms of actual days worked*	*Original budget*	*Efficiency variance*	*Capacity variance*	*Calendar variance*
1	2	3	4	5	6 (*2*−*3*)	7 (*3*−*4*)	8 (*4*−*5*)
11,334 hours at £0.50	60,000 at £0.50	50,000 at £0.50	$\frac{584{,}000}{240} \times 24$ = 58,400 × £0.50	$\frac{584{,}000}{240} \times 20$ = 48,666 × £0.50	10,000 at £0.50	8,400 at £0.50	9,734 at £0.50
£5,667F	£30,000	£25,000	£29,200	£24,333	£5,000F	£4,200A	£4,867F

CHAPTER TWENTY-TWO

Sales Variances and Income Statements

1.0 CALCULATION AND CAUSES OF SALES VARIANCES

1.1 Calculation of sales variances

There are two methods of calculating sales variances and they produce quite different final results.

(a) Turnover method
This shows the effect of a change in sales on turnover.

(b) Margin method
This shows the effect of a change in sales on profits.

An important assumption of the margin method is made in view of the fact that sales variances are prepared essentially in connection with the control of sales; the analyst therefore assumes that the *actual* cost of the product equals the standard cost of the product.

The cost variances (production, selling, distribution) are therefore calculated separately.

1.2 Causes of sales variances

Sales variances are caused by two basic variances:

(a) those due to price changes,

(b) those due to volume changes.

The volume variances may be fuller analysed into:

(a) the volume variance caused by a change in the sales mix;

(b) the volume variance caused by a change in sales quantities.

2.0 SALES VARIANCE ANALYSIS—THE TURNOVER METHOD

2.1 Definitions

(a) Total variance
The difference between the budgeted value of sales and the actual value of sales.

(b) Price variance
That portion of the total variance which is due to the difference between the actual quantity sold at actual prices and actual quantity sold at standard or budgeted selling prices.

(c) Volume variance
That portion of the total variance which is due to the difference between the budgeted quantity and actual quantity sold at standard or budgeted selling prices.

2.2 Turnover method—illustrations

Illustration 1

BUDGETED SALES

Product	*Quantity (units)*	*Unit price*	*Budgeted sales value*
MA	1,000	£5	£5,000
NO	500	£10	5,000
RE	400	£20	8,000
			£18,000

ACTUAL SALES

Product	*Quantity (units)*	*Unit price*	*Actual sales value*
MA	1,000	£5	£5,000
NO	600	£10	6,000
RE	400	£25	10,000
			£21,000

THE TOTAL SALES VARIANCE

Budgeted sales	£18,000
Actual sales	£21,000
	£3,000

SALES PRICE VARIANCE

Product	Budgeted price	Actual price	Price variance per unit
MA	£5	£5	nil
NO	£10	£10	nil
RE	£20	£25	£5

TOTAL SALES PRICE VARIANCE

Product	Price variance per unit	Actual quantity sold	Price variance
MA	nil	1,000	nil
NO	nil	600	nil
RE	£5	400	£2,000F

A *favourable price variance* occurs if the actual price is greater than the standard or budgeted price.

An *unfavourable price variance* occurs if the actual price is less than the standard or budgeted price.

SALES VOLUME VARIANCE

Product	Budgeted quantity	Actual quantity	Volume variance
MA	1,000	1,000	nil
NO	500	600	100
RE	400	400	nil

TOTAL SALES VOLUME VARIANCE

Product	*Volume variance (units)*	*Standard price per unit*	*Sales volume variance*
MA	nil	£5	nil
NO	100	£10	£1,000
RE	nil	£20	nil

A *favourable volume variance* occurs if the actual quantity sold is greater than the budgeted quantity.

An *unfavourable volume variance* occurs if the actual quantity sold is less than the budgeted quantity.

Illustration 2

SUMMARY BUDGET YEAR 7

Product	*Budgeted selling price per unit*	*Budgeted quantity (units)*	*Budgeted sales value*
MA	£5	4,000	£20,000
NO	£10	12,000	£120,000
RE	£8	4,000	£32,000
		20,000	£172,000

ACTUAL RESULTS YEAR 7

Product	*Actual selling price per unit*	*Quantity (units)*	*Actual sales value*
MA	£5.50	10,000	£55,000
NO	£11.00	10,000	£110,000
RE	£7.50	2,000	£15,000
		22,000	£180,000

SALES VARIANCE ANALYSIS—TURNOVER METHOD

Product	*Actual quantity sold at actual selling prices = Actual sales*	*Budgeted quantity at standard selling prices = Budgeted sales*	*Actual quantity sold at standard selling prices = Standard sales*	*Total sales variance*	*Variance analysis*	
					Price	*Volume*
	1	*2*	*3*	*4* (*1* − *2*)	*5* (*1* − *3*)	*6* (*3* − *2*)
MA	10,000 × £5.50 = £55,000	4,000 × £5.00 = £20,000	10,000 × £5.00 = £50,000	£35,000F	(10,000 × £0.50) = £5,000F	(6,000 × £5.00) = £30,000F
NO	10,000 × £11.00 = £110,000	12,000 × £10.00 = £120,000	10,000 × £10.00 = £100,000	£10,000A	(10,000 × £1.00) = £10,000F	(2,000 × £10) = £20,000A
RE	2,000 × £7.50 = £15,000	4,000 × £8.00 = £32,000	2,000 × £8.00 = £16,000	£17,000A	(2,000 × £0.50) = £1,000A	(2,000 × £8.00) = £16,000A
Total	£180,000	£172,000	£166,000	£8,000F	£14,000F	£6,000A

3.0 SALES VARIANCE ANALYSIS—THE MARGIN METHOD

The sales margin method shows the *effect* of a *change in sales* on the profits of the company. Sales variances are prepared essentially in connection with the control of sales. The analyst therefore assumes that the costs (production, administration, selling and distribution and other) remain constant. The cost variances are therefore calculated separately (Fig. 30). The method highlights the effect on budgeted profit of changes in sales and is essential in reconciling actual profit with budgeted profit.

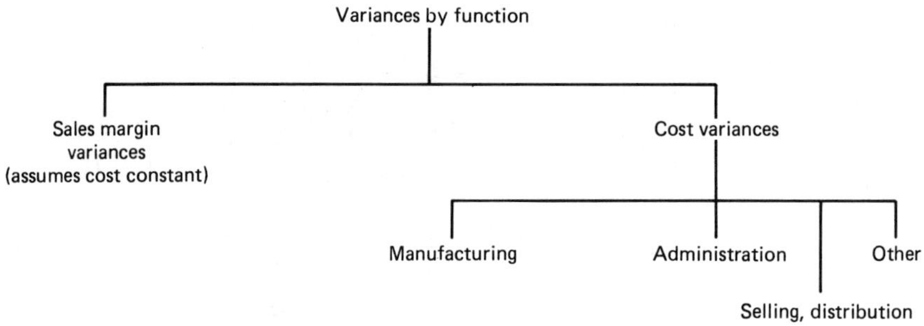

Fig. 30. *Separation of cost variances and sales margin variances.*

Note, with regard to Fig. 30:

Manufacturing cost variance: the difference between the standard cost of actual output and the actual cost;

Administration, selling, distribution and other: the difference between the budgeted cost and actual cost.

3.1 Note on the meaning of "margin"

The word is misleading. The margin refers to either

(a) standard gross profit *or*

(b) standard gross contribution.

In analysing the sales variances the analyst uses one of the product costing techniques:

(a) In standard absorption costing, margin refers to standard gross profit, i.e. budgeted standard price less standard cost.

(b) In standard marginal costing, margin refers to standard gross contribution, i.e. budgeted standard price less standard variable cost.

3.2 Total sales margin variance

The difference between the budgeted margin and the actual margin is as follows:

(a) budgeted margin = budgeted sales value less standard cost of budgeted sales;

(b) actual margin = actual sales value less standard of actual quantity sold.

3.3 Analysis of the total sales margin variance

(a) Sales margin variance due to price
This is that portion of the sales margin variance due to the difference between the budgeted selling price and the actual selling price of the actual quantity sold.

(b) Sales margin variance due to volume
This consists of that portion of the sales margin variance which is due to the difference between actual quantity sold and the budgeted quantity at standard margin per unit. Standard margin per unit is the difference between the budgeted selling price less standard total cost per unit.

3.4 Margin method—illustration (single product)

Illustration 3
From the following information calculate the sales margin variances:

Product MA	*Budget*	*Actual*
Quantity	10,000	11,000
Selling price per unit	£10	£12
Standard cost per unit	£6	£8

Suggested answer

Product	*Budgeted margin*	*Actual margin*	*Standard margin*	*Total variance*	*Variance analysis*	
					Price	*Volume*
	1	*2*	*3*	*4* (*2*−*1*)	*5* (*2*−*3*)	*6* (*3*−*1*)
MA	10,000 × (£10−6)	11,000 × (£12−6)	11,000 × (£10−6)	£26,000	11,000 × £2	1,000 × £4
	£40,000	£66,000	£44,000	£26,000	£22,000F	£4,000F

Notes

(*a*) *In calculating actual margin, assume actual costs were proportionate to standard costs.*

(*b*) *Actual quantity sold at budgeted margin per unit. Budget margin per unit is budgeted selling price less standard cost per unit.*

(*c*) *Standard cost refers to*

(*i*) *standard total manufacturing cost per unit (standard absorption costing)*

(*ii*) *standard variable manufacturing cost per unit (standard marginal costing)*

3.5 Marginal method—illustration (multi-product situation)

Illustration 4

SUMMARY BUDGET YEAR 1

Product	*Budgeted or standard selling price per unit*	*Quantity (units)*	*Budget sales value*	*Standard cost per unit*
MA	£5	4,000	£20,000	£2.00
NO	£10	12,000	£120,000	£5.00
RE	£8	4,000	£32,000	£4.00
		20,000	£172,000	

ACTUAL RESULT

Product	*Actual selling price per unit*	*Quantity (units)*	*Actual sales value*	*Actual cost per unit*
MA	£5.50	10,000	£55,000	£3.00
NO	£11.50	10,000	£110,000	£6.00
RE	£7.50	2,000	£15,000	£3.00
		22,000	£180,000	

SALES VARIANCE ANALYSIS—MARGIN METHOD

Product	Budgeted margin	Actual margin	Standard margin	Total variance	Variance analysis: Price	Variance analysis: Volume
	1	*2*	*3*	*4* (2 − *1*)	*5* (2 − *3*)	*6* (*3* − *1*)
MA	4,000 × (£5 − 2) = £12,000	10,000 × (£5.50 − 2.00) = £35,000	10,000 × (£5 − 2) = £30,000	£23,000F	10,000 × £0.50 = £5,000F	6,000 × £3 = £18,000F
NO	12,000 × (£10 − 5) = £60,000	10,000 × (£11 − 5) = £60,000	10,000 × (£10 − 5) = £50,000	nil	10,000 × £1 = £10,000F	2,000 × £5 = £10,000A
RE	4,000 × (£8 − 4) = £16,000	2,000 × (£7.50 − 4.00) = £7,000	2,000 × (£8 − 4) = £8,000	£9,000A	2,000 × £0.50 = £1,000A	2,000 × £4 = £8,000A
	£88,000	£102,000	£88,000	£14,000F	£14,000F	nil

4.0 INCOME STATEMENT—EXAMPLE

EW Limited manufactures one standard product and operates a system of variance accounting. As assistant accountant, you are responsible for preparing the monthly operating statements. Data from the budget and the standard product cost for the month ended 31st May year 7 are given below:

Budgeted and standard cost data
Budgeted sales and production for the month: 10,000 units.

STANDARD COST FOR EACH UNIT OF PRODUCT

	SQ	× SP	= SC
Direct material: A (lb)	2	1	2
Direct material: B (lb)	4	0.5	2
Direct labour	2	3	6
Variable production overhead	2	1	2
Fixed production overhead	2	4	8
			20

Budgeted sales price has been calculated to give a gross profit of 20 per cent of selling price.

Budgeted selling and administration—variable	£8,000
—fixed	£12,000

Actual data for month ended 31st May year 7

Units produced	11,000
Units sold	9,000 at 20 per cent higher than budgeted.

DIRECT MATERIALS

Purchases—A	24,000 at £1.50 per lb
B	50,000 at £0.60 per lb
Consumed—A	22,000 lb
B	40,000 lb

Stocks of raw materials are kept at standard prices.

Direct wages	*Paid*		*Worked*
Hours	25,000	(rate per hour: £2.50)	24,000
Variable production overhead	£20,000		
Fixed production overhead	£100,000		

Selling, distribution and administration—Variable £10,000
Fixed £15,500

Note: Production cost variances are transferred to the profit and loss statement of the period in which they are incurred.

Using the data given you are required to:

(a) Prepare the budgeted profit and loss statement.

(b) Calculate and present the production cost variances.

(c) Complete the preprinted profit and loss statement for the month.

(d) Present a statement for management reconciling the budgeted net profit with the actual net profit.

NOTE: FORMAT OF PROFIT AND LOSS STATEMENT FOR THE MONTH ENDED 31st MAY YEAR 7

		£
Budgeted sales	(1)	
Sales variances based on turnover (Schedule 1)		
Actual sales	(2)	
Standard cost of sales:		
Direct material A		
Direct material B		
Direct wages		
Variable overhead		
Fixed overhead		
Total	(3)	

Standard profit on actual sales	(2–3)	(4)	
Production cost variances (Schedule 2)			
Material cost variance A			
Material cost variance B			
Direct labour cost variance			
Variable overhead cost variance			
Fixed overhead cost variance			
			———
Total production cost variance		(5)	
			———
Actual gross profit	(4–5)	(6)	
Administration, selling and distribution expenses:			
Variable			
Fixed			
			———
Actual net profit			
			═══

Suggested answer

(a) *Budgeted profit and loss statement*

	£000	*£000*
Budgeted sales (10,000 at £25)	250	
Standard cost of sales (10,000 at £20)	200	50
	—	
Standard gross profit		
Administration, selling and distribution costs:		
Variable	8	
Fixed	12	20
	—	—
Budgeted net profit		30
		═

Type	*Actual cost of purchases*	*Actual price of product at SP*	*Standard cost of actual issues*	*Standard cost of actual output*	*Cost variance*	*Price (purchases)*	*Usage*
	1	*2*	*3*	*4*	*5* (*6+7*)	*6* (*2−1*)	*7* (*4−3*)
Material A	24,000 × £1.50 = £36,000	24,000 × £1.00 = £24,000	22,000 × £1.00 = £22,000	11,000 × 2 = 22,000 × £1 = £22,000	£(8,000)	£(8,000)	nil

Type	*Actual cost of purchases*	*Actual quantity bought at SP*	*Standard cost of actual issues*	*Standard cost of actual output*	*Cost variance*	*Price*	*Usage*
					5 (*6+7*)	*6* (*2−1*)	*7* (*4−3*)
Material B	50,000 × £0.66 = £30,000	50,000 × £0.50 = £25,000	40,000 × £0.50 = £20,000	11,000 × 4 = 44,000 × £0.50 = £22,000	£(3,000)	£(5,000)	£2,000

Type	*Actual wages paid*	*Actual hours paid at standard rate*	*Actual hours worked at standard rate*	*Standard cost of actual output*	*Cost variance*	*Rate*	*Idle time*	*Efficiency*
	1	*2*	*3*	*4*	*5* (*4−1*)	*6*	*7*	*8*
Labour	25,000 × £2.50 = £62,500	25,000 × £3.00 = £75,000	24,000 × £3.00 = £72,000	11,000 × 2 = 22,000 × £3 = £66,000	£3,500 +	£12,500	£3,000	£(6,000)

Type	*Actual cost*		*Actual hours worked × SR*	*Standard cost of actual output*	*Cost variance*	*Spending*	*Efficiency*
	1	*2*	*3*	*4*	*5* (*4−1*)	*6* (*3−1*)	*7* (*4−3*)
Variable overhead	£20,000	–	24,000 × £1.00 = £24,000	11,000 × 2 = 22,000 × £1 = £22,000	£2,000 +	£4,000 +	£(2,000)

Type	*Actual cost*	*Budget (Ref. Note 2)*		*Standard cost of actual output*	*Cost variance*	*Expenditure*	*Volume*
	1	*2*	*3*	*4*	*5* (*4−1*)	*6* (*2−1*)	*7* (*4−2*)
Fixed overhead	£100,000	£80,000		11,000 × 2 = 22,000 × £4 = £88,000	£(12,000)	£(20,000)	£8,000 +

NOTE 1 BUDGETED SELLING PRICE

Standard cost	£20
Profit: 20 per cent of SP	5
	£25

NOTE 2 BUDGETED FIXED PRODUCTION OVERHEAD

Budgeted output (units)	10,000
Fixed overhead per unit	£8
Budget	£80,000

SCHEDULE 1—SALES VARIANCES, TURNOVER METHOD

Product	*Budgeted sales*	*Actual sales*	*Standard sales*	*Sales variance*	*Analysis* *Price*	*Volume*
	1	2	*3*	*4* (2−*1*)	*5* (*3*−2)	*6* (*3*−*1*)
	£000	*£000*	*£000*	*£000*	*£000*	*£000*
	10,000 × £25	9,000 × £30	9,000 × £25			
	£250	£270	£225	£20+	£45+	(£25)

SCHEDULE 3—SALES MARGIN VARIANCE

Product	*Budgeted margin*	*Actual margin*	*Standard margin*	*Sales margin variance*	*Due to price*	*Due to volume*
	1	2	*3*	*4* (2−*1*)	*5* (2−*3*)	*6* (*3*−*1*)
	£000	*£000*	*£000*	*£000*	*£000*	*£000*
	10,000 × (25−20)	9,000 × (30−20)	9,000 × (25−20)			
	£50	£90	£45	£40+	£45+	(£5)

(c) *Profit and loss statement:*

Period/month ended 31st May year 7

			£000
(1)	Budgeted sales	10,000 at £25	250
	Sales variances based on turnover—(Schedule 1)		20+
(2)	Actual sales	9,000 at £30	270
	Standard cost of sales:		
	Direct materials A	9,000 × £2 = £18,000	
	Direct materials B	9,000 × £2 = £18,000	
	Direct labour	9,000 × £6 = £54,000	
	Variable overhead	9,000 × £2 = £18,000	
	Fixed overhead	9,000 × £8 = £72,000	
(3)	Total (9,000 × £20)		(180)
(4)	Standard profit on actual sales (2 − 3)		90
(5)	Production cost variances (Schedule 2)		
	Material A	£(8,000)	
	Material B	(3,000)	
	Labour	3,500	
	Variable overhead	2,000	
	Fixed overhead	(12,000)	
	Total production cost variance		(17.5)
(6)	(4 − 5) Gross profit		72.5
	Administration, selling and distribution expenses:		
	Variable		10.0
	Fixed		15.5
		Net profit	47.0

NOTE 1 STANDARD ABSORPTION COSTING

A reconciliation of the firm's budgeted and actual profit would reveal *three* possible sources for any difference between them:

(i) sales margin variance;

(ii) non-production cost variances;

(iii) production cost variances written-off.

NOTE 2 · UNDER STANDARD MARGINAL COSTING—FOUR POSSIBLE SOURCES

(i) sales margin variance;

(ii) non-production cost variances;

(iii) variable production cost variances;

(iv) fixed production cost variance.

(d) *Reconciliation statement—standard absorption costing*

				£000
Budgeted net profit				30
(i) Sales margin variance (Schedule 3)				
due to price				45+
due to volume				(5)
(ii) Non-production cost variances:				
	Budget (£000)	*Actual (£000)*	*Variance (£000)*	
Administration, selling and distribution:				
Variable	8	10.0	(2.0)	(2.0)
Fixed	12	15.5	(3.5)	(3.5)
(iii) Production cost variances (Schedule 2)				
	Planned (£000)	*Actual (£000)*	*Variance (£000)*	
Material A	–	(8.0)	(8.0)	(8.0)
Material B	–	(3.0)	(3.0)	(3.0)
Labour	–	3.5	3.5	3.5
Variable overhead	–	2.0	2.0	2.0
Fixed overhead	–	(12.0)	(12.0)	(12.0)
		Actual net profit		47.0

CHAPTER TWENTY-THREE

Budgetary Control

1.0 MEANING OF CONTROL

Control may be defined as the direction of current and future activities of the company to conform to plan. The control process involves five aspects:

(a) *Planning*. Planning is the basis for control. The word control carries no meaning without a plan.

(b) *Communication*, i.e. informing those involved of the proposed plan.

(c) *Motivation* of people to achieve the plans.

(d) *Comparison*, i.e. performance reporting. The comparison of actual with planned results, in order that corrective action may be taken if necessary.

(e) *Action*. If the events do not conform to plan corrective action has to be taken. Without action there will be no control.

Any control system must embody these five fundamental requirements, which show that *decision making* based on relevant information is the heart of the control process.

2.0 FUNCTIONS OF MANAGEMENT

The fundamental function of any business organisation is to achieve certain basic goals. Goals are often qualitative statements of the position the company would like to occupy in the long run.

2.1 Fundamental goal

The most important goal of a company is survival. This depends on the performance of the company measured in terms of earning a satisfactory return (profit) on capital employed in the long run. This in turn depends on the creation of a customer for its products.

2.2 Secondary goals

These include:

(a) a competitive position for the company;

(b) service to the community;

(c) defining the kind of products to be marketed;

(d) clarifying the type of market to be aimed at;

(e) relations with customers and employees.

2.3 Business objectives

Companies should know where they intend to go. Decision making is made easier if management spells out the boundaries within which the company is to operate. Business objectives are the boundaries set by management on its freedom of decisions. The objectives have two important characteristics:

(a) They quantify the goals of the company. They are not management's beliefs, but are specified targets to be achieved.

(b) In quantifying objectives, companies set the time limits in which these objectives should be achieved.

3.0 THE MANAGER'S JOB—BASIC CONSIDERATIONS

Business objectives cannot be achieved without effective and efficient direction. The manager's job is deciding what should be done to achieve the objectives set and motivating other people to do it.

To perform his functions effectively and efficiently, a manager needs to consider the following:

(a) *The plan.* That is, a scheme for accomplishing the objectives.

(b) *Organisation and co-ordination.* What activities are required at each level of the organisation to achieve the objectives and how the work should be allocated to various groups?

(c) *Communication and motivation.* A manager must encourage his staff to act in harmony with the objectives of the company and to be loyal to the company. He does this not only through constant communication but also through his own relations with the people he is responsible for.

(d) *Control.* This is done by comparing actual with planned results.

(e) *Development of people.* By and large, there is agreement among writers that in order to perform their functions efficiently and effectively managers need to plan, organise, motivate and control. To these four functions of management Drucker contributed another function, the development of people. He says:

> ". . . the function which distinguishes the manager above all others is his educational one. The one contribution he is uniquely expected to make is to give others vision and ability to perform. He directs people or misdirects them. He strengthens their integrity or he corrupts them. He trains them to stand upright and strong or he deforms them."

The manager's job is to decide *what should be done* to achieve the company objectives and to *motivate other people to do it*. To perform his functions he must have tools; budgetary control is one of them.

4.0 BUDGET AND BUDGETARY CONTROL

A budget is a financial and/or *quantitative statement*, prepared *prior to a given period of time*, of the *policy* to pursue during that period for the *purpose* of attaining a *given objective*.

The essential features of a budget are as follows:

(a) a statement;

(b) expression in *money* or *quantity* or both;

(c) a specified period of time—the *budget period*;

(d) preparation in advance;

(e) prior to preparation:

  (i) a definite objective, and

  (ii) a decided *policy* to be pursued in order to achieve the objective.

The budget is a managerial tool designed to assist in planning, communicating, organising, co-ordinating and controlling.

4.1 Budgetary control

To achieve the objectives, managers should act in harmony. The suitability of a budget should not be assessed in terms of the interest of one function but in terms of the company as a whole. One problem in business management is that the interests of the four main functions—sales, production, purchasing and financial—are often in conflict. What suits one does not suit the other. The sales function would prefer to have in stock most of the items so that customers' goodwill is retained. The production functions would prefer a small number of items and long production runs rather than a large number of items and short production runs. The purchasing function prefers to order in large quantities to reduce freight costs and take advantage of quantity discounts. Large stocks of raw materials and/or finished goods do not suit the finance function, which prefers less money to be tied up in stock.

The aim of budgetary control is to encourage and assist managers to act in harmony with the overall objectives of the company, rather than in terms of functional or individual objectives. Budgetary control is defined as the establishment of budgets relating the responsibilities of executives to the requirements of a policy and the continuous comparison of actual with planned results, either to secure by individual action the objectives of that policy or else to provide a basis for its revision. The purpose of budgetary control may be called goal congruence, whereby functional and individual objectives assist in achieving top management objectives.

5.0 ORGANISATION FOR BUDGETARY CONTROL

For the budgetary control system to be successful it must possess many requisites, as follows:

5.1 Support of top management

Budgeting is a management function designed to achieve the objectives of top management. To achieve goal congruence, managers have to act in harmony with top management goals, and it will be an impossible task if the programme lacks top management support.

5.2 Division of work

Management must consider the kind of organisational structure essential to attain the objectives of the business. A functional division of work should be followed by a further division into cost centres/departments. The authority and responsibility of each manager must be clearly established; and it is essential that the manager's responsibility and authority correspond and that he is held accountable only for activities over which he has control.

5.3 Co-ordination: budget officer

It is essential that a department headed by a responsible person (the budget officer) is appointed to co-ordinate the preparation and administration of the budgetary control system and the liaison between the large number of people involved. The budget officer is usually the accountant.

Principal duties of the budget officer
These are:

(a) To see that managers develop and accept responsibility for their budgets.

(b) To co-ordinate the work of those responsible for the preparation of the budget.

(c) To prepare and present budget reports.

(d) To advise the budget committee as to the financial effects of plans under consideration.

(e) To act as secretary to the budget committee.

(f) To prepare the budget programme and issue suitable instructions.

(g) To supervise the preparation of the budget manual.

5.4 Budget committee

We have already termed the purpose of budgeting as goal congruence, meaning that all functional and individual objectives should blend together in achieving top management goals. It is an accepted practice that the direction, control, responsibility, preparation and execution of the budget are delegated to a small body of executives known as the budget committee; in most companies this is made up of the main functional heads.

Principal duties of the budget committee
These may be listed as follows:

(a) To receive individual budgets from responsible executives and to consider them in relation to the overall objectives of the company, the master plan.

(b) To decide general policies affecting the budget of more than one department.

(c) To suggest and consider revisions of the budgets.

(d) To prepare and recommend the acceptance of the master budget.

(e) To receive and consider in the light of company objectives the budget reports showing actual results compared with the budget and to recommend corrective action where necessary.

5.5 Budget manual

This is a handbook in which the responsibilities of the executives responsible for the preparation of budgets, the forms and specific procedures to be followed and the objectives of the business are set forth.

Contents of a budget manual
The contents of a budget manual would include:

(a) *Objectives:* a statement of purpose for which the budgetary control system is devised.

(b) *Organisation chart:* the authority, responsibility and span of control of each executive who is responsible for the preparation of the budget.

(c) *Budget officer:* the functions and responsibilities of the budget officer.

(d) *Budget committee:* the composition, functions and duties of the budget committee.

(e) *Budget period:* the time period covered by the budget. It may not be the same for all budgets, yet it must be definitely established.

(f) *Timetable:* the schedule of dates for the receipt of estimates from various budget centres and the issue of performance reports.

(g) *Procedures and principles:* the procedures and principles governing the form and nature of budgets and performance reports.

5.6 Budget period

Practical considerations should prevail in determining the period of time covered by the budget. For example, capital expenditure budgets by necessity are long-term budgets whereas sales or production budgets may be for short periods. Although the period of time covered by budgets may differ, it must be established. The main objective of the budgetary control system which must not be lost sight of is the attainment of the company objectives within a certain time span.

Factors to be considered

In determining the budget period, the following factors should be considered:

(a) *Product.* With seasonal products such as footwear or clothing, the period should cover at least a season. In another industry, e.g. hi-fi equipment, it will be for a longer period to allow expenses to be spread evenly over the entire period.

(b) *Length of the production cycle.* It should at least cover the period required to manufacture the products.

(c) *Type of budget.* Sales, cash, production, capital expenditure, purchases, etc.

(d) *General economic conditions.* The ability to forecast the future at any particular time is influenced by general economic conditions. The budget period may reflect a likelihood of strikes or political unrest and by necessity be short.

(e) *Share of the market.* If the firm has a monopoly it can forecast its position with reasonable accuracy and the budget period can be longer than that of a firm which has a small share of the market.

(f) *Co-ordination of sales and production.* By co-ordinating production and sales, it is possible to determine the contribution made by each to the achievement of the company objectives. The budget period should, therefore, cover both production and sales. If the firm manufactures in summer for sale in winter and if the budget period ends in September then the company will not get the full benefits of budgeting. The interrelationship of other budgets, for example, the timing and availability of finance, will affect the selection of the budget period since in a budgetary control system all budgets should fit together within master budget.

(g) *Control aspect.* For control purposes the budget period is usually divided into shorter periods. This division of the budget period will make possible the comparison of actual with budget results so that corrective action may be taken very much earlier than the end of the budget period.

5.7 The principal budget factor

To achieve company overall objectives, managers should act in harmony. The suitability of a budget should not be assessed in terms of the interest of one function but in terms of the company as a whole. Due to this inter-link, the limitation affecting a particular budget has its influence on the rest of the budgets. A factor in the activities of a company which at a particular point in time or over a period will limit the volume of output is known as the principal budget factor.

The nature of the principal budget factor is such that it tends to affect all budgets. It is, therefore, essential in planning to establish the principal budget factor in order to ensure that the budgets are prepared in the light of this limitation, so that they have a reasonable chance of fulfilment. It may be a shortage of skilled labour, working capital, demand for products, plant capacity, shortage of raw materials or government restrictions. It can be seen that the principal budget factor is governed by both internal and external influences.

5.8 The human aspect

The manager's job is to decide what should be done to attain the objectives and motivating other people to do it. The targets must be realistically set. It is also essential that the managers understand employees' motivation. It depends on management's understanding of why people work and what people expect from working. There are two schools of thought on why people work and what they expect from work, as follows:

(a) The conventional view

The conventional view is based on the following assumptions:

(i) The willingness to work is essentially motivated by monetary rewards.

(ii) Work is not a pleasant task.

(iii) People naturally dislike work, are lazy and have to be motivated.

(iv) Human beings are ordinarily inefficient and wasteful.

On the basis of these assumptions, the conventional view holds that authority is the central means of management control. To attain the goals of the enterprise people have to be bribed because they are essentially lazy and dislike work. The budget serves to apply pressure to achieve the desired results.

The result is that employees tend to become suspicious of management moves and departmental heads may fail to see beyond their departmental responsibilities.

(b) Modern organisation theory

The modern organisation theory is based on the following assumptions:

(i) That most people want to work. To perform their functions better not only do they need reasonable rewards but also a favourable environment in which to perform their tasks.

(ii) Employees under proper working conditions not only work towards the achievement of objectives but also are prepared to seek responsibility.

(iii) Employees place a high value on social status. They have to be treated as people and not like machines. The "carrot and stick" theory of motivation does not work.

The modern organisation theory is a challenge to management. If employees dislike work, are lazy, inefficient and wasteful, will not willingly accept responsibility and are unco-operative, the modern theory places the responsibility on the shoulders of management. Management's responsibility is to provide the environment in which people will want to work and therefore will accept responsibility.

Most current management theorists have advocated participation by employees in the decisions on which the budget is established. Participation is fundamental to:

(i) acceptance of company goals;

(ii) goal congruence;

(iii) acceptance of challenge and responsibility for achieving the objectives;

(iv) increasing employee motivation;

(v) reducing organisational conflict.

6.0 BUDGET PREPARATION

6.1 Comprehensive budget plan

A comprehensive budget plan should cover the following types of budgets:

(a) Sales budget

According to products
sales territories
types of customers, salesmen.

(b) Production budget

According to products

(i) *Plant utilisation budget*
The plant utilisation budget in terms of machine hours, or direct labour hours required in each cost centre.

(ii) *Cost of production budget*
Direct materials cost budget.
Direct labour cost budget.
Production overhead budget.

(iii) *Purchases budget*
The quantity and value of the various items of raw materials to be purchased during the budget period.

(iv) *Stock budgets*
Raw materials.
Work in progress.
Finished goods.

(c) Operating expense budgets

(i) Selling cost budget.

(ii) Distribution cost budget.

(iii) Administration cost budget.

(iv) Finance expense budget.

(v) Research and development budget.

(d) Capital expenditure budget

(i) Plant equipment.

(ii) Land and building.

(iii) Other.

(e) Cash budget

(i) Cash receipt budget.

(ii) Cash expenditure budget.

(f) Master budget

(i) Budgeted profit and loss account.

(ii) Budgeted balance sheet.

6.2 Master budget—The basic steps

The budgeted profit and loss account and the balance sheet combine all the other budgets and show the overall budgeted profit plan. Upon acceptance by the board of directors, they are together termed the master budget. The basic steps in compiling the master budget are as follows:

STEP 1 THE SALES BUDGET

The forecast of goods to be sold is the starting point in budgeting. The forecast is prepared after consideration of the following factors:

(a) the quantity and value of past sales;

(b) competition and conditions within the particular industry;

(c) general economic conditions;

(d) market research and salesmen's estimates;

(e) sales mix—which is dependent on the relative product profitability.

Steps

(a) Sales forecast by product.

(b) Product mix by product—the most profitable mix, taking into consideration the manufacturing capacity and profitability of product lines.

(c) The sales budget—the products by type, area and mix which management believes it could sell to achieve company objectives.

STEP 2 THE PRODUCTION BUDGET

The production budget is expressed in terms of physical units of products. The basic information required is:

Sales budget	units
Add: Closing stock requirements of finished goods	units
Less: Opening stock of finished goods	units
Units to be produced	

The production budget assists in making provision for the following:

(a) The stock budget.

(b) Production planning—what, when and in what quantities shall it be produced?

(c) The productive capacity required.

(d) The plant utilisation.

(e) In the light of production capacity and plant utilisation, an estimate of additional facilities required.

(f) Labour and material requirements.

(g) Cash requirements.

STEP 3 COST OF PRODUCTION BUDGET

(a) *Direct materials cost/usage budget*
Basic information required:

(i) Production budget.

(ii) Raw materials per unit of product by type and quantity.

(iii) Allowances for waste and scrap.

(iv) Rate per unit of raw material.

(b) *Direct labour cost budget*
Basic information required:

(i) The production budget.

(ii) Hours per unit in various producing departments.

(iii) Rates per direct labour hour.

(iv) Labour related costs and their treatment.

(c) *Production overhead budget*
Basic information required:

(i) The behaviour of manufacturing overhead items of expenditure. A cost classification according to the behaviour of each element of cost.

(ii) The classification of overhead departmentally.

(iii) The production budget—the capacity required departmentally (both producing and service departments) to meet the production target.

STEP 4 PURCHASES BUDGET (BY TYPE OF MATERIAL)

Basic information required:

(a) *Production budget:* raw materials by type and quantity required for production during the budget period.

(b) Planned opening and closing stock requirements.

(c) Materials allocated for incomplete order or special jobs.

(d) Orders for materials already placed.

(e) Economic size of the order—the actual quantity purchased at one time.

(f) Availability of finance.

STEP 5 PLANT UTILISATION BUDGET

The plant utilisation budget is a forecast of the plant capacity required (expressed in machine hours, direct labour hours, weight, number of products) to carry out the production programme as per the production budget. It is essential that the aim should be the most effective utilisation of capacity.

The plant utilisation budget determines for the budget period:

(a) the machine load on individual machines within a cost centre (or group of machines if they are identical) and the machine load on departments;

(b) the bottlenecks created by over-loading;

(c) idle facilities;

(d) use of sub-contractors;

(e) purchase of additional plant and equipment;

(f) changes necessary to the sales and production budgets, if it is not possible in the short period to increase manufacturing capacity and the utilisation of idle facilities effectively.

STEP 6 CAPITAL EXPENDITURE BUDGET

The capital expenditure budget consists of the planned expenditures on the acquisitions of assets which will remain in the business for a considerable time and form part of the earning capacity of the business. Since they are long-term commitments of resources, many companies have laid down definite procedures and methods for project evaluation.

The capital expenditure budget serves the following purposes:

(a) It is a cash budget, stating the cash requirements for replacement of obsolete or worn-out facilities, expansion of facilities, and cash in-flow from the sale of such assets.

(b) It is the basis for the provision of depreciation and maintenance.

(c) It acts as the basis for long-term planning.

STEP 7 CASH BUDGET

STEP 8 MASTER BUDGET

(a) Profit and loss account.

(b) Balance sheet.

7.0 COMPREHENSIVE ILLUSTRATIONS

7.1 Budgeting material quantities

Illustration 1—production budget, direct materials cost budget, purchases budget

A sales budget for year 7 is given for a particular line manufactured by Smith and Wesson:

Sales budget (units)

Period 1	20,000	Period 7	50,000
2	30,000	8	40,000
3	40,000	9	20,000
4	20,000	10	30,000
5	20,000	11	60,000
6	40,000	12	40,000

The stock of finished products at the end of each period is to be equal to 25 per cent of the sales estimate for the next period. At the beginning of period one there were 4,000 units. There was no work in progress at the end of any period.

Each unit of product requires material type ROD in the following quantities:

Material ROD: 10 lb at £1.00 per lb.

Materials equal to 25 per cent of the next period's production are to be on hand at the end of each period. The stock of raw material at the beginning of period 1 met this requirement.

You are required to prepare for the first six periods:

(a) the production budget;

(b) the direct materials cost/usage budget;

(c) the purchases budget.

Suggested answer

(a) *Production budget*

Period	*Sales budget (units)*	*Opening stock (units)*	*Closing stock (units)*	*Production budget (units)*
	1	*2*	*3*	*4* (*1*+*3*−*2*)
1	20,000	4,000	7,500	23,500
2	30,000	7,500	10,000	32,500
3	40,000	10,000	5,000	35,000
4	20,000	5,000	5,000	20,000
5	20,000	5,000	10,000	25,000
6	40,000	10,000	12,500	42,500
7	50,000	12,500	10,000	47,500
8	40,000			

Note: The stock of finished products at the end of each period is to be equal to 25 per cent of the sales estimate for the next period: e.g. closing stock for period 1: 25 per cent × £30,000 (sales of period 2).

(b, c) *Direct materials cost/usage budget; purchases budget*

Period	*Production budget (units)*	*Direct materials usage budget (10 lb per unit of product) (lb)*	*Opening stock (lb)*	*Closing stock (lb)*	*Purchases budget (lb)*	*Cost per unit*	*Cost of purchases (£)*	*Direct materials cost budget (£)*
	1	*2*	*3*	*4*	*5*	*6*	*7*	*8*
					(2+4−3)		(5×6)	(2×6)
1	23,500	235,000	58,750	81,250	257,500	£1	257,500	235,000
2	32,500	325,000	81,250	87,500	331,250	£1	331,250	325,000
3	35,000	350,000	87,500	50,000	312,500	£1	312,500	350,000
4	20,000	200,000	50,000	62,500	212,500	£1	212,500	200,000
5	25,000	250,000	62,500	106,250	293,750	£1	293,750	250,000
6	42,500	425,000	106,250	118,750	437,500	£1	437,500	425,000
7	47,500							

Notes
(a) Each unit requires 10 lb of material type ROD.
(b) Materials equal to 25 per cent of the next period's production are to be on hand at the end of each period.

7.2 Labour budget

Illustration 2

RA Manufacturing Company produces three products, RB, RJ and RS, and is preparing its annual budget.

The production budget:

Product	*Units*
RB	40,000
RJ	80,000
RS	60,000

The production requirements are to be produced in three departments which plan to employ as follows:

Department	*Standard wage rate per hour*	*Number of employees*
One	£2.50	750
Two	£2.75	1,200
Three	£3.00	1,000

	Department		
	One (hours)	*Two (hours)*	*Three (hours)*
Product RB is scheduled to take (per unit)	10	–	15
Product RJ is scheduled to take (per unit)	–	10	20
Product RS is scheduled to take (per unit)	20	30	–

The company works a 5-day, 40-hour basic week and overtime is paid at the rate of time plus one-half. The annual paid holiday agreement is for 2 weeks and 4 days, which is additional to the 6 days' paid statutory holidays.

Standard allowances are budgeted for loss of productive hours for the following causes:

Annual—sickness—5 days per employee
Weekly—cleaning machines—75 minutes per employee
Weekly—personal—45 minutes per employee.

All holidays, absence and non-productive time is to be calculated at the standard wage rate per hour. Assume a year of exactly fifty-two weeks. It is the policy of the company to work overtime irregularly to meet commitments from time to time.

You are required to calculate and present:

(a) The annual payroll budget for each department.

(b) Each of the departmental budgets in money values, for:

(i) direct labour; (ii) holiday and sick pay; (iii) overtime premium; (iv) other.

(c) The standard direct wage cost for each product.

Suggested answer—see p. 435

NOTE 1 PRODUCTIVE HOURS PER EMPLOYEE PER ANNUM

Maximum possible hours: $52 \times 40 =$			2,080
Less:	holidays: $4 \times 40 =$ (2 weeks + 4 days + 6 days)	160.0	
	sickness: $1 \times 40 =$	40.0	
	cleaning machines: 1.25 hours per week × 47 weeks	58.75	
	personal: 0.45×47	35.25	(294)
Productive hours per employee per annum			1,786 hours

NOTE 2 CAPACITY REQUIRED—IN MAN-HOURS

		Dept One	*Dept Two*	*Dept Three*
Production budget (units)				
RB	(1)	40,000	–	40,000
RJ	(2)	–	80,000	80,000
RS	(3)	60,000	60,000	–
Hours per unit				
RB	(4)	10	–	15
RJ	(5)	–	10	20
RS	(6)	20	30	–
Capacity required				
RB	(1 × 4)	400,000	–	600,000
RJ	(2 × 5)	–	800,000	1,600,000
RS	(3 × 6)	1,200,000	1,800,000	–
Total hours		1,600,000	2,600,000	2,200,000

Suggested answer

(a) *Annual payroll budget summary*

Department	*Rate per hour (£)*	*Number of employees*	*Annual normal hours per employee (hours)*	*Total normal hours (hours)*	*Overtime hours (Note 4) (hours)*	*Overtime premium hours (hours)*	*Normal pay (£)*	*Overtime pay (£)*	*Overtime premium (£)*	*Total (£)*
One	2.50	750	2,080	1,560,000	261,000	130,000	3,900,000	652,500	326,250	4,878,750
Two	2.75	1,200	2,080	2,496,000	457,000	228,500	6,864,000	1,256,750	628,375	8,749,125
Three	3.00	1,000	2,080	2,080,000	414,000	207,000	6,240,000	1,242,000	621,000	8,103,000
Total	–	2,950	–	6,136,000	1,132,000	566,000	17,004,000	3,151,250	1,575,625	21,730,875

NOTE 3 CAPACITY AVAILABLE

	Dept One	*Dept Two*	*Dept Three*
Number of men	750	1,200	1,000
Productive hours per employee per annum (refer Note 1)	1,786	1,786	1,786
Available capacity (to nearest 1,000 hours)	1,339,000	2,143,000	1,786,000

NOTE 4 ADDITIONAL CAPACITY—IN MAN-HOURS

	Dept One	*Dept Two*	*Dept Three*
Capacity required (Note 2) (direct labour hours)	1,600,000	2,600,000	2,200,000
Capacity available (Note 3) (direct labour hours)	1,339,000	2,143,000	1,786,000
Overtime hours (additional capacity)	261,000	457,000	414,000
Overtime premium hours (payroll purposes) time plus one-half	130,500	228,500	207,000
Budgeted productive hours during: (wages analysis and effective hourly rate)			
Normal time	1,339,000	2,143,000	1,786,000
Overtime	261,000	457,000	414,000
	1,600,000	2,600,000	2,200,000

NOTE 5

DEPARTMENT ONE

Direct wages—normal hours (Note 1)	(1,786 × 750 × £2.50)	£3,348,750
Holidays (Note 1)	(160 × 750 × £2.50)	300,000
Sickness (Note 1)	(40 × 750 × £2.50)	75,000
Other (Note 1)	(94 × 750 × £2.50)	176,250
		£3,900,000

Suggested answer (continued)

(b) *Wages analysis sheet*

	Direct wages			*Production overhead*					*Total*
				Holiday and sick pay					
Department	*Normal (Note 3)*	*Overtime (refer to payroll)*	*Total*	*Holiday (Note 5)*	*Sick (Note 5)*	*Total*	*Overtime premium (refer to payroll)*	*Other (Note 5)*	*Total (refer to payroll)*
One	£3,348,750	£652,500	£4,001,250	£300,000	£75,000	£375,000	£326,250	£176,250	£4,878,750
Two	£5,893,800	£1,256,750	£7,150,550	£528,000	£132,000	£660,000	£628,375	£310,200	£8,749,125
Three	£5,358,000	£1,242,000	£6,600,000	£480,000	£120,000	£600,000	£621,000	£282,000	£8,103,000
	£14,600,550	£3,151,250	£17,751,800	£1,308,000	£327,000	£1,635,000	£1,575,625	£768,450	£21,730,875

DEPARTMENT TWO

Direct wages—normal hours	(1,786–1,200 × £2.75)	£5,893,800
Holidays	(160 × 1,200 × £2.75)	528,000
Sickness	(40 × 1,200 × £2.75)	132,000
Other	(94 × 1,200 × £2.75)	310,200
		£6,864,000

DEPARTMENT THREE

Direct wages—normal hours	(1,786 × 1,000 × £3.00)	£5,358,000
Holidays	(160 × 1,000 × £3.00)	480,000
Sickness	(40 × 1,000 × £3.00)	120,000
Other	(94 × 1,000 × £3.00)	282,000
		£6,240,000

Suggested answer (continued)

(c) *Standard direct wage cost for each product*

Product	RB	RJ	RS
Department/hours per unit			
Department One (hours)	10	–	20
Department Two (hours)	–	10	30
Department Three (hours)	15	20	–
	Dept One	Dept Two	Dept Three
Effective hourly rate (Note 6)	£2.5008	£2.7502	£3.00
Direct wage cost—product	RB	RJ	RS
Department One	£25.008	–	£50.016
Department Two	–	£27.502	£82.506
Department Three	£45.000	£60.000	–
Total	£70.008	£87.502	£132.522

NOTE 6 EFFECTIVE DIRECT LABOUR HOURLY RATE FOR PRODUCT COSTING PURPOSES

Department	One	Two	Three
Direct wages (refer wages analysis sheet)	£4,001,250	£7,150,550	£6,600,000
Direct labour hours (Note 3—budgeted productive hours)	1,600,000	2,600,000	2,200,000
Effective hourly rate	£2.5008	£2.7502	£3.00

7.3 Master budget

Illustration 3

Joslin Manufacturing Company manufactures three products, extracts from the standard cost data relating to which are appended:

MATERIALS USED IN MANUFACTURING OF THE PRODUCTS

Material type:	M111	M222	M333	M444
Cost per lb	£5.00	£4.00	£3.00	£2.00

CONTENT OF EACH UNIT OF PRODUCT

Product: HO	3	2	2	5
Product: RA	4	4	4	3
Product: NA	5	3	4	2

LABOUR TIMES

Two types of labour are used, U12 grade A and grade B, the standard unit times for each product being:

Product	*Labour type grade A (hours per unit)*	*Labour type grade B (hours per unit)*
HO	5	3
RA	6	5
NA	8	6

The direct labour hourly rates are grade A, £3.50; grade B, £2.50.

Stocks at the beginning of period one are expected to be:

Finished goods	*Quantity*	*£*
HO	2,000	145,621
RA	4,000	398,457
NA	6,000	668,509
		£1,212,587

Raw materials	*Quantity (lb)*
M111	50,000
M222	20,000
M333	10,000
M444	20,000

The company plans an increase of 20 per cent in the quantities of finished stocks held and a reduction of 10 per cent in the quantities of raw material stocks.

Work in progress is negligible and may be ignored at anticipated volume levels. The following costs will be incurred:

	Factory overhead
Factory supplies	£20,640
Building occupancy	150,000
Indirect wages	70,000
Equipment utilisation	520,000
Materials handling	15,000
Production planning and control	19,000
Supervision and administration	30,000

	Selling, distribution and general administration
Commission	£150,000
Advertising	300,000
Salaries	400,000
Wages and travel	120,000

BUDGETED SALES OF THE PRODUCTS

Product	*Quantity*	*Price per unit*
HO	10,000	£100
RA	20,000	£200
NA	30,000	£250

You are required to prepare a budgeted profit statement for the period showing the amount of profit contributed by each product. Include the following detailed schedules:

(a) Sales budget.

(b) Production budget.

(c) Direct materials usage budget.

(d) Direct material purchase budget.

(e) Direct labour utilisation and cost budget.

(f) Factory overhead budget.

(g) Closing stock budget.

(h) Cost of goods sold budget.

(i) Selling and administration expenses budget.

Suggested answer

SCHEDULE 1 SALES BUDGET

Product	*Sales budget (units)*	*Selling price*	*Total sales*
HO	10,000	£100	£1,000,000
RA	20,000	200	4,000,000
NA	30,000	250	7,500,000
			£12,500,000

SCHEDULE 2 PRODUCTION BUDGET—UNITS

	Product		
	HO	*RA*	*NA*
Planned sales (Schedule 1)	10,000	20,000	30,000
Closing stock (20 per cent increase)	2,400	4,800	7,200
Total needs	12,400	24,800	37,200
Less: Opening stock	(2,000)	(4,000)	(6,000)
Units to be produced	10,400	20,800	31,200

SCHEDULE 3 DIRECT MATERIAL USAGE BUDGET

	Production budget (units)	*M111 (lb per unit)*	*M222 (lb per unit)*	*M333 (lb per unit)*	*M444 (lb per unit)*
Product HO	10,400	3	2	2	5
Product RA	10,800	4	4	4	3
Product NA	31,200	5	3	4	2
		(lb)	*(lb)*	*(lb)*	*(lb)*
Product HO	–	31,200	20,800	20,800	52,000
Product RA	–	83,200	83,200	83,200	62,400
Product NA	–	156,000	93,600	124,800	62,400
Total usage		270,400	197,600	228,800	176,800
Price per lb		£5.00	£4.00	£3.00	£2.00
Cost of materials consumed		£1,352,000	£790,400	£686,400	£353,600

Total cost of materials consumed £3,182,400.

SCHEDULE 4 DIRECT MATERIAL PURCHASE BUDGET

	M111 (lb)	*M222 (lb)*	*M333 (lb)*	*M444 (lb)*
Units needed for production (Schedule 3)	270,400	167,600	228,800	176,800
Add: Closing stock requirements (less 10 per cent reduction)	45,000	18,000	9,000	1,800
Total needs	315,400	185,600	237,800	194,800
Less: Opening stock	(50,000)	(20,000)	(10,000)	(20,000)
Units to be purchased	265,400	165,600	227,700	174,800
Unit price	£5.00	£4.00	£3.00	£2.00
Purchase budget	£1,327,000	£662,400	£683,100	£349,600

SCHEDULE 5 DIRECT LABOUR UTILISATION AND COST BUDGET

Product	*Production budget (units)*	*Grade A (hours per unit)*	*Grade B (hours per unit)*
HO	10,400	5	3
RA	20,800	6	5
NA	31,200	8	6
HO	10,400	52,000	31,200
RA	20,800	124,800	104,000
NA	3,100	249,600	187,200
Total hours	–	426,400	322,400

	Total	*Grade A*	*Grade B*
Total direct labour hours	748,800	426,400	322,400
Budgeted labour rate per hour	–	£3.50	£2.50
Total direct labour cost	£2,298,400	£1,492,400	£806,000

SCHEDULE 6 FACTORY OVERHEAD BUDGET

Anticipated level of activity (grades A and B): 748,800 direct labour hours.

Factory supplies	£20,640
Building occupancy	150,000
Indirect wages	70,000
Equipment utilisation	520,000
Materials handling	15,000
Production planning and control	19,000
Supervision and administration	30,000
Total factory overhead	£824,640

Overhead rate of absorption:

$$\frac{\text{Budgeted overhead}}{\text{Budgeted level of activity}} = \frac{£824,640}{748,800} = £1.1013 \text{ per direct labour hour.}$$

SCHEDULE 7 STOCK BUDGET

Direct materials	*Closing stock*	*Unit cost*	*Total*
M111 (Schedule 4)	£45,000	£5.00	£225,000
M222 (Schedule 4)	18,000	4.00	72,000
M333 (Schedule 4)	9,000	3.00	27,000
M444 (Schedule 4)	18,000	2.00	36,000
			£360,000

FINISHED GOODS

Product	*Units (Schedule 2)*	*Unit cost (Note 1)*	*Amount*
HO	2,400	£72.8104	£174,745
RA	4,800	£99.6143	478,149
NA	7,200	£111.4182	802,211
			£1,455,105

SCHEDULE 8 COST OF GOODS SOLD BUDGET

	Source of information	*Amount*
Direct materials	Schedule 3	£3,182,400
Direct labour	Schedule 5	2,298,400
Factory overhead	Schedule 6	824,640
Total manufacturing cost		£6,305,440
Add: Finished goods—at the beginning (given)		1,212,587
Less: Finished goods—at the end (Schedule 7)		(1,455,105)
Cost of goods sold		£6,062,922

NOTE 1 UNIT COST CALCULATION

		HO	*RA*	*NA*
Direct materials:				
M111	3 × £5.00	£15.00		
	4 × £5.00		£20.00	
	5 × £5.00			£25.00
M222	2 × £4.00	£8.00		
	4 × £4.00		£16.00	
	3 × £4.00			£12.00
M333	2 × £3.00	£6.00		
	4 × £3.00		£12.00	
	4 × £3.00			£12.00
M444	5 × £2.00	£10.00		
	3 × £2.00		£6.00	
	2 × £2.00			£4.00
Direct materials		£39.00	£54.00	£53.00
Direct labour:				
Grade A	5 × £3.50	£17.50		
	6 × £3.50		£21.00	
	8 × £3.50			£28.00
Grade B	3 × £2.50	£7.50		
	5 × £2.50		£12.50	
	6 × £2.50			£15.00
Prime cost		£64.00	£87.50	£96.00
Production overhead:				
	8 × £1.1013	£8.8104		
	11 × £1.1013		£12.1143	
	14 × £1.1013			£15.4182
Cost per unit		£72.8104	£99.6143	£111.4182

SCHEDULE 9 SELLING AND ADMINISTRATION EXPENSES BUDGET

Commission	£150,000
Advertising	300,000
Salaries	400,000
Wages, travel	120,000
	£970,000

Budgeted profit and loss account (summary)

Sales—Schedule 1	£12,500,000
Cost of goods sold—Schedule 8	£6,062,922
Gross profit	£6,437,078
Selling and administration—Schedule 9	970,000
Profit	£5,467,078

Budgeted profit and loss account

	Total	*HO*	*RA*	*NA*
Budgeted sales (units) (Schedule 1)		10,000	20,000	30,000
Selling price per unit		£100	£200	£250
Manufacturing cost per unit (Note 1)		£72.8104	£99.6143	£111.4182
Sales	£12,500,000	£1,000,000	£4,000,000	£7,500,000
Cost of goods sold	£6,062,922	£728,104	£1,992,286	£3,342,546
Gross profit	£6,437,078	£271,896	£2,007,714	£4,157,454
Selling and administration	£970,000	–	–	–
Net profit	£5,467,078			

8.0 CASH BUDGETS

A schedule of the expected cash inflow and outflow for the budget period. There are many approaches to the preparation of a cash budget, e.g.

(a) cash receipts and disbursements method;

(b) adjusted profit and loss method, or the income method.

In preparing the cash budget it is essential that continuing sources and application of funds are separated from other cash flows.

8.1 Basic information required

(a) The time period

The cash budget is a planning device rather than a control tool. Consequently, the period covered may vary with the cash position of the company. If the inflow and outflow of cash are more or less stable throughout the year then the cash budget may be prepared annually. If the business is seasonal then a cash budget by months for the year.

(b) Inflow of funds—sales budget

(i) Cash sales—less discounts.

(ii) Credit sales:

Credit is allowed to customers for varying periods and on varying terms. On the basis of the past average collection period, an estimate is made of the collection of accounts receivable. Collections from debtors during a period will be the result of the current period's sales plus collections from debtors of previous periods. The following illustration provides an example.

Illustration

10 per cent of this month's sales will be collected this month;
50 per cent of this month's sales will be collected next month;
30 per cent of this month's sales will be collected in the second month;
8 per cent of this month's sales will be collected in the third month;
2 per cent will never be collected.

ESTIMATED CREDIT SALES

January	£240,000
February	£300,000
March	£400,000
April	£600,000
May	£800,000
June	£500,000

COLLECTIONS FOR THE MONTH OF APRIL

10 per cent × £600,000 (April)	£60,000
50 per cent × £400,000 (March)	£200,000
30 per cent × £300,000 (February)	£90,000
8 per cent × £240,000 (January)	£19,200
Total collections for April	£369,200

(iii) Inflow of funds—other sources

Other sources of receipts are dividends, interest, royalties, sales of fixed assets, issue of shares and debentures, loans, sale of investments, sale of obsolete stock etc.

(c) Outflow of cash

(i) Payments to trade creditors—payments for purchases of materials (purchases budget).

(ii) Payments to other creditors—various types of overhead expense budgets.

(iii) Wages and salaries—labour budget.

(iv) Capital expenditure—purchase of plant and equipment.

(v) Dividend, loans, donations, corporation tax, investments etc.

(d) Non-cash expenses are excluded

(i) Depreciation provisions.

(ii) Accruals.

8.2 Purpose of the cash budget

(a) To indicate that sufficient cash is available as and when required for running the business.

(b) To determine when, if any, funds are necessary.

(c) To determine the availability of surplus funds for short-term and long-term investments.

(d) To determine whether funds for capital projects are available from internal sources.

(e) To take advantage of cash discounts.

(f) To determine whether the company is over-trading.

(g) To indicate the effect on the cash position of seasonal requirements, unusual receipts and slowness in collecting accounts receivables.

(h) To assist in planning the cash requirements for the redemption of long-term loans, corporation tax instalments, and payments to pension funds.

Illustration 4—Manufacturing concern

On the basis of the sales budget for the year, the production, planning and control department has prepared the following Production Schedule for the coming month.

PRODUCTION SCHEDULE

Product RS	50,000 units
Product RR	40,000 units

The factory variable cost per unit of product is expected to be:

Product RS

5 lb of material S at £2.00	£10.00
10 lb of material R at £2.50	25.00
5 hours of direct labour at £4.00	20.00
5 hours of variable overhead at £2.00	10.00
	£65.00

Product RR

30 lb of material S at £2.00	£60.00
20 lb of material R at £2.50	50.00
10 hours of direct labour at £4.00	40.00
10 hours of variable overhead at £2.00	20.00
	£170.00

Fixed factory overhead for a month is estimated as follows:

Depreciation	£60,000
Insurance	20,000
Rent and rates	20,000
Other	50,000
Indirect wages and salaries	500,000
	£650,000

Standard allowances are budgeted for loss of direct labour hours for the following causes:

Sickness (monthly)	15,000 hours
Normal idleness	20,000 hours
Variable overhead rate per unit includes sickness and normal idle time	£140,000 per month.

It is planned to increase the stock of material S by 50,000 lb and to decrease the stock of material R by 200,000 lb as of the beginning of next month.

You are required to prepare an estimate of the amount of cash necessary for the manufacturing operations of the month.

Suggested answer

SUMMARY OF CASH REQUIREMENTS

Raw materials—Schedule 1	£5,750,000
Direct wages—Schedule 2	2,600,000
Indirect wages and salaries—Schedule 3	640,000
Variable overhead—Schedule 4	1,160,000
Fixed factory overhead—Schedule 5	90,000
	£10,240,000

SCHEDULE 1 RAW MATERIALS—PURCHASE AND PAYMENT

	Production budget (units)	*Production budget requirements (lb)*	*Plus closing stock (lb)*	*Less opening stock (lb)*	*Total purchases (lb)*	*Price per unit*	*Amount*
Product RS	50,000						
Product RR	40,000						
Material S							
50,000 × 5		250,000	50,000				
40,000 × 30		1,200,000	Stock increase				
		1,450,000	50,000		1,500,000	£2.00	£3,000,000
Material R							
50,000 × 10		500,000	(200,000)				
40,000 × 20		800,000	Stock decrease				
		1,300,000	(200,000)		1,100,000	£2.50	£2,750,000
Total		–	–		–	–	£5,750,000

SCHEDULE 2 DIRECT WAGES

Product	*Production budget (units)*	*Hours per unit (hours)*	*Total hours (hours)*	*Rate per hour (£)*	*Total cost (£)*
RS	50,000	5	250,000	4.00	1,000,000
RR	40,000	10	400,000	4.00	1,600,000
	–	–	650,000	4.00	2,600,000

SCHEDULE 3 INDIRECT WAGES

Indirect wages and salaries	£500,000
Sickness and normal idle time	
(350,000 × £4.00)	£140,000
	£640,000

Total expected payroll

Direct wages	£2,600,000
Indirect wages	£640,000
	£3,240,000

SCHEDULE 4 VARIABLE OVERHEAD

Product	*Budgeted production*	*Hours per unit*	*Total hours*	*Rate per hour*	*Amount*
RS	50,000	5	250,000	£2.00	£500,000
RR	40,000	10	400,000	£2.00	£800,000
Total					£1,300,000
Less: Normal idle time and sickness					(140,000)
Total estimated outflow					£1,160,000

SCHEDULE 5 FIXED FACTORY OVERHEAD

Insurance	£20,000
Rent and rates	£20,000
Other	£50,000
	£90,000

9.0 EXAMPLES

Example 1

The management of RA and RB Limited has set aside, on 1st January year 8, £400,000 for working capital to commence manufacture of a new product. Using the information given below, prepare a cash budget for the 6 months, January, February, March, April, May and June, year 8.

The following information is available:

(a) *Variable manufacturing cost per unit of product*
This is expected to be:

Direct materials	£20.00
Direct labour	80.00
Variable production overhead	40.00
Variable production cost per unit	£140.00

(b) *Fixed production overhead per annum*
Assume fixed production overhead is incurred uniformly and paid in the month used.

Depreciation—plant and machinery	£40,000
Depreciation—building	£50,000
Insurance	£40,000
Salaries and wages	£300,000
Other	£80,000

(c) *Estimated sales for the first 6 months*
After production commences in January, and sales on 1st February, year 8, these are expected to be:

	Units	*Sales value*
February	3,000	£900,000
March	5,000	£1,500,000
April	7,000	£2,100,000
May	8,000	£2,400,000
June	10,000	£3,000,000
July	12,000	£3,600,000

(d) *Finished goods stock*
75 per cent of each month's invoiced sales are produced in the previous month and 25 per cent are produced in the month of sale.

(e) *Raw material stocks*
50 per cent of direct materials required for each month's production are purchased

in the previous month. Direct materials are paid for in the month following purchase.

(f) *Direct wages*
Paid in the month used.

(g) *Variable overhead*
80 per cent is paid in the month of usage and the balance the following month.

(h) *Collections from debtors*
20 per cent received in the month of sale.
40 per cent received in the following month.
25 per cent received in the third month.
10 per cent received in the fourth month.
5 per cent not recovered.
5 per cent cash discount is allowed for payment in the current month.

Suggested answer

SCHEDULE 1 COLLECTION FROM DEBTORS—MONTHLY RECEIPTS

	February	*March*	*April*	*May*	*June*	*July*
Sales	£900,000	£1,500,000	£2,100,000	£2,400,000	£3,000,000	£3,600,000
20 per cent in the month of sale	180,000	300,000	420,000	480,000	600,000	720,000
Less 5 per cent discount	(9,000)	(15,000)	(21,000)	(24,000)	(30,000)	(36,000)
40 per cent in the following month	–	360,000	600,000	840,000	960,000	1,200,000
25 per cent in the third month	–	–	225,000	375,000	525,000	600,000
10 per cent in the fourth month	–	–	–	90,000	150,000	210,000
Total inflow	£171,000	£645,000	£1,224,000	£1,761,000	£2,205,000	£2,694,000

SCHEDULE 2 PRODUCTION BUDGET

	January	*February*	*March*	*April*	*May*	*June*	*July*
Sales budget (units)	–	3,000	5,000	7,000	8,000	10,000	12,000
Production (units):							
75 per cent—previous month	2,250	3,750	5,250	6,000	7,500	9,000	–
25 per cent—same month	–	750	1,250	1,750	2,000	2,500	3,000
Production budget	2,250	4,500	6,500	7,750	9,500	11,500	3,000

SCHEDULE 3 PURCHASES BUDGET

	December	*January*	*February*	*March*	*April*	*May*	*June*	*July*
Production budget (units)	–	2,250	4,500	6,500	7,750	9,500	11,500	3,000
Direct material cost per unit		£20	£20	£20	£20	£20	£20	£20
Cost of materials		£45,000	£90,000	£130,000	£155,000	£190,000	£230,000	£60,000
Purchases								
50 per cent previous month	£22,500	£22,500	£45,000	£65,000	£77,500	£95,000	£115,000	–
50 per cent same month	–	£45,000	£65,000	£77,500	£95,000	£115,000	£30,000	£30,000

SCHEDULE 4 PAYMENTS

	January	*February*	*March*	*April*	*May*	*June*	*July*
Payments—month following purchase	£22,500	£67,500	£110,000	£142,500	£172,500	£210,000	£145,000

SCHEDULE 5 DIRECT WAGES

	January	*February*	*March*	*April*	*May*	*June*	*July*
Production budget (units)	2,250	4,500	6,500	7,750	9,500	11,500	3,000
Cost per unit	£80	£80	£80	£80	£80	£80	£80
Cost of production	£180,000	£360,000	£520,000	£620,000	£760,000	£920,000	£240,000
Payments: in the month used	£180,000	£360,000	£520,000	£620,000	£760,000	£920,000	£240,000

SCHEDULE 6 VARIABLE OVERHEAD

	January	*February*	*March*	*April*	*May*	*June*	*July*
Production budget (units)	2,250	4,500	6,500	7,750	9,500	11,500	3,000
Cost per unit	£40	£40	£40	£40	£40	£40	£40
Cost of production	£90,000	£180,000	£260,000	£310,000	£380,000	£460,000	£120,000
Payments:							
80 per cent—same month	£72,000	£144,000	£208,000	£248,000	£304,000	£368,000	–
20 per cent—following month	–	£18,000	£36,000	£52,000	£62,000	£76,000	£92,000
	£72,000	£162,000	£244,000	£300,000	£366,000	£444,000	£92,000

SCHEDULE 7 FIXED PRODUCTION OVERHEAD

Insurance	£40,000
Salaries and wages	300,000
Other	80,000
	£420,000
Per month	£35,000

Cash budget 6 months year 8

	January	*February*	*March*	*April*	*May*	*June*
Cash balance—opening	£400,000	£90,500	£(363,000)	£(627,000)	£(500,500)	£(73,000)
Sales (Schedule 1)	nil	171,000	645,000	1,224,000	1,761,000	2,205,000
Other	–	–	–	–	–	–
(A) Total	£400,000	£261,500	£282,000	£597,000	£1,260,500	£2,132,000
Payments:						
Trade creditors (Schedule 4)	22,500	67,500	110,000	142,500	172,500	210,000
Direct wages (Schedule 5)	180,000	360,000	520,000	620,000	760,000	920,000
Variable overhead (Schedule 6)	72,000	162,000	244,000	300,000	366,000	444,000
Fixed overhead (Schedule 7)	35,000	35,000	35,000	35,000	35,000	35,000
(B) Total	£309,500	£624,500	£909,000	£1,097,500	£1,333,500	£1,609,000
(C) Cash balance carried forward (A−B)	£90,500	£(363,000)	£(627,000)	£(500,500)	£(73,000)	£523,000

Example 2

From the following information relating to a departmental store you are required to prepare a cash budget for the six months ending 30th June year 9.

Budgeted balance sheet as at 30th June year 9

31st December year 8 (£000)		*Budgeted 30th June year 9 (£000)*
	Fixed assets	
85,000	Fixed assets at cost	113,750
19,800	*Less:* Depreciation	21,000
65,200	Net fixed assets	92,750
	Current assets	
20,650	Stock	20,000
10,350	Debtors	20,000
250	Short-term investments	250
200	Loan to associated company	400
500	Cash	9,430
31,950	Total current assets	50,080
	Current liabilities	
11,000	Trade creditors	10,350
400	Other creditors	500
8,870	Taxation	12,000
450	Debentures interest	450
20,720	Total current liabilities	23,300
11,230	Net current assets	26,780
76,430	Total:	119,530
	Financed by:	
62,000	Ordinary share capital	62,000
8,430	Reserves	17,530
6,000	15 per cent debentures	40,000
76,430		119,530

(a) Capital expenditure (new fixed assets) amounting to £30,000,000 is expected to be incurred during the period.

(b) New debentures are to be issued on 30th June year 9. Interest is payable half-yearly, 30th June and 31st December.

Budgeted profit statement Six months ended 30th June year 9

			(£000)
Sales	Credit	100,000	
	Cash	20,000	120,000
Cost of sales			40,000
Gross profit			80,000
Less: Debenture interest			450
Wages, salaries			12,000
Other expenses			38,000
Depreciation			2,400
Trading profit prior to tax			27,150
Corporation tax			12,000
			15,150
Proposed 10 per cent interim dividend payable on 30th June			6,200
			8,950
Profit on sale of fixed assets			150
Profit retained			9,100

Suggested answer

Cash budget Half-year ending 30th June year 9

	(£000)
Balance as at 31st December year 8	500
Add inflow:	
Cash sales—profit and loss account	20,000
Cash received from debtors (Note V)	90,350
Sale of fixed assets (Note III)	200
Issue of debentures (Note IX)	34,000
	145,050
Deduct outflow:	
Purchases of fixed assets (Note I)	30,000
Trade creditors (Note IV)	40,000
Loans to associated company (Note VII)	200
Taxation (Note VIII)	8,870
Debenture holders (Note VIII)	450
Other creditors (Note VIII)	56,100
Expected cash balance as at 30th June year 9	9,430

The budgeted balance sheet shows an increase of £8,930,000 in cash.

ANALYSIS OF £8,930,000

(I) *Fixed assets*	(£000)
Fixed assets as at 31st December year 8	85,000
Add: Purchases during the period	30,000
	115,000
Less: Carried forward 30th June year 9	113,750
Sale of assets	1,250

(II) *Provision for depreciation*	(£000)
Provision as at 31st December year 8	19,800
Profit and loss: charge for the period	2,400
	22,200
Provision as at 30th June year 9	21,000
Sale of assets	1,200

(III) *Sale of assets*	(£000)
At cost	1,250
Provision for depreciation	1,200
Net book value	50
Profit on the sale of fixed asset	150
Cash received (cash inflow)	200

(IV) *Stock and trade creditors*

Purchases	(£000)
Cost of goods sold (profit and loss)	40,000
Stock carried forward 30th June (balance sheet)	20,000
	60,000
Less: Stock as at 31st December year 8 (balance sheet)	20,650
Purchases during the period	39,350

Trade creditors	(£000)
Balance as at 31st December year 8	11,000
Purchases	39,350
	50,350
Less: Balance as at 30th June (balance sheet)	10,350
Payments to trade creditors (outflow)	40,000

(V) *Debtors*

	(£000)
Balance as at 31st December year 8 (balance sheet)	10,350
Credit sales (profit and loss)	100,000
	110,350
Less: Balance as at 30th June year 9	20,000
Cash received (inflow)	90,350

(VI) *Short-term investments*

	(£000)
As at 30th June year 9	250
Less: As at 31st December year 8	250
No change	nil

(VII) *Loans to associated company*

	(£000)
As at 30th June year 9	400
As at 31st December year 8	200
Additional loans to associated company (outflow)	200

(VIII) *Creditors*

	Taxation (£000)	*Debenture holders* (£000)	*Other creditors* (£000)
Balance as at 31st December year 8 (balance sheet)	8,870	450	400
Profit and loss account			
Add:			
Debenture interest		450	
Wages and salaries			12,000
Other expenses			38,000
Corporation tax	12,000		
Proposed dividend			6,200
	20,870	900	56,600
Deduct balance as at 30th June (balance sheet)	(12,000)	(450)	(500)
Payments (cash outflow)	8,870	450	56,100

(IX) *Issue of debentures*

	(£000)
Balance as at 30th June year 9	40,000
Less: Balance as at 31st December year 8	6,000
Issue during the period (cash inflow)	34,000

CHAPTER TWENTY-FOUR

Non-Integration and Integration Accounting Systems

1.0 TWO SEPARATE ACCOUNTING SYSTEMS

If a company maintains two separate accounting systems for its financial and its cost accounting then the profits shown by the respective systems will probably differ. It is therefore essential that the profit shown in one system should be reconciled with that shown in the other system. For example, there are costs with no financial outlays which are recorded in the cost ledger and not recorded in the financial ledger.

2.0 REASONS FOR THE DIFFERENCE

2.1 Transactions of a purely financial nature recorded in the financial ledger but not in the cost ledger

(a) Purely financial income

(i) profit on sale of fixed assets;

(ii) dividends received;

(iii) discounts received;

(iv) bank interest received.

(b) Purely financial charges

(i) loss on sale of fixed assets;

(ii) fines and penalties;

(iii) interest on bank loans and mortgages;

(iv) discounts given;

(v) debenture interest.

2.2 Appropriation of profits which are not reflected in the cost accounts

Corporation tax; dividends payable; transfers to reserves; amount written off goodwill; donations to political parties and charities.

2.3 Items of income/expenditure which appear in the cost ledger and not in the financial ledger, i.e. notional income or expenditure

(a) Interest on capital with which a business is financed.

(b) Charges in lieu of rent—which represents the cost of the use of own premises.

Note: These items will not cause a difference in profit between financial and cost ledgers.

Illustration

A notional rent of £3,000 is charged in the cost accounts. Follow the journal entries carefully.

TO RECORD THE CHARGE

Debit:	Factory overhead control account	£3,000	
Credit:	Notional rent account		£3,000

AT THE END OF THE ACCOUNTING PERIOD THE FOLLOWING ENTRY WOULD BE MADE

Debit:	Notional rent account	£3,000	
Credit:	Costing profit and loss account		£3,000

2.4 Factory overheads over-/under-absorbed which have been carried forward to the next period in the cost ledger but not in the financial ledger

If the under-/over-absorbed overhead is written off in the same period and not carried forward then it will not affect the reconciliation.

Illustration 1

The cost accountant of Sri Nimal Manufacturing Company estimated the factory overhead costs for year 8 at £40,000.

The company planned to produce 20,000 units. At the end of the year the actual factory overhead costs were £45,000 and actual units produced were 22,000.

(*a*) *Cost ledger entries*

Actual cost

Debit:	Factory overhead control account	£45,000	
Credit:	Various accounts		£45,000

Overhead absorbed

Debit:	Work in progress account 22,000 units at £2 per unit	£44,000	
Credit:	Factory overhead control account		£44,000

Under-absorbed overhead

Debit:	Factory overhead under-absorbed account	£1,000	
Credit:	Factory overhead control account		£1,000

(*b*) *Financial ledger entries*

Actual cost

Debit:	Factory overhead—various accounts	£45,000	
Credit:	Other creditors and provision for depreciation		£45,000

End of the period

Debit:	Manufacturing account	£45,000	
Credit:	Factory overhead—various accounts		£45,000

(*c*) *Cost of production (overhead)*

	Financial accounts	*Cost accounts*
Actual charge	£45,000	–
Actual charge is based on a predetermined rate of overhead absorption	–	£44,000
	£45,000	£44,000

If the under-absorption is carried forward then the cost of production in the cost ledger is understated by £1,000. Therefore the cost profit will be overstated by the same amount.

2.5 Valuation of raw materials: work in progress and finished goods as per cost accounts may not agree with the financial ledger balances owing to the use of different bases of stock valuation

In financial accounts, valuation of stocks is normally on the basis of market value or cost, whichever is lower. In cost accounts, stocks may be at standard cost or historical cost in accordance with the method of accounting in use, e.g. average (simple average, weighted average), FIFO, LIFO etc.

Illustration 2

OPENING STOCK AND WORK IN PROGRESS

	Financial ledger	*Cost ledger*	*Difference*
Raw materials	£20,000	£18,000	£2,000
Work in progress	30,000	27,000	3,000
Finished goods	40,000	41,000	1,000

(*a*) *Raw materials (opening stock)*
In the preparation of final accounts, the financial accountant would charge £20,000 as opening stock of raw materials, whereas the cost accountant would charge £18,000. Therefore the financial profit will be £2,000 less than the costing profit.

(*b*) *Work in progress (opening stock)*
The figure used in the preparation of the final accounts in the financial accounts is £30,000, which is £3,000 more than the cost ledger balance. Since opening stock is a charge against income, financial profit will be £3,000 less than the costing profit.

(*c*) *Finished goods (opening stock)*
In the financial accounts the charge against income is £40,000, which is £1,000 less than the cost accounts. The financial profit will be £1,000 more than the cost profit.

CLOSING STOCK AND WORK IN PROGRESS

	Financial ledger	*Cost ledger*	*Difference*
Raw materials	£15,000	£14,000	£1,000
Work in progress	20,000	22,000	2,000
Finished goods	25,000	23,000	2,000

Closing stock should always be deducted from the opening stock plus purchases, thus revealing the cost of goods sold. Raw materials stock, work in progress and finished goods closing stock all reduce the cost of goods sold.

(*a*) *Raw materials (closing stock)*
Financial accounts show £15,000 which is £1,000 more than in cost accounts, so costing profit must be £1,000 less than the financial profit.

(*b*) *Work in progress (closing stock)*
Financial accounts £20,000 is £2,000 less than in the cost accounts, so costing profit must be £2,000 more than the financial profit.

(c) *Finished goods (closing stock)*
Financial accounts £25,000 is £2,000 more than in the cost accounts, so costing profit must be £2,000 less than the financial profit.

SUMMARY

PROFIT AS PER FINANCIAL ACCOUNTS				£ FP
	Financial ledger	*Cost ledger*	*Difference*	
Opening stock				
Raw materials	£20,000	£18,000	£2,000	
Work in progress	30,000	27,000	3,000	
Finished goods	40,000	41,000	(1,000)	
Total	£90,000	£86,000	£4,000	
Add: £4,000 as the opening stock is £4,000 less in the cost ledger				4,000
Closing stock				
Raw materials	£15,000	£14,000	£1,000	
Work in progress	20,000	22,000	(2,000)	
Finished goods	25,000	23,000	2,000	
Total	£60,000	£59,000	£1,000	
Deduct: £1,000 as the closing stock is £1,000 less in the cost ledger				(1,000)
Profit as per cost accounts				CP

2.6 Reasons for the difference—summary

(a) Purely financial income.

(b) Purely financial charges.

(c) Appropriation of profit.

(d) Notional charges.

(e) Under-/over-absorbed factory overhead.

(f) Stock valuation differences.

(g) Different methods of depreciation.

3.0 MEMORANDUM RECONCILIATION STATEMENT

				£
Profit as per financial accounts				
Purely financial charges				*Add*
Purely financial income				*Deduct*
Appropriations				*Add*
	Financial ledger	*Cost ledger*	*Difference*	
Stock valuation:				
Opening stock				
Raw materials				
Work in progress				
Finished goods				

If the financial ledger balance is *greater* than the cost ledger balance, *add* the difference. If the financial ledger balance is *less* than the cost ledger balance, *deduct* the difference. — *Add* / *Deduct*

Closing stock				
Raw materials				
Work in progress				
Finished goods				

If the financial ledger balance is *greater* than the cost ledger balance, *deduct* the difference. If the financial ledger balance is *less* than the cost ledger balance *add* the difference. — *Add* / *Deduct*

	Financial ledger	*Cost ledger*	*Difference*	£
Depreciation charge				
If, for example (a)	10,000	9,000	1,000	*Add*
(b)	9,000	10,000	1,000	*Deduct*

If, as in example (a), the financial ledger charge is *greater* than the cost ledger, the difference must be *added.* If, as in example (b), the financial ledger charge is *less* than the cost ledger charge, the difference must be *deducted.*

Under-absorption of factory overhead which has not been written off in the cost ledger.	*Add*
Over-absorption of factory overhead which has not been written off in the cost ledger.	*Deduct*
Notional charges—These items will not cause a difference	–
Profit as per cost accounts	

4.0 COMPREHENSIVE ILLUSTRATION

Illustration 3

(a) NIA Limited operates a non-integrated accounting system. At the end of April, the financial accountant has produced the final accounts, shown below. Based on these accounts and data supplied by the cost accountant, a reconciliation statement has been prepared, also as shown below.

You are required to prepare the following accounts as they would appear in the cost ledger:

(i) raw materials stores;

(ii) work in progress;

(iii) finished goods.

Manufacturing, trading and profit and loss account
for month of April 19_9

Raw materials:			Cost of goods manufactured, carried down	£602,000
Opening stock	£60,500			
Purchases	320,000			
	380,500			
Closing stock	65,000	£315,500		
Direct wages		125,000		
Production overhead		160,000		
Work in progress:				
Opening stock	36,700			
Closing stock	35,200	1,500		
		£602,000		£602,000
Finished goods:			Sales	£1,000,000
Opening stock	£45,600			
Goods manufactured	602,000			
	647,600			
Closing stock	47,600	£600,000		
Gross profit, carried down		400,000		
		£1,000,000		£1,000,000
Administration expenses		£110,000	Gross profit, brought down	£400,000
Selling and distribution expenses		150,000	Discount received	30,000
Discount allowed		50,000		
Debenture interest		20,000		
Net profit		100,000		
		£430,000		£430,000

Statement reconciling the profit of financial accounts and cost accounts

Profit as per financial accounts				£100,000
Differences in stock valuation				
Add: Raw materials:	closing stock	£750		
Work in progress:	opening stock	900		
Finished goods:	opening stock	1,300		
	closing stock	500	3,450	
Less: Raw materials:	opening stock	1,100		
Work in progress:	closing stock	500	1,600	1,850
Other items				
Add: Discount allowed		50,000		
Debenture interest		20,000	70,000	
Less: Discount received			30,000	40,000
				141,850
Production overhead, over-absorbed				2,000
Profit, as per cost accounts				£139,850

(b) Explain briefly why you think that the balances of work in progress shown in the financial accounts above differ from those in the cost accounts.

Suggested answer

(a) Cost ledger accounts

(i) *Raw materials stores account*

Opening stock (£60,500 + £1,100)	£61,600	Work in progress account	£315,850
Purchases	320,000	Closing stock (£65,000 + £750)	65,750
	£381,600		£381,600

(ii) *Work in progress account*

Opening stock (£36,700 − £900)	£35,800		
Raw material stores	315,850	Finished goods account	£603,950
Direct wages	125,000	Closing stock (£35,200 − £500)	34,700
Production overhead (£160,000 + £2,000)	162,000		
	£638,650		£638,650

(iii) *Finished goods account*

Opening stock (£45,600 − £1,300)	£44,300	Cost of sales account	600,150
Work in progress account	603,950	Closing stock (£47,600 + £500)	48,100
	£648,250		£648,250

(b) Work in progress balances in the financial accounts may differ from those in the cost accounts for the following reasons:

(i) Fixed production overheads may be included in the financial accounts while work in progress is valued at marginal cost in the cost accounts.

(ii) Administration overhead may be added in financial accounts but not in cost accounts.

(iii) The use of standard costing in the cost accounts may give rise to differences with financial accounting figures.

5.0 INTEGRATED ACCOUNTING

5.1 Double-entry cost book-keeping

It is quite possible to have a detailed cost analysis outside a system of double-entry book-keeping, but most firms keep their costing records within such a system.

There are two basic systems:

(a) Integrated or integral: a unified system including both financial and cost accounts, theoretically in a single ledger.

(b) Interlocking: a system in which the cost accounts are distinct from the financial accounts. The cost ledger is kept independently of the financial ledger, there being no double-entry connection but since the basic data is the same the two sets of accounts should be readily reconcilable.

Thus, the cost accounts may be integrated with, or kept separately from, the financial accounts. The question of interlocking accounts was dealt with in the previous chapter and it is now necessary to explain integrated accounting.

5.2 Integrated accounts

In financial books there are three basic types of accounts:

(a) real, e.g. fixed assets, cash, stocks;

(b) personal, e.g. debtors, creditors;

(c) nominal, e.g. wages, rent and rates, lighting and heating.

In cost books there are no personal accounts, because cost accounts do not show relationships with outsiders, and stocks are the only real accounts. The emphasis is on the nominal accounts where costs are analysed in detail and charged directly to production or to the relevant overhead accounts.

Integrated accounts attempt to show the overall picture shown separately in an interlocking system by the financial books and the cost books. In an integrated system the usual financial real and personal accounts exist but the nominal accounts follow the principles of a cost accounting system. Thus there are accounts for raw materials, work in progress, and finished goods stocks and production, administration, selling and distribution overhead followed by the cost of sales and profit and loss account.

5.3 Control accounts

In an integrated system, control accounts are often used as the vehicle for the double entry. The figures in the control account are the subject of much more detailed analysis in subsidiary records outside the double-entry system, the entries in these subsidiary records often being known as "third entries". For example, the figures in the work in progress control account are analysed in greater detail in a subsidiary work in progress ledger showing the cost of the individual production jobs in progress. Therefore, this is a similar principle to the individual debtor accounts showing the make-up of the figures in the sales ledger control account.

5.4 Comprehensive illustration

Illustration 4

B Limited operates an integrated accounting system and the following details given relate to one year.

You are required from the details given to:

(a) enter in the appropriate ledger accounts the transactions for the year;

(b) prepare a profit and loss account for the year; and

(c) prepare a balance sheet as at the end of the year.

Trial balance at beginning of the year:

	£000	£000
Capital	–	1,000
Reserves	–	200
Creditors	–	150
Expense creditors	–	20
Freehold buildings at cost	500	–
Plant and machinery at cost	300	–
Provision for depreciation of plant and machinery	–	100
Stock of: Raw materials	220	–
Work in progress	40	–
Finished goods	60	–
Debtors	200	–
Bank	150	–
	£1,470	£1,470

The following data for the year are given:

			£000
Materials:	Purchased on credit		990
	Returned to suppliers		40
	Issued to production		850
Production:	Wages incurred		250
	Salaries		60
	Expenses incurred		320
Carriage inwards			45
Provision for depreciation of plant and machinery			50
Production:	Overhead absorbed		425
Production:	At standard cost		1,600
Administration:	Salaries		100
	Expenses incurred		260
	Overhead absorbed in finished goods		380
Selling and distribution:	Salaries		80
	Expenses incurred		120
	Absorbed in cost of sales		210
Finished goods sold			2,000
Sales on credit			2,500
Sales returns			60
Variance:	Direct material:	price (adverse)	35
		usage (favourable)	20
	Direct wages rate (favourable)		15
	Direct labour efficiency (favourable)		30
	Production overhead:	expenditure (adverse)	25
		efficiency (favourable)	40
Abnormal loss of raw material stock, insurance claim agreed and cash received			60
New machinery purchased, paid by cheque			50
Paid:	Creditors		895
	Expense creditors		730
Cash discount received from trade creditors			25
Paid wages and salaries			425
Deduction from wages and salaries			50
Received cheques from debtors			2,350
Cash discount allowed			35
Bad debts written off			25

All "price" variances (i.e. direct material price, direct wages rate and production overhead expenditure) are recorded in the relevant expenditure accounts; "quantity" variances (i.e. direct material usage, direct labour efficiency, production overhead efficiency) are recorded in the work in progress account.

Suggested answer

(a) *Ledger accounts*

Capital account

	£000		£000
		Balance b/d	1,000

Reserve account

		Balance b/d	200

Creditors account

Returns	40	Balance b/d	150
Bank	895	Raw materials	990
Cash discount	25		
Balance c/d	180		
	1,140		1,140

Expense creditors account

Bank	730	Balance b/d	20
Balance c/d	35	Production expenses	320
		Carriage inwards	45
		Administration expenses	260
		Selling and distribution expenses	120
	765		765

Freehold buildings account

Balance b/d	500		

Plant and machinery account

Balance b/d	300		
Bank	50		
	350		

Provision for depreciation of plant and machinery

		Balance b/d	100
		Production o.h.	50
			150

Raw material control account

	£000		£000
Balance b/d	220	Returns	40
Creditors	990	Work in progress	850
		Price variance	35
		Bank (insurance)	60
		Balance c/d	225
	1,210		1,210

Work in progress control account

Balance b/d	40	Finished goods	1,600
Raw material	850	Balance c/d	55
Salaries and wages control	250		
Production o.h.	425		
Material usage variance	20		
Labour efficiency variance	30		
Production o.h. efficiency variance	40		
	1,655		1,655

Finished goods control account

Balance b/d	60	Cost of sales	2,000
Work in progress	1,600	Balance c/d	40
Administration o.h.	380		
	2,040		2,040

Debtors account

Balance b/d	200	Sales returns	60
Sales	2,500	Bank	2,350
		Cash discount	35
		Bad debts	25
		Balance c/d	230
	2,700		2,700

Cash account

Balance b/d	150	Plant and machinery	50
Material (ins.)	60	Creditors	895
Debtors	2,350	Expense creditors	730
		Salaries and wages control	425
		Balance c/d	460
	2,560		2,560

Salaries and wages control account

	£000		£000
Wages rate variance	15	Work in progress	250
Bank	425	Production o.h.	60
Deductions	50	Administration control	100
		Selling and distribution control	80
	490		490

Production overhead control account

Salaries and wages control	60	Work in progress	425
Expense creditors	320	Expenditure variance	25
*Expense creditors (carriage)	45	Under-absorbed overheads	25
Provision for depreciation	50		
	475		475

*Carriage inwards may be charged to raw material control account

Administration overhead control account

Salaries and wages control	100	Finished goods	380
Expense creditors	260		
Over-absorbed overheads	20		
	380		380

Selling and distribution overhead control account

Salaries and wages control	80	Cost of sales	210
Expense creditors	120		
Over-absorbed overheads	10		
	210		210

Cost of sales account

Selling and distribution	210	Profit and loss account	2,210
Finished goods	2,000		
	2,210		2,210

Sales account

Returns	60	Debtors	2,500
Profit and loss	2,440		
	2,500		2,500

Direct material price variance account

	£000		£000
Raw materials	35	Profit and loss	35

Direct material usage variance account

Profit and loss	20	Work in progress	20

Direct wages rate variance account

Profit and loss	15	Salaries and wages control	15

Direct labour efficiency variance account

Profit and loss	30	Work in progress	30

Production overhead expenditure variance account

Production overhead	25	Profit and loss	25

Production overhead efficiency variance account

Profit and loss	40	Work in progress	40

Deductions from salaries and wages account

		Salaries and wages control	50

Cash discount allowed account

Debtors	35	Profit and loss	35

Cash discount received account

Profit and loss	25	Creditors	25

Bad debts account

Debtors	25	Profit and loss	25

Over-/under-absorbed overhead account

Production overhead	25	Administration overhead	20
Profit and loss	5	Selling and distribution overhead	10
	30		30

(b) *Profit and loss account for the year*

		£000	£000
Sales			2,440
Less: Cost of sales			2,210
			230
Variances:			
Direct material:	price	−35	
	usage	+20	
Direct wages rate		+15	
Direct labour efficiency		+30	
Production overhead:	expenditure	−25	
	efficiency	+40	
Total			+45
Other items:			
Cash discount:	allowed	−35	
	received	+25	
Bad debts		−25	
Over-absorbed overhead		+ 5	−30
Net profit			245

(c)

B Ltd
Balance Sheet

	£000	£000
Employment of capital:		
Fixed assets:		
Freehold buildings, at cost		500
Plant and machinery, at cost	350	
Less: Depreciation	150	200
		700
Current assets:		
Stocks: Raw materials	225	
Work in progress	55	
Finished goods	40	
	320	
Debtors	230	
Bank	460	
		1,010
Less: Current liabilities:		
Creditors	180	
Expense creditors	35	
Deductions from salaries and wages	50	265
Net current assets		745
		1,445
Sources of capital:		
Capital		1,000
Profit and loss account	245	
Reserves	200	445
		1,445

Appendix: Glossary of Terms

Note: The chapter and paragraph numbers indicated in brackets show where a full explanation is given in the text.

Absorption costing. Method of costing where the fixed manufacturing overhead is included in the cost of inventory. (1, 5.5)

Average costing. See under Unit costing.

Batch costing. Costing for a particular unit of identical items which can maintain its identity throughout one or more stages of production. (9, 3.0)

Break-even point. Point at which sales volume equals total revenue from the sales, i.e. no profit or loss is made. (15, 3.0)

Budget. A financial and/or quantitative statement prepared prior to a given period of time of the policy to be pursued during that period to attain a given objective. (23, 4.0)

Cash budget. The estimated amount of cash which should be available during the budget period. (1, 8.3)

Contribution. The measurement of sales revenue less variable costs of production. (15, 3.0)

Cost. A measure of the amount of scarce resources used for some purpose. (1, 2.1)

Cost allocation. Charges a cost centre with those overheads which result solely from the existence of that cost centre. (7, 3.1)

Cost apportionment. The allotment of proportions of cost items to cost centres or cost units. (7, 3.1)

Cost centre. A location, person or item of equipment in relation to which costs may be ascertained. (1, 3.2)

Cost unit. A unit of product, service or time in relation to which costs may be ascertained or expressed. (1, 3.2)

Differential costing. See under Incremental costing.

Direct costs. Those costs which can readily be identified with a product. (2, 3.0)

Economic order quantity. The amount of inventory which should be ordered at one time so that all other associated costs can be minimised. (3, 6.0)

Expired costs. See under Period costs.

Financial accounting. Area of accounting concerned with the provision of information to external users to aid decision-making. (1, 1.2)

Fixed budget. A plan to achieve the objectives of the enterprise or the particular cost centre. (1, 8.3)

Flexible budget. A budget which is designed to change in relation to the level of activity attained during the budgetary period. (1, 8.4)

Historic costing. The ascertainment of costs after they have been incurred. (1, 5.4)

Incremental costing. A technique which compares the profit before a particular decision is taken, with the total profit including the effect of the decision. (1, 10.2)

Indirect costs. Those costs which cannot be easily identified with a product. (2, 4.0)

Job costing. Method of costing where expenditure is linked to a particular job, batch or contract. (9, 1.1)

Joint product costing. Costing for a number of products which are manufactured simultaneously from the same raw materials. (12, 1.0)

Management accounting. Concerned with how information can be used to aid internal users. (1, 3.1)

Marginal costing. Technique which highlights contribution as the indicator of profitability. (1, 10.1; see also 1, 5.5)

Normal costing. Method of charging actual direct labour, actual direct materials and predetermined factory overhead, to products. (1, 5.4)

Operating budget. A forecast of the economic resources to be used, products to be produced, or services to be rendered during the budget period. (1, 8.3)

Opportunity cost. The alternative revenue foregone when a given course of action is taken. (1, 10.3)

Overheads. Term used for indirect cost elements which cannot be charged directly to cost units. (2, 4.0)

Period costs. Those costs incurred in a period independent of the level of activity. (2, 5.1)

Primary distribution. Allocation and/or apportionment of overhead costs on various bases deemed reasonable to all cost centres or departments to which they apply. (7, 3.1)

Prime cost. The sum of direct cost elements which can be identified with and allocated to cost units. (2, 3.4)

Process costing. System whereby costs are applied to similar products which are mass produced in a continuous manner through several production steps. (11, 2.0)

Product cost. Costs which are attached to products. (2, 5.2)

Responsibility accounting. A system of accounting which recognises various decision centres throughout the organisations and traces costs, incomes, assets and liabilities to the respective managers responsible for making decisions about the factors involved. (1, 9.1)

Secondary distribution. Apportionment of costs charged to service departments to the producing departments on a suitable basis. (7, 4.1)

Split-off point. The point at which joint products become individually identifiable. (12, 3.2)

Standard costing. A scientifically predetermined unit cost which should be attained. (1, 5.4)

Static budget. See under Fixed budget.

Unit costing. Expenditure is charged to departments or processes and not directly to cost units. (9, 1.1)

Variance. The difference between actual and expected results. (6, 3.3)

Index